PREFACE

Entrepreneurship has become a major force in the global economy. Policymakers across the world are discovering that economic growth and prosperity lies in the hands of entrepreneurs-those dynamic-driven men and women who are committed to achieving success by creating and marketing innovative, customer-focused new products and services. Not only are these entrepreneurs creating economic prosperity, but many of them are also striving to make the world a better place in which to live. Those who possess this spirit of entrepreneurial leadership will continue to lead the economic revolution that has proven time and again, its ability to raise the standard of living for people everywhere. Entrepreneurial activity, if undertaken in full spirits, certainly activates one's dormant talents into successful action. We hope that you will join this economic revolution to bring about lasting, positive changes around the world.

We are pleased to present the book of *"Fundamentals of Entrepreneurship Development and Project Management"* to students, teachers, management consultants, budding entrepreneurs and other readers interested in today's world of small business development and management. This book has been written with a purpose to develop an inclination towards entrepreneurial activities and to set up small business. It will help everyone to get more knowledge and awareness about entrepreneurship, project management, entrepreneurship development programs and many such more. This book can be used as a text book by the commerce, arts and engineering students of various universities. Our hope is that this book will answer all the questions, students and professionals have when they conduct and undertake entrepreneurship and project management study or course. Moreover, the text will be of immense use to those who intend to venture in innovative business activities and to set up their own small business. To provide an understanding of entrepreneur and the process of creating and growing a new venture, this book is divided into seventeen chapters.

We would like to express our special appreciation and thanks to our colleagues and family members who gave us inspiration and the moral support to convert our dreams into reality in the shape of this book. We would like to extend our special thanks to multiple departments of Panjab University — University School of Open Learning, University Institute of Hotel Management and Tourism and University Business School and to Applied Sciences Department, Punjab Engineering College. We are more than thankful to Himalaya Publishing House Pvt. Ltd., specially Mr. Veer Singh who coordinated this project from the start and helped us to bring this work to fulfillment.

Due to constraint of space, we could not name people who deserve mention but we recognize the fact that working with every author team is a stuff of professionals who work extremely hard to bring a book to life. They handle thousands of details involved in transforming a rough manuscript into the finished product. Our special thanks to everyone who assisted us in our task and are real heroes of this assignment.

Lipika K.Guliani
R.K. Gupta

CONTENTS

FUNDAMENTALS OF ENTREPRENEURSHIP DEVELOPMENT AND PROJECT MANAGEMENT

Lipika K. Guliani

Assistant Professor,

University Institute of Hotel Management and Tourism,

Panjab University, Chandigarh

R.K. Gupta

Professor, (Department of commerce & Management) and

Director (University Institute of Hotel Management & Tourism)

Panjab University, Chandigarh

HPH

Himalaya Publishing House

MUMBAI • NEW DELHI • NAGPUR • BENGALURU • HYDERABAD • CHENNAI • PUNE

LUCKNOW • AHMEDABAD • ERNAKULAM • BHUBANESWAR • INDORE • KOLKATA • GUWAHATI

First Edition : 2014

Published by : Mrs. Meena Pandey for **Himalaya Publishing House Pvt. Ltd.,**
"Ramdoot", Dr. Bhalerao Marg, Girgaon, Mumbai - 400 004.
Phone: 022-23860170/23863863, Fax: 022-23877178
E-mail: himpub@vsnl.com; Website: www.himpub.com

Branch Offices :

New Delhi : "Pooja Apartments", 4-B, Murari Lal Street, Ansari Road, Darya Ganj, New Delhi - 110 002. Phone: 011-23270392, 23278631; Fax: 011-23256286

Nagpur : Kundanlal Chandak Industrial Estate, Ghat Road, Nagpur - 440 018. Phone: 0712-2738731, 3296733; Telefax: 0712-2721216

Bengaluru : No. 16/1 (Old 12/1), 1st Floor, Next to Hotel Highlands, Madhava Nagar, Race Course Road, Bengaluru - 560 001. Phone: 080-22286611, 22385461, 4113 8821, 22281541

Hyderabad : No. 3-4-184, Lingampally, Besides Raghavendra Swamy Matham, Kachiguda, Hyderabad - 500 027. Phone: 040-27560041, 27550139

Chennai : 8/2 Madley 2nd street, T. Nagar, Chennai - 600 017. Mobile: 09320490962

Pune : First Floor, "Laksha" Apartment, No. 527, Mehunpura, Shaniwarpeth (Near Prabhat Theatre), Pune - 411 030. Phone: 020-24496323/24496333; Mobile: 09370579333

Lucknow : House No 731, Shekhupura Colony, Near B.D. Convent School, Aliganj, Lucknow - 226 022. Phone: 0522-4012353; Mobile: 09307501549

Ahmedabad : 114, "SHAIL", 1st Floor, Opp. Madhu Sudan House, C.G. Road, Navrang Pura, Ahmedabad - 380 009. Phone: 079-26560126; Mobile: 09377088847

Ernakulam : 39/176 (New No: 60/251) 1st Floor, Karikkamuri Road, Ernakulam, Kochi – 682011. Phone: 0484-2378012, 2378016; Mobile: 09387122121

Bhubaneswar : 5 Station Square, Bhubaneswar - 751 001 (Odisha). Phone: 0674-2532129, Mobile: 09338746007

Indore : Kesardeep Avenue Extension, 73, Narayan Bagh, Flat No. 302, IIIrd Floor, Near Humpty Dumpty School, Indore - 452 007 (M.P.). Mobile: 09303399304

Kolkata : 108/4, Beliaghata Main Road, Near ID Hospital, Opp. SBI Bank, Kolkata - 700 010, Phone: 033-32449649, Mobile: 7439040301

Guwahati : House No. 15, Behind Pragjyotish College, Near Sharma Printing Press, P.O. Bharalumukh, Guwahati - 781009, (Assam). Mobile: 09883055590, 08486355289, 7439040301

DTP by : Elite Art, Delhi.

Printed at : M/s. Aditya Offset Process (I) Pvt. Ltd., Hyderabad. On behalf of HPH.

1

CONCEPT OF THE ENTREPRENEUR

1.1. INTRODUCTION

Entrepreneur is an Economic Agent who plays a vital role in the economic development of a country. Economic development of a country refers to steady growth in the income levels. This growth mainly depends on its entrepreneurs. An Entrepreneur is a person who perceives a need and brings together manpower, material and capital required to meet that need. An **Entrepreneur is an individual with knowledge, skills, initiative, drive and spirit of innovation who aims at achieving goals**. An entrepreneur identifies opportunities, gathers the necessary resources, seizes opportunities for economic benefits and ultimately becomes responsible for the performance of the organization.

Entrepreneur is an organizer who combines various factors of production to produce a socially viable product and uses his initiative, skill and motivation to set up a business or enterprise of his own and who always looks for high achievements. He is the catalyst for social change and works for the common good. The entrepreneurial spirit has been described as the most significant development in recent economic history. Entrepreneurial ventures are having impact on the economy of the whole world.

1.2. CONCEPT OF AN ENTREPENEUR

The concept of an entrepreneur varies from country to country as well as from period to period. The term **entrepreneur** is a loanword from **French**, and is commonly used to describe an individual who organizes and operates a business or businesses, taking on financial risk to do so. Entrepreneur in French literally means "between taker" or "go between". The term was first defined by the Irish-French economist Richard Cantillon as the person who pays a certain price for a product to resell it at an uncertain price, thereby making decisions about obtaining and using the resources while consequently admitting the risk of enterprise. The term first appeared in the French Dictionary

"*Dictionnaire Universel de Commerce*" of Jacques des Bruslons published in 1723 and the word "**Entrepreneur**" is derived from "*entreprendre*" which means "**to undertake**" (Fig. 1.1). So, Entrepreneur is a person who brings in overall change through innovation for maximum social betterment.

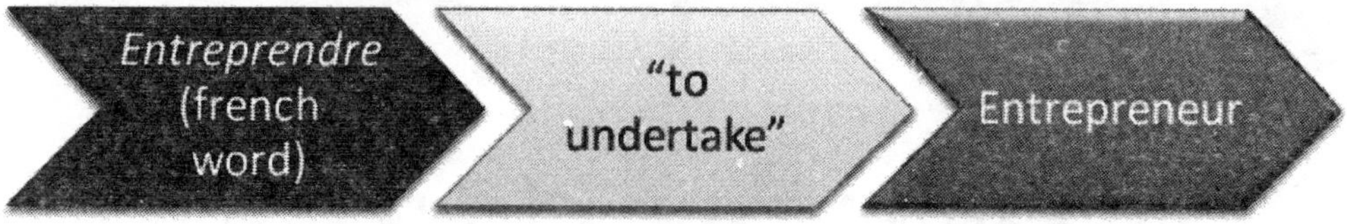

Fig. 1.1.

1.3. MEANING OF ENTREPRENEUR

Entrepreneur is an innovator who recognizes the opportunities and converts these opportunities into marketable ideas. Schumpeter defined an entrepreneur as a dynamic agent of change, a catalyst who transforms increasingly physical, natural and human resources into corresponding production possibilities.

The entrepreneur is a catalyst for the economic change and uses purposeful searching, planning and judgment in order to carry on entrepreneurial process. Entrepreneur brings overall change through innovation for the maximum social benefit. He is a visionary and an integrated person with outstanding leadership qualities, who conceives an enterprise for the purpose, displays required initiative to bring the project into action.

1.4. EVOLUTION OF ENTREPRENEURIAL THEORY

Hoselitz (1960) suggests that it originated during the Middle Ages when the term entrepreneur was applied to "*...the man in charge of the great architectural works: castles and fortifications, public buildings, abbeys and cathedrals*" (Hoselitz, 1960, p. 237). Given the origins of the word it should not be surprising that the early thinkers were French economists. In most entrepreneurship texts, Cantillon is recognized as the first to use the term 'entrepreneurship' in an economic context (Hébert and Link, 1988; Binks and Vale, 1990). His *Essai Sur la Nature du Commerce en Général* was published in 1732. Cantillon introduced an economic system based on classes of actors and entrepreneurs are one of the three classes. There are 'landowners' who are financially independent aristocracy. 'Hirelings' and 'entrepreneurs' were viewed to be financially dependent on others. Hirelings earned fixed incomes while entrepreneurs were "*...set up with a capital to conduct their enterprise, or are undertakers of their own labour without capital, and they may be regarded as living off uncertainty*" (Cantillon, 1931, p. 55). For Cantillon individuals who purchased a good at a certain price, used that good to produce a product and then sold that product at an uncertain price could be considered 'entrepreneurs'. Risk and uncertainty play central parts in his theory of the economic system. Successful entrepreneurs were those individuals who made better judgments about changes in the market and who coped with risk and uncertainty better than their counterparts. Schumpeter's theories of the economic system and the role of entrepreneurship within it, have been widely discussed (MacDonald, 1971; Shionoya,

1992; 1997). His principle contribution can be found in his book *'The Theory of Economic Development'* and an article *'The Fundamental Phenomenon of Economic Development'*. Schumpeter introduced a concept of entrepreneurship which is quite different from the others discussed so far. His theory is focused on economic development and the role of the entrepreneur in the development process. Schumpeter argues, somewhat contrary to the established thought of the time, that the important question in capitalism is not how it supports existing structures and markets but how it creates and destroys them. In contemporary thought 'creative destruction' is now seen as one of the crucial functions of entrepreneurial activity within an economy. The function of the entrepreneur in this new theory was the person who innovates or makes 'new combinations' of production possible. The concept of 'new combinations' covered five potential cases: The introduction of a new good or a new quality of a good; The introduction of a new method of production; The opening of a new market;The development of a new source of supply or raw-materials or half manufactured goods; The carrying out of a new organization of any industry (Kilby, 1971).

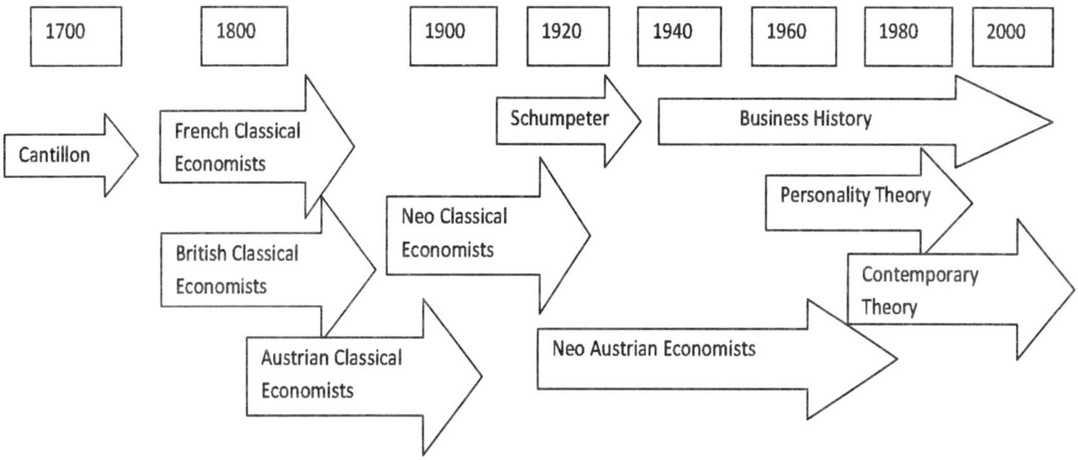

Fig. 1.2. Timeline of Entrepreneurship Thought

Jean-Baptiste Say was both a professor and a business person founding a cotton spinning mill in Pas de Calais. Perhaps because of his business experience Say made the entrepreneur the pivot on which his views about the economic system turned (see Figure 1.2).

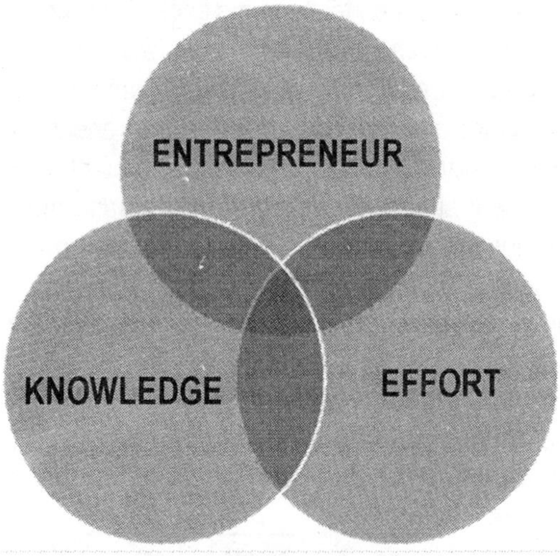

Fig. 1.3

Say proceeded to make a tripartite division of human industry into "...effort, knowledge and the applications of the entrepreneur" (Koolman, 1971, p. 271). The entrepreneur was viewed by Say as the coordinator of the system, acting as an intermediary between all of the other agents of production and taking on the uncertainty and risk. The profit the entrepreneur gained was the reward for the risk undertaken. Successful entrepreneurship needed significant qualities. The most important was judgment or the ability to assess the needs of the market and understand how these needs could be met.

1.5. EMERGENCE OF ENTREPRENEURIAL CLASS

Earliest Period

An early example of the earliest definition of an entrepreneur as a go-between is Marco Polo, who attempted to establish trade routes to the Far East. As a go-between, Marco Polo would sign a contract with a moneyed person to sell his goods. A common contract during this time provided loan to the merchant – including insurance. While the capitalist was a passive risk taker.

Middle Ages

In the middle ages, the term entrepreneur was used to describe both an actor and a person who managed large production projects. A typical entrepreneur in the middle ages was the cleric — the person in charge of great architectural work such as -public buildings, castles etc. In early 16th century, the Frenchmen who organized and led military expeditions were referred as 'entrepreneur'.

17th Century

In the 17th century an entrepreneur is termed as a person who entered into a contractual arrangement with the government to perform a service or to supply stipulated products. In late 17th century, proto-entrepreneurs were offered chances to involve themselves in trade formerly reserved for kings, members of the royal family, aristocrats and high dignitaries. They can be seprated into four groups as follows:

1. The private merchants and tan farmers.
2. The trading expert official and court merchants.
3. The trader and peddlers
4. The local officials.

18th Century

In the 18th century Richard Cantillon is the French economist who used the term 'entrepreneur' to business activities. According to Richard Cantillon, "An entrepreneur is the agent who buys factor of production at certain prices in order to combine them into a product with a view to sell it at uncertain price in future. " The necessity of entrepreneurship for production was first formally recognized by Alfred Marshall in 1890. In his famous treatise, *Principles of Economics*, Marshall asserts that there are four factors of production: land, labor, capital and organization. Organization is the coordinating factor, which brings the other factors together, and Marshall believed that entrepreneurship is the driving element behind the organization. Many entrepreneurs came into existence in 18th century like;- Samuel Crompton (Spining Mule), Great Britain, Thomas Newcomen (Steam Engine), Great Britain, James Watt (Steam Engine), Great Britain, etc.

19th Century (onwards)

Jean Baptiste Say, who was a French economist, coined the term "entrepreneur" in the 19th century. According to him, "an entrepreneur is an economic agent who unites all means of production — land of one, the labour of another and capital of yet another and thus produces a product. By selling the product in market,he pays rent of land, wages to labour, interest on capital and what remains is his profit." According to Marshall, entrepreneurs create new commodities or improve the plan of producing an old commodity. In order to do this, Marshall believed that entrepreneurs must have a thorough understanding about their industries and they must be natural leaders. Additionally, Marshall's entrepreneurs must have the ability to foresee changes in supply and demand and be willing to act on such risky forecasts in the absence of complete information (Marshall, 1994). In the 20th century, many successful entrepreneurs have led their firms, organizations or business entities to outstanding levels of success. Common factors in their success are: the capabilities to select competent management, build a cohesive and object-oriented team, and lead it to achieve the goal. Examples, (19th century) Thomas Alva Edison (General electrical), Richard Trevithick (Mining and steam engines) etc. (20th century) - Steve Jobs (Computers), Dhirubhai Ambani (Reliance industries), Kiran Mazumdar-Shaw (Biotechnology), etc.

1.6. DEFINITIONS

The term "entrepreneur" is defined in a variety of ways. Overtime, scholars have defined the term in different ways. Here are some prominent definitions.

- **(1803): Jean-Baptiste Say:** An entrepreneur is an economic agent who unites all means of production, — *i.e.,* land of one, the labour of another and the capital of yet another and thus produces a product. By selling the product in the market he pays rent of land, wages to labour, interest on capital and what remains is his profit. He shifts economic resources out of an area of lower productivity and into an area of higher productivity and greater yield.

- **(1934): Schumpeter:** Entrepreneurs are innovators who use a process of shattering the *status quo* of the existing products and services, to set up new products, new services.
- **(1961): David McClleland:** An entrepreneur is a person with a high need for achievement [N-Ach]. He is energetic and a moderate risk taker.
- **(1964): Peter Drucker:** An entrepreneur searches for change, responds to it and exploits opportunities. Innovation is a specific tool of an entrepreneur hence an effective entrepreneur converts a source into a resource.

Peter F. Drucker opines that:

(a) An entrepreneur must be an **innovator** as well as a **leader**

(b) He must be **capable of analyzing the opportunities** and **exploit** them successfully.

(c) He should **innovate for present** period but not for future.

(d) Innovation must be very **simple to understand,** otherwise, it may not give the desired results.

(e) Entrepreneur must **possess the knowledge, diligence, pesistence and commitment to innovation.**

(f) He must **mobilise resources** and allocate them to make a **commercial gain** from the opportunities identified

- **(1971): Kilby:** Emphasizes the role of an imitator entrepreneur who does not innovate but imitates technologies innovated by others.
- **(1975): Albert Shapero:** Entrepreneurs take initiative, accept risk of failure and have an internal locus of control.
- **(1985): W. B. Gartner:** Entrepreneur is a person who started a new business where there was none before.

Other Definitions:

(a) According to J. S Mill, An entrepreneur is a organizer who was paid for his non-manual type of work. Extraordinary skills acted as the bedrock in production process that ought to be processed by the entrepreneur.

(b) According to F. A Walker, Entrepreneur is one who is endowed with more than average capacities in the task of organizing and coordinating the factors of production, *i.e.*, land, labour, capital and enterprise.

(c) According to E. E Hagen, An entrepreneur is an economic man who tries to maximize his profits by innovation, involve problem solving and gets satisfaction from using his capabilities on attacking the problems.

(d) Frank Young defines entrepreneur as a change agent.

(e) International Labour Organization (ILO) defines entrepreneurs as those people who have the ability to see and evaluate business opportunities, together with the necessary resources to take advantage of them and to initiate appropriate action to ensure success.

(f) Marx regarded entrepreneur as a social parasite.

(g) Leon Walrus, in his papers, *The Theory of Social Wealth,* pointed out that entrepreneur is the coordinator of basic factor of production. He treated entrepreneur as the fourth factor of production who combines other factors such as land, labour and capital. (Fig. 1.4)

Fig. 1.4

So an entrepreneur is someone who exercises initiative by organizing a venture to take benefit of an opportunity and as the decision maker, decides what, and how much of a good or service will be produced. An entrepreneur supplies risk capital as a risk taker, and monitors and controls the business activities. The entrepreneur is usually a sole proprietor, a partner, or the one who owns the majority of shares in an incorporated venture.

According to economist Joseph Schumpeter, entrepreneurs are not necessarily motivated by profit but regard it as a standard for measuring achievement or success. Schumpeter discovered that they

(1) greatly value self-reliance

(2) strive for distinction through excellence

(3) are highly optimistic (otherwise nothing would be undertaken)

(4) always favor challenges of medium risk (neither too easy, nor ruinous).

1.7. NEW CONCEPT OF ENTREPRENEUR

So the new concept of entrepreneur is, a person who conceives a new idea, explores the environment, evaluates the situation and starts a project according to the need of the society. It includes much more:-

(a) Explores opportunities;

(b) Evaluates the environment;

(c) Conceives an idea;

(d) Arranges initial capital;

(e) Arranges latest technology;

(f) Does social-cost benefit analysis;

(g) Obtains necessary licences;

(h) Promises to provide the best to the customers.

To be an entrepreneur, the basic requirements are innovation, risk, enterprise, resources(men, money, machinery etc), skill, urge to grow and organizing all together. (Fig. 1.5)

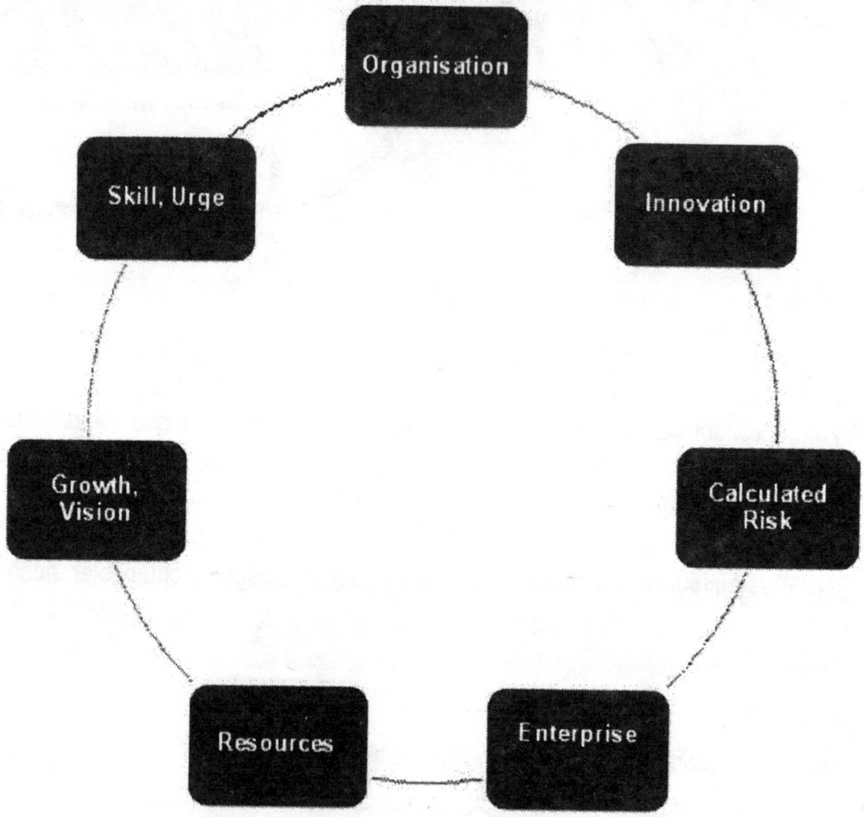

Fig. 1.5. Basics of Entrepreneur

1.8. QUALITIES / SKILLS OF AN ENTREPRENEUR

An entrepreneur is oriented, creative, innovative and energetic individual, who has following qualities:

1.Imagination and creativity: A successful entrepreneur is imaginative and creative. He looks outside the square and see things others do not. He offer solutions to difficult problems as well as being able to brainstorm ideas for their products and be able to create a business that will set them apart from others.

2. An achiever: Another key quality of a successful entrepreneur is that they are achievers. Getting things done is important. Remember you need to keep driving your business vehicle until you are satisfied with the result and achieved your goal. Those that stop halfway will never see what they can really achieve. Successful entrepreneurs are the ones that are persistent, motivated, independent and hardworking. They have a clear vision of what they want to achieve and set out to form a plan, followed by an action in order to reach their goals. They are proactive and get things done.

3. Self Discipline: Those who are self disciplined are one step closer to becoming a successful entrepreneur. When you want to succeed in anything, not just business, you must teach yourself time management, stress management and also be able to separate work from play.

4. Independence: Not only do successful entrepreneurs have to possess self discipline but they must also show independence. Being independent means that they are aware of the decisions needed to be made and can make them on their own. They are not afraid of being alone and being different. They understand what is required of the business and are the decision makers.

5. Patience: Patience is the key to success. We all know that a business needs time to build-up. Success does not happen overnight (unless extremely lucky). Entrepreneurs understand this and often like to put ideas into actions and wait to see the results. Whatever the results may be they often go back and tweak their ideas to produce better results. This is what differentiates a successful entrepreneur from one that is not so successful.

6. Determination: Another quality that entrepreneur must have in order to succeed is determination. In the business world it comes without saying that competition is everywhere and this can lead people to lack the confidence and motivation required to succeed. A successful entrepreneur can take failure as it is and then tries again, maybe using a different approach. Point is they believe in their ability to become successful and it is this belief that allows them to stand up again after they fall.

7. Motivation: Motivation is a skill that entrepreneurs cannot lack. In any business venture there is bound to be both success and failure. A successful entrepreneur must not let failure block their view of what could be a successful business. If they can put aside the disappointment and motivate themselves to try again, they are one step closer to reaching their goal. When all enthusiasm and motivation is lost then this is when the business is also lost.

8. Self-starter: Entrepreneurs know that if something needs to be done, they should start it themselves. They set the parameters and make sure that projects follow that path. They are proactive, not waiting for someone to give them permission.

9. Competitive: Many companies are formed because an entrepreneur knows that they can do a job better than any other. They need to win at the sports they play and need to win at the businesses that they create. An entrepreneur will highlight their own company's track record of success.

10. Calculated Risk Taker: An entrepreneur is having ability to take calculated risks. A risk situation involves potential gain or loss. Entrepreneurs are truly risk bearing agents as they take the responsibility for the loss that may arise due to uncertainties of future.

11. Innovative: An entrepreneur is always innovative. He adapts modern techniques of production and is not reluctant to changes. He keep on innovating new products or new techniques of production and tries to give the best to the society.

12. Decision Making: Entrepreneur has to take right decision at a right time by showing his promptness. Quick decisions are expected but hasty decisions should not be taken. Delay in decisions may increase cost of project and reduce the profits and the entrepreneur takes many decisions in day to day activities.

13. Negotiation skills: Businessman regularly comes into contact with various persons like consumers, workers, government officials, etc. An entrepreneur uses his negotiation skills well in order to deal with these persons in order to get his work done.

14. Organising Skills: An entrepreneur has to bring together all the required factors of production. An entrepreneur by using his organising skill combines land, labour and capital to produce a product. As an organizer, he perform various functions like planning, controlling and coordinating.

15. Information Seeker: An entrepreneur is ready to learn from the experiences of others and enriches his business information to help him reach his goals. He tries to seek maximum information from the environment which can help him in the attainment of his objectives.

1.9. CHARACTERISTICS OF ENTREPRENEUR

"The five essential entrepreneurial skills for success are concentration, discrimination,organisation, innovation and communication. " –Henry Reed.

There is no such thing as a typical entrepreneur. Some entrepreneurs are quiet and hard-working, while others are more outgoing and flamboyant. The key to being a successful entrepreneur lies in the ability to take an idea and then, through the process of innovation, develop it in such a way that it becomes a marketable product or service. Research indicates that there are a number of characteristics that are quite likely to be present in high-achieving entrepreneurs.

Entrepreneur is a key figure in economic progress. He is the person who introduces new things in the economy. **M. M. P. Akhouri,** formerly Executive Director, National Institute for Entrepreneurship and Small Business Development (NIESBUD), New Delhi, describes entrepreneur "as a character who combines innovativeness, readiness to take risk, sensing opportunities, identifying and mobilizing potential resources, concerns for excellence and who is persistent in achieving the goal. " To be successful, an entrepreneur should have the following characteristic features.

1. Innovative: Innovation means doing things in a new and better way. As an innovator, the entrepreneur foresees the potentially profitable opportunity and tries to exploit it. He is always involved in the process of doing new things. Innovation may take in following way:

(a) Introduction of new products;
(b) Introduction of new techniques of production;
(c) Opening of a new markets for products;
(d) New source of raw material;
(e) New type of organization and industry.

Innovation is the specific tool of entrepreneur, the means by which they exploit change as an opportunity for a different business or services.

2. Need to Achieve: Entrepreneurs have got strong desire to achieve higher goals. The high achievement motive strengthened them to face the obstacles, problems and difficulties. They have a high need of achievement called n-Ach' which means they want to excel in whatever they do. Their inner self motivates their behaviour towards high achievement; most of the people dream of success but do not take any action towards achieving these dreams. Entrepreneurs with high n-Ach factor act continuously to achieve the goal and make their dreams come true. For them, winning is achievement.

3. Risk Taking: Entrepreneurs are the persons who take decisions under conditions of uncertainty and therefore are willing to bear risk. This the important characteristic of an entrepreneur as he has to assume all possible risks of business which emerges due to possibility of changes in demand, modern techniques of production and new inventions. Successful entrepreneurs has ability to take calculated risk to achieve pre-determined industrial objectives. A risk situation involves potential gain or loss. They constantly put their efforts in introducing new products, new methods of production, opening new markets and recognizing the enterprise and it's very risky that the new product will be accepted by the market or not. So he takes the responsibility for loss that may arise due to uncertainties of future.

4. Independence: Most of the entrepreneurs start on their own because they do not like to work for others. The nature to be independent pushes them to start something of their own. They prefer to be their own boss and want to be responsible for their own decisions.

5. Optimistic: The successful entrepreneurs do not get disturbed by the present problems faced by them. They are optimistic for future that the situation will become favorable to business in future. They always keep positive view about the business.

6. Locus of Control: According to Rotter's locus of control theory, Individuals with a high internal locus of control believe that events in their life derive primarily from their own actions; for example, if a person with an internal locus of control does not perform as well as they wanted to on a test, they would blame it on lack of preparedness on their part. If they performed well on a test, they would attribute this to ability to study. Entrepreneurs believe in their own ability to control the consequences of their endeavor by influencing their socio-economic environment rather than leave everything to luck.

7. Mental Ability: Entrepreneur consist of creative thinking and intelligence and both are part of their mental ability. He has to be creative so that he can be innovative enough to lead the market and to give the best to the community. Entrepreneur must be intelligent enough to face the problems of the business so that he can take the right decisions at the right time.

8. Ability to Explore Opportunities: Entrepreneurs must always be alert and has to keep their eyes open for the forthcoming opportunities. They must be eager to grab opportunities. They must have the ability to explore the new opportunities to earn the maximum profit in the future.

9. Visionary: An entrepreneur has vision for growth and development so he explores new ideas, start his enterprise and provides added value to the society. On the basis of the visionary quality, an entrepreneur creates new idea, starts his enterprise and provides added value to the society.

10. Insight: The most successful entrepreneurs have been those who gained a key insight into the area of the business world that they are entering. They are able to identify a key advantage that they have over their competitors if they start a new business. Either from a new technique, a new technology or from a simple discovery of something like a new bookkeeping method. The entrepreneurs who changed business offered new important insights.

11. Social Responsibility: An entrepreneur must take social responsibility as his priority. All the innovations and creativity must be done for the welfare of the society and the whole economy. He must think of the projects of social significance and must make his profits alongwith benefits to the society.

12. Openness to Feedback and Learning from Experience: Entrepreneurs are always open to have immediate feedback for their performance. They learn from their experience and the feedback from the society and modify their plans accordingly. They keep on learning from their experiences in the journey of the venture set up and growth.

13. Human Relation Ability: An entrepreneur always maintains good and healthy relationships with his employees, customers, shareholders, creditors, etc. He has the ability to maintain and sustain these relationship for the growth of his business.

Entrepreneurs are always comfortable while dealing with people at all levels. They interact with raw material suppliers, customers, bankers, etc., for different activities. As successful entrepreneurs, they should be persons who like working with others possessing the much needed quality of interpersonal skill to deal with people.

14. Stress Takers: Entrepreneurs are capable of working for long hours and have good capacity to take stress. An entrepreneur faces a number of problems and at the right time he takes a right decision which involves a lot of stress. So an entrepreneur must be able to take this stress positively and must not loose heart at the tough time.

15. Perseverance: Entrepreneur has got the quality of sticking to the job he decides to undertake. Once committed to a specific goal, an entrepreneur tries to fulfill the same. Entrepreneur personally solves the problems that come across his way while setting up the project. He put his full efforts and works sincerely until the whole project is successfully implemented.

16. Effective Communication Ability: An entrepreneur must have good communication ability as good communication means the sender and receiver receives the message in the same manner without any confusion. So, if an entrepreneur will have good communication ability only then he can interact well with his employees, customers, suppliers, etc. Also, in order to motivate others in the business entrepreneurs must possess good communication skill. Both written and oral communication skills are necessary for the entrepreneurs for running the enterprise efficiently.

17. Leadership: Entrepreneurs must have the quality of leadership. Entrepreneurs as leaders should provide the necessary spark to motivation by guiding, inspiring, assisting and directing the members of the group for achievement of unity of action, efforts and purpose. Entrepreneur as a leader leads the organization and effectively handles the problems of the employees.

18. Planner: Planning implies deciding in advance what to do, when to do and how to do a thing. Entrepreneurs must have skill and knowledge to prepare their business plan. A successful entrepreneur always plans in advance and the planning starts from the day an entrepreneur conceives an idea to start something on their own. Planning provides a sense of vision to the entrepreneurs to cope with risky situations.

19. Desire for responsibility: Entrepreneurs feel deep sense of responsibility for the outcomes of their venture. They take the full responsibility of the venture they start and prefer to take responsibility of their resources in order to achieve self determined goals.

20. Future Orientation: Entrepreneurs are future-oriented as they always look ahead. They keep on looking for opportunities and always remain focused on the future. Traditional managers were concerned with managing available resources but modern entrepreneurs are more interested in spotting future opportunities.

1.10. TYPES OF ENTREPRENEURS

Following are the classification of entrepreneurs (Fig. 1.6) on the basis of common characteristics:-

TYPES OF ENTREPRENEURS

A. Clarence Danhof classification
1. Aggressive/Innovative
2. Imitative/ Adoptive
3. Fabian
4. Drone

B. Arthur H. Cole classification
1. Empirical
2. Rational
3. Cognitive

C. On the basis of ownership
1. Private
2. Public
3. Large-scale

D. On the basis of scale of enterprise
1. Small-scale
2. Medium-scale

E. According to type of businesses
1. Business Entrepreneurs
2. Trading Entrepreneurs
3. Corporate Entrepreneurs
4. Agriculture Entrepreneurs
5. Industrial Entrepreneurs

F. On the basis of gender
1. Men Entrepreneurs
2. Women Entrepreneurs

G. Others
1. Solo Operators
2. Active Partners
3. Serial Entrepreneurs
4. Buyers (Entrepreneurs)
5. Technical Entrepreneurs
6. Prime Movers
7. Minor Innovators
8. Based on Entrepreneur
9. Early Starters
10. Experienced Entrepreneurs
11. 1st Generation Entrepreneurs
12. Novice Business

Fig. 1.6.

A. Clarence Danhof Classification

Clarence Danhof classifies entrepreneurs into four types.

1. Innovating Entrepreneurs: Innovative entrepreneurs are aggressive by nature. These are ones who assembles and synthesis information and introduces new combinations of factors of production. They are characterized by the smell of innovativeness. These entrepreneurs sense the opportunities for introduction of new ideas, new methods of production, new technology, discovers new markets and creating new organizations. For this one need not be inventive only but can be one who convert even old established products and services, by changing their utility, their value, their economic characteristic into new, attractive and more utility product. These entrepreneurs experiments and converts the attractive possibilities into practice. Innovative entrepreneurs are very much helpful to their country because they bring about a transformation in lifestyle, *e.g.*, new product, new ways of product, new markets and reorganise the enterprise.

2. Imitative/Adoptive Entrepreneurs: Imitative entrepreneurs are also known as adoptive entrepreneurs. They are characterized by readiness to adopt successful innovation inaugurated by innovating entrepreneurs. He simply adopts successful innovations introduced by other innovators. These entrepreneurs imitate the existing entrepreneurs and set up their enterprise in the same manner. Instead of innovating, they just imitate the technology and methods innovated by others. These types of entrepreneurs are found in underdeveloped countries. These entrepreneurs are very helpful in less developed countries or developing countries as they contribute significantly in the growth of enterprise and entrepreneurial culture in these countries. Further by adopting the technology, which is already tested, they generate ample employment avenues for the youth and therefore, they are treated as agents of economic development. In some cases, these entrepreneurs make some changes in the innovations made by the innovative entrepreneurs so as to suit their requirements. E.g. Chinese mobiles.

3. Fabian Entrepreneurs: The Fabian entrepreneurs are very cautious, timid and skeptical in experimenting any change in their enterprise. These entrepreneurs have neither the will to introduce new changes nor desire to adopt new methods innovated by the most enterprising entrepreneurs. He imitates other innovations only if he is certain that failure to do so may damage his business. They are very much skeptical in their approach in adopting or innovating new technology in their enterprise. They are not adaptable to the changing environment. They love to remain in the existing business with the age-old techniques of production as they are termed as lazy and shy. They only adopt the new technology when they realize that failure to adopt will lead to loss or collapse of the enterprise.

4. Drone: These entrepreneurs are conservative in outlook. They are characterized by refusal to adopt opportunities to make changes. These entrepreneurs are rigid and they resist change. They never like to get rid of their traditional business and traditional machinery or systems of the business. They always feel comfortable with their old fashioned technology of production even though the environment as well as the society have undergone considerable change. They are laggards as they continue to operate in their traditional way and resist changes. His entrepreneurial activity may be restricted to just one or two innovations. They refuse to adopt changes in production even at the risk of reduced returns. They struggle to exist, not to grow. They continue in their traditional way and their product loses its marketability or their operations becomes uneconomical and they are pushed out of the market.

B. Arthur H. Cole Classification

Arthur H. Cole divides the history of American entrepreneurship into three stages of entrepreneurial thought processes:

Stage	Style of thought	Dates
1. Empirical	Rule of thumb	From scratch to 1860
2. Rational	Informed	1860-1890
3. Coginitive	Sophisticated	From 1890 onwards

1. Empirical: He is an entrepreneur who hardly introduces anything revolutionary and follows the principle of rule of thumb.

2. Rational: The rational entrepreneur is well informed about the general economic conditions and introduces changes which are more revolutionary.

3. Cognitive: Cognitive entrepreneur is well informed, draws upon the advice and services of experts and introduces changes that reflect complete break from the existing scheme of enterprise.

C. Classification on the Basis of Ownership

1. Private: Private Entrepreneur is when the enterprise is set up by an individual or group of individuals privately by arranging finance. Private entrepreneur is motivated by profit and will not enter those sectors of the economy in which prospects of monetary rewards are not very bright.

2. Public: In the underdeveloped countries, government will take the initiative to share enterprises. These enterprises are owned by the government.

D. Classification Based on the Scale of Enterprise

1. Small-scale: This classification is especially popular in the underdeveloped and developing countries. An undertaking having investment plan in plant and machinery is more than ₹ 25 lakhs but does not exceed ₹ 5 crores. Small entrepreneurs do not possess the necessary resources to initiate large-scale production and introduce revolutionary technological changes.

2. Medium-scale: According to "MICRO, SMALL AND MEDIUM ENTERPRISES DEVELOPMENT ACT, 2006" under subsection (1) of section 7, Medium enterprise is where the investment in plant and machinery is more than ₹ five crores but does not exceedes ₹ ten crores.

3. Large-scale: In the developed countries most entrepreneurs deal with large-scale enterprises. They possess the financial and necessary enterprise to initiate and introduce new technical changes. The result is that the developed countries are able to sustain and develop a high level of technical progress. Under large-scale industries, the investment in plant and machinery is more than ₹ ten crores.

E. According to Type of Business

1. Business Entrepreneurs: These are those individuals who conceive an idea for a new product/ service and then create a business to materialize their idea into reality. They are known as either small, medium or large-scale business entrepreneurs and this scale is according to the amount of investment made. In majority of cases entrepreneurs are found in small trading and manufacturing business.

2. Trading Entrepreneurs: These are those entrepreneurs who are not into manufacturing business but undertakes trading activities. They are simply in the trading of goods according to the potential and need of the market. They are engaged in both domestic and international trade. Due to some of the geographical limitations in some cases only trading entrepreneurs helps in development of trade.

3. Corporate Entrepreneurs: These are those entrepreneurs who use their skills and innovations in organizing and managing a corporate undertaking. A corporate enterprise is a business organization but it has separate legal entity. Corporate undertakings can be a company under Companies Act or a trust under Trust Act.

4. Agriculture Entrepreneurs: Agricultural entrepreneurs are those entrepreneurs who are involved in agricultural activities. They do innovations in agriculture like: raising of new type of crops, fertilizers and other inputs of agriculture. They are innovative and is motivated to increase productivity of agriculture through application of new technology. It includes agriculture and allied activities.

5. Industrial Entrepreneurs: These are those entrepreneurs who are into manufacturing business. These entrepreneurs sense the need of the customer and manufacture the product accordingly. Industrial entrepreneurs starts the industrial units if there is possibility of making of new product.

F. On the Basis of Gender

1. Men Entrepreneurs: These are those entrepreneurs who do innovation, start their enterprises and set up businesses. It can be classified as young entrepreneurs, old entrepreneurs, middle aged entrepreneurs etc. It includes any enterprises started by male member of the society.

2. Female Entrepreneurs: Any women or group of women who initiate, organize, and operate a business enterprise is known as women entrepreneur. Government of India, defined women entrepreneurs as an enterprise owned and controlled by women and having minimum financial interest of 51% of the capital and giving at least 51% of the employment generated in the enterprise to women.

G. Others

In recent years, some new classifications have been made regarding entrepreneurs, which are discussed further.

1. Solo Operators: These entrepreneurs prefer to set up their business individually. They introduce their own capital, intellect and other resources to run the enterprise successfully. This is basically proprietorship type of concern. They are the owners of the concern and are liable for their actions.

2. Active Partners: Entrepreneurs of this type jointly put their efforts to build the enterprise pooling together their own resources. They actively participate in managing the daily routine of the business concern. As such, the business houses or the firms which are managed by active partners become more successful in their operation.

3. Serial Entrepreneurs: These are those entrepreneurs who repeatedly start businesses and grow them to a sustainable size. The majority of serial entrepreneurs start a company, manage its growth and then sell it to start another one and few of them are jugglers(parallel entrepreneurs), people who start and manage several companies at one time.

4. Buyers (Entrepreneurs): These entrepreneurs explore opportunities to purchase the existing units which may be seized or are in running condition. If the units they purchase are sick they turn them around using their experiences, expertise and business acumen. By purchasing these units they make themselves free from the hassles of building infrastructures and other facilities.

5. Technical Entrepreneurs: A technical entrepreneur develops new and improved quality of goods due to his craftsmanship. The skill in production techniques is the greatest strength of technical entrepreneurs.

6. Prime Movers: This entrepreneur sets in motion a powerful sequence of development, expansion and diversification of business. E.g. Ambani

7. Minor Innovators: This entrepreneur contributes to economic progress by finding better use for existing resources. E.g. : Minimum wastage, maximum production.

8. Based on Entrepreneurs Business

(1) **Manufacturing:** An entrepreneur who manufacture the product by using the available resources and supplies. E.g. : Chemical and related products, textile products, etc

(2) **Wholesaling:** The entrepreneur who sells product to the middle man.

(3) **Retailing:** An entrepreneur with such business sells goods directly to the consumers.

(4) **Service:** In this an entrepreneurs sells services instead of goods.

9. Early Starters: This classification is based on the timing of the venture creation. Early starters start their business with no full time or little work experience. Normally they are from the business families or the persons who are having great potential. Example: Suhas Gopinath, who started his company Global Inc., at the age of 14. Moreover, he incorporated his company in USA as Indian law do not permit minor to run a company on their own.

10. Experienced Entrepreneurs: Theses types of entrepreneurs has spent few years working in the family business or any other large company. In this the entrepreneur brings a lot of experience &skill into the venture.

11. First Generation Entrepreneurs: These are those entrepreneurs whose families are not at all in the business or who are new in the business. These are those entrepreneurs who with their innovation and new ideas set up their own enterprise. Example: Dhirubhai Ambani, Narayan Murthy.

12. Novice: These are those entrepreneurs who are classified on the bases of entrepreneurial activity. They are someone who started his/her first entrepreneurial venture but they must not be confused with early starters. A novice can be anyone, he can be 50 years old with 25 years of experience. Example: Vishamber Saran who was the director of raw material for Tata Steel. He resigned from Tata Steel after serving the company for 35 years and started his own venture as Visa Steel.

1.11. FUNCTIONS OF AN ENTREPRENEURS

An entrepreneur is an opportunity seeker. He is also the organizer and coordinator of the agents of production. He has to execute many functions while establishing an enterprise. He not only perceives the business opportunities but also mobilizes other resources like 5Ms — man, money, machine, materials and methods.

However, the main functions of the entrepreneurs are discussed further.

1. Risk bearing function: The functions of an entrepreneur as risk bearer is specific in nature. The entrepreneur assumes all possible risks of business which emerges due to the possibility of changes in the tastes of consumers, modern techniques of production and new inventions. Such risks are not insurable and calculable. In simple terms such risks are known as uncertainty concerning a loss.

The entrepreneur, according to Knight, "is the economic functionary who undertakes such responsibility of uncertainty which by its very nature cannot be insured nor capitalised nor salaried too. " Richard Cantillon conceived of an entrepreneur as a bearer of non-insurable risk because he described an entrepreneur as a person who buys things at a certain price and sells them at an uncertain price.

Thus, risk bearing or uncertainty bearing still remains the most important function of an entrepreneur which he tries to minimise by his initiative, skill and good judgement. J. B. Say and others have stressed risk taking as the specific function of the entrepreneur.

2. Idea generation: This is the most important and most critical function of the entrepreneur as the whole project depends on idea generation. Idea generation can only be possible through vision, insight, observation, experience, education, training and exposure of the entrepreneur. There are many opportunities in the world of business which are based on human needs like food, fashion, education, etc. It help an entrepreneur in the generation of an idea. Idea generation precisely implies product selection and project identification. Ideas can be generated by scanning the environment and market survey. An entrepreneur has to generate as many ideas as he can for the purpose of selecting the best business opportunities.

3. Innovative function: The basic function an entrepreneur performs is to innovate new products, services, ideas and informations for the enterprise. As an innovator, the entrepreneur foresees the potentially profitable opportunity and tries to exploit it. He is always involved in the process of doing new things. According to Peter Drucker, "Innovation is the means by which the entrepreneur either creates new wealth producing resources or endows existing resources with enhanced potential for creating wealth". Whenever a new idea occurs entrepreneurial efforts are essential to convert the idea into practical application. J. A. Schumpeter considered economic development as a descrete dynamic change brought by entrepreneurs by instituting new combinations of production, *i.e.*, innovation. According to him innovation may occur in any one of the following five forms:

(a) The introduction of a new product in the market with which the customers are not get familiar with.

(b) Introduction of a new method of production technology which is not yet tested by experience in the branch of manufacture concerned.

(c) The opening of a new market into which the specific product has not previously entered.

(d) The discovery of a new source of supply of raw material, irrespective of whether this source already exists or has first to be created.

(e) The carrying out of the new form of organisation of any industry by creating of a monopoly position or the breaking up of it.

4. Determination of objectives: The next function of the entrepreneur is to determine and lay down the objectives of the business. In other words, entrepreneur should be very much clear about the various objectives to be achieved, nature of business and the type of business.

5. Organisational function: Entrepreneur as an organiser and his organising function is described by J. B. Say, as a function whereby the entrepreneur brings together various factors of production, ensures continuing management and renders risk bearing functions as well. His definition associates entrepreneur with the functions of coordination, organisation and supervision. According to him, an entrepreneur is one who combines the land of one, the labour of another and the capital of yet another and thus, produces a product. By selling the product in the market, he pays interest on capital, rent on land and wages to labourers and what remains is his/her profit. In this way, he describes an entrepreneur as an organiser who alone determines the lines of business to expand and capital to employ judiciously. He is the ultimate judge in the conduct of the business.

6. Raising of funds: Fund raising is the most important function of an entrepreneur. All the activities of a business depends upon the finance and its proper management. The entrepreneur decides about the capital structure of the enterprise and the requirement of finance. Then the sources are determind, which can be either internal or external. In this matter, he should be aware of the different sources of funds and the formalities to raise funds. He should have the full knowledge of different government sponsored schemes by which he can get government assistance in the form of seed capital, fixed and working capital for his business. Moreover, different banks are also helpful in providing finance for short as well as long period.

7. Procurement of raw materials: Another important function of the entrepreneur is the procurement of raw material. Raw material is basic resource, so entrepreneur has to identify the better and regular sources. Easy availability of raw material reduces the cost of the product and it will help him to face the competition. So an entrepreneur has to check accessibility of raw material with due care.

8. Managerial function: Entrepreneur also performs a variety of managerial function like determination of business objectives, formulation of production plans, product analysis and market research, organisation of sales, procuring machine and material, recruitment of men and undertaking, of business operations. He also undertakes the basic managerial functions of planning, organising, coordinating, staffing, directing, motivating and controlling the enterprise.

9. Market research: The next important function of the entrepreneur is market research and product analysis. Market research is any organized effort to gather information about markets or customers. It includes, systematic collection of data regarding the product which the entrepreneur wants to manufacture. Market research is a key factor to get advantage over competitors. Market research provides important information to identify and analyze the market need, market size and competition. Entrepreneur has to undertake market research persistently in order to know the details of the intending product, *i.e.*, the demand for the product, the supply of the product, the price of the product, the size of the customers, etc., while starting an enterprise.

10. Recruitment of manpower: This function involves manning the positions created by the organization process. It is concerned with the human resources of an enterprise. Entrepreneur has to perform the following activities while undertaking this function:

(a) Assessing manpower need of the organization in terms of quality and qualtity.

(b) Laying down of recruitment, selection and training procedure

(c) Placement of manpower

(d) Devising scheme of compensation

11. Feasibility study: The entrepreneur conducts studies to assess the market feasibility of the proposed product or services. He anticipates problems and assesses quantity, quality, cost and sources of inputs required to run the enterprise. Such a blueprint of all the activities is termed as a 'business plan' or a 'project report'.

12. Implementation of the project: Entrepreneur has to work on the implementation schedule of the project. Implementation of project is very important activity and has to done within the time limit. All the activities from the conception stage to the commissioning stage are to be accomplished by him in accordance with the implementation schedule to avoid cost and time overrun, as well as competition.

13. Decision making function: The most vital function an entrepreneur discharges refers to decision making in various fields of the business enterprise. He is the decision maker of all activities of the enterprise. A. H. Cole described an entrepreneur as a decision maker and attributed the following functions to him.

He determines the business objectives suitable for the enterprise, he develops an organization and creates an atmosphere for maintaining a cordial relationship with subordinates and all employees of the organization, he decides in securing adequate financial resources for the organisation and maintains good relations with the existing and potential investors and financiers, he decides in introducing advanced modern technology in the enterprise to cope up with changing scenario of manufacturing process, he decides the development of a market for his product, develops new product or modify the existing product in accordance with the changing consumer's fashion, taste and preference.

14. Determining the size of the enterprise: The size of the firm or the scale at which the proposed enterprise is to be started is an important function performed by an entrepreneur. It is essential for an entrepreneur to prepare both short and long-term forecast of sales before taking any decision about the size of the firm. Size of the enterprise is very important as on the basis of size. Rest of the decisions regarding finance, manpower, machinery, etc., can only be taken.

1.12. REASONS FOR ENTREPRENEURIAL FAILURE

Entrepreneurial success is very important for the growth of the economy. But that is not possible without team efforts and the team is made up of various investors, partners, employees, clients, etc.

All are very important for the success of the enterprise, but there are many reasons for the failure of the enterprise. It can be because of limited resources, inexperienced management, new venture, less confidence by the customers, etc. These are:

1. Poor Management: Many a report on business failures cites poor management as the number one reason for failure. New business owners frequently lack relevant business and management expertise in areas such as finance, purchasing, selling, production, and hiring and managing employees. Unless they recognize what they do not do well, and seek help, business owners may soon face disaster. They must also be educated and alert to fraud, and put into place, measures to avoid it.

Neglect of a business can also be its downfall. Care must be taken to regularly study, organize, plan and control all activities of its operations. This includes the continuing study of market research and customer data, an area which one may be more prone to disregard it once a business has been established.

A successful manager is also a good leader who creates a work climate that encourages productivity. He or she has a skill of hiring competent people, training them and is able to delegate. A good leader is also skilled at strategic thinking, able to make a vision a reality, and able to confront change, make transitions, and envision new possibilities for the future.

2. Insufficient Capital: A common fatal mistake for many failed businesses is having insufficient operating funds. Business owners underestimate how much money is needed and they are forced to close before they even have had a fair chance to succeed. They also may have an unrealistic expectation of incoming revenues from sales.

It is imperative to ascertain how much money your business will require; not only the costs of starting, but the costs of staying in business. It is important to take into consideration that many businesses take a year or two to get going. This means you will need enough funds to cover all costs until sales can eventually pay for these costs. This business start-up calculator will help you predict how much money you will need to launch your business.

3. Location: Location is critical to the success of your business. Whereas a good business location may enable a struggling business to ultimately survive and thrive, a bad location could spell disaster to even the best managed enterprise.

Some factors to consider:

- Where your customers are
- Traffic, accessibility, parking and lighting
- Location of competitors
- Condition and safety of building
- Local incentive programs for business start-ups in specific targeted areas
- The history, community flavor and receptiveness to a new business at a prospective site

4. Lack of Planning: Anyone who has ever been in charge of a successful major event knows that were it not for their careful, methodical, strategic planning — and hard work — success would not have followed. The same could be said of most business successes.

It is critical for all businesses to have a business plan. Many small businesses fail because of fundamental shortcomings in their business planning. It must be realistic and based on accurate, current information and educated projections for the future.

Components may include:

- Description of the business, vision, goals, and keys to success
- Workforce needs
- Potential problems and solutions
- Financial capital, equipment and supply list, balance sheet, income statement and cash flow analysis, sales and expense forecast
- Analysis of competition
- Marketing, advertising and promotional activities
- Budgeting and managing company growth

5. Overexpansion: A leading cause of business failure, overexpansion, often happens when business owners confuse success with how fast they can expand their business. A focus on slow and steady growth is optimum. Many a bankruptcy has been caused by rapidly expanding companies.

At the same time, you do not want to repress growth. Once you have an established solid customer base and a good cash flow, let your success help you set the right measured pace. Some indications that an expansion may be warranted include the inability to fill customer needs in a timely basis, and employees having difficulty in keeping up with production demands.

If expansion is warranted after careful review, research and analysis, identify what and who you need to add in order for your business to grow. Then with the right systems and people in place, you can focus on the growth of your business, not on doing everything by yourself.

6. Lack of Information: Information is very important for any type of business. But some times due to lack of information or incorrect information act as a source of business failure. In this era, information is needed at each and every step but blockage in this information, act as hurdle in the entrepreneurship growth and may lead to failure of the venture.

7. Lack of Understanding of Technical Requirement: In order to become a successful entrepreneur there must be innovation of new products and it mostly involves new techniques. But lack of understanding of the need for technology can sink a new venture. Sometimes unexpected occurrence of technical difficulties consumes much of the time and can halt the new venture.

1.12.1. The Four Entrepreneurial Pitfalls-by Peter Drucker

Peter Drucker pointed out in his book, *Managing in the Next Society*, that there are four entrepreneurial pitfalls where the new and growing business typically gets into trouble.

The first pitfall *comes when the entrepreneur has to face the fact that the new product or service is not successful where he or she thought it would be but is successful in a totally different market.* The pitfall is that it is often entrepreneurs who reject success. The majority of successful new product or service does not succeed in the market as the founder-entrepreneur thought it would. But it succeeds in a totally different market. Many businesses fail because the founder-entrepreneur is so obsessed with his or her original plan and refuse to grab the opportunity in the unexpected market. According to Drucker, "The majority of successful new inventions or products do not succeed in the market for which they were originally designed"

Novocaine was invented in 1905 by German chemist Alfred Einhorn for use in major surgery, but it was not suitable. Dentists immediately wanted the product, but the inventor actually tried to stop them from using it for the "mundane purpose" of drilling teeth. To the end of his days, Einhorn travelled all over the world preaching the merits of novocaine as a general anesthetic.

The second pitfall is that entrepreneurs do not pay enough attention to cash flow. Entrepreneurs believe that profit is what matters most in a new enterprise. But profit is secondary. Cash flow matters most. Many businesses are getting caught in a cash crunch because entrepreneurs are financially illiterate and have a hard time grasping the concept of cash flow.

The third pitfall is that the entrepreneur outgrows his management base when business grows rapidly beyond expectations. Starting out, the typical founder does everything by himself. He sees the sales figures, and he sees profit forecasts. When business grows, the entrepreneur begins running around like the proverbial one-armed paperhanger. Unfortunately, the entrepreneur does not realize he has outgrown his management capabilities. He does not get the management team in place quick enough. Then all the sudden, everything goes wrong. The quality falls out of bed. Customers do not pay. Deliveries are missed. The business is eventually hit hard by management crunch.

According to Drucker, "To avoid a crisis, you should sit down and create a management team. By that time you have, maybe 40 people working for you. Look them over to see who shows management ability. You call in those 4 or 5 people (you're not likely to have more), and you say, "I want each of you to sit down alone next weekend and look at the other people here, including me. Don't look at yourself. Look at the others, and think about what each of them is good at. " And then you all sit down together, take a fresh sheet of paper, and list the key activities of the business. Today we call this - establishing our core competencies. "

The fourth pitfall is the most difficult one. In this entrepreneur begins to put himself and his needs before his business when the business is a success. He has worked eighteen hours a day for fourteen years. He does not enjoy it anymore. He knows he's not concentrating on the right things. But it is difficult for him to face up to the harsh reality and start asking "What does the business need at this stage?" and "Do I have those qualities?" He does not realize that it is time to bring in an outsider. He ends up killing himself and the business.

There can be many more reasons and pitfalls which act as failure for entrepreneurial venture but sometimes these failures act as a pillar for success. Here are some case studies:

(1) Henry Ford: While Ford is today known for his innovative assembly line and American-made cars, he was not an instant success. In fact, his early businesses failed and left him broke five times before he founded the successful Ford Motor Company.

(2) Bill Gates: Gates did not seem like a shoe-in for success after dropping out of Harvard and starting a failed first business with Microsoft co-founder Paul Allen called Traf-O-Data. While this early idea did not work, Gates' later work did, creating the global empire, that is, Microsoft.

(3) Soichiro Honda: The billion-dollar business that is Honda began with a series of failures and fortunate turns of luck. Honda was turned down by Toyota Motor Corporation him after interviewing for a job as an engineer, leaving him jobless for quite some time. He started making scooters of his own at home, and spurred on by his neighbors, finally started his own business.

(4) Walt Disney: Today Disney rakes in billions from merchandise, movies and theme parks around the world, but Walt Disney himself had a bit of a rough start. He was fired by a newspaper editor because, "he lacked imagination and had no good ideas. " After that, Disney started a number of businesses that did not last too long and ended with bankruptcy and failure. He kept plugging along, however, and eventually found a recipe for success that worked.

1.13. DISTINCTION BETWEEN AN ENTREPRENEUR AND A MANAGER

The terms Entrepreneur and Manager are considered one and the same. But the two terms have different meanings. The following are some of the differences between a manager and an entrepreneur:

1. The main reason for an entrepreneur to start a business enterprise is because he comprehends the venture for his individual satisfaction and has personal stake in it whereas a manager provides his services in an enterprise established by someone.

2. An entrepreneur and a manager differ in their standing, an entrepreneur is the owner of the organization and he bears all the risk and uncertainties involved in running an organization whereas a manager is an employee and does not accept any risk.

3. An entrepreneur and a manager differ in their objectives. Entrepreneur's objective is to innovate and create and he acts as a change agent whereas a manager's objective is to supervise and create routines. He implements the entrepreneur's plans and ideas.

4. An entrepreneur is faced with more income uncertainties as his income is contingent on the performance of the firm whereas a manager's compensation is less dependent on the performance of the organization.

5. An entrepreneur is not induced to involve in fraudulent behavior whereas a manger does. A manager may cheat by not working hard because his income is not tied up to the performance of the organization.

6. Entrepreneur is required to have certain qualifications and qualities like high accomplishment motive, innovative thinking, forethought, risk bearing ability, etc. Conversely, it's mandatory for a manager to be educated in the fields of management theories and practices.

7. An entrepreneur deals with faults and failures as a part of learning experience whereas a manager make every effort to avoid mistakes and he postpones failure.

8. "An entrepreneur could be a manager but a manager cannot be an entrepreneur". An entrepreneur is intensely dedicated to develop business through constant innovation. He may employ a manager in order to perform some of his functions such as setting objectives, policies, rules, etc. A manager cannot replace an entrepreneur in spite of performing the allotted duties because a manager has to work as per the guidelines laid down by the entrepreneur.

9. An Entrepreneur gets uncertain rewards but a manager gets fixed salary.

10. An Entrepreneur is driven by perception of opportunity and a manager is driven by the resources he currently possesses.

1.14. DISTINCTION BETWEEN AN ENTREPRENEUR AND BUSINESSMAN

Businessman	Entrepreneur
1. Starts a business from an existing idea or concept	1. Starts a business from his own unique idea or concept
2. Focuses on competition	2. Focuses on cooperation
3. Usually plays safe	3. Bold and ambitious
4. Profit-oriented	4. People-oriented (*i.e.*, employee, customer, public)
5. Hires people to increase business productivity	5. Hires people to give them productivity
6. A market player	6. A market leader
7. May be purchased, donated or inherited	7. Creates his own ideas and realizes it as a business
8. Traditional businessmen, as the name suggest, like to stick to crowded markets.	8. Entrepreneurs tend to pick up niches that are not overcrowded. In fact, they create new niche and market segments.

1.15. DISTINCTION BETWEEN AN ENTREPRENEUR AND AN INTRAPRENEUR

Entrepreneur

An entrepreneur is a person who starts a business venture with his own business idea. He/she funds the venture, that is, invests all of the necessary capital. He/she also assumes the associated risk and is the primary decision maker and decides how much of the goods or service will be produced, where it will be produced, how it will be produced and who the target market is. An entrepreneur is a single owner, a partner or the individual who owns the most shares in a corporation, *Business Dictionary* reports. In the process of bringing the new project into market, the entrepreneur undertakes number of responsibilities such as perceiving opportunities for profitable investment, explores the prospects of starting an enterprise, obtains the license, arranges the required capital, etc. So entrepreneur is an economic agent who unites all means of production to maximize his profits by innovations.

Intrapreneur

Organizations sometimes give creative employees the opportunity to act as entrepreneurs. This is called intrapreneurship, according to U. S. Legal. The term intrapreneur was put to use in America in the late 70s. In America some of the business executives left their jobs and started their own business because they do not get to chance to explore their innovative ideas earlier and these executive turned entrepreneurs posed threat to the organizations they left. So, Gifford Pinchot III in his book used the word 'Intrapreneur' who left their jobs and launched their own business. So nowadays these executives are provided with enough opportunities within the firm to come up with the innovative ideas, suggestions, proposals and enable them to grow. E.g.: A company is launching a new product, such as a new type of cellphone. The company may give a certain employee the authority to decide where the parts for the cellphone are obtained; where the cell phone is manufactured; and who the target market is, *i.e.*, teenagers, young adults or middle-aged adults. Therefore, the employee is acting as an entrepreneur within the organization.

Intrapreneurs have a different mindset. They can perform many similar acts to entrepreneurs, but they tend to do so without taking the personal financial risk. Intrapreneurs live within established organisations and whilst their ego may be dented and indeed their career prospects may be dented if their intrapreneurial project does not work, they are unlikely to suffer the financial consequences that befall the entrepreneur when their venture fails.

1.16. HOW TO BECOME A SUCCESSFUL ENTREPRENEUR?

In order to become successful, an entrepreneur must possess the following qualities:

- Knowledge of Organisation
- Technical Knowledge
- Administrative Ability
- Ability to Instruct and Inspire
- Creative
- Ability to Listen and Judge People
- Leadership Qualities
- Social Sensibility
- Physical Qualities

1.17. SUMMARY

Entrepreneur is an important agent for economic development. Economic growth and development means steady growth in income levels. This growth mainly depends upon entrepreneurs. An entrepreneur is a person who identifies opportunities and exploits it for economic development. An entrepreneur can be regarded as a person who has the initiative skill and motivation to set up a business or enterprise of his own and who always looks for high achievements. The word "Entrepreneur" is derived from the French verb '*entrepredre*'. It means '**to undertake**'. Since that time the word entrepreneur means one who takes the risk of starting a new organization or introducing a new idea, product or service to society.

1.18. SELF ASSESSMENT QUESTIONS

1. Define Entrepreneur. Discuss the nature and characteristics of an entrepreneur.
2. Does an entrepreneur have to be a business owner?
3. Explain how to become a successful entrepreneur and what are the functions of an entrepreneur?
4. Are entrepreneurs born or to made? Explain along with the qualities of a successful entrepreneur.
5. Explain the different types of entrepreneurs.
6. How does an entrepreneur contribute to the economy and the society?
7. Outline the causes of entrepreneurial failure.
8. What are usually the personal considerations that drive a person to be an entrepreneur?

SOURCE/NOTES

1. Center for Entrepreneurial Learning and Leadership: Working Paper Series Working Paper 01–2011: *The Evolution of Entrepreneurship Theory.*
2. Center for Entrepreneurial Learning and Leadership: Working Paper Series Working Paper 01–2011: *The Evolution of Entrepreneurship Theory.*
3. J.A Schumpeter, *The Theory of Economic Development: An Enquiry into Profits, Capital, Interests and The Business Cycle.*
4. http://kalyan-city.blogspot.com/2010/11/what-is-entrepreneur-qualities-or.html
5. Carlson, N.R., *et al.* (2007). Psychology: *The Science of Behaviour* - 4th Canadian ed. Toronto, ON: Pearson Education Canada. (And) https://en.wikipedia.org/wiki/Locus_of_control
6. Acharyan N.G. Ranga, Agricultural University-Entrepreneurship Development (study material) - Dr. V.Sudharani.
7. Arthur Cole, *Entrepreneurial History,* Johnathan R.T. Hughes Northwestern University
8. Acharyan N.G Ranga, Agricultural University-Entrepreneurship Development (study material)- Dr.V.Sudharani & http://www.preservearticles.com/201101143322/functions-of-an-entrepreneur.html
9. http://www.proccounting.com/resources/articles/49-the-four-entrepreneurial-pitfalls.html
10. www.businessknowhow.com & www.inc.com

2

THE FOUNDATIONS OF ENTREPRENEURSHIP

2.1. INTRODUCTION

Entrepreneurship comes from the French verb *'entreprendre'* which means 'to undertake'. It is the act and art of being an entrepreneur or one who undertakes innovations or introducing new things, finance and business acumen in an effort to transform innovations into economic goods. This may result in new organizations or may be part of revitalizing mature organizations in response to a perceived opportunity. So it is the process of creating something new with value by devoting the necessary time and effort, assuming the accompanying financial, social risk and receiving the resulting monetary rewards and personal satisfaction. The most obvious form of entrepreneurship is that of starting new businesses; however, in recent years, the term has been extended to include social and political forms of entrepreneurial activity. Entrepreneurship is a process of action an entrepreneur undertakes to establish his enterprise. So, is the process of exploring the opportunities in the market place and arranging resources required to exploit these opportunities for long-term gain. It is a dynamic activity which helps the entrepreneur to bring changes in the process of production, innovation in production, new usage of materials, creator of markets, etc.

Entrepreneurial ventures are having heavy impact on the economy of the whole world. In India too, there has been significant change in the mindset of society. Earlier, entrepreneurship preferred by socio-ethnic groups but nowadays the mindset of youth has been changed and they are turning their attention to emerging business opportunities. Many more are opting for entrepreneurial venture as their career.

2.2. HISTORY OF ENTREPRENEURSHIP

The entrepreneur is a factor in microeconomics, and the study of entrepreneurship reaches back to the work of Richard Cantillon and Adam Smith in the late 17th and early 18th centuries, but was largely ignored theoretically until the late 19th and early 20th centuries and empirically, until a profound resurgence in business and economics in the last 40 years.In the 20th century, the understanding of entrepreneurship owes much to the work of economist Joseph Schumpeter in the 1930s and other Austrian economists such as Carl Menger, Ludwig von Mises and Friedrich von Hayek

The early history of entrepreneurship in India reflects from the culture, customs and tradition of the Indian people. It is divided into two sections:-

(a) Entrepreneurship during pre-Independence

(b) Entrepreneurship during post-Independence

(a) Entrepreneurship during pre-Independence: The evolution of the Indian entrepreneurship can be traced back to even as early as Rigveda, when metal handicrafts existed in the society. Before India came into contact with west, people were organized in a particular type of economic and social system of the village community. Evidently, organized industrial activity was observable among the India artisans in a few recognizable products in the cities of Banaras, Allahabad, Gaya, Puri and Mirzapur which were established on their river basins. The process of entrepreneurship therefore passed through the potential roots of the society and all those who accepted entrepreneurial role had the cultural heritage of trade and business. Occupational pursuits opted by the individual under the caste system received different meaning of value attached to entrepreneurship. Which is based on social sanctions. Vaishyas are considered to venture into business pursuits. As society grew and the process of business occupation depended and the value of work tended towards change and the various occupational role interchanged with non-role group and subgroups. People from different castes and status also entered into the entrepreneurial role. The emergence of entrepreneurship in this part of the country got localized and spread effect took its own time.

Ranchodlal Chotalal, a Nagar Brahman, was the first Indian to think of setting up the textile manufacturing on the modern factory lines in 1847, but failed. In his second attempt, he succeeded in setting up a textile mill in 1861 at Ahmadabad. But before this, the first cotton textile manufacturing unit was already setup by a Parsi, Cowasjee Nanabhoy Dabar in Bombay in 1854, followed by Nawrosjee Wadia who opened his textile mill in Bombay in 1880. The credit for the expansion of textile industries upto 1915 goes to the Parsis. Out of 96 textile mills existing in 1915, 43% (41) were set up by Parsis, 24% (23) by Hindus, 10% (10) By Muslims and 23% (22) by British citizens. Later, the Parsis invaded other fields, mainly iron and steel industry, also Jamshedjee Tata was the first Parsi entrepreneur who established the first steel industry in Jamshedpur in 1911.

In the first wave of manufacturing entrepreneurship, except Parsis, all others hailed from non-commercial communities. Why the well-known commercial communities, namely, Jains and Vaishyas of Ahmadabad and Baroda, lagged behind in entrepreneurial initiative throughout the nineteenth century can be explained by two factors. Firstly, the improvement of business climate in the countryside during this period results in an increase in the quantum of trade which assumed quick returns on investments. This proved the commercial activity was more lucrative during the period, Secondly; it can also beat tribute to their conservative attitude to change from commercial entrepreneurship to industrial entrepreneurship.

The second wave of entrepreneurial growth in India began after the First World War. For various reasons, the Indian Government agreed to 'discriminating' protection to certain industries, even requiring that companies receiving its benefits should be registered in India with rupee capital and have a proportion of their directors as Indians. The advantages of these measures were mostly enjoyed by the Indians. The Europeans failed to harness the protectionist policies to their interests." These measures helped in establishing and extending the factory manufacturing in India during the first four decades of the twentieth century. During these decades, the relative importance of Parsis declined and Gujaratis and Marwari Vaishyas gained that pendulum in India's entrepreneurial scene.

The concept of growth theory seems to be closely related in explaining the theory of entrepreneurship development as well. After the Second World War, entrepreneurship received new meaning for attaining economic development within the shortest possible time. But in the process they were seriously handicapped by the rigid institutional set up, political instability, marketing imperfection and traditional value system. Britishers for their own ulterior motive destabilized the then self-sufficient Indian economy. England flourished and India had to pay for that. In the process India suffered heavy industrial loss.

(b) Entrepreneurship during post-Independence: After taking a long sigh of political relief in 1947, the Government of India tried to spell out the priorities to devise a scheme for achieving balanced growth. For this purpose, the Government came forward with the first Industrial Policy, 1948 which was revised from time to time." The Government in her various industrial policy statements identified the responsibility of the State to promote, assist and develop industries in the national interest. It also explicitly recognised the vital role of the private sector in accelerating industrial development and, for this, enough field was reserved for the private sector.

A steady growth can be observed on the business of long cherished history of entrepreneurial development in the country is certainly promised or the environment to be created by the state and its agencies. For this, Government set three important objectives to be achieved through industrial resolutions

(i) to maintain a proper distribution of economic power between private and public sector.

(ii) to encourage the tempo of industrialisation by spreading entrepreneurship from the existing centres to other cities, towns and villages,

(iii) to disseminate the entrepreneurship acumen concentrated in a few dominant communities to a large number of industrially potential people of various social strata.

To achieve these objectives, the Government accorded emphasis on the development of small-scale industries in the country through various 5 year plans. **During 1st Five Year Plan**, diversified development of industry takes place but there was high progress in the field of textile and iron and steel industry. **During 2nd Five Year Plan,** major task in industry was building of three steel plants in Orissa, Madhya Pradesh and West Bengal and the production of heavy electrical and heavy machine tool industries, heavy machine building and the production of machine for the cement and paper industry began for the first time in India. New industrial items, e.g., industrial boilers, milling machines, tractors, motorcycles and scooters were produced in large quantity. **During the 3rd Five Year Plan**, the Government started to provide various incentives and concessions in the form of capital, technical know-how, markets and land to the potential entrepreneurs to establish industries in the industrially potential areas to remove the regional imbalances in development. This was, indeed, a major step taken by the Government to initiate interested people of varied social strata to enter the small-scale manufacturing field. Several institutions like Directorate of Industries, Financial Corporation, Small-scale Industries Corporations and Small Industries Service Institute were also established by the Government to facilitate the new entrepreneurs in setting up their enterprises. Expectedly, the small-scale units emerged very rapidly in India, witnessing a tremendous increase in their number from 121,619 in 1966 to 190,727 in 1970 registering an increase of 17,000 units per year during the period under reference. Under this plan, mining and extractive industries, automobile industries, textile and cement industries showed a considerable progress. **4th Five Year Plan** aimed at increasing the existing capacities upto the level required for future developments. The plan aimed at sustained increase of exports by 7% per year but the performance was much short of set targets. Stagnation in the industries like sugar, textiles, fluctuating agricultural output acted as constraints on rapid growth. So, the main objective of **5th Five Year Plan** was to achieve self-reliance and growth with social justice. It was intended to diversify the industry rapidly and make reservation of certain items for the development of small-scale industries. During this plan considerable progress was seen in the industries like steel, aluminum, fertilizers, engineering goods and petroleum products. **During 6th and 7th Five Year Plans**, emphasis was on the development of village and small scale industries. **During 8th and 9th and further Five Year plans,** Government of India established various entrepreneurship development institutes and strengthened the role of entrepreneurs in the economic development of the country as the developments of entrepreneurship will optimize the use of the unexploited resources, generate self-employment and a self-sufficient economy. Government also reserved 821 items for small-scale industries. During this period training was provided all over the country through various EDP's and young entrepreneurs were motivated to come out with determination to do something of their own and also to contribute to the national income and wealth in the economy.

But the most important is the period of post-liberalization, the number of new companies formed during the 1980-2006 period points to a possible growth in entrepreneurship. Figures from the Ministry of Corporate Affairs show that from 1980 to 1991, the average number of companies formed each year was 14,379, while from 1992 to 2006, the average number of companies formed per year was 33,835. Liberalization itself kick-started the growth of entrepreneurship in India for it presented businesses in the country with new market opportunities. According to Dr.Mani, "Post-liberalization, entrepreneurship has generally increased in India"

Moreover, liberalization increases the opportunities for the entrepreneurs and reduced regulatory measures like, licensing. Similarly, improved availability of financial support from both official and private sources boosted the growth of entrepreneurship.

2.3. CONCEPT OF ENTREPRENEURSHIP

The term 'entrepreneurship' is often used synonymously with the term 'Entrepreneur' though, they are two sides of the same coin, conceptually they are different. Entrepreneurship is the process of identifying opportunities in the market place, arranging the resources required to pursue these opportunities and investing the resources to exploit the opportunities for long-term gains. It involves creating wealth by bringing together resources in new ways to start and operate an enterprise

It has assumed super importance for accelerating economic growth both in developed and developing countries. It promotes capital formation and creates wealth in the country. It is hope and dreams of millions of individuals around the world. It reduces unemployment and poverty and it is a pathway to prosperity. Entrepreneurship is the process of exploring the opportunities in the market place and arranging resources required to exploit these opportunities for long-term gain. It is the process of planning, organising, and assuming opportunities. Thus, it is a risk of business enterprise. It may be distinguished as an ability to take risk independently to make utmost earnings in the market. It is a creative and innovative skill and adapting response to environment. There are different approaches for the same:

1. Economic Approach[1]: Joseph Schumpeter is the person behind the economic approach of entrepreneurship. The theory given by Joseph Schumpeter is versatile. According to him, all the problems in economic theory could be solved with the equilibrium theory in his book *'The Theory of Economic Development'*. Schumpeter starts in *The Theory of Economic Development* with a treatise of circular flow which, excluding any innovations and innovative activities, leads to a stationary state. The stationary state is, according to Schumpeter, described by Walrasian equilibrium and Walrasian equilibrium is not adequate to capture the key mechanisms of economic development. The hero of his story is the entrepreneur. The entrepreneur disturbs this equilibrium and is the prime cause of economic development, which proceeds in cyclic fashion along several time scales.

Some other economists proves that entrepreneurship and economic growth will take place in those situation where particular economic conditions are prevailed. Economic incentives are the main motivators for entrepreneurial activities. Economic incentives include taxation policy, industrial policy, sources of finance and raw material, infrastructure availability, investment and marketing opportunities, access to information about market conditions, technology, etc

2. Sociological Approach[2]: The phenomenon of entrepreneurship development has been viewed, explained and interpreted differently by social scientists. According to social scientists, entrepreneurship can be conceptualized as a social movement. Entrepreneurs are the important part of society and they are role performer according to the role expectations of a society. Entrepreneurship is likely to get boost in a particular social culture and society's values, beliefs, religion, culture, customs, etc., influences the behavior of individuals in a society.

3. Psychological Approach[3]: A Psychological Approach enriches our understanding of entrepreneurship from a psychological perspective. From a psychological point of view, the study is interesting because entrepreneurs have to work on a complex set of tasks, such as development of the organization, leadership and organizational issues. The common theme of this special issue is to look at personality predictors of success and entrepreneurial behaviour. Psychological approaches to entrepreneurship have experienced a revitalization recently because of the future importance of small-scale entrepreneurs and because the entrepreneur is at the boundary line of individual work psychology (personality, work activities, etc.), organizational psychology (founders of the organization have an enormous influence on it), and market psychology (economic activities in the market). Many organizational issues, for example, the influence of human resource practice, can also be studied in entrepreneurs. Essentially, all aspects of psychology are implicated when studying entrepreneurs (Rauch and Frese, 2000).

2.4. DEFINITIONS

1. According to Arthur H.Cole, "Entrepreneurship is the purposeful activity of an individual or a group of associated individuals undertaken to initiate, maintain and aggrandize profit by production or distribution of economic goods and services".

2. According to Higgins "Entrepreneurship is meant the function of foreseeing investment and production opportunities, organizing an enterprise to undertake a new production process, raising capital, hiring labour, arranging the supply of raw materials, finding site, introducing a new technique, discovering new resources or raw materials and selecting top managers for day to day operations of the enterprise".

3. According to Joseph A. Schumpeter,"Entrepreneurship is essentially a creative activity or it is an innovation function. The process of innovation may be in form of (1) Introduction of new product; (2) Use of new method of production; (3) Opening of new market; (4) The conquest of new source of supplying raw material 5) A new form of organization."

4. According to Peter Drucker, "Entrepreneurship is neither a science nor an art. It is a practice. It has a knowledge base. Knowledge in entrepreneurship is a means to an end. Indeed, what constitutes knowledge in practice is largely defined by the ends, that is, by the practice."

5. According to William Diamond, "Entrepreneurship is equivalent to 'enterprise' which involves the willingness to assume risks in undertaking an economic activity particularly a new one.

6. According to Robert K. Lamb, "Entrepreneurship is that form of social decision which is performed by economic innovators."

7. According to John J. Kao, "Entrepreneurship is the attempt to create value through regulation of business opportunity, the management of risk-taking appropriate to the opportunity, and through the communicative and management skills to mobilise human, financial and material resources necessary to bring a project to fruitition."

Thus, entrepreneurship is defined as purposeful activity to initiate, maintain, and develop a profit-oriented business. The above definitions highlights risk bearing, innovating and resource organizing aspects and an individual or group of people achieve goal through production or distribution of products or services. To conclude entrepreneurship is set of activities performed by an entrepreneur, thus, entrepreneur proceeds entrepreneurship.

2.5. DIFFERENCE BETWEEN ENTREPRENEUR, ENTERPRISE AND ENTREPRENEURSHIP

The term entrepreneur refers to the persons or individual, who conceive, start and manage a business or an enterprise, individually. He is the person who is the creator of an enterprise. Entrepreneur is the key individual, central to entrepreneurship who makes things happen.

The term entrepreneurship refers to a process by which the organization is created; decisions are made, leadership is displayed, risk is undertaken, initiative is displayed and motivation takes place. Entrepreneurship is an abstraction whereas entrepreneurs are tangible people. Entrepreneurship is a process and an entrepreneur is a person. Entrepreneurship is the most effective way of bridging the gap between science and the market place by creating new enterprises. An entrepreneur is the catalyst who brings about this change.

The enterprise is the objective behind the whole process i.e the organization. It refers to any form of organization, with any type of ownership .

2.6. CHARACTERISTICS OF ENTREPRENEURSHIP

CHARACTERISTICS OF ENTREPRENEURSHIP →

(1) INNOVATION
(2) ECONOMIC ACTIVITY
(3) RISK BEARING ACTIVITY
(4) ORGANIZATION BUILDING
(5) FUNCTION OF HIGH ACHIVEMENT
(6) GOAL-ORIENTED ACTIVITY
(7) GAP FILLING ACTIVITY
(8) DYNAMIC PROCESS
(9) TO MANAGE CHANGING SCENARIO
(10) CREATIVE ACTIVITY

1. Innovation: Entrepreneurship is an innovative activity as it involve doing things in new and better way. Joseph Schumpeter argued that the defining characteristic of entrepreneurial ventures was innovation. By finding a new "production function" in an existing resource, a previously unknown means through which a resource could produce value, the entrepreneur was innovating. An innovation could take place in product design, organization of the firm, marketing devices, or process design. Nevertheless, innovation was what separated the entrepreneur from others who undertook closely related endeavors.

2. Economic Activity: Entrepreneurship is an economic activity because it involve creation and operation of new enterprise. An entrepreneur adds wealth (or at least the potential for gain) to the economy when he or she presents the economy with new ways to use the resource as a means of gaining some kind of value. It is concerned with the processing and satisfying the needs of customers with the help of production and distribution of goods and services.

3. Risk Bearing Capacity: Risk is the inseparable part of entrepreneurship. Entrepreneurs assume the risks because they make significant investments in their ventures. These risks include market uncertainties (whether customers will actually buy a new product or service), production uncertainties, and resource uncertainties. Prof. Knight defines in his theory –'Risk uncertainty and profit' that there are two types of risks.i.e.:

(a) Foreseeable risks: The risk which can be insured and capable of being calculated.

(b) Unforeseeable risks : The risk which cannot be insured and very tough to calculate.

So, the entrepreneur has to calculate both the risks and has to play safe because the supreme motive of an entrepreneur is to earn maximum profits by minimizing the associated risks.

4. Organization Building: Entrepreneurship implies the skill to build an organization. Entrepreneurship is a process which helps in creation of an organization.

Entrepreneur (individual) ⟶ Entrepreneurship (process of action) ⟶ Organization (object)

5. Function of high achievement: People having high need for achievement are more likely to become successful entrepreneurs. Many entrepreneurs start their business from scratch but they accept challenges and have high need for achievement only then the they become successful entrepreneurs. E.g.: Dhirubai Ambani.

6. Goal-oriented Activity: Entrepreneurship is a goal-oriented activity as the basic aim behind this is the creation of an enterprise and profit maximization through satisfaction of customers.

7. Gap Filling Function: Entrepreneurship is a process which helps in the filling of gap between the human needs and available products and services. Normally entrepreneurs identify the need of the customers and takes necessary steps to fulfill the same by doing some innovations. They manufacture the products and provide the services as per the needs of the customers and fill the gap between the needs and availability of resources.

8. Dynamic process: Entrepreneurship is a dynamic process as it involves innovations as per the needs of the market. Entrepreneurs identify the opportunities and needs of the customers and change the process accordingly. If it is flexible and dynamic only then an entrepreneur will be termed as successful.

9. To Manage Changing Scenario: In present era in order to compete and sustain, entrepreneurs has to cope with changing scenario. Entrepreneurship is based on innovation and everyday new developments takes place so entrepreneurship helps to cope with the changing needs of the market. If an entrepreneur cannot manage this change then he cannot survive.

10. Creative Activity: Entrepreneurship is a creative activity. More and more creativity helps in more and more innovations. Entrepreneurship is concerned with maximizing the profits by innovating, producing and distributing the goods to the ultimate consumer. So more creativity helps in providing maximum satisfaction to the customer .

2.7. FACTORS INFLUENCING ENTREPRENEURSHIP

There are various factors which influence entrepreneurship. Some of these are as under:

Economic Factors

Economic factors have due importance for an entrepreneur and entrepreneurial activities because the driving force for any entrepreneurial activity is the amount of available economic incentive. In other words, attractive economic environment encourages people to take entrepreneurial activities in the society. Following are the economic factors which influence people to move towards entrepreneurship:

(a) Capital: Capital is the most important factor in any entrepreneurial activity. Most of the times deserving and capable person are not able to enter into any entrepreneurial activity due to non-availability of capital and easy availability of capital helps the person with innovative ideas to bring that ideas into reality. So, if the capital is available without any obstacles and barriers then entrepreneurship can be increased.

(b) Availability of Manpower: Manpower in the form of employees, labour or managers is basic necessity of any entrepreneurial activity. Easy availability of manpower makes entrepreneurship attractive. More than the availability of abundance human resource, the presence of skilled labour force is very important. If the entrepreneurial activities are initiated at/near the areas where skilled manpower is available, then its easy to carry out the entrepreneurship more comfortably and profitably.

(c) Availability of Raw Material: Raw material is the important resource for manufacturing unit and the easy availability of raw material draws people towards entrepreneurial activities. Easy availability of raw material also helps in the reduction of the prices of the end product.

(d) Market Opportunities: Ready available market also influence entrepreneurship. The main objective of any entrepreneurial activity is the profit which can be achieved from the market only. If the product is having demand in the market then it will ultimate attract more and more entrepreneurs to start entrepreneurial activities as the market is the only source to fetch revenues for any business. If sufficient market is not there, people will hesitate to start any business activity.

Non-economic Factors

Entrepreneurship needs both economic and non-economic factors in order to grow. Entrepreneurship development also needs positive social environment. The society and its dynamics decide the fate of entrepreneurship to a great extent. These are as under:

(a) Social Norms and Values: Society is very important for the existence of entrepreneurship. A society sets certain norms and values for the behaviour of people who are the part of that society. If that norms or values are violated then either will push you out or impose some restrictions. If a society has an open and flexible approach towards various types of jobs then people will feel free to do their job as well as they will feel free to innovate. Openness in society pushes entrepreneurship.

(b) Respect and Status: If societies accord recognition and respect to people who dare to do something different and creative, then it will always attract others to do the same. In order to get respect and status in society, a number of entrepreneurial activities are started.Thus, societies where there is respect and recognition for people to do different things are more, there entrepreneurial activities develop at faster rate.

(c) Role Models: Successful entrepreneurs always act as role models to others. Societies that appreciate and encourage entrepreneurial activities always help upcoming entrepreneurs to come up with their innovative ideas and these upcoming entrepreneurs always set successful entrepreneurs as their role models and tries to follow their path.

2.8. ROLE OF ENTREPRENEURSHIP IN ECONOMIC DEVELPOMENT[4]

An entrepreneur is an enterprising individual who builds capital through risk and/or initiative. The true spirit of entrepreneurship is providing solutions to the problems and needs of humanity. The number of people embracing entrepreneurship as a vocation has sprouted up in the last few years. Many people are becoming entrepreneurs with the aim of following their passion of doing something good for the Indian society. This new drive is sequentially leading to the overall development of the Indian society. At the present, a widely accepted fact is that energetic and excited entrepreneurs only can look at the potentials of the country's scope for resources such as labour, capital and technology. Entrepreneurial efforts have been found to create a broad array of economic benefits, together with new businesses, new jobs, new products and services, and increased assets for investment in future. These are as under:

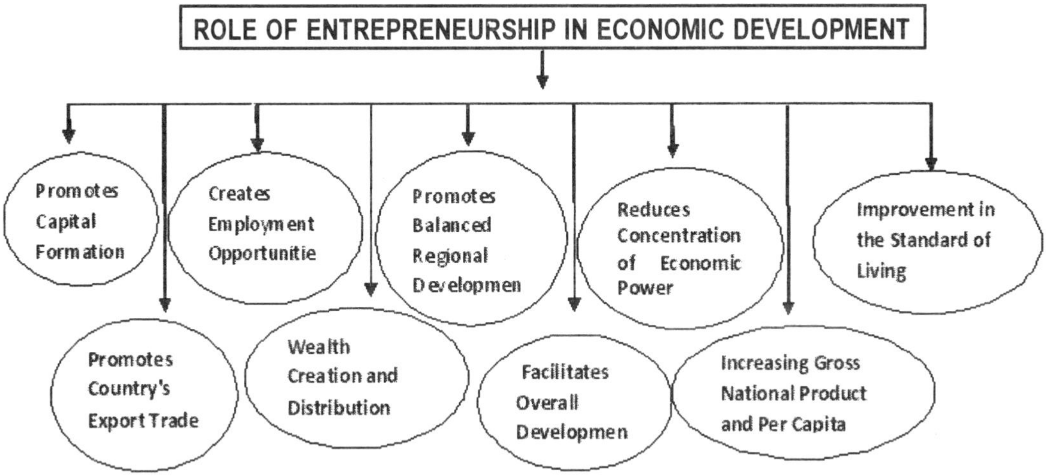

1. Promotes Capital Formation: Entrepreneurs promote capital formation by mobilising the idle savings of public. They employ their own as well as borrowed resources for setting up their enterprises. Such type of entrepreneurial activities lead to value addition and creation of wealth, which is very essential for the industrial and economic development of the country.

2. Creates Large-scale Employment Opportunities: Entrepreneurs provide immediate large-scale employment to the unemployed which is a chronic problem of underdeveloped nations. With the setting up of more and more units by entrepreneurs, both on small and large-scale, numerous job opportunities are created for others. As time passes, these enterprises grow, providing direct and indirect employment opportunities to many more. In this way, entrepreneurs play an effective role in reducing the problem of unemployment in the country which in turn clears the path towards economic development of the nation.

3. Promotes Balanced Regional Development: Entrepreneurs help to remove regional disparities through setting up of industries in less developed and backward areas. The growth of industries and business in these areas lead to a large number of public benefits like road transport, health, education, entertainment, etc. Setting up of more industries lead to more development of backward regions and thereby, promotes balanced regional development.

4. Reduces Concentration of Economic Power: Economic power is the natural outcome of industrial and business activity. Industrial development normally lead to concentration of economic power in the hands of a few individuals which results in the growth of monopolies. In order to redress this problem a large number of entrepreneurs need to be developed, which will help reduce the concentration of economic power amongst the population.

5. Wealth Creation and Distribution: It stimulates equitable redistribution of wealth and income in the interest of the country to more people and geographic areas, thus giving benefit to larger sections of the society. Entrepreneurial activities also generate more activities and give a multiplier effect to the economy.

6. Increasing Gross National Product and Per Capita Income: Entrepreneurs are always on the lookout for opportunities. They explore and exploit opportunities,, encourage effective resource mobilisation of capital and skill, bring in new products and services and develops markets for growth of the economy. In this way, they help increasing gross national product as well as per capita income of the people in a country. Increase in gross national product and per capita income of the people in a country, is a sign of economic growth.

7. Improvement in the Standard of Living: Increase in the standard of living of the people is a characteristic feature of economic development of the country. Entrepreneurs play a key role in increasing the standard of living of the people by adopting latest innovations in the production of wide variety of goods and services in large-scale that too at a lower cost. This enables the people to avail better quality goods at lower prices which results in the improvement of their standard of living.

8. Promotes Country's Export Trade: Entrepreneurs help in promoting a country's export-trade, which is an important ingredient of economic development. They produce goods and services on a large-scale for the purpose earning huge amount of foreign exchange from export in order to combat the import dues requirement. Hence import substitution and export promotion ensure economic independence and development.

9. Induces Backward and Forward Linkages: Entrepreneurs like to work in an environment of change and try to maximise profits by innovation. When an enterprise is established in accordance with the changing technology, it induces backward and forward linkages which stimulate the process of economic development in the country.

10. Facilitates Overall Development: Entrepreneurs act as catalytic agents for change which results in chain reaction. Once an enterprise is established, the process of industrialisation is set in motion. This unit will generate demand for various types of units required by it and there will be so many other units which require the output of this unit. This leads to overall development of an area due to increase in demand and setting up of more and more units. In this way, the entrepreneurs multiply their entrepreneurial activities, thus creating an environment of enthusiasm and conveying an impetus for overall development of the area.

In short, the development of the entrepreneurship is inevitable in the economic development of the country. The role played by the entrepreneurship development can be expressed in the following words:

"Economic development is the effect for which entrepreneurship is a cause."

2.9. ENTREPRENEURS AND COMPANIES WHO SHAPED INDIA[5]

Here are a few entrepreneurs and companies who actually defined new businesses/products and shaped India:

(a) Jamsetji Tata (1839–1904): Founder of the Tata group, this entrepreneur from Gujarat is honoured by many as the father of Indian industry. The multi billion company, we see today had its first phase in a trading firm started by J N Tata in 1869 with an initial capital of ₹ 21,000.

(b) Dhirajlal Hirachand Ambani (Dhirubhai Ambani) (1932–2002): Dhirubhai Ambani was an Indian rags-to-riches business tycoon who founded Reliance Industries in Mumbai with his cousin. From a poor worker in the fifties to one of the country's largest megacorp, Ambani's journey to the pinnacle was at flashing speed.

(c) Verghese Kurien (1921–2012): Verghese Kurien, born at Kozhikode, Kerala, was the founder of the Gujarat Cooperative Milk Marketing Federation (GCMMF) that manages the Amul food brand. He was recognised as the man behind the success of the Amul brand. He helped modernise the Anand model of cooperative dairy development and thus, engineered the White Revolution in India, and made India the largest milk producer in the world.

(d) N. R. Narayana Murthy (1946): A co-founder of Infosys, N. R. Narayana Murthy is the man who is often attributed for much of India's IT revolution. He left no stone unturned to put Bengaluru on the global map and make India a softwere power. Infosys, the company he co-founded in 1981, with ₹ 10,000 in capital is now a $7 billion company and also the second largest software exporter from India.

Above mentioned are the names of few entrepreneurs who have hit the glamour circuit. There are many other entrepreneurs and companies who changed the face of India, but are being talked about in low tones, in rare columns and in rarer features.

2.10. DIFFICULTIES FACED IN THE DEVELOPMENT AND GROWTH OF ENTREPRENEURSHIP IN INDIA

In India, most of the entrepreneurs face peculiar problems like illiteracy, fear of risk, lack of training and experience, limited purchasing power and competition from established entrepreneurs. Some of the major problems faced by entrepreneurs are as under:

1. Finance: A sound understanding of business finance, access to capital, and relationships with lenders are integral to the success of any business. When starting a business, approximately one-third of the entrepreneurs found cash flow, finance, insufficient sales volume, and pricing goods or services to be the most problematic. Most of the entrepreneurs fail to get external funds due to absence of tangible security and credit in the market. The procedure to avail the loan facility is too time-consuming that its delay often disappoints the entrepreneurs.

2. Competition: New entrepreneurs face severe completion from large sized organizations and established entrepreneurs. They incur high cost of production due to high input cost.

3. Legal formalities: There are large number of legal formalities like: licensing, registration, government approvals, etc., and entrepreneurs find it extremely difficult in complying with various legal formalities in obtaining licenses due to ignorance.

4. Procurement of raw materials and other inputs: Procurement of raw materials, power and skilled manpower is really a tough task for entrepreneur. They may end up with poor quality raw materials and they also face the problem of storage and warehousing.

5. Lack of support and counseling: New and budding entrepreneurs fails to get counseling assistance or support by various agencies, as in India there is lack of support by the government. Although government has taken various steps to remove this problem by starting various entrepreneurship development programs but still they are not up to the mark and most of the entrepreneurs are facing this problem.

6. Lack of technical knowledge: Indian entrepreneurs suffer a severe problem of lack of technical knowledge, lack of training facilities and extension services etc. It creates a hurdle for the development of entrepreneurship.

7. Lack of infrastructural facilities: The growth of entrepreneurs in India is not very healthy in spite of efforts made by government due to lack of proper and adequate infrastructural facilities. It's due to poor follow–up support of primary institutes which creates hurdle in the development and growth of entrepreneurship in the country.

8. Poor quality of products: Another important problem in growth of entrepreneurship is the inferior quality of products produced due to lack of availability of standard tools and equipment and poor quality of raw materials.

9. Negative attitude: The environment in the family, society and support system is not conducive to encourage people to take up entrepreneurship as a career. It may be due to lack of awareness and knowledge of entrepreneurial opportunities.

10. Poor and incompetent management: Poor and incompetent management act as a big hurdle in the development of entrepreneurship. As per the study, in beginning of business, about one-quarter of the entrepreneurs stated that their management problems were diverse and focused on themselves (like: controlling my own time, setting goals and measuring performance), their employees (finding, exloiting and retaining qualified employees) and accessing helpful information.

2.11. GLOBAL ENTREPRENEURSHIP MONITOR 2007[6]

The 2007 Global Entrepreneurship Monitor, an annual assessment of entrepreneurship around the world conducted by London Business School and Babson College. Some of the key findings this year include:

- Many low-income countries are exhibiting high rates of early-stage entrepreneurial activity. The top three hotspots for early-stage entrepreneurship are Thailand, Peru and Colombia. The lowest activity was in Russia, Romania and Latvia.

- Among high-income countries, Iceland, Hong Kong and the United States lead the way in early-stage entrepreneurial activity, while the lowest rates were found in Austria, Puerto Rico and Belgium. (I was a little surprised to see Puerto Rico listed in the high-income category.)
- In Latin America and the Caribbean, gender differences are relatively small. In high-income countries, though, men are about twice as likely as women to be involved in early-stage entrepreneurial activity. For countries in Eastern Europe and Central Asia the gender gap is even more pronounced: men are 2.3 times as likely to be early-stage entrepreneurs as women.
- The report, debunks some of the common misconceptions that hign number of entrepreneurial businesses, particularly new ones, fail. One of the common reasons for the misconception uncovered by the study is that, on average, about one-third of businesses that were "discontinued" actually continued in some other form or with different ownership. Also, financial problems were cited as the reason for quitting the business by no more than 55% of all respondents.
- While regulatory red tape has very little impact on the launch of micro businesses, it is a significant barrier to the creation of high-growth, ambitious enterprises. Previous studies have shown a strong link between high-potential entrepreneurship and subsequent economic growth. The vast majority of entrepreneurial businesses offer products or services that people are already familiar with. Only around 10% offer products or services that are considered new or unfamiliar to all of their potential customers.

2.12. SUMMARY

Entrepreneurship is the cycle of actions, an entrepreneurs undertakes to start a new enterprise. It is described at process of handling economic activity, undertaking risk, creating something new and organizing resources. So it's a purposeful activity of an individual or a group of associated individuals undertaken to initiate, maintain or organize a profit-oriented business unit. It is an innovative and creative activity which include the search of business idea and opportunity recognition. But it's different from intrapreneurs/corporate entrepreneurs.

The corporate entrepreneur is an individual that exists within an organisation to generate product and process ideas that will create value for the organization.

2.13. SOME CASE STUDIES OF FAMOUS ENTREPRENEURS[7]

Larry Page

Larry Page was born in March of 1973 in Michigan. He maintained an interest in computers for the better part of his life, and was encouraged to follow this interest by his father, Dr. Carl Victor Page, a professor of computer science at the University of Michigan.

Larry Page and partner Sergey Brin changed the world in a rented garage where they worked on a project called "The Anatomy of a Large-scale Hypertextual Web Search Engine," or as they say in press releases for simplicity sake: "The Anatomy of a Search Engine." They developed a method of "web-crawling" perform a a quicker method of web search.

Page graduated in honors standing from East Lansing High School, and was accepted by the University of Michigan where he acquired a bachelor's degree in computer engineering, and a master's degree from Stanford. He took a leave of absence from his Ph.D. studies to further develop the PageRank technology, and later form Google. According to Forbes, Page maintains a 7.2 billion dollar net worth, making the tycoon, the 55th richest man in the world, following closely behind by Brin.

Because of Google's success, Page never returned to the Ph.D, program at Stanford where, to this day, he remains "on-leave."

Azim Premji

Wipro Products Ltd., was run by Premji's father. In 1966, Premji was completing his degree in engineering at Stanford University when his father died. He later was able to finish getting his degree in electrical engineering with correspondence course. Just 21, Premji took over the family oil business.

Under Premji's leadership Wipro Corporation began to expand and diversify. General Electric used Wipro to manufacture light bulbs, shampoo, baby care products and powder. By 1975, Premji started Wipro Fluid Power to make hydraulic cylinders and also truck tippers.

In the 1980s, IMBM was kicked out of India creating a vacuum in the technology field. With Pemji's interest in electrical engineering, Wipro was a natural entry into the IT field. Wipro was issued a special license from Sentinel. They began manufacturing hardware for computers and then branched out to software development.

Wipro is the largest outsourcing company in India and its research and development unit is the world largest independent group. Under Pemji's guidance, Wipro grew from a $1.5 million oil company to a $662 million diversified conglomerate.

Premji believes in growth through delivering value with integrity to the customer. Wipro became the first Indian company to implement the Six Sigma program. It also achieved SEI CMM Level 5 (the first software company to earn this distinction), and it also achieved PCMM Level 5 (People Capability Maturity Model), the world's first organization to gain this level.

Pemji has been awarded numerous honors. Honors in 2000, included an honorary doctorate by both the Manipal Academy of Higher Education in India and Roorkee and the Business Man of the Year by *Business India.* In 2003, Forbes named Premji to two distinguished lists – one of the 10 people globally, who have the most "power to effect change" and one of the 25 most powerful business leaders outside the US, Also in 2003, and *Business Week* had Premji's picture on its October cover titled "India's Tech King". In 2004, his honors included top 25 billionaires who have done most to bring about significant and lasting social, political or cultural changes by the *Financial Times,* and as one of the 100 most influential people in the world. In 2005, he received one of his country's highest honor for a civilian, the Padmabhushana. He is a member of the Prime Minister's Advisory Committee for Information Technology in India.

Bill Gates

William Gates III, the former CEO of Microsoft, for short period of time, had assets worth over 100 billion dollars, making him the world's first centibillionaire. Today his assets are half of that but he remains, the world's wealthiest man according to Forbes.

Gates was born on 28 October, 1955 in Seattle, Washington to a successful family and was able to attend a Seattle private school. His mother was a schoolteacher and his father a Seattle attorney. He developed interest in software and began programming at age 13, when the school acquired an ASR-33 teletype terminal from a mother's rummage sale. Because of their exploits of bugs in the school's second computer: a DEC PDP-10, owned by Computer Center Corporation, Gates and a number of other students, including Paul Allen, Microsoft's co-founder, were offered unlimited computer time in exchange for debugging the company's computers. After CCC went out of business, the students were hired by Sciences Inc. to write a payroll program. The students were successful and received royalties for the program.

Gates scored a close-to-perfect score of 1590 on the SAT and was accepted by Harvard. He studied pre-law but spent the majority of his time with the school's computers. Here, he met Steve Balmer, who was to become a prominent business partner in Microsoft. Gates and Allen understood the computer market was erupting. They contacted Micro Instrumentation and Telemetry Systems, or MITS: and lied claiming they had developed a BASIC (a programming language). MITS were intrigued but Allen and Gates had not developed the code, nor had Altair for themselves or even had touched one. They worked day and night for eight weeks writing the code for their promised computer and with a single yoke, worked perfectly in a demonstration for MITS. Gates and Allen had already dropped out of college. When MITS purchased the rights to their BASIC for the Altair, Microsoft was formed.

Gates announced in 2008, he will leave Microsoft, but will remain as a chair, to follow philanthropy.

Dhirubhai Ambani

Dhirubhai Ambani built India's largest private sector company. Created an equity cult in the Indian capital market. Reliance is the first Indian company to feature in Forbes 500 list.

Dhirubhai Ambani was the most enterprising Indian entrepreneur. His life journey is reminiscent of the rags to riches story. He is remembered as the one who rewrote Indian corporate history and built a truly global corporate group.

Dhirubhai Ambani alias Dhirajlal Hirachand Ambani was born on December 28, 1932, at Chorwad, Gujarat, into a Modh family. His father was a schoolteacher. Dhirubhai Ambani started his entrepreneurial career by selling "bhajias" to pilgrims in Mount Girnar over the weekends.

After doing his matriculation at the age of 16, Dhirubhai moved to Aden, Yemen. He worked there as a gas-station attendant, and as a clerk in an oil company. He returned to India in 1958, with ₹ 50,000 and set up a textile trading company.

Assisted by his two sons, Mukesh and Anil, Dhirubhai Ambani built India's largest private sector company, Reliance India Limited, from scratch. Over time his business has diversified into a core specialisation in petrochemicals with additional interests in telecommunications, information technology, energy, power, retail, textiles, infrastructure services, capital markets and logistics.

Dhirubhai Ambani is credited with shaping India's equity culture, attracting millions of retail investors in a market till then dominated by financial institutions. Dhirubhai revolutionised capital markets. From nothing, he generated billions of rupees in wealth for those who put their trust in his companies. His efforts helped create an 'equity cult' in the Indian capital market. With innovative instruments like the convertible debenture, Reliance quickly became a favorite of the stock market in the 1980s.

In 1992, Reliance became the first Indian company to raise money in global markets, its high credit-taking in international markets limited only by India's sovereign rating. Reliance also became the first Indian company to feature in Forbes 500 list.

Dhirubhai Ambani was named the Indian Entrepreneur of the 20th Century by the Federation of Indian Chambers of Commerce and Industry (FICCI). A poll conducted by *The Times of India* in 2000, voted him "greatest creator of wealth in the century".

Dhirubhai Ambani died on July 6, 2002, at Mumbai.

Steve Jobs

Steven Paul "Steve" Jobs (February 24, 1955 – October 5, 2011) was an American entrepreneur and inventor, best known as the co-founder, chairman, and CEO of Apple Inc. Through Apple, he was widely recognized as a charismatic pioneer of the personal computer revolution and for his influential career in the computer and consumer electronics fields, transforming "one industry after another, from computers and smartphones to music and movies..." Jobs also co-founded and served as chief executive of Pixar Animation Studios, he became a member of the board of directors of The Walt Disney Company in 2006, when Disney acquired Pixar. Jobs was among the first to see the commercial potential of Xerox PARC's mouse-driven graphical user interface, which led to the creation of the Apple Lisa and, one year later, the Macintosh. He also played a role in introducing the LaserWriter, one of the first widely available laser printers, to the market.

After a power struggle with the board of directors in 1985, Jobs left Apple and founded NeXT, a computer platform development company specializing in the higher-education and business markets. In 1986, he acquired the computer graphics division of Lucasfilm, which was spun off as Pixar. He was credited in *Toy Story* (1995) as an executive producer. He served as CEO and majority shareholder until Disney's purchase of Pixar in 2006. In 1996, after Apple had failed to deliver its operating system, Copland, Gil Amelio turned to NeXT Computer, and the NeXTSTEP platform became the foundation for the Mac OS X. Jobs returned to Apple as an advisor, and took control of the company as an interim CEO. Jobs brought Apple from near bankruptcy to profitability by 1998.

As the new CEO of the company, Jobs oversaw the development of the iMac, iTunes, iPod, iPhone, and iPad, and on the services side, the company's Apple Retail Stores, iTunes Store and the App Store. The success of these products and services provided several years of stable financial returns, and propelled Apple to become the world's most valuable publicly traded company in 2011. The reinvigoration of the company is regarded by many commentators as one of the greatest turnarounds in business history.

In 2003, Jobs was diagnosed with a pancreas neuroendocrine tumor. Though it was initially treated, he reported a hormone imbalance, underwent a liver transplant in 2009, and appeared progressively thinner as his health declined. On medical leave for most of 2011, Jobs resigned in August that year, and was elected Chairman of the Board. He died of respiratory arrest related to his metastatic tumor on October 5, 2011.

Jobs received a number of honors and public recognition for his influence in the technology and music industries. He has been referred to as "legendary", a "futurist" or simply "visionary", and has been described as the "Father of the Digital Revolution", a "master of innovation", "the master evangelist of the digital age" and a "design perfectionist".

2.14. SELF ASSESSMENT QUESTIONS

1. Explain Entrepreneurship and explain its main characteristics?
2. What do you mean by innovation and what are its characteristics?
3. What is innovation and how it is different from invention?
4. What are the various sources and barriers of innovation?
5. What do you mean by business idea and what are its different sources?
6. What do you mean by corporate entrepreneurs? What are the various roles, responsibilities and essentials of corporate entrepreneurs?

SOURCE/NOTES

1. http://en.wikipedia.org/wiki/Schumpeter
2. http://wi.uni-giessen.de/wps/pgn/dl/down/open/ebme_de and *Entrepreneurship and Small Business–Purnima Sehgal*

   Entrepreneurship Development—Dr. V.Sudharani, Acharaya N.G Ranga, agricultural university
3. http://wi.uni-giessen.de/wps/pgn/dl/down/open/ebme_de

   Entrepreneurship and small Business–Purnima Sehgal,

   Entrepreneurship Development-Dr. V.Sudharani, AcharayaN.G Ranga, agricultural university
4. http://www.preservearticles.com
5. http://www.co-founder.co.in
6. From Scott Allen, Former About.com Guide-http://entrepreneurs.about.com/b/2008/01/23/global-entrepreneurship-monitor-2007.htm
7. www. topbusinessentrepreneurs.com and www. wikipedia.org

3

WOMEN ENTREPRENEUR

3.1. INTRODUCTION

The emergence of entrepreneurs in a society depends to a great extent on the social, economic, religious, cultural, psychological and environmental factors prevailing in a society. Entrepreneurs with their inherent intelligence, drive and hard work making the best use of the opportunities that are made available in the above factors. Women entrepreneurs are no exception to this.

Though women, in traditional societies are confined to the four walls of houses doing all the household works including taking care of the children and are treated as property of men, the concept and status of women in the modern society has changed substantially. Modern age has lifted the veil of ignorance. Slowly and subtly changes are creeping in. Women have come out of the four walls to participate in all sorts of activities. They are growing and blossoming as successful persons in their own right. They have proved that they are no less than men in efficiency, hard work or intelligence. They are treated equally in teaching jobs, IT firms, hospitals and administrative jobs, military and defence fields, law, science, medicines and even aeronautics and space exploration. Now they have jumped into industrial activities and run their enterprises successfully. They are emerging as potential entrepreneurs. They have been making significant impact in all segments of the economy. Indian women also do have vast entrepreneurial talent which could be harnessed to join in the race for development. Therefore, it is now quite significant to discuss about the concept, meaning, growth, problems and its solutions of women entrepreneurs in India.

3.2. MEANING AND CONCEPT OF WOMEN ENTREPRENEURS

In the simplest sense, women entrepreneurs are those women who take the lead and organise the business or industry and provide employment to others. It signifies that section of female population who venture out into industrial activities. It may be defined as a woman or group of women who initiate, organise and run a business enterprise.

However, Government of India has given a broader definition of the term women entrepreneur. It defined women entrepreneur as "an enterprise owned and controlled by women having a minimum

G

H

I

J

K

L

E

F

financial interest of 51% of the capital and giving at least 51% of the employment generated in the enterprise to women".

So women entrepreneur has following points:

1. The women entrepreneur should have contributed to the equity of the concern.
2. The women entrepreneur should be actively participating in running the organization in all functional areas of management.

3.3. DEFINITIONS

According to J.A. Schumpeter, "Woman who innovates, imitates, or adopts a business activity is called woman entrepreneur."

Thus, women entrepreneur are those women who initiate, organise and operate business enterprise and want to prove their mettle in innovative and competitive jobs. She also wants to oversee and control every aspects of her business for its overall success.

Government of India has given a broader definition of the term women entrepreneur. It defined women entrepreneur as "an enterprise owned and controlled by women having a minimum financial interest of 51% of the capital and giving at least 51% of the employment generated in the enterprise to women".

In a nutshell, women entrepreneurs are those women who think of a business enterprise, initiate it, organize and combine the factors of production, operate the enterprise and undertake risks and handle economic, uncertainty involved in running a business enterprise.

In India, women entry into business is a new phenomenon. Women entry into business or entrepreneurship is traced out as an extension of their kitchen activities mainly to 3Ps, *viz.*, Pickles, Powder and Pappad. With growing awareness about business and spread of education among women over the period, women have started shifting from 3Ps to engross to 3 modern Es, *viz.*, Engineering. Electronics and Energy. They have excelled in these activities. Women entrepreneurs manufacturing solar cookers in Gujarat, running small foundaries in Maharashtra and making T.V. capacitors in Odisha have proved beyond doubt that given the opportunities, they can excel their male counterparts.

3.4. REASONS WOMEN BECOME ENTREPRENEURS

Women in India plunged into business for both pull and push factors:-

1. Pull factors. It implies that factors which encourage women to start an occupation or venture with an urge to do something independently. (In push factors women engaged in business activities due to family compulsion and the responsibility is thrust upon them.)

2. Push factors. It refers to those factors which compel women to take, up their own business to tide over their economic difficulties and responsibilities. Saddled with household chores and domestic responsibilities, women want independence. (Under the influence of these factors the women entrepreneurs choose a profession as a challenge and as an urge to do something new. Such situation is described as pull factors.)

Many studies indicate that women start businesses for fundamentally different reasons than their male counterparts. While men start businesses primarily for growth opportunities and profit potential, women most often found businesses in order to meet personal goals, such as gaining feelings of achievement and accomplishment. In many instances, women consider financial success as an external confirmation of their ability rather than as a primary goal or motivation to start a business, although millions of women entrepreneurs will grant that financial profitability is important in its own right.

Women also tend to start businesses about ten years later then men, on an average. Motherhood, lack of management experience, and traditional socialization have all been cited as reasons for delayed entry into entrepreneurial careers. Many women start a business due to some traumatic event, such as divorce, discrimination due to pregnancy or the corporate glass ceiling, the health of a family member, or economic reasons such as a layoff. But a new talent pool of women entrepreneurs is forming today, as more women opt to leave corporates to chart their own destinies. These women have developed financial expertise and bring experience in manufacturing or nontraditional fields. As a result, the concentration of women business owners in the retail and service sectors—and in traditional industries such as cosmetics, food, fashion, and personal care — is slowly changing.

The role of women entrepreneurs in the process of economic development has been recognized from nineties in various parts of the world. Today, in the world of business, women entrepreneurship has become an essential movement in many countries and has been accepted in all areas of working. The United Nations report has also concluded that economic development is closely related to the advancement of women. In nations where women have advanced, economic growth has usually been steady. By contrast, in countries where women have been restricted, the economy has been stagnant. The data on correlation between Gender-related development index and GDP per capita reinforces the above fact.[1]

TABLE 3.1. GENDER-RELATED DEVELOPMENT INDEX AND ITS COMPONENT[2]

Rank	Country	Gender-related development	As a per % of HDI	GDP per Capital (US$)
1	Australia	0.966	98.9	34923
2	Norway	0.961	99.6	53433
3	Iceland	0.959	99.0	44613
4	Canada	0.959	99.2	35812
5	Sweden	0.956	99.3	36712
6	France	0.956	99.4	33674
7	Netherland	0.954	98.9	38694
8	Finland	0.954	99.5	34526
9	Spain	0.949	99.4	31560
10	Ireland	0.948	98.2	44613
11	India	0.594	97.1	4102

As shown in the above table, Gender-related development index is significantly correlated with GDP per capita. The value of correlation coefficient comes 0.857371. Therefore, It can be treated as one of the parameter to show the economic condition and growth of the country.

3.5. GROWTH OF WOMEN ENTREPRENEURSHIP[3]

Almost half of India's population consists of women. But they constitute a very negligible proportion of the total entrepreneurs. Entrepreneurial traits and competencies have not been well developed amongst the women entrepreneurs. They are very shy in nature and emotionally attached to the family. They are treated as weak and dependent on men. They are the neglected sections in the society. The much low literacy rate 39%, low work participation rate 28% and low urban population share 10% of women as compared to 63%, 52% and 18% respectively of their male counterpart well confirm their precarious position in the society.

In spite of the above, in sixties, women have started entrepreneurial activities as one- woman enterprises at home and from home for self-occupation and engagement. The number of women entrepreneurs were only 6,000 which was miserably low during the period.

Indian women started their entrepreneurial work in 1970s. Their entrepreneurship is traced out as an extension of kitchen activities mainly pickles, powder and pappad. Women are encouraged to start an occupation or venture with an urge to do something independently, started to tide over their economic difficulties and responsibilities.

In the seventies, Government of India has also brought a change in its policy objective of welfare approach of women to development approach of women. Women were given priorities in all the sectors including small-scale industries sector. As a result, the number of women entrepreneurs has increased over the years.

During 1980s, government and non-government bodies have paid increasing attention to women entrepreneurs through formulation of various policies and programmes and introduction of new schemes and incentives. It adopted a multidisciplinary approach for development of women entrepreneurs. Women entrepreneurs were given top priority for implementation of programmes under agricultural and its allied activities of dairy farming, poultry, animal husbandry, handlooms, handicrafts and small-scale industries, etc.

In the nineties, out of the total women population of 437.10 millions, there are 126.48 million women workforce of which only 1,85,900 women accounting for self-employed in the country. This indicates a dismally low level of women participation in the entrepreneurial activities.

Further women entrepreneurs in India accounted for 9.01% of the total 1.70 million entrepreneurs during 1988-89. There were more than 2,95,680 women entrepreneurs claiming 11.2% of the total 2.64 million entrepreneurs in India during 1995-96. The number of women entrepreneurs have increased to 3,28,000 in 1996-97.

During the ninth five year plan, the government had introduced in 1998s an important scheme on Trade-related Entrepreneurship of Assistance and Development (TREAD) aiming at economic empowerment of women in rural, urban and semi-urban areas. It developed their entrepreneurial skill and eliminated the constraints faced by women entrepreneurs.

The TREAD programme was operated through Small Industries Development Bank of India (SIDBI). SIDBI has initiated various schemes for the growth of women entrepreneurs through Mahila Udyam Nidhi (MUN), Mahila Vikash for Nidhi (MVN), Micro Credit Scheme (MSC), Women Entrepreneurial Development Programme (EDP), and Marketing Development Fund (MDF) for women entrepreneurs.

In the context of the opening up of the economy and the need for upgradation of technology, the Consortium of Women Entrepreneurs of India (CWEI) is a common platform to help every women entrepreneurs in finding innovative techniques of production and marketing and finance.

Prime Minister Rozgar Yojna (PMRY), National Rural Employment Programme and (NREP), Rural Landless Employment Guarantee Programme (RLEGP) are some of the important schemes floated by the Government which encourage women to enter into work entrepreneurial activities.

With growing awareness about business and due to growth of educational level, in professional education, industrialisation, urbanisation and democratic values awareness, the tradition-bound Indian society has undergone a change and women entrepreneurs have shifted their entrepreneurial activities to engineering, electronics and energy. They made personal choices, stood up for their convictions and had the courage and strength to enter into new ventures. As a result of these efforts, number of women entrepreneurs have increased over the years.

3.6. PROBLEMS OF WOMEN ENTREPRENEURS [4]

1. External Finance: Finance is regarded as "lifeblood" for any enterprise, be it big or small. In general, women have lower personal financial assets than men. However, women entrepreneurs suffer from shortage of finance on two counts. Firstly, women do not generally have property on their names to use them as collateral for obtaining funds from external sources. Thus, their access to the external sources of funds is limited. Secondly, the banks also consider women less creditworthy and discourage women borrowers on the belief that they can at any time leave their business. This means that for a given opportunity and equally capable individual, women must secure additional resources compared to men in order to exploit the opportunity because they control less capital. A question that has developed into its own sub-field in the women's entrepreneurship literature, is why women have a harder time getting finance than men for the same business opportunity.

2. Obstacles Specific to managing a small firm: Studies on women entrepreneurs show that women have to cope with stereotypic attitudes towards women on a daily basis. Business relations as customers, suppliers, banks, etc., constantly remind the entrepreneur that she is different, sometimes in a positive way such as by praising her for being a successful entrepreneur even though being a woman. Employees tend to mix the perceptions of the manager with their images of female role models leading to mixed expectations on the woman manager to be a manager as well as a "mother". The workload associated with being a small business manager is also not easily combined with taking care of children and a family. However, even if the revenues are somewhat smaller, women entrepreneurs feel more in control and happier with their situation than if they worked as an employee.

3. Scarcity of Raw Material: Most of the women enterprises are plagued by the scarcity of raw material and necessary inputs. Added to this is the high price of raw material, on the one hand, and getting raw material at the minimum of discount, on the other.

4. Stiff Competition: A specific problem of women entrepreneurs seems to be their inability to achieve growth especially sales growth. In other words, as women often have a difficult time to assemble external resources, they start less ambitious firms that can be financed to a greater degree by their own available resources. This also has consequences for the future growth of the firm. Basically, firms with more resources at start-up have a higher probability to grow than firms with fewer resources. By resources, it is meant here societal position, human resources and financial resources. This initial endowment in the firm is therefore of great importance for firm's survival and especially for firm's growth. Women entrepreneurs do not have organizational set-up to pump in a lot of money for canvassing and advertisement. Thus, they have to face a stiff competition for marketing their products with both organized sector and their male counterparts. Such a competition, ultimately results in the liquidation of women enterprises. Many business women find it difficult to capture the market and make their products popular. They are not fully aware of the changing market conditions.

5. Male Dominated Society: Male chauvinism is still the order of the day in India. The Constitution of India speaks of equality between sexes. But, in practice, women are looked upon as *abla,* i.e., weak in all respects. Moreover, male ego never supports women in any business activites. In a nutshell, in the male dominated Indian society, women are not treated equal to men. This, in turn, serves as a barrier to women's entry into business.

6. Sociocultural Barriers: Women are always seen with suspicious eyes and particularly in rural areas. There are number social barriers which restricts the growth of women entrepreneur. Religion and racism has already restricted the boundaries for women and in many areas they believe that women is meant only for household work and not for any outdoor activity. So, the society never supports women in starting any entrepreneurial activity.

7. Family Responsibilities: Women having family responsibility like – looking after the kids, husband and other family members and man play a secondary role only. Her success is dependent upon the support of her family. Support and approval of husbands seem necessary condition for women's entry into business. Generally its difficult for women to maintain a balance between family and business and ultimately it slows down her performance.

8. Lack of Education: In our society, more importance is given to educating the male child as compared to female child. This results in lack of schooling, training and awareness. Due to the lack of education and that too qualitative education, women are not aware of business, technology and market knowledge. Also, lack of education causes low achievement motivation among women.

9. Low Risk Bearing Ability: Women in India lead a protected life. They are less educated and economically not self-dependent. All these reduce their ability to bear risk involved in running an enterprise. Risk bearing is an essential requisite of a successful entrepreneur.

10. Lack of information: Women entrepreneurs generally do not get proper information about the market, business and competitors as they fail to make their network. Women spend most of the time with their family so do not get the chance to make and increase their network. Moreover women mostly depend upon men for the information, so it slows down their progress. Various institutions in the financial sector extend their maximum support in the form of incentives, loans, schemes, etc. Even then every woman entrepreneur may not be aware of all the assistance provided by the

institutions. So, sincere efforts taken towards women entrepreneurs may not reach the entrepreneurs in rural and backward areas.

11. Lack of Training: Training is the basic need for setting up of an enterprise. But due to lack of social and government support women does not get proper training for setting and extension of the enterprise. Lack of training always lower down the confidence. So it act as major barrier in the setting of women entrepreneurial venture.

12. High Cost of Production: As women lack information, government subsidies, discounts about the market. Hence, sometimes they have to pay higher rates for production .

13. Lack of Confidence: In general, women lack confidence in their strength and competence. The family members and the society are reluctant to stand beside their entrepreneurial growth. To a certain extent, this situation is changing among Indian women and yet face a tremendous change to increase the rate of growth in entrepreneurship

14. Motivational Factors: Self motivation can be realized through a mind set for a successful business, attitude to take up risk and behavior towards the business society by shouldering the social responsibilities. Other factors are family support, Government policies, financial assistance from public and private institutions and also the environment suitable for women to establish business units.

15. Identifying the Available Resources: Women are hesitant to find out the access to cater their needs in the financial and marketing areas. In spite of the mushrooming growth of associations, institutions, and the schemes from the government side, women are not enterprising and dynamic to optimize the resources in the form of reserves, assets, manpower or business volunteers.

16. Limited Mobility: Women mobility in India is highly limited and has become a problem due to traditional values and inability to drive vehicles. Moving alone and asking for a room to stay out in the night for business purposes are still looked upon with suspicious eyes. Sometimes, younger women feel uncomfortable in dealing with men who show extra interest in them than work-related aspects.

17. Legal formalities: Fulfilling the legal formalities required for running an enterprise becomes an upheaval task on the part of women entrepreneurs because of the prevalence of corrupt practices in government offices and procedural delays for various licenses, electricity, water and shed allotments. In such situations, women entrepreneurs find it hard to concentrate on the smooth working of the enterprise.

3.7. "WOMEN" AS ENTREPRENEUR IN INDIA

Women owned businesses are highly increasing in the economies of almost all countries. The hidden entrepreneurial potentials of women have gradually been changing with the growing sensitivity to the role and economic status in the society. Skill, knowledge and adaptability in business are the main reasons for women to emerge into business ventures. 'Women Entrepreneur' is a person who accepts challenging role to meet her personal needs and become economically independent. A strong desire to do something positive is an inbuilt quality of entrepreneurial women, who is capable

of contributing values in both family and social life. With the advent of media, women are aware of their own traits, rights and also the work situations. The glass ceilings shattered and women are found indulging in every line of business from pappad to power cables. The challenges and opportunities provided to the women of digital era are growing rapidly that the job seekers are turning into job creators. They are flourishing as designers, interior decorators, exporters, publishers, garment manufacturers and still exploring new avenues of economic participation. In India, although women constitute the majority of the total population, the entrepreneurial world is still a male dominated one. Women in advanced nations are recognized and are more prominent in the business world. But the Indian women entrepreneurs are facing major constraints as discussed earlier.

So, highly educated, technically sound and professionally qualified women should be encouraged for managing their own business, rather than be dependent on wage employment outlets. The unexplored talents of young women can be identified, trained and used for various types of industries to increase the productivity in the industrial sector. A desirable environment is necessary for every woman to inculcate entrepreneurial values and involve greatly in business dealings. The additional business opportunities that are recently approaching women entrepreneurs are: Eco-friendly technology, Biotechnology, IT enabled enterprises, Event Management, Tourism industry, etc.

3.8 ROLE OF WOMEN AS AN ENTREPRENEUR

1. Imaginative: It refers to the imaginative approach or original ideas with competitive market. Wellplanned approach is needed to examine the existing situation and to identify the entrepreneurial opportunities. It further implies that women entrepreneur's have association with knowledgeable people and contracting the right organization offering support and services.

2. Attribute to work hard: Enterprising women have further ability to work hard. The imaginative ideas have to come to a fair play. Hard work is needed to build up an enterprise..

3. Persistence: Women entrepreneurs must have an intention to fulfill their dreams. They have to make a dream transferred into an idea enterprise; Studies show that successful women work hard.

4. Ability and desire to take risk: The desire refers to the willingness to take risks and ability to the proficiency in planning, making forecast estimates and calculations.

5. Profit earning capacity: She should have a capacity to get maximum return out of invested capital.

A Woman entrepreneur has also to perform all the functions involved in establishing an enterprise.These include idea generation, and screening, determination of objectives, project preparation, product analysis, determination of forms of business organization, completion of formal activities, raising funds, procuring men, machine, materials and operations of business.

Fredrick Harbiscon, has enumerated the following five functions of a woman entrepreneur:

- Exploration of the prospects of starting a new business enterprise.
- Undertaking a risk and handling of economic uncertainties involved in business.
- Introduction of innovations, imitations of innovations.

- Coordination, administration and control.
- Supervision and leadership.

In a nutshell, women entrepreneurs are those women who think of a business enterprise, initiate it organize and combine the factors of production, operate the enterprise, undertake risk and handle economic uncertainties involved in running a business enterprise.

With education and training, the women have gained confidence to do all the work, which was the prerogative of men and do it excellently, rather, better than men. Over the years, the educated women have become ambitious, acquired experience and basic skills of competency and self-assurance.

3.9. HOW TO DEVELOP WOMEN ENTREPRENEURS?[5]

Right efforts on from all areas are required in the development of women entrepreneurs and their greater participation in the entrepreneurial activities. Following efforts can be taken into account for effective development of women entrepreneurs.

1. Consider women as specific target group for all developmental programmes.
2. Better educational facilities and schemes should be extended to women folk by the government.
3. Adequate training programme on management skills to be provided to women community.
4. Encourage women's participation in decision making.
5. Vocational training to be extended to women community that enables them to understand the production process and production management.
6. Skill development to be done in women's polytechnics and industrial training institutes. Skills are put to work in training-cum-production workshops.
7. Training on professional competence and leadership skills to be extended to women entrepreneurs.
8. Training and counselling on a large-scale of existing women entrepreneurs to remove psychological causes like lack of self-confidence and fear of success.
9. Counselling through the aid of committed NGOs, psychologists, managerial experts and technical personnel should be provided to existing and emerging women entrepreneurs.
10. Continuous monitoring and improvement of training programmes.
11. Activities in which women are trained should focus on their marketability and profitability.
12. Making provision of marketing and sales assistance from the government.
13. To encourage more passive women entrepreneurs the women's training programme should be organised that teacher them to recognize their own psychological needs and express them.
14. State finance corporations and financing institutions should permitted by statute to extend purely trade-related finance to women entrepreneurs.

15. Women's development corporations have to gain access to open-ended financing.
16. The financial institutions should provide more working capital assistance both for small-scale venture and large-scale ventures.
17. Making provision of microcredit system and enterprise credit system to the women entrepreneurs at local level.
18. Repeated gender sensitisation programmes should be held to train financiers to treat women with dignity and respect as persons in their own right.
19. Infrastructure, in the form of industrial plots and sheds, to set up industries is to be provided by state run agencies.
20. Industrial estates could also provide marketing outlets for the display and sale of products made by women.
21. A Women Entrepreneur's Guidance Cell be set up to handle the various problems of women entrepreneurs all over the State.
22. District Industries Centres and Single Window Agencies should make use of assisting women in their trade and business guidance.
23. Programmes for encouraging entrepreneurship among women are to be extended at local level.
24. Training in entrepreneurial attitudes should start at the high school level through well designed courses, which build confidence through behavioral games.
25. More governmental schemes to motivate women entrepreneurs to engage in small-scale and large-scale business ventures.
26. Involvement of Non-governmental Organisations in women entrepreneurial training programmes and counseling.

3.10. INCENTIVES AND SCHEMES FOR WOMEN ENTREPRENEURS

According to the Third All India Census of Small-scale Industries conducted in 2001-02 and subsequent estimates made, only 10.11% of the Micro and Small Enterprises in India are owned by women, while 9.46% of the MSE enterprises are managed by women. As per the latest available estimates, the number of women owned and women managed enterprises are 12.99 lakhs and 12.15 lakhs respectively.

In order to encourage more and more women enterprises in the MSE sector, several schemes have been formulated by this Ministry and some more are in the process of being finalized, targeted only at the development of women enterprises in India. Women entrepreneurs have achieved remarkable success. The Micro, Small and Medium Enterprises Development Organization (MSME-DO), the various State Small Industries Development Corporations (SSIDCs), the nationalized banks and even NGOs are conducting various programmes including Entrepreneurship Development Programmes (EDPs). To cater to the needs of potential women entrepreneurs, who may not have adequate educational background and skills, MSME-DO has introduced process/product-oriented EDPs in areas like TV repairing, printed circuit boards, leather goods, screen printing, etc. A special prize to "Outstanding Woman Entrepreneur" of the year is being given to recognize achievements made by and to provide incentives to women entrepreneurs. The Office of DC (MSME) has also opened a Women Cell to provide coordination and assistance to women entrepreneurs facing specific problems. Various schemes[6] are as under;-

1. Trade related Entrepreneurship Assistance and Development Scheme for Women (Tread): With a view to encourage women in setting up their own ventures, government implemented a scheme, namely, "Trade-related Entrepreneurship Assistance and Development (TREAD) during the 11th Plan. The MSME (Micro, Small and Medium Enterprises) Ministry runs a scheme in both urban and rural areas to help overcome the developmental hurdles faced by women. This organization helps develop the entrepreneurship skills of women in non-farm activities by providing them with information and counselling with respect to trade. The scheme envisages economic empowerment of women through the development of their entrepreneurial skills in non-farm activities. There are three major components of the scheme-

(i) Govt. of India (GoI) grant upto 30% of the total project cost to the Non-government Organisations (NGOs) for promoting entrepreneurship among women. The remaining 70% of the project cost is financed by the lending agency as loan for undertaking activities as envisaged in the project.

(ii) GoI grant upto ₹ 1 lakh per programme to training institutions /NGOs for imparting training to the women entrepreneurs, subject to these institutions/NGOs bring their share to the extent of minimum 25% of GoI grant and 10% in case of NER.

(iii) Need-based GoI grants upto ₹ 5 lakhs to National Entrepreneurship Development Institutions and any other institutions of repute for undertaking field surveys, research studies, evaluation studies, designing of training modules, etc.,

2. Credit Guarantee Fund Scheme: The Government introduced the Credit Guarantee Fund Scheme for Small Industries in May, 2000, with the objective of making available credit to SSI units, particularly tiny units, for loans up to ₹ 25 lakhs without collateral/third party guarantees. The Scheme is being operated by the Credit Guarantee Fund Trust for Small Industries (CGTSI) set up jointly by the Government of India and SIDBI. The Scheme provides for collateral free credit facility (term loan and/or working capital) extended by eligible lending institutions to new and existing SSI units/ small scale Service and Business (industry related) Enterprises (SSSBEs) including Information Technology and Software Industry up to ₹ 25 lakhs per borrowing unit. In the case of women enterprises, the guarantee cover is up to 80% of the credit subject to maximum guarantee limit of ₹ 20 lakhs. The member lending institutions (MLI) availing of guarantee from the Trust have to pay a one-time guarantee fee of 1.5% of the credit facility (comprising term loan and/or working capital) sanctioned by the lending institution to the borrower and annual service fee of 0.75% per annum on the amount of credit facility extended by the MLI, which is covered under the scheme.

3. Support for Entrepreneurial and Management Development: MSME DIs regularly conduct EDPs/MDPs for existing and prospective entrepreneurs and charge fee for such courses. To encourage more entrepreneurs from among the SC/ST, women and physically challenged groups, it is proposed that such beneficiaries will not be charged any fees but, instead pay a stipend of ₹ 500/-per month.

50,000 entrepreneurs will be trained in IT, Fashion Technology, Catering, Agro and Food Processing, Pharmaceutical, Biotechnology, etc., through specialized courses run by MSME DIs. 20% of courses conducted by these Institutions shall be exclusively for women.

4. Creation of Physical Infrastructure: This Ministry implemented the IID Scheme to provide developed sites with infrastructural facilities like power distribution network, water, telecommunications, drainage and pollution control facilities, roads, exhibition/display centres, raw materials, storage and marketing outlets, common service facilities and technological back-up services, etc. This scheme has been subsumed in the MSME-Cluster Development Programme. All the features of IID Scheme have been retained. To create physical infrastructure exclusively for women enterprises central grant of 40% of the project cost subject to a maximum of ₹ 2 crores is available. The Ministry of MSME is making efforts to enhance the quantum of grant to 80% in a project of ₹ 10 crores.

There are also several other schemes of the government like the Income Generating Scheme, implemented by the Department of Women and Child Development, which provides assistance for setting up training-cum-income generating activities for needy women to make them economically independent. The Small Industries Development Bank of India (SIDBI) has been implementing two special schemes for women namely Mahila Udyam Nidhi which is an exclusive scheme for providing equity to women entrepreneurs and the Mahila Vikas Nidhi which offers developmental assistance for pursuit of income generating activities to women. The SIDBI has also taken initiative to set up an informal channel for credit needs on soft terms giving special emphasis to women. Over and above this, SIDBI also provides training for credit utilisation as also credit delivery skills for the executives of voluntary organisations working for women. Grant for setting up a production unit is also available under Socio-economic Programme of Central Social Welfare Board.

3.11. NATIONAL ORGANIZATIONS EMPOWERING WOMEN ENTREPRENEURS

1. FIWE[7]: The Federation of Indian Women Entrepreneurs: Based out of Delhi, FIWE was established in 1993, is today, one of India's premier institution for women thoroughly devoted towards entrepreneurship development. It now has over 15,000 members and around 28 member associations. The aim of this organization is to help empower women entrepreneurs through trainings on technical know-how, industry research, expertise, and skill development. They concentrate largely on the SME segment. FIWE endeavors to provide: Networking platform for women, Technical know-how, Industry research and expertise, Skill development and training and brings the businesswomen on a Common Forum; and ensures that their opinions, ideas and visions are collectively and effectively taken up with policymakers and various other agencies respectively for the development of enterprise in women.

The Federation of Indian Women Entrepreneurs (FIWE) is an outcome of the decisions taken at the International Conference of Women Entrepreneurs held in December 1993 at Hyderabad (India). The idea was that the women's wing of the erstwhile National Alliance of Young Entrepreneurs (NAYE) converts itself into an autonomous national-level women entrepreneur's organization whose main function would be networking and to provide a package of services to the associations of women entrepreneurs in different parts of the country.

It was accordingly announced that NAYE's womens wing will henceforth be known as Federation of Indian Women Entrepreneurs (FIWE) and will have no chapters. Associations of women entrepreneurs in various districts and States will be provided to women entrepreneurs in India. Individual women entrepreneurs could also be eligible for general membership.

2. CWEI[8]: Consortium of Women Entrepreneurs of India: A leading organization in the field, CWEI works with UN Women, the MSME Ministry and the Ministry of Rural Development. Consortium of Women Entrepreneurs of India – was registered in 1996 as a civil society nonprofit organization in New Delhi with a mandate to work in the sub continent. CWEI is accredited to Govt. of India and is a Member of National Board, Ministry of MSME and is working closely with Ministry of Rural Development in the PPP mode to support BPL families in India. It is also the Knowledge Partner to the State Govt. of Andhra Pradesh, working for the sustainable economic empowerment of women and their families through income generating activities and entrepreneurship development.

CWEI strongly claims to have achieved success in motivating women to opt for entrepreneurship as a challenging career – the only answer to unemployment. Outreach Entrepreneurship and Skill Development trainings (ESDP), financial inclusion and support services are being provided to set up micro enterprises amongst women minorities, SC and tribals in various States in the country.

CWEI launched SAWE with the help of UN Women in 1996, with the aim to reach every corner of the country, SAARC and Asia Pacific region and developing countries. SAWE delivers technological know-how, new design techniques, skill development and training by acting as a catalyst providing all escort services leading to higher productivity, competitive prices and monitoring stringent quality control.

MOHA, 4 Rajiv Gandhi Handicrafts Bhawan, Baba Kharag Singh Marg, Connaught Place, New Delhi 110001, Indias the marketing center is an initiative to provide retail sales and showcase products for market linkages, product development and design, build alliances and network with other women entrepreneurs globally.

IWEM&C - International Women Entrepreneurs Meet and Conference the annual event of Consortium of Women Entrepreneurs of India was initiated in 1996 by UN Women in South Asia. It has been a successful endeavour for over a decade and has partnered with their focal points in almost 42 countries around the globe within 14 years of their fruitful existence.

IWEM&C highlights issues pertaining to marketing, finance, training, product design and development and a host of other critical problems in order to bring the issues to the notice of policy-makers, implementing agencies and women entrepreneurs themselves forming fruitful alliances and a chain of networks.

They are in the forefront of all initiatives concerned with assisting women entrepreneurs – help them learn better marketing skills, work with tribal and backward women to integrate them with urban organizations and devising new and innovative methods for arranging financing for women-run businesses.

Keeping in view the main concern of empowerment of rural, illiterate and under privileged women, "SHASHWAT" – the rural system of CWEI was launched.

SHASHWAT provides common facilities and acts as an incubator in rural clusters. It has been established to make women self-reliant by educating them about the technologies, training them to access new opportunities, use better tools, thereby upgrading their skills for sustainable income generation in clusters

3. Stree Shakti by TIE: The Indus Entrepreneurs (TIE), was founded in 1992 in Silicon Valley by a group of successful entrepreneurs, corporate executives, and senior professionals with roots in the Indus region. There are currently 13,000 members, including over 2,500 charter members in 57 chapters across 14 countries. TIE's mission is to foster entrepreneurship globally through mentoring, networking, and education. Dedicated to the virtuous cycle of wealth creation and giving back to the community, TIE's focus is on generating and nurturing our next generation of entrepreneurs.The Indus Entrepreneurs, movement 'Stree Shakti' aims at connecting and enabling enterprising women from different classes of society through a series of on-ground focused programmes. They are a leading organization in mentoring, educating and providing inspiration.

4. NWEA, The Noida Womens' Entrepreneur Association: It was set up to help businesswomen in Noida deal with the hurdles that come with their ventures. The organization plays the role of a mentor and lobbyist for its members. "The association was started in the year 1986 by a group of nine women who faced similar problems while starting out in Noida," said Rekha Gupta, president and one of the founding members of NWEA. Gupta is also the managing director of Delhi Control Devices, based out of Noida, which manufactures electrical and electronics parts, According to Rekha Gupta. "An association for women was the need of the hour to tackle all the issues which were unique to women entrepreneurs."

5. Best Price Members Women's Council: Retail giant Walmart, which came into India in collaboration with Bharti, has launched a forum in Chandigarh in order to help women understand the issues they will face with a start-up and to help scale up the business.

Women's Web has recently launched Women's Haat, a listing space for women entrepreneurs to be featured on and gain visibility to our growing tribe of readers.

While most women in the metros and other large towns have access to events such as TIE meetings or all forms of media.

3.12. GLOBAL ORGANIZATIONS EMPOWERING WOMEN ENTREPRENEURS[9]

1. Goldman Sachs – ISB 10000 Women Program: The Goldman Sachs 10,000 Women initiative operates through a network of more than 80 academic and non profit institutions. These partnerships help develop locally relevant coursework and improve the quality and capacity of business education worldwide.

The women selected for the program enroll in customized certificate programs ranging from five weeks to six months. Topics covered include marketing, accounting, writing business plans and accessing capital.

Students are offered mentoring and post-graduate support by partner institutions, local businesses and the people of Goldman Sachs.

The unique aspect of this program is that it strives to provide women with an education in business management – one that will help them succeed in their venture. 10,000 women from across the globe learn the basic skills of **running a business** like writing a business plan, accounting, marketing and seeking investments for their business. The program is supported by various non-profit organizations across the world.

2. The Cherie Blair Foundation for Women: Based in London, this non-profit organization was set up to benefit women entrepreneurs. They facilitate access to technology, business skills training, networks and finance by working in partnership with other organisations through three programmes: Enterprise Development, Mobile Technology and Mentoring. This organization lays special emphasis on investing in women from developing regions like Africa, Asia and the Middle East. While providing access to finances is the foundation's main area, they also provide business and technical knowledge and networking platforms for women. The charity was set up in 2008 in response to Cherie's experiences meeting women around the world and the realisation that, with the right support, women can overcome the challenges they face and play an important part in the economies and societies in which they work and live.

3. Carma – Creating Access to Resources and Markets: A profit company, Carma helps nurture aspiring entrepreneurs – anyone who has an idea they want to execute. While a large number of their mentees are women, Carma does its work across genders, ages and geographies. They charge a fee depending on the whether the business is just starting up or has already been in the market and then conduct virtual mentoring for a period of 6 months. Carma's approach is a logical, practical and ROI driven one.

4. WeConnect International: This is a corporate led non-profit organization which helps empower women entrepreneurs by connecting them with other corporates and helping to accelerate their growth.

5. Google launches Women Entrepreneurs on the Web (WEOW): Bengaluru: Google, the search engine giant that offers Gmail, YouTube and other Google+ products, has launched ' Women Entrepreneurs on the Web ' (WEOW), an initiative aimed at helping women entrepreneurs across India grow their online presence.

The program will provide women entrepreneurs support on using various web-based technologies and eventually help them increase their outreach to the customer base, the company said in a statement.

3.13. SUMMARY

Women constitutes around half of the total population of the world but still has no power to take decisions. But in the modern era the concept of women is changed. She is stepping out of the house and exploring new opportunities. Moreover our constitution has given equal rights to women and irrespective of the problems faced by women entrepreneur, she is moving forward. And Government of India has given many incentives and schemes to them.So according to Government of India – women entrepreneur is defined as an enterprise which is owned and controlled by women entrepreneur having minimum financial interest of 51% of capital and giving atleast 51% of the employment to women only.

3.14. CASE STUDIES

Shahnaz Husain

"I do not sell products. I sell an entire civilization in a jar." **- Shahnaz Husain**

Shahnaz Husain belongs to a royal Muslim family which migrated from Samarkhand to India and later held high positions in the princely kingdoms of Bhopal and Hyderabad before India's independence. Shahnaz received her schooling in an Irish convent and because of the influence of her father, Chief Justice N.U. Beg, she developed a love for poetry and English Literature. Born in a royal Muslim family, Husain was introduced to both modern schooling as well as traditions. She got married at a tender age of 16 and gave birth to a daughter within a year. However, the monotony of her life made her do something more than a housewife.

It was during her husband's posting in Iran that she realized her keen interest in beauty and cosmetology. She pursued it with great passion in many leading institutes like Helena Rubinstein, Arnould Taylor, Swarzkopf, Christine Valmy, Lancome and Lean of Copenhagen and supported her education by writing for the Iran Tribune. She realized that chemical treatments are harmful and have long lasting negative effects. She was thus attracted towards the ancient treasure of Ayurveda. She came up with many natural Ayurvedic chemical free products for beauty care. She firmly believes in the power of 'care and cure' of the nature than chemicals.

The Turning Point — Saloon to Shahnaz Husain Herbal INC: She started her saloon on a humble budget of ₹ 35,000/- in Delhi and soon she was booked for 6 months in advance. She stopped advertising her services, thereafter, as she believed firmly in the word of mouth publicity by satisfied customers. Turning point came in her career when she was given an opportunity to represent India in London during The Festival of India in 1980. Her products created a huge stir and soon she captured a huge market there. Now, her company produces more than 400 different products which have a market in over 138 countries. Husain expanded her consumer base by entering the retail markets in 1990's. Her new below ₹ 250 range is targeted towards the masses which is a very lucrative market segment. The Shahnaz group has diversified into health resorts, spas as well as low calorie health drinks.

She captured the markets around the world and now she wants to conquer space. In an innovative move, Shahnaz Husain has started work on formulations that astronauts could carry with them in their extraterrestrial sojourns to protect their skin from the ravages of space travel and slow down the ageing process. She has sent National Aeronautics and Space Administration (NASA) free samples of her moisturizers, hoping that they will be used on space expeditions. Shahnaz Husain is one of India's most successful women entrepreneurs. Her company, Shahnaz Husain Herbals is one of the largest manufacturers of herbal products in the world. It formulates and markets over 400 products for various beauty and health needs and has a strong presence across the globe, from the USA to Asia.

- Shahnaz has a long list of recognition in her kitty; a few of them are-
- She was awarded Padma Shree in 2006, by President Dr.Abdul Kalam.

- She has been honoured with two prestigious international awards for Quality Excellence and Outstanding Woman Entrepreneur 2002, by Global Quality Management, in London.
- Awarded 'The 2000 Millennium Medal of Honour'.
- Awarded 'The Arch of Europe Gold Star Award for Quality'.
- She was awarded the Golden America Award and the Indian Government Awards for Export Excellence.
- She was awarded Success Magazine's 'World's Greatest Woman Entrepreneur' award in 1996.

Kiran Mazumdar Shaw—Biocon

Kiran Mazumdar-Shaw (born 23 March 1953) is an Indian entrepreneur. She is the Chairman and Managing Director of Biocon Limited a biotechnology company based in Bengaluru, India. Kiran Mazumdar-Shaw completed her schooling from the city's Bishop Cotton Girl's High School. She took up biology and completed her BSc Zoology Honours course from Mount Carmel College, Bangalore University (1973). She later did her postgraduation as a brewmaster in Malting and Brewing from Ballarat College, Melbourne University (1975).

She worked as a trainee brewer in Carlton and United Breweries, Melbourne and as a trainee at Barrett Brothers and Burston, Australia. She also worked for some time as a technical consultant at Jupiter Breweries Limited, Calcutta and as a technical manager at Standard Maltings Corporation, Baroda between 1975 and 1977.

In 1978, she joined Biocon Biochemicals Limited, of Cork, Ireland as a Trainee Manager. In the same year, she started Biocon in the garage of her rented house in Bengaluru with a seed capital of ₹ 10,000.

Initially, she faced credibility challenges because of her youth, gender and her untested business model. Not only was funding a problem as no bank wanted to lend to her, but she also found it difficult to recruit people for her start-up. With single-minded determination, she overcame these challenges only to be confronted with the technological challenges associated with trying to build a biotech business in a country facing infrastructural woes. Uninterrupted power, superior quality water, sterile labs, imported research equipment, and advanced scientific skills were not easily available in India during the time.

She is responsible for steering Biocon on a trajectory of growth and innovation over the years. Within a year of its inception, Biocon became the first Indian company to manufacture and export enzymes to USA and Europe. In 1989, Biocon became the first Indian biotech company to receive US funding for proprietary technologies. In 1990, she upgraded Biocon's in-house research program, based on a proprietary solid substrate fermentation technology.

In the same year, she incorporated Biocon Biopharmaceuticals Private Limited to manufacture and market a select range of biotherapeutics in a joint venture with the Cuban Centre of Molecular Immunology.

She also established two subsidiaries: Syngene (1994) to provide development support services as an outsourcing firm for discovery research and Clinigene (2000) to cater to clinical development services. In 2004, she decided to access the capital markets to develop Biocon's pipeline of research programs. Biocon's IPO was oversubscribed 32 times and its first day at the bourses closed with a market value of $1.11 billion, making Biocon only the second Indian company to cross the $1-billion mark on the first day of listing.

Her pioneering work in the sector has earned her several awards, including the prestigious Padma Shri (1989) and the Padma Bhushan (2005) from the government of India. She was recently named among TIME magazine's 100 most influential people in the world. She is on the Forbes list of the world's 100 most powerful women and the *Financial Times*' top 50 women in business list. She is also a member of the board of governors of the prestigious Indian School of Business and Indian Institute of Technology Hyderabad.

Chitra Rajan—Founder, Radix Lifespaces[10]

Her father passed away when she was doing an MA in Bhopal. Her family needed to be supported and that meant Chitra Rajan could not do a PhD as she was hoping. She moved to Chennai and started a software firm in 1988. She and her partner, who later became her husband, got good clients like Glaxo, Crompton Greaves and the United Nations. In 1996, they realised the business could go forward only with substantial investments. They did not have the resources, so sold the business, and moved to Bengaluru, where Chitra worked in IT roles in companies including ITC, Cambridge Technology Partners and Digital GlobalSoft.

In 2004, the entrepreneurship bug bit her again and she started a construction firm that did not last long. "Our second project was a large one, and the demands we faced from officials put us off. So we sold it," Chitra says. She then bought a 200-acre coffee plantation in Somwarpet near Coorg. There she saw coffee husk being wasted in massive quantities. She did research and found a commercially viable way to convert such organic waste into methane. "Today we have four plants running in different cities and more are coming up. The gas is being used in cooking, and in our Mumbai project, we are experimenting with the use of this gas in automobiles," Chitra says. Two years ago, she even completed the PhD she had longed to do in 1987.

Pallavi Gupta–Co-founder, Mast Kalandar[11]

In her restaurants she uses the ingredients that most of us use at home - top brands like MDH masalas, Annapurna atta and Amul dairy products. Most restaurants use inferior products. It is this, combined with the freshness of the products served that has made Pallavi Gupta's Mast Kalandar so popular, and why the 'home cooked' branding works so well for it. She, together with her husband Gaurav Jain, has now established 42 outlets serving vegetarian, north Indian fare across Bengaluru, Hyderabad, Chennai and Pune. And the chain, having attracted venture capital, is expected to grow to 100 outlets by next year.

Gupta grew up in Ludhiana in Punjab, did engineering from Patiala, and then a MBA from IMT, Ghaziabad. Immediately after that she moved to Bengaluru where she worked as a retail consultant, first with Wipro and then TCS. She would travel to the top retailers around the world building their IT systems. That's when she and Gaurav (who was in Wipro and Planetasia and who she married in 2002) thought of starting their own business in retail. "I realised that retail was a sunrise industry and that people's busy lives would create a home meal replacement market in India," Pallavi says. Thus Mast Kalandar was born in 2005.

Pallavi says it was challenging for her as a woman entrepreneur. "People often do not take you seriously. But perseverance is the most important thing, everything else then falls into place," says Pallavi, adding that being a woman also has its advantages: "Women bond with people more easily, and they win the trust of staff more easily."

Chetna Gala Sinha

Chetna Gala Sinha is an Indian social entrepreneur. She is empowering women in drought prone areas of rural India by inculcating entrepreneurial skills and providing them access to land and other means of production. The greatest mark of a successful social entrepreneur is the impact that she can have on other aspiring entrepreneurs. By the yardstick, Chetna Gala Sinha is a resounding success. **In 1997, she founded the Mann Deshi Mahila Sahkari Bank, a microfinance bank that lends to women in drought-prone areas in Maharashtra, and inspires them on a journey towards economic self-sufficiency.** The organization provides both financial and non financial (vocational) help to improve the standard of living of women in rural India. She has also started several linked initiatives, such as the Mann Deshi Udyogini (a Rural Business School for Rural Women), and the 1000 Deshi Entrepreneurs Program (which aspires to create business role models of 1,000 promising rural women entrepreneurs by helping them achieve significant economic growth.)

Ms Sinha has won many accolades for her work as the chairperson of Mann Deshi Mahila Bank, including the recognition as a "Bridge Builder" by Harvard University and as a "World Fellow" by Yale University. Her story is a message of empowerment and dedication for all social entrepreneurs. India's rural women often bear the brunt of climatic factors and stringent government regulations, making it appear as if there is no way out of the cycle of poverty. **Ms Sinha's persistent efforts have proven that even in one of the most arid areas of India, prosperity is an achievable reality.**

Ela Bhatt

India's microfinance success story owes much to Ela Bhatt's grit and social consciousness. Bhatt is the founder of the Self-employed Women's Association (SEWA) which provides microfinance funding and entrepreneurial training to thousands of women across India.

Bhatt, a noted Gandhian, started SEWA in 1972, to support the large number of women working in India's unorganized labour sector. From traditional garments and textiles to solar-powered bulbs and lighting products, SEWA women have found entrepreneurial success through a diverse line of ventures. SEWA supports more than 9,00,000 women in their business journeys through financing, publicity, legal help and other social and justice-based issues.

Ela Bhatt has been awarded the Padmashri, the Padmabhushan and the Magsaysay Award, in recognition of her contribution to women's economic and social empowerment in India. Her story is the best example there is of small things making a huge difference. SEWA began by giving out small loans to women to start their entrepreneurial journeys. Today, it has led a revolution in microfinancing and even impacted India's regulations within the unorganized sector, in favour of the countless self-employed women. Most importantly, SEWA has taught women that anything is possible: it is possible to be a woman and succeed in a largely male-dominated society, it is possible to grow large enterprises even if you start small, it is possible to do good while doing well for yourself, and it is possible (and very beneficial) for women to support and strengthen each other in their journey towards economic freedom and social well-being.

Shalini Ahuja Agarwal's Safe Baby:

India's first professional child safety company[12]

Safe Baby was started by Agarwal and her husband Sachin Agarwal upon their return from the US to Mumbai in 2011. The company offers baby-proofing audits where the duo identifies probable risks of accidents in a child's room, a play or preparatory school. "We have safety equipment such as door guards, cabinet locks, safety gates, cord shorteners and many others which are installed on the spot to reduce risks instantly. We also offer workshops on preventing accidents, first-aid and CPR," says Agarwal. Audits and workshops are on offer for parents, day-cares and playschools.

The Agarwals claim that the response to their workshops on preventing accidents and first-aid has been phenomenal. However, since it is a relatively new business idea, it is difficult to estimate the market size, she adds. The idea to start such a service emerged from the idea that Indians have begun to spend a lot of money on their children. In addition to customized audits, the company offers workshops for nannies, teachers, architects and other interested people. These workshops can be held in group or a suitable venue of the client. "Sometimes a carpenter is required to make certain changes. In such cases, we work with the carpenters or architects for making the product or place safe for a baby."

3.15 SELF ASSESSMENT QUESTIONS

1. Define women entrepreneur. Explain the various problems faced by women entrepreneurs.
2. What are the various functions performed by women entrepreneurs?
3. What the recent trends in the development of women entrepreneurship in India?
4. Define women entrepreneurs and discuss the main reasons for the slow progress of women entrepreneurs in India.

SOURCE/NOTES

1. Women Entrepreneurship in India: Opportunities and Challenges(Research paper)-Gurendra Nath Bhardwaj, Swati Parashar, Babita Pandey, Puspamita Sahu.
2. Women Entrepreneurship in India: Opportunities and Challenges(Research paper)-Gurendra Nath Bhardwaj, Swati Parashar, Babita Pandey, Puspamita Sahu.

3. http://www.preservearticles.com/201101153364/meaning-and-growth-of-woman-entrepreneurship-in-india.html
4. Acharyan N.G Ranga Agricultural University-Entrepreneurship Development(study material)- Dr. V.Sudharani
5. www. swapnaraju wordpress.com
6. dcmsme.gov.in andmsmediagra.gov.in
7. www.fiwe.org
8. www.cwei.org
9. womensweb.inand google.com
10. www.timesofindia.indiatimes.com
11. www.timesofindia.indiatimes.com
12. http://economictimes.indiatimes.com/articleshow/21036435.cms

4

THEORIES OF ENTREPRENEURSHIP

4.1. INTRODUCTION

The concept of entrepreneurship is as old as civilization. But theories of entrepreneurship have been evolved over a period of three centuries. Different authors have explained entrepreneurship in different ways. The concept of entrepreneurship has evolved and undergone tremendous change and the topic of entrepreneurship has been surveyed by many economists. So the theories of entrepreneurship has advanced from the classical economists to the post Keynesian analysts. A consistent universal theory does not exist in entrepreneurship, but rather it consists of several different approaches including psychology, sociology, anthropology, regional science and economics.

The concept of entrepreneurship is complex and its content is not influenced only by economical aspects but also by sociological, political, psychological, ethical, religious and cultural values. The concept also bears testimony to courage, creativity, determination, networking, hardworking, etc., Over the years the social scientists have interpreted the phenomenon of entrepreneurship differently in accordance with their perception and economic environment. Entrepreneurship as a process has and is undergoing changes and keeping these changes, different theories of entrepreneurship have been evolved by different thinkers.

4.2. ROLE OF DIFFERENT THEORIES IN EXPLAINING ENTREPRENEURSHIP

1. Psychological Theories and the Need for Achievement: Psychological theories such as those developed by McLelland pay attention to personal traits, motives and incentives of an individual and conclude that entrepreneurs have a strong need for achievement (McLelland and Winter, 1971). A similar focus is found in locus of control theories that conclude that an entrepreneur will probably have strong internal locus of control (Low and MacMillan 1988, 147, Amit, *et.al.*, 1993, 821). This means that an entrepreneur believes in his or her capabilities to commence and complete things and events through his or her own actions. Brockhaus (1982, 42-45) suggests that an internal locus of control, even if it fails to distinguish entrepreneurs, may serve to distinguish the successful entrepreneur from the unsuccessful one. How do we measure success of entrepreneur? Success is a relative concept that can also be measured differently in different contexts. If success is measured in relation to the fulfillment of the goals and objectives of a particular entrepreneur, self-employed could also be classified as successful if their businesses generate continuously a satisfactory (in relation to their goals) level of living. On the other hand, high-growth ventures may be considered unsuccessful if they are not able to offer high enough ROI to their investors. Davidsson (1989, 210-211) states that achievement motivation is the most important factor contributing in explaining variation of growth rates and entrepreneurship. Shaver and Scott (1991, 31) believe that achievement motivation is perhaps the only convincing personological variable associated with new venture creation. Why is it convincing? If the concept will be defined broadly as Murray (1938, "Explorations in Personality") it is no wonder, why Johnson (1990) found a relationship between achievement motivation and entrepreneurship in 20 of 23 studies According to Shaver and Scott (1991, 31) Murray (1938) saw a need as a force "in the brain region" and the specific need for achievement was defined as: "To accomplish something difficult. To master, manipulate, or organize physical objects, human beings or ideas. To do this as rapidly, and as independently as possible. To overcome obstacles and attain a high standard. To excel oneself. To rival and surpass others. To increase self-regard by the successful exercise of talent"

This definition compared with the others includes most of the characteristics listed above.

- Internal locus of control is included in "To master and manipulate physical objects, human beings, or ideas," in "To overcome obstacles and attain a high standard," and in "To excel oneself."
- High risk taking propensity is connected with "To overcome obstacles and attain a high standard."
- Tolerance of ambiguity is associated with "To accomplish something difficult."
- High needs for autonomy, dominance, and independence coincide with "To master, manipulate, or organize physical objects, human beings or ideas..as independently as possible."
- The capacity for endurance or capability for intense effort is parallel to "To overcome obstacles and attain a high standard," "To accomplish something difficult," "To rival and surpass others," "To do this as rapidly," and to "To excel oneself."

In addition to the above traits, the definition of need for achievement includes traits as competitive mind ("To rival and surpass others"), self-consciousness, and an itch to self development and learning ("To increase self-regard by the successful exercise of talent") (c.f. Sexton and Bowman 1985, 134, Low and MacMillan 1988, 147, Amit, *et. al.,* 1993, 821). In analyzing entrepreneurial behavior we should pay more attention to expectations, motives and incentives. "The forces in the brain region" (needs) foster expectations, motives and incentives to take some action. What kind of motives and incentives are required to enforce entrepreneurial activity? Why would someone start a new venture? The reasons, as well as the businesses, may differ from case to case. Thus, to systematically approach the question, we should conceptualize the phenomenon into some controllable pieces and to define the concepts.

2. Entrepreneurship and Sociological Theories: To complement the definition of the entrepreneur, the role of the entrepreneur could be described as Cantillon did (Murphy 1986, 255): "The entrepreneur scouts around, he sniffs out potentially profitable ventures, he forms hunches, and he reacts quickly if his hunches prove incorrect - otherwise he goes out of business. He is the highly visible hand that ensures coordination between producers and consumers."

The characterization of an entrepreneur's role points out the meaning of environmental context (scouts around). This links different approaches to different environments that provide profit potential for different ventures. Thus the entrepreneur's role as the highly visible hand depends on the environmental (social) context. Johnson's (1990) study refers to the sociological perspective of entrepreneurship by proposing that a detailed description of the environmental context is required before achievement motivation research will make further progress. Reynolds (1991, 61-62) states that the inability of trait theories to predict entrepreneurship could result from the ignorance of social context and choices confronting the individual when the decision is made. Thus, describing situations where seizing the opportunity to be an entrepreneur takes place will be useful. In addition to sociological entrepreneurship theories opportunity recognition could be described by anthropological theories. Anthropological entrepreneurship studies concentrate on social and cultural processes. The outcome and the degree of entrepreneurial activity depend on opportunity structure. Opportunity structure consists of "both objective structure of economic opportunity and a structure of differential advantage in the capacity of the system's participants to perceive and act upon such opportunities."

The main focus of sociological enterprise is to identify this social context. Reynolds (1991) differentiates with four social contexts in relation to entrepreneurial opportunity; (1) social networks, (2) life course stage, (3) ethnic identification and (4) population ecology stage. For the entrepreneur, involvement in casual informal networks may produce a major advantage (Reynolds, 1991, 63, c.f also Granovetter, 1973). In contrast to the transaction cost approach, social network theories emphasize trust, not opportunism, as an integral part of the relationship (Larson, 1992, 90, Reynolds, 1991, 63). Social control and economic exchange factors interact closely in long-term relationships. The life course context involves analyzing the life situations and characteristics of individuals who have decided to become entrepreneurs. Social context and life course stages associated with entrepreneurial behavior are unique and to some extent even predictable (Reynolds, 1991, 63). Sociologists argue that entrepreneurship is most likely to emerge under specific social culture. According to them social sanctions, cultural values and role expectations are responsible for the emergence of entrepreneurship.

Sociological theories that start from ethnic identification, try to explain entrepreneurship as a process where the individual's sociological (disadvantageous) background is one of the decisive "Push" factors to become an entrepreneur. Low and MacMillan (1988, 149) suggest that current examples of technology clusters and high-tech companies offer contradictory evidence regarding disadvantageous backgrounds of entrepreneurs and no confident generalizations should be made about entrepreneurship being a response to inferior social conditions even though some cases exist. This conclusion, however, is applicable only in the category of special ventures that usually have high-growth and value added objectives and expectations. The population ecology perspective is dynamic and process-oriented, thus might be a good analogy to describe the entrepreneurial process. In recent years, it has developed from a simplistic and deterministic metaphor to a rich theoretical framework capable of incorporating other theoretical perspectives (Low and MacMlillan 1988, 145). Population ecology examines the survival of organizations in relation to environmental factors (c.f Amit, *et al.,* 1990, 823). However, population ecology theory excludes the most important criterion used for example in venture capitalist's financing decisions: the entrepreneur and management team. If the entrepreneur and management team are the most important determinants of success in the minds of venture capitalists, then as Amit, *et al.,* (1990, 823) asked: "Further, to what extent is success determined by the environment rather than the skill and ingenuity and decision of the entrepreneur?" However, ecological models could be developed more in the direction of entrepreneurial ecology by making the entrepreneur rather than the organization as the unit of analysis. Boime (1976, 181) states that:"If it is feasible to speak of an 'entrepreneurial psychology', it is also appropriate to speak of an 'entrepreneurial ecology. The entrepreneur, insofar as his activities transform the physical nature of the environment and thus the conditions of experience,creates what I call the entrepreneurial ecology. The term as used, expresses the changing character of the contemporary world through material signs of modernity. Not only do entrepreneurs furnish conspicuous evidence of change, they are the first to call attention to it by their lifestyle." This approach would not exclude the entrepreneur from the development process but in fact emphasizes his or her role in it. Boime highlights the reason why we believe entrepreneurial talents are crucially important: an entrepreneur's activities transform the physical nature of the environment. He introduces an interesting ingredient to roles of entrepreneurs (c.f Chandler and Jansen 1992): entrepreneurs may also act as early adopters on the consumer side.

4.3. INNOVATIVE THEORY OF ENTREPRENEURSHIP

Joseph Schumpeter has been pioneering work in the field of entrepreneurship. Innovation theory is the given by Joseph Schumpeter only. According to him, entrepreneurship is essentially a creative activity. It refers to do things which are generally not done in ordinary course of business. The basics of Schumpeter's theory of innovation are found in his economic model of the circular flow. This circular flow describes a stationary situation of equilibrium and perfect competition similar to a so-called Walrasian state of equilibrium. Innovation is defined as the stage of successful introduction of new products and processes. In explaining, the change over from routine economic growth to 'dynamic' economic development, Schumpeter introduced the notion of so-called 'new combinations'. These new combinations refer to the introduction of new product or a new quality of a product, a new method of production, a new market, a new source of supply of raw material or half manufactured goods, and finally implementing the new organization of any industry. According to him, entrepreneurs are essentially motivated and talented class of people. The innovative entrepreneur forsees the potentially profitable opportunity and tries to exploit it. Although Schumpeter referred to innovation as new combinations in most of his writings, he also defined innovation 'as setting up of a new production function'. In that context, it is worth noting that Schumpeter introduced three broad definitions of production function, i.e., as the given technological possibilities as seen by producers, blueprints with 'cost neutral' technical alternatives and a 'realistic' production function constructed on the basis of factual observations distinct from 'logically pure' production function. Innovations involve problem solving and entrepreneur is a problem solver. An entrepreneur gets satisfaction from using his capabilities in attaching problems.

4.3.1. Schumpeter's Classification of Innovations and the Walrasian System

1. **Product innovation:** A new product is introduced in a new firm's production function and in some of the consumers' consumption functions, i.e., introduction of new product with which consumers are not yet familiar or introduction of a new quality of an existing product.

2. **Process innovation:** New production function for an existing consumption product, i.e., the introduction of a new method of production that has not been yet tested in the branch of manufacture concerned. This need not be scientific discovery and can also be a new way of handling a commodity commercially.

3. **Market innovation:** An existing consumption product is introduced in the consumption function of a new group of buyers (e.g., in a new country), i.e., the opening of a new market, into which the particular branch of manufacture of the country in question has not previously entered, whether or not this market has existed before.

4. **Input innovation:** The supplying firm introduces a new production function and some buyers introduce the novelty in their production functions, i.e., the conquest of a new source of supply of raw materials or semi-finished goods, irrespective of whether this source already exists or whether it has first to be created.

5. **Organisational innovation:** A change in the routine for the economic behavior of a firm – typically by changing the market structure (e.g., a new cartel), i.e., the carrying out of a new organization, like the creation of a monopoly situation or the breaking up of a monopoly position.

Schumpeter has made the distinction between innovator and inventor. An inventor discovers new methods and new materials, whereas, an innovator is one who uses and applies inventions and discoveries in order to make new combinations and to produce new and better goods which yield both satisfaction and profits. The innovator implements the new ideas produced by inventor as the invention refers to new concepts or products that derive from individual's ideas or from scientific research. The innovation on the other hand, represents the commercialization of the invention itself. Moreover an inventor is concerned with his technical work of innovation whereas an entrepreneur converts the technical work into economic performance. Schumpeter's definition of innovation as 'new combinations' is broad as it relates to technical, marketing and organizational aspects of subjects. All three aspects are important for understanding the complexity of innovation.

Moreover, Schumpeter stressed the role of the entrepreneurial function in economic development. Schumpeter's innovating entrepreneur represents the most vigorous type of enterprise. In the view of above, Schumpeter's theory of entrepreneurship has got the following features:

(a) Distinction between invention and innovation

(b) Emphasis on entrepreneurial functions, i.e., Schumpeter has given emphasis on the role of entrepreneurial functions in economic development.

(c) Presentation of disequilibrium situation through entrepreneurial activity.

(d) Characteristic motives of the entrepreneurial conduct.

4.3.2. Limitations of Innovative Theory of Entrepreneurship

Schumpeter's focus on innovation and innovation theory, however, ignores the entrepreneur's risk taking ability and organizational skills, and place undue importance on innovation. This theory applies to large-scale businesses, but economic conditions force small entrepreneurs to imitate rather than innovate. Schumpeter's focus only innovation without much attention for pre-market conditions of technological development resulted not only in the abstraction from early phases of technology; it also meant that minor technological changes were somewhat neglected. Furthermore, Schumpeter's understanding of innovations as more or less radical changes with a great impact on sectors of industry and business cycles made minor day to day technical improvements apparently less important. Schumpeter's concept of innovation is too restricted. Some other limitations of the theory are as under:-

1. **Emphasis on Innovative Function only:** The theory stressed much on the innovation function of an entrepreneur and it neglects the other important functions like;- risk taking, decision making, managerial function of organization and leadership which are equally vital to perform entrepreneurial activity effectively.

2. **Study of Large Businessman:** This theory assumes entrepreneur as a big businessman running a large-scale enterprise. According to Schumpeter, entrepreneur is a person who always creates something new. But in reality an entrepreneur cannot always creates new things and cannot operate on a large-scale in the beginning rather it has to start from a small scale only and later it got extended to large-scale.

3. **Non-practicable in Developing Countries:** Innovative entrepreneurs are non–practicable in developing countries. Entrepreneurs in developing countries generally imitate techniques of production from the developed economy. So they never go for innovation on their own and therefore, imitative entrepreneurs are more suitable than innovative entrepreneurs for developing countries.

4. **No Study on Established Businessmen:** The theory excludes the individuals who merely operate an established business without performing any innovative activity.

4.3.3. Systematic Innovation Theory

Systematic innovation theory has been developed by Peter Drucker (1909-2005).Peter Drucker holds innovation, resources, and an entrepreneurial behavior as the keys to entrepreneurship. Drucker treats entrepreneurship as practice or discipline that has a knowledge base. It is a purposeful task that can be organized and learnt. The focus should not be on psychology or character traits of entrepreneurs but on their actions and behavior. Systematic innovation consists in the purposeful and organized search for changes and in the systematic analysis of the opportunities, such changes might offer for economic or social innovation. According to him entrepreneurship involves

1. increase in value or satisfaction to the customer from the resource
2. creation of new values
3. combination of existing materials or resources in a new productive combination

According to Drucker, systematic innovation means monitoring sources of Innovative Opportunity, these are

1. internal: unexpected, incongruity, process need, changes in industry structure.
2. external: demographics, changes in perception, mood, and meaning, new knowledge.
3. the unexpected success, unexpected failure and unexpected outside event.
4. the incongruity between reality what it is actually and reality what is assumed to be or as it ought to be.
   - between different economic realities.
   - between industry reality and assumptions.
   - between industry effort and values and expectations of customers.
   - internal logic of a process.
5. new knowledge both scientific and non-scientific.
6. innovation in industry structure or market structure that catches everyone unaware.
7. changes in perception, mood and meaning.
8. innovation is based on process need.

Outside of the Enterprise are: demographic changes in perception and new knowledge (both scientific and non scientific).

4.3.4. Principles of Innovation

- Begin with analysis of opportunities.
- Innovation as conceptual and perceptual.
- Simple and focused.
- Start small.
- Aims at leadership

Further, Peter Drucker laid down three basic conditions of systematic innovation which often go disregarded by the majority. These are :

(a) Innovation is work. It requires knowledge. It requires great ingenuity. When all is said and done innovation becomes hard, focused on purposeful work, working very great demands on diligence on persistence and on commitment.

(b) To succeed, innovation must build on their strengths.

(c) Innovation always has to be close to the market, focused on market and indeed market-driven.

4.3.5. Limitations of Systematic Innovation Theory

1. The sources of innovative opportunities are not very reliable and cannot be predicted with accuracy.

2. The theory stresses on market–driven innovation and ignores the innovation in production or technology.
3. It demands too much diligence, persistence and commitment, which may be a hard fact to find in today's youth .

4.3.6. Dynamic Entrepreneurship Innovation Theory

This theory was given by Schumpeter. He considered entrepreneurship as the catalyst that disrupts the stationary circular flow of the economy and thereby, initiates and sustains the process of development. According to Schumpeter, the entrepreneur can activate the economy to a new level of development by embarking upon new combinations of the factors of production which terms as innovation. The concept of innovation and its corollary development embraces five functions— Introduction of new product, introduction of new method of production, opening of new market, conquest of new source of supply of raw materials and carrying out a new organization of any industry.

Schumpeter represents a synthesis of different notions of entrepreneurship. His concept of innovation included the elements of risk taking, superintendence and coordination. Therefore, Schumpeter stressed the fact that these attributes unaccompanied by the ability to innovate would not be sufficient to account for entrepreneurship.

4.4. THEORY OF HIGH ACHIEVEMENT BY McCLELLAND

Over the years behavioral scientists have observed that some people have an intense need to achieve; others, perhaps the majority, do not seem to be as concerned about achievement. This phenomenon has fascinated David C. McClelland. For over twenty years he and his associates at Harvard University studied this urge to achieve. McClelland's research led him to believe that the need for achievement is a distinct human motive that can be distinguished from other needs. More important, the achievement motive can be isolated and assessed in any group. The theory of entrepreneurship developed by McClelland has identified two characteristics of entrepreneurship namely

(a) 'doing things in a new and better way' and

(b) 'decision making under uncertainty'.

David McClelland (1917-1988) considers entrepreneurs as people who do things in a better way and makes decisions in times of uncertainty. The dream to achieve big things overpowers monetary or other external incentives. McClelland's experiment revealed that traditional beliefs do not inhibit an entrepreneur, and that it is possible to internalize the motivation required for achievement orientation through training.

McClelland stressed the need for achievement or achievement-oriented as the most directly relevant factor for explaining economic behavior. Mc Clelland made efforts to identify the motivational factors that motivates a person to become an entrepreneur, to exploit the business opportunities and to take advantage of favourable trade conditions. According to him, the strong desire for high achievement is one of the motivational factors among successful entrepreneurs. Achievement-motivated people is that they seem to be more concerned with personal achievement than with the rewards of success. They do not reject rewards, but the rewards are not as essential as the accomplishment itself. They get a bigger "kick" out of winning or solving a difficult problem than they get from any money or praise they receive. Money, to achievement-motivated people, is valuable primarily as a measurement of their performance. It provides them with a means of assessing their progress and comparing their achievements with those of other people. They normally do not seek money for status or economic security.

4.4.1. Detail of Theory

The theory suggests that motivation for human behavior stems from the underlying assumption that we have a natural or instinctive need to attain high levels of success in our various pursuits.

The theory was proposed by David Clarence McClelland in 1941, while he was working towards achieving his doctorate. Dr. McClelland is known as one of the pioneers of the motivational thinking designed for the environment of the workplace. He is also one of the first to encourage the use of competency-based assessments for employers, which he felt were much more effective than the standard personality-based and IQ tests. Actually observing and testing the ability of the employee to do his or her current job, McClelland theorized, was a better way to determine immediate job skills. His theory is broken into three main points or groups of motivational needs. These three groups are the "n-ach, the "n-pow," and the "n-afil" needs. The presence of these needs can be examined in various ways, but McClelland's drew upon Murray's use of projective pictures as a way of identifying the position of these needs in a leader.

Achievement Need (N-ACH)

Achievement is reflected in stories about attaining challenging goals, setting new records, successful completion of difficult tasks, and doing something not done before.

High need achievers prefer a job in which success depends on effort and ability rather than on chance and factors beyond their control (locus of control). They prefer tasks that enable them to exercise their skills and initiation in problem solving. They want frequent and specific feedback about performance so they can enjoy the experience of making progress toward objectives. People scoring high are often found in jobs such as sales representative, real estate agent, producer of entertainment events, and owner-manager of small business. For managers in large organizations, moderate to high achievement is secondary to higher power needs. If achievement is dominant, the manager may try to achieve objectives alone rather than through team development.

Power Need (N-POW)

Yukl (1989) reviewed the results of McClelland's theory in predicting leadership. Power stories reflect influencing others, defeating an opponent or competitor, winning an argument, or attaining a position of greater authority. Persons with low need for power may lack the assertiveness and self-confidence necessary to organize and direct group activities effectively.

A high need for power may be expressed as "personalized power" or "socialized power." People with high personalized power may have little inhibition or self control, and they exercise power impulsively. Correlated with this are tendencies to be rude, excessive use of alcohol, sexual harassment, and collecting symbols of power (e.g., big offices, desks, fancy cars, etc.). When they give advice or support, it is with strategic intent to further bolster their own status. They demand loyalty to their leadership rather than to the organization. When the leader leaves the organization there is likely disorder and breakdown of team morale and direction. Socialized power need is most often associated with effective leadership. These leaders direct their power in socially positive ways that benefit others and the organization rather than only contributing to the leader's status and gain. They seek power because it is through power that tasks are accomplished. They are more hesitant to use power in a manipulative manner, are less narcissistic and defensive, accumulate fewer material possessions or symbols of power or status, have a longer range perspective, and are more willing to receive consultation and advice. They realize that power must be distributed and shared, and that everyone must have a sense of influence over their own jobs. Effective leaders empower others who use that power to enact and further the leader's vision for the organization. For technical managers, need for achievement was predictive of advancement through lower levels of management, but power was predictive of higher levels of attainment.

Affiliation Need (N-AFFIL)

Affiliation themes are revealed in stories about establishing or restoring close and friendly relationships, joining groups, participating in pleasant social activities, and enjoying shared activities with family or friends. It reflects behaviors toward others that are cooperative, supportive, and friendly and which value belonging and conformity to the group. They obtain great satisfaction from being liked and accepted by others, and prefer to work with others who prefer group harmony and cohesion (e.g.., relationship-centered, Jungian Type Fs).

A person low in affiliation tends to be a loner who is uncomfortable socializing with others except for a few close friends or family (introversion?). They may lack motivation or energy to maintain high social contacts in networking, group presentations, public relations, and building close personal relations with peers and subordinates so necessary for most managers.

Those with strong N-AFFIL are reluctant to let work interfere with harmonious relationships. Moderate N-AFFIL is related to effective management, since strong needs often lead to avoidance of unpopular decisions, permitting exceptions to rules, and showing favoritism to friends. This often leads to subordinates feeling confused about rules, playing to the manager's likes, and becoming anxious about what might happen next (inequity).

Let's take a closer look at how to manage team members who are driven by each of McClelland's three motivators: -

(a) Need for Achievement: Entrepreneurs having a high need for achievement always feel ambitious to be successful. People motivated by achievement need challenging, but not impossible, projects. They thrive on overcoming difficult problems or situations, so make sure you keep them engaged this way. People motivated by achievement work very effectively either alone or with other high achievers.

When providing feedback, give achievers a fair and balanced appraisal. They want to know what they're doing right – and wrong – so that they can improve. They like to face challenges, decide high aims for achievement and take calculated risk.

(b) Need for Power: An entrepreneur has high need for power. He always desires dominance and control. The need for power in an entrepreneur has the features like:-excels in position with status and prestige, prefer to be placed into highly competitive and status-oriented situation, likes to order others and demand obedience.Those with a high need for power work best when they are in charge. Because they enjoy competition, they do well with goal-oriented projects or tasks. They may also be very effective in negotiations or in situations in which another party must be convinced of an idea or goal

When providing feedback, be direct with these team members and keep them motivated by helping them further their career goals

(c) Need for Affiliation: According to Mcclelland, entrepreneurs desire to be liked and accepted by others.These types of entrepreneurs develop and maintain cordial and friendly relations with their employees. People motivated by affiliation work best in a group environment, so try to integrate them with a team (versus working alone) whenever possible. They also do not like uncertainty and risk. Therefore, when assigning projects or tasks, save the risky ones for other people.

When providing feedback to these people, be personal. It's still important to give balanced feedback, but if you start your appraisal by emphasizing their good working relationship and your trust in them, they will likely to be more open to what you say. Remember that these people often don't want to stand out, so it might be best to praise them in private rather than in front of others.

McClelland stressed the need for achievement as the most directly relevant factor for explaining economic behaviour. This motive is defined as the tendency to strive for success in a situation which involves an evaluation of performance of one person against some standard of excellence. People having high need for achievement are more likely to succeed as entrepreneur. McClelland's Human Motivation Theory states that every person has one of three main driving motivators: the needs for achievement, affiliation or power. These motivators are not inherent; we develop them through our culture and life experiences. Achievers like to solve problems and achieve goals

4.4.2. Thematic Apperception Test

McClelland used the Thematic Apperception Test (TAT) as a tool to measure the individual needs of different people. The TAT is a test of imagination that presents the subject with a series of ambiguous pictures, and the subject is asked to develop a spontaneous story for each picture. The assumption is that the subject will project his or her own needs into the story.

Psychologists have developed fairly reliable scoring techniques for the Thematic Apperception Test. The test determines the individual's score for each of the needs of achievement, affiliation, and power. This score can be used to suggest the types of jobs for which the person might be well suited.

4.5. X-EFFICIENCY THEORY BY LEIBENSTEIN

This theory has recently used to analyse the role of the entrepreneur. The concept of X-efficiency was proposed by economist Harvey Leibenstein in a 1966 paper and in his 1968 AER paper "Entrepreneurship and Development", and in his 1978 book, *General X-Efficiency Theory and Development*, Leibenstein applied his theory of X-efficiency to the study of development. It is worth mentioning that his (initial) presentation of the theory of X-efficiency had nothing to do with the study of development. Rather, as argued by Heinz Arndt, he developed this concept: "in the context of the efficiency of resource use within the (modern) firm, to explain why some firms in a given industry are more efficient than others" . The X in X-efficiency represents an unknown factor responsible for a non-allocative type of inefficiency. X-Efficiency is the degree of inefficiency in the use of resources within the firm. It measures the extent to which the enterprise fails to realize its productive potential. These (X) unexploited opportunities are due to factors such as lack of motivation, human inertia, and biases in human decision making that lead to non-maximizing behavior, suboptimal performance and waste. These unexploited opportunities are a form of inefficiency, but not allocative inefficiency. These inefficiencies are not related to prices and markets *per se*. They are related to intra firm activities and to both type-1 and type-2 errors made by individuals, which affect the firm's performance. Productive potential is identified with the point on Neo-classical production frontiers for a given set of inputs. X-efficiency arises either because the resources of the enterprises are used in the wrong way or because they are wasted which means not used at all.

Leibenstein identifies two main roles for the entrepreneur:-

1. Input Completion: It involves making available inputs that improve the efficiency of existing production method or facilitates the introduction of new ones. The role of the entrepreneur is to improve the flow of information in the market.

2. Gap Filling: The second role is closely asking to the arbitrage function emphasized by Kirzner. Leibenstein provides a very vivid description of gap filling, visualizing the economy as a net made up of nodes and pathway

Moreover, it explains how the individual's "internal" environment (personality) and "external" environment can produce both these types of behaviors. XE theory will be discussed in the following sequence. First, we will discuss the psychology and behavior of the individual. Second, we will discuss the individual as a group member. Third, we will present the implications of the theory. Fourth, we will provide an application of the theory to the determination of productivity.

4.5.1. The Individual in X Efficiency Theory

XE theory is largely a reaction to two things: orthodox economic theory which presents production as technologically determined, and formal and anecdotal evidence seemingly inconsistent with this theory. If production is not the outcome of merely technological forces, then what does determine input-output relations? In part, XE theory explains both these issues by exploring the component parts, or meanings, of some commonly used words and terms, including decision making, effort (physical and/or mental), pressure, maximization and rationality. In each case, the reader will see a tendency to think of these as being defined by a range of possibilities; for example, decision making can be either "tight" or "loose," and effort and pressure can vary from a little to a great deal. The reader will also recognize a tendency for XE theory to inquire about the behavioral or procedural aspects of these words.

For example, what are the component parts of effort, and under what conditions is a high effort level more likely to be forthcoming? Similar to Herbert Simon, rationality is used in a procedural sense. That is, what procedures are necessary for a rational decision to be made?

4.5.2. The Dual Personality

The concept that an individual can contribute to X-(in)efficiency arises from the dual nature of the human personality. On the one hand, we want to adhere to standards, to strive for the maximum, and to strive by being calculating and attentive to details. In other words, this aspect of the personality is our rational self, the part of us that uses "tight," focused, or rational decision-making procedures. Leibenstein refers to this aspect of our personality as the "superego function." (Although this term was used by Freud, it would be incorrect to assess its use here as implying that Leibenstein is attempting to incorporate Freudian psychology into economic theory.) The other tendency is for each of us to "kick back," to use "loose" decision making procedures, to follow our "animal spirits." Leibenstein refers to as the "id function." It is the id function that leads us to be "unconstrained," that is, unwilling but not necessarily unable to be calculating, attentive, rational. XE theory assumes that, on the average, each individual is influenced by both functions in a way that leads to a compromise between the two. That is, each of us forges a compromise between the way we feel we must behave and the way we would like to behave were it not for a sense of obligation to duty or to a set of standards. In other words, each individual strikes a compromise that provides them with a sense of (psychological) "comfort." The words "constrained" and "unconstrained" have been used in the context of an individual's ability and willingness to be attentive to details, to calculate, to be rational. "Constrained" and "unconstrained" are now going to be considered as the two end points of a personality trait that could be measured on a continuous scale. That is, the personality could exhibit complete constraint concern, at one end of the spectrum, and a complete lack of concern for constraints at the other end. Thus, an individual could employ the full power of his or her attention to details and to calculating costs and benefits. Such an individual would be completely or fully rational. On the other hand it is possible to imagine an individual placing less than 100% of this power on the details and calculations necessary to make a fully informed decision. Such an individual is referred to as "selectively rational." Rationality is, thus, a continuous variable with an "economic person" exhibiting complete constrain concern. The economic person is thus a limiting case: a characteristic of the decision making procedures used by some people at some times but not necessarily characteristic of all people at all times.

4.6. VARIOUS THEORIES OF PROFIT

There are various theories of profits given by different economists. These are as under:

(a) The Dynamic Theory : Prof. JB Clark propounded the dynamic theory of profit and according to him; profit is the difference between the price and the cost of production of the commodity. But the profit is the result of dynamic change. In a dynamic state, "five generic changes are going on, every one of which reacts on structure of society." They are (1) population is increasing (2) Capital is increasing (3) Methods of production are improving (4) The forms of industrial establishment are changing the less efficient shops etc. are passing from the field and the most efficient are surviving (5) The wants of consumers are multiplying.

(b) The Innovative Theory: Prof. Schumpeter attributes profit to dynamic changes resulting from an innovation. To start with, he takes a capitalist closed economy which is in a stationary equilibrium.

This equilibrium is characterised by what Schumpeter calls a "circular flow" which continues to repeat itself for ever. In such a static state, there is perfectly competitive equilibrium. The price of each product just equals its cost of production and there is no profit.

Only exogenous factors like whether conditions can cause changes in the circular flow position. In the circular flow position goods are being produced at a constant rate. This routine work is being performed by the salaried managers. It is the entrepreneur who disturbs the channels of this circular floe by the introduction of an innovation. Thus, Schumpeter assigns the role of an innovator not to the capitalist but to the entrepreneur.

(c) The Risk Theory: The risk theory of profit is associated with FB Hawley who regards risk taking as the main function of the entrepreneur. Profit is the residual income which the entrepreneur receives for the reason that he assumes risks. The entrepreneur exposes his business to risk and receives in turn a reward in the form of profit since the task of risk taking is infuriating. Profit is an excess of payment above the actuarial value of risk. No entrepreneur will be willing to undertake risks if he gets only the normal return. Hence, the reward for risk taking must be higher than the actual value of risk.

(d) The Uncertainty Bearing Theory: Prof. Frank H. Knight regards profit as the reward of bearing non insurable risks and uncertainties. He distinguishes amidst insurable and non-insurable risks. Certain risks are measurable in as much as the probability of their occurrence can be statistically calculated. The risk of fire theft of merchandise and of death by accident is insurable. Such risks are borne by the insurance company. There are certain unique risks which are incalculable. The probability of their occurrence cannot be statistically computed for the reason that of the presence of uncertainty in them.

Such unforeseen risks relate to changes in prices, demand and supply etc. No insurance company can calculate the loss expected from such risks and hence they are non-insurable. Profit according to Knight is the reward of bearing non-insurable risks and uncertainties. It is a deviation arising from uncertainty between earning ex post and ex ante.

(e) Shackle's Theory: Prof. GLS Shackle has extended Knight's theory of profit by introducing expectations under conditions of uncertainty. According to him, expectations are of two types: general and particular. General expectations relate to variables general to the economy as a whole. They are associated with such micro variables as the future reaction of a particular marketing strategy adopted by a firm, the future pricing policy of a competitive firm etc.

The decisions of the business community are generally based on general expectations. If it regards them favourable investments are made. But there is subjective certainty in the case of general expectations. Their time horizon is about 12 months. As the general expectations have subjective certainty and their time horizon is also of reasonable duration, the business community is able to anticipate price and income increases correctly for the economy as a whole and by adopting appropriate inventory policies it earns windfall profit.

(f) Rent Theory of Profit: The rent theory was developed by an American economist Francis L Walker. Walker maintains that profit is the rent of ability. Like different grades of land, entrepreneurs are also of different abilities. Entrepreneurs of superior ability earn profit just as superior lands earn rent. According to Walker just as there is the marginal or no rent land, similarly there exists a marginal or no profit entrepreneur who earns only wages only wages of management. The marginal or no profit entrepreneur is the least efficient one earning profit not beyond an amount just sufficient to keep him in his present industry.

The industry managed by the marginal entrepreneur is similar to the marginal land. Just as land at the margin is no rent land, similarly the marginal entrepreneur earns no profit.

4.6.1. Theory of Profit - Knight

Frank H. Knight held two different concepts of uncertainty. The first is based on the possibility of insuring against an outcome. The second refers to all instances where individuals have subjective expectations about the future. The second meaning forms the basis of Knight's (1921) theory of profit and entrepreneurial action (Knight I). Knight I is limited; it provides no explanation of the incentive for entrepreneurial action. Knight's (1942) much neglected second theory of profit (Knight II) highlights the deficiencies of Knight I by offering a clear incentive for entrepreneurial action. The differences between the two theories of profit reflect the impact of incorporating historical timing into economic analysis. The discussion of Knight's contribution to these related literatures has been based almost entirely on *Risk, Uncertainty and Profit* (1921, RUP hereafter).

Knight (1921, 1942) is consistent in defining profit as a residual. Providing productive services, labour and capital, and earning marginal products is the economic equivalent of a closed mechanical system. Profit is outside of this system, it is a residual that is not determined by any activity within the system. Uncertainty is the condition necessary for profit to exist. If the future is merely risky, then profit cannot exist. It is uncertainty, and not risk ... which forms the basis of a valid theory of profit since risk, in the ordinary sense, does not preclude perfect planning, such risk cannot prevent the complete realization of the tendencies of competitive forces, or give rise to profit".Knight continues by claiming that even if the future is risky, no profit can be earned if: "all the alternative possibilities are known and the probability of occurrence of each can be accurately ascertained" (1921, p. 198).

According to Frank Knight, profit is a residual; the reward for bearing risk is a factor payment for an economic activity, earned in proportion to the amount of risk borne. Thus, even though all incomes are not necessarily certain in advance, they are always a reward for a measurable function or activity. Further according to Knight, The economy is static, free from all "progressive" changes (technology, population, etc.), and exogenous forces are assumed away. When uncertainty is absent no profits can be earned. When introduced, the amount of uncertainty is determined by the length of the production period, the level of the economic activity (more complex societies have greater uncertainty), and the extent to which uncertainty has been reduced by insurance and hedging. Entrepreneurs, facing uncertainty, must forecast demand before contracting the factors of production and producing output. The production period that is strictly positive, and consumer preferences change through time. Profit arises as a result of errors in forecasting future demand.

Knight claims the entrepreneur as the owner of the firm and the bearer of risk/uncertainty. Knight (1921, p. 293) justifies the claim of the entrepreneur as owner on the basis that all decisions are made by agents appointed by the owner, who bears ultimate responsibility for all decisions made within the firm. It is worth summarizing the elements of the theory. First, profit arises out of short-term fluctuations, not "progressive" changes. Progressive changes include invention and innovation. Entrepreneurs earn profits by forecasting the future better than other entrepreneurs. In addition to forecasting the future, entrepreneurs have the responsibility of bearing uncertainty. The decision to become an entrepreneur is then based on the belief of superior ability in forecasting, as well as an appetite for bearing uncertainty. The profit itself is the result of a contracting error; the owners of the factors of production negotiate fixed incomes different to their marginal value in the eventual output. Net profits for all entrepreneurs are probably negative, and this is a reflection of the likely over optimism of entrepreneurs. Finally, this activity occurs in a very specific setting, a static economy in which production takes time, consumer preferences change over time, and all other factors are held constant. Knight defines "progressive" as changes in the population, technology and business organization, wants, and the accumulation of capital. The role of innovation is perhaps the most important, as this forms the basis of Schumpeter's (1961) theory of entrepreneurial action. To Knight (RUP, p. 148) long run changes are not the primary cause of profits. Successful entrepreneurs have characteristics that correspond with their role as entrepreneurs. The first is the ability to forecast the future: Men differ in their capacity by perception and inference to form correct judgments as to the future course of events in the environment. This capacity, furthermore, is far from homogeneous, some persons excelling in foresight in one kind of problem situations, others in other kinds, in almost endless variety" (1921, p. 241). The decision to become an entrepreneur relies not only on this inherent ability, but also on one's degree of faith in one's ability. The second attribute of the entrepreneur is a willingness to bear uncertainty: Any degree of effective exercise of judgement or making decisions, is in a free society coupled with a corresponding degree of uncertainty bearing, or taking responsibility for those actions" (1921, p. 271).

In short the above theory can summarized as follows:

F.H Knight , in his book *Risk, Uncertainty and Profit* propounded the theory of profit. He points out that entrepreneurs are a specialized group of people who bears risk and deals with uncertainty. Given the construction of the theory Knight (1921, p. 284) arrives at profit as being: a residue after deduction of the payment for the other agencies ... . The residue ... is not a product residue, but a margin of error in calculation on the part of the non-entrepreneurs who do not force the successful entrepreneurs to pay as much for the productive services as they could be forced to pay. The choice of the word error is perhaps unfortunate as it detracts from the role of expectations and gives profit the appearance of a mistake. Knight identifies the entrepreneur as a recipient of pure profits. According to Knight, pure profit is bearing the cost of uncertainty with regard to the entrepreneur. Knight identifies uncertainty with a situation where the probabilities of alternatives outcomes cannot be determined. Knight argues that business uncertainty can be reduced through 'consolidation'. Consolidation is a method of reducing total uncertainty by pooling individual instances. Consolidation is to uncertainty is what insurance is to risk. So Knight's theory has following features:-

(a) Pure profits: Knight identified entrepreneurs as the recipient of pure profit. Pure profit refers to the reward for bearing the cost of uncertainty.

(b) Situation of uncertainity: Uncertainity, according to Knight is identified with a situation where the probability of alternative cannot be determined either by a prior reasoning or by statistical inferences.

(c) Risk bearing capabilities: Risk bearing implies assuming the responsibilities of loss or gain that may occur due to unforeseen contingencies of the future. According to Knight, an entrepreneur is a person who willingly carries on those responsible activities which are neither insured nor salaried.

(d) Guarantee of specified sum: While undertaking the responsibility of the business enterprise, entrepreneur guarantees interest to lender, wages to employees and rent to landlord. Thus, specified sums of money are guaranteed by the entrepreneur for the assignment made to them. However, the supply of entrepreneurship depends upon the following three factors as per his opinion:-

1. Ability of the entrepreneur
2. Willingness of the entrepreneur
3. The power to extend guarantees to others.

(e) Identification of socio-economic and psychological factors: Knight identified the social, economic and psychological factors which influence the supply of entrepreneur since entrepreneurial motivation and abilities are long run problems. Economic, social and psychological factors should be combined to promote entrepreneurship.

(f) Use of consolidation technique to reduce business uncertainty: Knight's entrepreneurs specifically commit their capital and bear the resultant risk and uncertainty. He argued that business uncertainty can be reduced by using the technique of consolidation to increase the profits. Through the help of consolidation in which individual instances are pooled, total uncertainty can be reduced.

4.7. THEORY OF SOCIAL CHANGE – EVERETT HAGEN

The problem which Professor Hagen has posed is, why in the contemporary world, some of the technologically undeveloped nations are quick to adopt Western technology while others are resistant. The solution he proposes, after a rapid survey and discarding of existing theories of the causes for economic growth, is found in his idiosyncratic version of personality theory. Everett Hagen in his work "Theory of Social Change" explains how economic growth begins? His creative personality is an individual characterized by a high need for achievement , order and autonomy. He view the entrepreneur as a creative problem solver interested in things in the practical and technological realm, and driven by a duty to achieve.

Hagen considers the withdrawal of status, of respect, as the trigger mechanism for changes in personality formation. Status withdrawal occurs when members of some social group perceive that their purposes and values in life are not respected by the groups in the society they respect, and whose esteem they value. Hagen postulates four types of events which can produce status withdrawal:-

(a) Displacement of a traditional elite group from its previous status by another traditional supply physical force.

(b) Denigration of valued symbols through some change in the attitude of the superior group.

(c) Inconsistency of status symbols with a changing distribution of economic power.

(d) Non-acceptance of expected status on migration to a new society.

Following McClelland's concept that a level of development is correlated with achievement motivation, Hagen tried to explain why this achievement motivation varies between societies and their classes and strata. He argues that in traditional societies, the status of individuals is fixed. Children learn to act according to established norms, and deviations (initiative) are punished. If by external influences a new group gains power, the status of the old elite is challenged and weakened. The insecurity and frustration leads to changed behavior which has consequences on the family structure. Children tend to become dissatisfied with the society and readily accept new values. In time, they become innovative personalities. If these persons become dominant groups in the society, this causes economic development. Similar phenomena may happen as far as the changing situation of marginal groups or minorities is concerned.

Moreover, Traditional agricultural societies have begun to rapidly progress technologically, which in turn impacts both economic growth and social change. In order for countries, including those with low incomes, to experience economic growth, two factors must exist:-

1. Extensive levels of creativity, including the identification of and implementation of problem solving skills, and
2. Viewpoints which promote creative approaches towards production technology.

The characteristics of a traditional agricultural society are discussed, including the typical hierarchical, authoritarian social structure and the impact of family status upon an individual's perceived social status. Additionally, an individual's personality may also impact their role and status within a society, as well as their impact upon a society's economic growth. Utilizing a Freudian, psychoanalytic approach, personality development of the individual is analyzed at length by studying the function of parental influence, as well as environmental factors, upon child personality development. Several examples of social change among historically authoritarian societies are presented. As an explanation for social change within these traditional societies, the study theorizes that alienated, creative individuals often seek to break away from traditional social patterns after being marginalized by society for being different. As a result, they pursue projects which will utilize their creative talents, while also allotting them the power and retribution they seek against their elitist society.

In short, the above theory can be summarized as follows:

Everett E. Hagen, in his theory of social change, propounded how a traditional society becomes one in which continuing technical progress takes place.The theory exhorts the following features which presumes the entrepreneur's creativity as the key element of social transformation and economic growth.

1. Presentation of general model of the society: The theory reveals a general model of the society which considers interrelationship among physical environment, social structure, personality and culture.

2. Economic growth: Product of social change and political change:- According to Hagen, most of the economic theories of underdevelopment are inadequate. He viewed entrepreneur as a creative problem shooter who brings about economic development which is mingled with political and social change.

3. Historic shift as a factor of initiating change: Hagen, in his book *'How Economic Growth Begins'*, depicts historic shift as the crucial force which has bought about social change and technological progress thereby leading to the emergence of entrepreneurial class from different castes and communities. The historic shift caused some groups of the lesser elite, who previously held commanding position in the social hierarchy, feel that they were no longer valued and regarded. As a result of this, their inner urge was kindled to take up entrepreneurial venture through personality formation and thus they become competent enough to take up any kind of venture.

4. Withdrawal of status respects as the mechanism for rigorous entrepreneurial activity: Closely consistent with the historic shift, it is the social group that plunges into rigorous entrepreneurism which experiences the status withdrawal or 'withdrawal of status respect '. According to Hagen, they are a group of individuals, creative and alienated from traditional values, driven by burning drive to prove themselves, preferably an area in which they can gain power. Their inner urge will culminate into entrepreneurism disregarding their traditional values and turning to innovative entrepreneurship. When withdrawal of status respect occurs, it leads to four different responses and creation of four different personality types:-

(a) Retreatist : One who constantly does his work in the society but remains indifferent to his own position.

(b) Ritualist: One who adopts a kind of defensive personality and acts in the ways accepted and approved in his society without any hope of improving his opposition.

(c) Reformist: One who initiates rebellion and attempts to establish a new order in the society.

(d) Innovator: A creative individual who converts all odds into opportunities and is likely to become an entrepreneur.

Hence, Hagen's creative personality is the admixture of Schumpeter's innovation and McClelland's high need for achievement.

4.7.1. Limitations of theory

Hagen's analysis fails to give policy measures for backward countries which are striving for economic development as he identifies status withdrawal as the causal factor in the emergence of creative personality and withdrawal of status. Hagen's thesis of disadvantaged minority groups has its own limitations. There are many disadvantaged minority groups in India which have not supplied a good number of entrepreneurs.

4.8. OTHER THEORIES OF ENTREPRENEURSHIP

4.8.1. Theory of Religious Belief — Max Weber

Max Weber has propounded the theory of religious belief. According to him, entrepreneurism is a function of religious belief and the impact of religious shapes the entrepreneurial culture. He emphasized that the entrepreneurial energies are exogenous supplied by means of religious belief. The central features of Weberian theory of social change, therefore, consists in his treatment of the protestant ethics and the spirit of capitalism.

4.8.2. Leadership Theory

This theory of entrepreneurship was developed by Huselitz. According to him, entrepreneurship is a function of managerial skills and leadership. An entrepreneur must possess leadership qualities to perform his entrepreneurial activities. According to this theory, entrepreneurial leadership involved the following attributes:-

(a) Entrepreneurial leadership is the process of influencing behavior of workforce, superiors, suppliers and competitors.

(b) It directs the people to attain entrepreneurial goals.

(c) It influences work team

(d) Entrepreneurial leadership directs and coordinates the activities of an enterprise.

4.8.3. Theory of Social Behaviour

The social behavior theory of entrepreneurship was developed by John H.Kunkel. According to him, the most critical factor towards the success of entrepreneurship is the behavior of entrepreneur under different social systems and structures and physical conditions. In the view of Kunkel, entrepreneur has to perform many activities. Some activities of entrepreneur are accepted by the society while others are discarded by the society. Therefore, the social behavior found in the society directly affects the supply of entrepreneurship.

4.8.4. Theory of Adjustment

Israel M.Kirzner, has coined the theory of adjustment of price. According to him, the essential entrepreneurial element is the alertness to information rather than its possession alone. He contends that those entrepreneurs who have the superior telescopic faculty keep themselves all the while alert to confront any disequilibrium in the market. His theory has got the following features:

(a) Adjustment of price

(b) Alertness to disequilibrium.

4.9. SUMMARY

Major theories view the entrepreneur as performing various functional roles as risk taker, decision maker, organizer or coordinator, innovator, gap seeker, etc. All the theories ascribe a functional role to entrepreneur in the productive process and entrepreneurial rewards are explained by degree of success attained by fulfilling that function.

According to Schumpeter an entrepreneur is an innovator and Innovation is defined as the stage of successful introduction of new products and processes. Schumpeter is the first major theorist to put human agent at the centre of the process of economic development and according to him an entrepreneur is the prime mover in economic development and his function is to innovate and to carry out new combinations. McClelland identified two characteristics of entrepreneurship namely — doing things in a new and better way and decision making under uncertainty. Moreover, he stressed upon need for achievement, power and affiliation as relevant factor for explaining economic behavior. So different economists give different view about the entrepreneur and entrepreneurship.

Entrepreneurship is an evolved thing. With the advancement of science and technology ,it has undergone metamorphosis and emerged as a critical input for socio-economic development. Various writers have developed various theories on entrepreneurship and popularized the concept among the common people. The theories propounded by them can be categorized as — Sociological, economic, cultural and psychological theories. Each of the entrepreneurship theories discussed are inter-disciplinary and are influenced by multitude of factors. It is intergration of external environment, dreams, ambition, passion, achievement, motivation etc.

4.10. SELF ASSESSMENT QUESTIONS

1. Critically analyses the theory of innovation given by Schumpeter.
2. Give detailed explanation of the theory of high achievement given by McClelland.
3. Explain different theories of entrepreneurship.
4. Explain various theories of entrepreneurship?
5. Give detail explanation of X-Efficiency Theory by Leibenstein.
6. Give views about the different theories of profit.
7. Discuss the Theory of Profit by Knight and Theory of Social change by Everett Hagen.

SOURCE/NOTES

1. Frantz, Roger. 1997, *X-Efficiency: Theory, Evidence and Application,* second edition, Boston/ New York: Kluwer Academic Publishers.
2. Leibenstein, Harvey, 1978, *General X-Efficiency Theory and Economic Development,* New York, Harvard University Press.
3. *Fundamentals of Entrepreneurship*-Sangam Keshari.
4. *Entrepreneurship and Small Business*-Rajesh Marwaha and J.S Mehandipur.
5. *The Dynamics of Entrepreneurial Development and Management*-Vasant Desai.

5

ENTREPRENEURIAL CULTURE

5.1. INTRODUCTION

Culture, a broad word that one defines as "The collective programming of the mind which distinguishes the members of one human group from another. Culture, in this sense, includes systems of values; and values are among the building blocs of culture," (Geert Hofstede). Organizational culture is the collective behavior of humans who are part of an organization and the meanings that the people attach to their actions. Culture includes the organization values, visions, norms, working language, systems, symbols, beliefs and habits. It is also the pattern of such collective behaviors and assumptions that are taught to new organizational members as a way of perceiving, and even thinking and feeling. Organizational culture affects the way people and groups interact with each other, with clients, and with stakeholders. Although a company may have "own unique culture", in larger organizations, there is a diverse and sometimes conflicting cultures that coexist due to different characteristics of the management team. The organizational culture may also have negative and positive aspects.

In this chapter, we will examine the nature of culture and the role it plays in sustaining the entrepreneurial spirit within a company.

5.2. NATURE OF CULTURE

Ravasi and Schultz (2006) state that organizational culture is a set of shared mental assumptions that guide interpretation and action in organizations by defining appropriate behavior for various situations. Culture have certain characteristics, regardless of the business. A culture reflects the unique history of a group of people interacting over time, but it also is subject to continuous change as people come and go and also based on the developments in external environment.

According to Edward Burnett Tylor," Culture of civilization is that complex whole which includes knowledge, belief, art, morals, law, custom and other capabilities and habits acquired by man as a member of society."

According to Clyde, culture is" the total life way of people." The culture is customs, ideas and attitudes shared by a group and which is transmitted from generation to generation. Each human group has its own distinctive culture, but a complex society contains many subcultures.

Every company has a culture. It can be ' positive' or 'negative', 'strong ' or 'weak'. Companies that innovate well, often share in common a culture of optimism. This type of culture exemplifies a company's belief that its employees are extremely capable and serves as fertile breeding ground for extraordinary innovation and entrepreneurial spirit.

5.3. FEATURES OF CULTURE

1. It relates to 'how to behave in certain circumstances'. So it includes 'programmed responses'.This 'Programming' of human beings takes place on its own, with the help of rewards for desired behavior (e.g., going to religious place) and punishment for undesirable behavior.

2. These programmed responses re handed down from generation to generation. When family, ethnic congregations, educational system and religious group etc., reinforce such responses, they became the value system.

3. Culture caters to physiological and emotional needs of the people.Those who confirm to such behaviour are given importance and recognition in the society. This acts as reinforcement, however if a particular element does not remain desirable in the society people may stop assigning importance honor and recognition to such actions. Such elements automatically are extinguished from the culture.

4. Culture is evolutionary and rarely revolutionary. Culture usually evolves from existing value systems. If some values become hinderance in welfare of society, they are rejected by people and a new value system evolves. Sometimes when only a fraction of society benefits from existing value system the disadvantaged sections usually replace them with revolutionary methods.

5.4. COMPONENTS/ELEMENTS OF CULTURE[1]

The components of culture are symbols, language, values and beliefs, knowledge, ideals, preferences and norms. The components of culture are extremely important to all aspects of a society. These components are passed down from generation to generation. The actions of people can provide information on the culture they come from. Sometimes, being submerged into another culture can lead to culture shock. There are many components of culture, some of them are:—

1. Values and Beliefs: Values are anything members of a culture aspire to or hold in high esteem. Values are things to be achieved, things considered of great worth or value.These are human creations. ***Values*** are defined as the standards by which people assess desirability, goodness, and beauty; they are broad principles which underlie ***beliefs,*** specific statements that people hold to be true. Beliefs are the things members of a culture hold to be true. They are the "facts" accepted by all or most members. Beliefs are not limited to religious statements, but include all the things a people know and accept as true, including common sense everyday knowledge. Beliefs are learned through socialization and help shape how we perceive our surroundings and how our personality develops. Indeed they provide the cultural capital by which we evaluate our future possibilities.

2. Norms: Norms are defined as rules that guide behaviour. It is humanly created rules for behavior. They can be proscriptive, mandating what we should not do, or prescriptive, stating what we should do. They can change over time, as illustrated by norms regarding sexual behaviour. Some are meant to apply to all situations and all people, while others apply to only certain people and vary from situation to situation.

3. Ethics: Ethics provides the basic rules for conducting any activity in an acceptable manner. More specifically, ethics represents a set of principles prescribing a behavioral code that explains what is right or wrong, good or bad. Ethics outline moral duty and obligations.

4. Knowledge: Knowledge is a familiarity with someone or something, which can include facts, information, descriptions, or skills acquired through experience or education. It can refer to the theoretical or practical understanding of a subject. It can be implicit (as with practical skill or expertise) or explicit (as with the theoretical understanding of a subject); it can be more or less formal or systematic. It is the state or fact of knowing and the familiarity, awareness, or understanding gained through experience or study. It is the sum or range of what has been perceived, discovered, or learned and it passes from one generation to other or from one part of society to other.

5. Language: Language is a set of symbols used to assign and communicate meaning. It enables us to name or label the things in our world, so we can think and communicate about them. It is the cornerstone of culture. All cultures have a spoken language (even if there are no developed forms of writing). People who speak the same language often share the same culture. There are many societies which include large number of people who speak different languages and each language can have several different dialects.

6. Social Collectives: Social collectives such as groups, organizations, communities, institutions, classes, and societies are also collectively produced symbolic social constructions. Social collectives are symbolic entities. They are defined into existence when people define themselves as a group or are defined as a group by others. They can and do become reified over time, such that they are seen and treated as real objective entities. However, they remain fundamentally symbolic entities and as such can be renegotiated and redefined.

7. Ideologies: Ideologies are integrated and connected systems of beliefs. Sets of beliefs and assumptions connected by a common theme or focus. They are often are associated with specific social institutions or systems and serve to legitimize those systems. Some prominent American ideologies are:—Capitalism, Christianity (Protestantism), Individualism, Scientism, Racism etc., Ideologies are, themselves, often related and connected to each other in complex ideological systems, such that one ideology "makes sense" when considered with another. They also often serve to legitimize each other. Religious ideologies often encompass or subsume many of a culture's ideologies, giving them added legitimacy. However, it is also possible for a culture to hold ideologies that are conflicting and contradictory.

8. Status and Role in Society: A status or a social role is nothing but a slot or position within a group or society, which gives an overall idea of the social structure and hence is an important element of culture. This can also include traditional gender-based or age-based roles.

9. Cultural Integration: This includes the degree of harmony or integration within the various elements of culture. This can include elements like subcultures, local cultures and the difference between historical and cultural traditions.

5.5. ENTREPRENEURIAL CULTURE

Culture defines how human beings behave and various behavioral sciences like psychology explain why they behave like that. Cultural factors determine how the business is conducted and the limits in which entrepreneur acts. Culture is a complex of values, attitudes, ideas and pre-programmed responses. Culture does not concern itself with instinctive behavior of individuals rather it is the group behavior of human beings, i.e., how does the group of persons behave under given circumstances. In an entrepreneurial culture, work is more than a job, it's a lifestyle. Employees are more like a team than in most companies, and in some cases, we are even like a family. Entrepreneurial culture includes organizational culture. Organizational culture is the collective behavior of humans who are part of an organization and the meanings that the people attach to their actions. Culture includes the organization values, visions, norms, working language, systems, symbols, beliefs and habits. It is also the pattern of such collective behaviors and assumptions that are taught to new organizational members as a way of perceiving, and even thinking and feeling.

5.5.1. Essentials of Entrepreneurial Organisational Culture

An Entrepreneurial Organizational Culture (EOC) is a system of shared values, beliefs and norms of members of an organization, including valuing creativity and tolerance of creative people, believing that innovating and seizing market opportunities are appropriate behaviors to deal with problems of survival and prosperity, environmental uncertainty, and competitors' threats, and expecting organizational members to behave accordingly. Any employee however efficient will be a misfit if he is unable to adapt himself to the work culture. Organizations are laying emphasis on culture since growth and success depends on the kind of culture prevalent in the company. Do employees feel threatened or cherished, is there a desire to work and grow, do they want to evolve as a group or go their separate ways? These questions can be answered by a careful examination of the organizational culture.

5.5.2. Ethical Side of Entrepreneurship

Ethics are very important for business these days. Business ethics refers to the moral principles which are considered right by the society, and so, should govern and guide the activities of a business. They are the moral principles and rules of conduct which should guide the activities of a business. Business ethics are derived from social values. Every organization has to go through various ethical issues. Entrepreneurs has to face various ethical decisions specially in case of early stages of business. Sir Adrian Cadbury[2] observed, "There is no simple universal formula for solving ethical problems .We have to choose from our own codes of conduct whichever rules are appropriate to the case in hand; the outcome of these choices make us who we are." Ethics provides basic parameters for conducting any activity in an acceptable manner and it outlines moral duty and obligations. But the society operates in dynamic environment so deciding the right or wrong is situational. Organization has to survive in the environment which includes-shareholders, customers, managers, employees, government, peers and many more. So an entrepreneur has to take many ethical decisions depending upon the circumstances and the situations.

5.5.3. Formation of Ethics

An individual's ethics are formulated through the operation of forces in the individual's environment. These are discussed below:—

1. Family influence: Family has deep impact on the formation of ethics. The formation of ethics begins when the individual is a child. Thus the family environment has a significant influence in determining what the child learns about good and bad, right and wrong.

2. Experiences: As a human being grows, he learns from the day to day experiences. As a human he/she has to exposed to many critical issues that affect his/her ethical standards. These experiences help in formation of ethics according to the situation.

3. Peer influences: As a person moves in the outer world, he /she get in contact with peers/ friends. In school, college, at work peers exert considerable influence on the individual's ethical beliefs.

4. Morals and values: Morals and values has high impact on the ethical standards. Morals and values helps in formation of ethics as it helps in choosing the right or the wrong.

5. The legal system: Laws are rules of conduct, approves by legislatures, that guide human behavior in any society. Whenever ethics the law codifies, it is binding on businesses. The society expects businesses to abide by the law. Obeying the law is presumed to be ethical behavior.

5.5.4. Application of Ethics to Business[3]

Business ethics is the study of good and evil, right and wrong, and just and unjust actions of businessmen. What is right or wrong is a personal individual matter, but is still influenced by socially accepted norms. Basically ethics includes individual consciousness. Ethics are very important for an organization and every organization should have a culture which can influence the employees to follow the same. A company culture is a blend of ideas, customer traditional practices, company values and shared meanings that help define normal behaviour for everyone who works in a company. The Council for Fair Business Practices (CFBP) established in 1966, by leading private sector industrialists in western India, have given certain ethics applicable to business. They are:

1. To charge only fair and reasonable price and take every possible step to ensure that the prices to be charged to the consumer are brought to his notice.
2. To take every possible step to ensure that the agents or dealers do not charge prices higher than fixed.
3. In times of scarcity, not to withhold or suppress stocks of goods with a view to hoarding or profiteering.

4. Not to produce or trade in spurious goods of standards lower than specified.
5. Not to adulterate goods supplied.
6. Not to publish misleading advertisements.
7. To invoice goods exported or imported at their correct prices.
8. To maintain accuracy in weights and measures of goods offered for sale.
9. Not to deal knowingly in smuggled goods.
10. Providing after-sales service where necessary or possible.
11. Honoring the fundamental rights of the consumers like, Right of safety, Right to choose, Right to information and Right to be Heard.
12. Discharging social responsibilities and the responsibility to protect the environment and nature's infrastructure.
13. Ensuring that the product warranty is offered in simple, unambiguous and concise language, highlights the rights of consumer under it.

The CFBP has instituted a set of prizes and awards called **'Jamnalal Bajaj Uchit Vyavahar Puraskar'** to promote exemplary application of the above norms.

The CFBP president claimed that sustained pressure from his council has resulted in creation of Advertising Standards Council of India (ASCOI) and in promulgation of the Consumer Protection Act (CPA),1986. The Federation of Indian Chambers of Commerce and Industry (FICCI, which includes the MNCs) has recently issued a declaration on norms of business consisting of ten points. The Punjab, Haryana and Delhi Chamber of Commerce has also formulated a code of ethics. The code says:

1. Business must maintain the highest standards of behaviour for the benefit of industry, employees, customers, shareholders and the society.
2. Goods and services must conform to the commitment promised to customers. Business must be realistic and truthful in stating claims.
3. Customers must be given best possible service and treated with respect and fairness.
4. Business must understand and respect the needs, concerns and welfare of the community and society. It should use knowledge and experience for upgrading the quality of life. All business endeavors must combine the qualities of private excellence for public good.
5. The best way of promoting high standard of business practices is through self regulation.

Therefore, it is mandatory for all business firms to follows Business Ethics, which will result in its own welfare.

5.5.5. Types of Organizational Culture

By organization culture, we mean, the strategies and attitudes deemed constant, and prevalent throughout the workforce hierarchy. Different organizations follow different work cultures in their workplace, and culture is what makes a workplace an organization. Here are the various organizational cultures that define even the minutiae of an aspect in the organization.

The diverse organizational cultures that mold the structure of a business acumen are as follows[4]:

1. Normative Culture: In a normative organization, the organization stresses on implementing the organizational procedures in the correct manner, and according to the norms and rules defined. This kind of culture is perceived to portray a high standard of business ethics.

2. Pragmatic Culture: In contrast to normative cultures, stress is laid on satisfying the wish of their clients. In this type of organizational structure, the client is virtually deified. The prime concern of every employee is to cater to the needs of the client, attain, and retain the business they may invite through the clients.

3. Academy Culture: In this kind of culture, employees are highly skilled, and the organization provides an environment for the development, and honing of employee skills. Examples of this kind of culture are hospitals, universities, and large corporations. Employees tend to stay with the organization, and grow with(in) it.

4. Collaborate Work Culture: Often referred to as clan culture, an organization that adopts a collaborate culture offers a congenial and amiable environment to work in. The feeling one derives while working in this type of organization is that of comfort and coercive motivation. This organization consists of superiors who provide more of guidance, and less of governance. The organization is based on worker-welfare, where you have the employees' interest in the foreground with his skills valued, and performances handsomely rewarded. Insinuating and developing teamwork is the most vital element of the organization.

5. Adhocracy Work Culture: It is a type of organization that is altered to provide an environment to accrue one's creative acumen. Ideas are encouraged, and out-of-the-box thinking is an appendage-cum-motto. Dynamism is defined best when the workforce has the free will to conceive an out-of-the-ordinary idea; the development of which, may lead to success; inadvertently, to higher levels of morale, and monetary incentives.

6. Baseball Team Culture: In this kind of culture, the employees are 'free agents', and are highly prized. These employees find employment easily in any organization, and are highly in demand. There is, however, a considerable amount of risk attached to this culture, as it is very fast-paced. Examples of this kind of culture are advertising and investment banking.

7. Club Culture: Usually, the employees stay with the organization for a long time, and get promoted to a senior post, or level. These employees are hand-picked, and it is imperative that they possess the specific skills required and desired, by the organization. Examples of this kind of organization are law firms, the military, etc.

8. Fortress Culture: Employees are not sure if the will be laid off or not by the organization. Very often, this organization undergoes massive changes. Few examples of this type of culture are loans and savings, large car companies, etc.

9. Macho Culture: The most important aspect of this kind of culture is big rewards, and quick feedback. This kind of culture is mostly associated with quick financial activities; like, brokerage, and currency trading. It can also be related to activities, like, a sports team, a police team, or branding of an athlete. This kind of culture is does not eschew high levels of stress; instead they are known to reach the apotheosis of efficiency. The employees are expected to possess a strong mentality for survival in the organization.

10. Work Hard/Play Hard Culture: This type of organization does not involve much risk, as the organizations, already, consist of a firm base coupled with a strong client relationship. This kind of culture is predominantly opted by the large-scale organizations that have gained their customers' trust and support; subsequently rolling out a steadfast customer help service. The organization, with this kind of culture, is equipped with specialized jargon, and is qualified with multiple-team meetings.

11. Bet Your Company Culture: In this kind of culture, the company makes big, and important decisions over high stake endeavors. It takes time to see the consequence of these decisions. Companies that postulate experimental projects, and researches as their core business proposition, adopt this kind of culture; for instance, a company designing experimental military weapons may implement the said type of culture.

12. Process Culture: This type of culture does not include the process of feedback. In this kind of culture, the organization is extremely cautious about the adherence to laws, and prefers to abide by them. This culture bestows consistency upon the organization, predominantly meant for public services.

One of the most difficult tasks to undertake in an organization, is to change its work culture. A change in the organizational culture requires an organization to make amendments to its policies, workplace ethics, and management system. It needs to start right from its base functions; including, support functions, operations, and the production floor, which finally affects the overall output of the organization. It requires a complete overhaul of the entire system, and not many organizations prefer it as the process is a long, and tedious one, which requires patience, and endurance. However, when an organization succeeds in making a change on such a massive level, the results are almost always positive, and fruitful. The different types of organizational cultures aforementioned, surely, must have helped you to understand them. You can also adopt one of them for your own organization; however, persistence and patience ultimately, is the essence.

5.5.6. Various Essentials of Organisational Culture

1. People and empowerment focused: In the oragnisation there must be full focus on people i.e employees. This is still one of the most contentious issues in organizational culture today. How much should be the management focus on the people? Some organizations are famous for being employee oriented as they focus more on creating a better work environment for its 'associates' to work in. Others still are feudal in nature, treating employees no better than work-machines. The culture must prevail in the organization in which employees must be focused, encouraged and empowered so that they can give their maximum to the organization

2. Value creation through innovation and risk taking: Culture must prevail in the organization which will be open to innovations and must accept the change as it will help in value creation. Risk and returns go hand in hand. Places where you take a risk (calculated risk of course!), the chances of returns are higher. Same goes for innovation. You could either be a follower or a pioneer. Pioneering has its share of risks, but at times it can also have a breakthrough outcome for the organization.

Thus, innovation and risk taking is one of the main characteristics of organizational culture defining how much room the business allows for innovation.

3. Doing the right thing at right time: There must be culture of doing the right thing at the right time so that no opportunity can be missed .

4. Freedom to grow: The individuals must get freedom to take initiative.

5. Risk tolerance: There must be a culture in which employees are encouraged to be aggressive and risk seeking.

6. Emphasis on the future: Organizational culture must have emphasis on future activitie, i.e., there must be organizational culture in which there must be emphasis on future activities.

(a) **Management support:** These culture should prevail in which management must provide full support and assistance to their employees.

7. Rewards: There must be proper reward system so that the employees get motivation to work. The reward allocation must be based on the performance of the employees and not on the seniority basis.

8. Communication system: There must be proper communication in the organization so that the information can move in the right way and right direction. There must prevail formal as well as informal way of communication.

9. Control: Control means rules and regulations and amount of supervision that is used to oversee the employee. So culture must be prevail where the control must not be too high or too less, i.e., the number of rules and regulations must be appropriate in which employees can breathe.

10. Aggressiveness: Every organization also lays down the level of aggressiveness with which their employees work. Some businesses like Microsoft are known for their aggression and market dominating strategies.

11. Stability: While some organizations believe that constant change and innovation is the key to their growth, others are more focused on making themselves and their operations stable. The managements of these organizations are looking at ensuring stability of the company rather than looking at indiscriminate growth.

5.6. CORPORATE SUBCULTURES

Corporate culture is the total sum of the values, customs, traditions, and meanings that make a company unique. Corporate culture is often called "the character of an organization", since it embodies the vision of the company's founders. The values of a corporate culture influence the ethical standards within a corporation, as well as managerial behavior.

Senior management may try to determine a *corporate culture.* They may wish to impose corporate values and standards of behavior that specifically reflect the objectives of the organization. In addition, there will also be an extant internal culture within the workforce. Work groups within the organization have their own behavioral quirks and interactions which, to an extent, affect the whole system. Roger Harrison's four-culture typology, and adapted by Charles Handy, suggests that unlike organizational culture, corporate culture can be 'imported'. For example, computer technicians will have expertise, language and behaviors gained independently of the organization, but their presence can influence the culture of the organization as a whole.

5.7. METHODS TO CLASSIFY ORGANIZATIONAL CULTURE

Several methods have been used to classify organizational culture. While there is no single "type" of organizational culture and organizational cultures vary widely from one organization to the next, commonalities do exist and some researchers have developed models to describe different indicators of organizational cultures. Some are described below:

5.7.1. Hofstede's Cultural Dimensions Theory

Hofstede (1980) looked for global differences between over 100,000 of IBM's employees in 50 different countries and three regions of the world, in an attempt to find aspects of culture that might influence business behavior. He suggested about cultural differences existing in regions and nations, and the importance of international awareness and multiculturalism for the own cultural introspection. Cultural differences reflect differences in thinking and social action, and even in "mental programs", a term Hofstede uses for predictable behaviour. Hofstede relates culture to ethnic and regional groups, but also organizations, profession, family, to society and subcultural groups, national political systems and legislation, etc.

Hofstede demonstrated that there are national and regional cultural groupings that affect the behavior of organizations and identified four dimensions of culture (later five) in his study of national cultures:

1. Power distance (Mauk Mulder, 1977): Different societies find different solutions on social inequality. Although invisible, inside organizations power inequality of the "boss-subordinates relationships" is functional and according to Hofstede reflects the way inequality is addressed in the society. "According to Mulder's Power Distance Reduction theory, subordinates will try to reduce the power distance between themselves and their bosses and bosses will try to maintain or enlarge it", but there is also a degree to which a society expects there to be differences in the levels of power. A high score suggests that there is an expectation that some individuals wield larger amounts of power than others. A low score reflects the view that all people should have equal rights.

2. Individualism vs. collectivism: Hofstede brings that society's expectations of Individualism/ Collectivism will be reflected by the employee inside the organization. This dimension measures the amount of emphasis a society places on "individual" achievement over "group" achievement. The natural finding that Individualistic cultures tend to have more entrepreneurial activities comes as "no surprise". In this category, the worlds greatest supplier of entrepreneurs, the United States, had the single highest score. On the other hand we had India and Mexico scoring 48 and 30 respectively. Relating it back to the Arab culture, we can understand why such a factor would influence our drive towards success. Simply put we rather emphasize group values over individual success. Collectivist societies will have more emotional dependence of members on their organizations, when in equilibrium, organization is expected to show responsibility on members.

3. Masculinity vs. femininity: This dimension deals with gender/work relationships. In masculine cultures, sex roles were sharply differentiated whereas in feminine cultures little distinction is made between males and females doing the same job.

Although both India and Mexico had scores somewhere in the middle range, suggesting that such distinction does not exist, I believe the Arab culture would have scored much higher. This is due in part to the traditional view that a female role is to be housewives and full time mothers.

4. Uncertainty avoidance: Out of the four factors, this is the most important dimension. Uncertainty avoidance deals with how members of different cultures deal with ambiguous situations. Higher scoring nations feel uncomfortable with ambiguous situations and vice versa.

What makes a culture entrepreneurial?

As one of our engineers once put it, What also evolved was a set of rules for creating and maintaining NDA's petri dish. In creating your own, consider these rules:

- *Treat people with respect.* This is a very simple premise, which threads through each and every complicated issue that can arise within a company. Respect and trust provide the necessary base for a vibrant and sustainable corporate culture.
- *Help employees stay healthy.* When employees get sick, they miss work, so it makes sense to offer health insurance as a benefit. We covered 100% of employee health plans. I never want an employee to experience a catastrophic illness and not be covered by insurance. We also offered unlimited sick time. While I had seen this type of policy backfire elsewhere, it nonetheless allowed people to be sick when they really were sick, and not feel obligated to gobble up each "allotted" sick day. You may also want to add a wellness allowance for health-club membership.
- *Open doors to communication.* Create an environment where people can interact with each other, support each other and recognize each other's efforts and achievements. Provide positive rewards for positive behavior. Share information, so that employees are aware of the direction of the company and are involved in it. Use all-hands meetings for financial and operational information, team-building and social events. Offer incentive programs to reward effort and improve quality of life.
- *Build camaraderie.* Make time for people to get to know each other and the company. We held an annual off-site meeting to build team spirit and discuss where the company was going. At such events you can also distribute and share your business plan and discuss issues and ideas raised by your strategies.

Maintaining Entrepreneurial Culture

Once you have healthy, trusted and informed employees, don't let the culture that's evolving just be. It needs to be watched so that it grows as you intended. The trick is standing back, but not too far back. In maintaining your culture, consider these rules.

- *Let the team build itself.* Within that safe, comfortable, open environment, let employees grow together without being made to.
- *Participate without controlling.* Let the culture thrive, without your either meddling with it or ignoring it.

- *Don't forget the little things.* Culture is made up of many small actions that, when put together, create something larger than the sum of the parts. There are many things a CEO can do to make employees feel a part of the company. Some are just common courtesies: hallway conversations, saying "hello" in the morning, opening doors, asking after people's families and partners. Others are little extras, such as flowers to say thank you and happy-birthday e-mail messages. Eating lunch with employees, helping spouses find jobs and participating in team events show that you, the CEO, are involved with your employees.

Treating employees with respect helps enable them to do their jobs to the best of their abilities. If you challenge people to raise their bars, provide fun activities, keep people informed and humanize your management, you get culture. From these basics, you will grow in your petri dish a strong, healthy culture that will allow you, your company and your employees to flourish.

5.7.2. Charles Handy

Charles Handy (1976), popularized Roger Harrison (1972) with linking organizational structure to organizational culture. The described four types of culture are:

1. **Power culture:** concentrates power among a small group or a central figure and its control is radiating from its center like a web. Power cultures need only a few rules and little bureaucracy but swift in decisions can ensue.

2. **Role culture:** authorities are delegated as such within a highly defined structure. These organizations form hierarchical bureaucracies, where power derives from the personal position and rarely from an expert power. Control is made by procedures (which are highly valued), strict roles descriptions and authority definitions. These organizations have consistent systems and are very predictable. This culture is often represented by a "Roman Building" having pillars. These pillars represent the functional departments.

3. **Task culture:** teams are formed to solve particular problems. Power is derived from the team with the expertise to execute against a task. This culture uses a small team approach, where people are highly skilled and specialized in their own area of expertise. Additionally, these cultures often feature the multiple reporting lines seen in a matrix structure.

4. **Person culture:** formed where all individuals believe themselves superior to the organization. It can become difficult for such organizations to continue to operate, since the concept of an organization suggests that a group of like-minded individuals pursue organizational goals. However some professional partnerships operate well as person cultures, because each partner brings a particular expertise and clientele to the firm.

5.8. SUMMARY

Culture includes the organization values, visions, norms, working language, systems, symbols, beliefs and habits. It is also the pattern of such collective behaviors and assumptions that are taught to new organizational members. Culture is very important in entrepreneurship. Culture includes values, norms, behavior of an entrepreneur within the enterprise. A good culture always attract new employees and retains the old employees within the firm.

5.9. SOME CASE STUDIES

1. Work Culture in Singapore: Singapore is considered to be one of the best places in the world to work. Expatriates from all over the globe are flocking to this international city-state today to work. This tiny region is one of the world's freest economies. Singapore is also highly ranked when it comes to business competitiveness and economic growth, ranking well above countries like the United States. It also beats many western countries in areas like city infrastructure, technology, lifestyle, education, health care, safety, etc., due to which people around the planet want to work and settle there.

All countries have a different business culture. The history, traditions, past, geography, climate, society, economy and lifestyle affect and form a particular business culture. That is why, the way a business is managed differs so much from nation to nation and continent to continent. Singapore is believed to have a very efficient working population and no wonder they have some of the best companies like Singapore Airlines and Temasek. Let us see how different factors influence the work culture in Singapore.

Work culture in Singapore is of a high-power distance, which means there are clear authority structures and social status is defined by your position in the society and workplace. People at lower levels respect higher authorities. Respecting elders and seniors comes from Confucianism that still exists in the Chinese culture and Asian cultures. In such a hierarchical society or workplace, juniors do not openly question or argue with superiors. Using of surnames or titles while addressing is also important like in any other Asian country

2. Work Culture in Google: At Google, they are committed to a supportive work environment, where employees have the opportunity to reach their fullest potential. Each Googler is expected to do his or her utmost to create a respectful workplace culture that is free of harassment, intimidation, bias and unlawful discrimination of any kind. Collaboration isn't just about working together to solve problems or overcome challenges. At Google, it's also about sharing knowledge and helping your fellow Googlers grow their skills. Technology changes quickly and our Googlers-to-Googlers (G2G) education program empowers Googlers to learn throughout their careers. The program invites any Googler to teach a class about...well, just about anything—from Python programming and project management to spin classes and parenting. See what Fast Company learned about G2G and the power of employee-to-employee learning when they enrolled in a data visualization class at our NYC office.

In 2009, a group of Googlers organized an event at the Google headquarters in Mountain View, CA, designed to celebrate the culture of diversity with food, music, dance performances, and executive speakers. This group of passionate Googlers launched the first event in a series of Sum of Google Celebrations with over 1,000 Googlers attending. The Sum of Google has since grown - for the entire month of July in 2012, over 5,000 Googlers in 70 offices across Asia, Europe, Latin America, and North America engaged in global Diversity and Inclusion conversations through panel discussions and speakers. They celebrated Diversity and Inclusion in local offices with good food and cultural dance performances.

Some of the programs and benefits that are specifically focused on creating an inclusive environment for all employees:-

- Adoption Assistance
- Day Care
- Mother's Rooms
- Maternity / Paternity Leave Programs
- Baby-bonding bucks
- New parents support group
- Children centers in Mountain View
- Domestic Partnership Programs
- Accommodation Policies (including those for visually, mobility and hearing impaired Googlers)
- Transgender and Transitioning Workplace Support

For new parents, Google provides time off to bond with their new Googlet, plus tools and resources to help the transition back to work following maternity and paternity leaves. Google also partners with Care.com to provide US Googlers acccess to annual premium memberships. Care.com offers families a trusted place to easily connect to babysitters, nannies, special needs care, senior care givers, pet sitters, dog walkers, housekeepers, and more.

Moreover,the annual Global ERG Leadership Summit brings together 100+ leaders and members of Google's 18 ERGs for 2 days dedicated to sharing, collaborating, strategy planning, and connecting with the larger diversity community. Attendees at the 2011 summit selected custom content in one of three areas: career development, business diversity, and ERG strategy planning.

3. Work Culture in Facebook: Internal culture of Facebook seems to differ most significantly *from other similar Silicon Valley companies* or competitors:

- the culture is more oriented around **trying things out rather than debating** the merits of a course of action
- the culture values **getting things to work** rather than ensuring an optimal solution
- the culture is more oriented around **long-term plans**
- the culture is **younger** than most other companies; even older employees "act younger" than their peers at other companies (not more immature, just younger; the young people at the company actually act more mature than most people of their age)
- the culture is more oriented around a **very strong product leader** at the top
- the culture is more open about **knowing details about people's personal lives**
- the culture is more oriented around improving the **user experience over revenue generation**

According to one of the employee of facebook: In my experience at Facebook mistakes are viewed as positives events to learn from and this attitude allows us all to work outside of our comfort zone and push ourselves to accomplish more.

A related part of our culture is based on open communication and transparent decision making. (Don't get this confused with democratic group based decision making). We know that victory in the social space is about speed and execution. This means communicate openly to ensure that information is surfaced to the right people and the best decisions get made as quickly as possible.

5.10. SELF ASSESSMENT QUESTIONS

1. What do you mean by culture? What are the important features of entrepreneurial culture?
2. What are the various types of cultures?
3. What do you mean by entrepreneurial culture and why its important?
4. What do you mean by ethics and how is it different from one organization to the other? Explain with the help of case study.
5. What are the various types of organization culture. With the help of case study explain which? types of culture exist over there?

SOURCE/NOTES

1. http://capone.mtsu.edu AND http://www.buzzle.com
2. Source:-Sir Adrian Cabury, "Ethical managers make their own rules,"

   Harvard Business Review, Oct., 1987.
3. Acharyan N.G Ranga Agricultural University-Entrepreneurship Development(study material)-Dr. V.Sudharani
4. www.buzzle.com/articles/types-of-organizational-culture

6

ENTREPRENEURSHIP AND INTRAPRENEURSHIP — COMPARATIVE ANALYSIS

6.1. INTRODUCTION

In the past decades both the entrepreneurship and the management literature have paid increasing attention to entrepreneurship within existing organizations. This phenomenon is usually called 'corporate entrepreneurship', 'corporate venturing'or 'intrapreneurship'. Entrepreneurship in existing organizations can be studied at the individual, the organizational and the macro level. Entrepreneurs and intrapreneurs play a decisive role as they help the company (newly established or existing) to engage in new business and enter new markets. Intrapreneurship represent the initiation and implementation of innovative systems and practices within an organization, by some of its staff under the supervision of a manager who takes the role of an intrapreneur, in order to improve the economical performance of the organization, by using a part of its resources, namely those that previously have not been used in an appropriate manner. Intrapreneurship improves the economical and financial performance of the company, by applying a more efficient use of resources and by using a suitable motivational system for its employees (Istocescu, 2003).

6.2. MEANING OF INTRAPRENEURS/CORPORATE ENTREPRENEURS

We operationalize intrapreneurship as employees developing new business activities for their employer, including establishing a new outlet or subsidiary and launching new products or product-market combinations . Phenomenon is usually called 'corporate entrepreneurship', 'corporate venturing' or 'intrapreneurship. Intrapreneurship refers to initiatives by employees in organizations to undertake new business activities. Although intrapreneurship is related to corporate entrepreneurship, these concepts differ in the following sense. Corporate entrepreneurship is usually defined at the level of organization and refers to a top-down process, i.e., a strategy that management can utilize to foster more initiatives and/or efforts to achieve improvement from their workforce and organization. Intrapreneurship relates to the individual level and is about bottom up, proactive work-related initiatives of individual employees. Intrapreneurship represent the initiation and implementation of innovative systems and practices within an organization, by some of its staff under the supervision of a manager who takes the role of an intrapreneur, in order to improve the economical performance of the organization, by using a part of its resources, namely those that previously have not been used in an appropriate manner. Intrapreneurs have been credited with increasing the speed and cost-effectiveness of technology transfer from research and development to the marketplace. While intrapreneurs are sometimes considered inventors, inventors come up with new products. Intrapreneurs come up with new processes that get that product to the market.

Intrapreneurship is a special type of entrepreneurship and thus, shares many key behavioral characteristics with this comprehensive concept, such as taking initiative, pursuit of opportunity, and some element of 'newness'. At the same time, intrapreneurship also belongs to the domain of employee behavior and thus, faces specific limitations that a corporate hierarchy and an intraorganizational context may impose on individual initiative, as well as specific possibilities for support that an existing business may offer to a nascent intrapreneur.

Intrapreneurship improves the economical and financial performance of the company, by applying a more efficient use of the resources and by using a suitable motivational system for its employees.

So, corporate entrepreneurship is defined as a "process whereby an individual or a group of individuals, in association with an existing organization or do innovation within that organization." Popular terms includes–organizational entrepreneurship, intrapreneurship and corporate venturing. Authors use many terms to refer to different aspects of corporate entrepreneurship: intrapreneurship (Kuratko *et al.*, 1990), internal corporate entrepreneurship (Schollhammer, 1982), corporate ventures (Ellis and Taylor, 1987; MacMillan *et al.*, 1986), venture management (Veciana, 1996), new ventures (Roberts, 1980) and, internal corporate venturing (Burgelman, 1984).

6.3. HISTORY OF INTRAPRENEURS

The first written use of the terms 'intrapreneur', 'intrapreneuring,' and 'intrapreneurship' date from a paper written in 1978 by Gifford and Elizabeth Pinchot. Later, the term was credited to Gifford Pinchot III by Norman Macrae in the April 17, 1982, issue of *The Economist.* Under their model a person wishing to develop an intrapreneurial project would initially have to risk something of value to themself — a portion of their salary, for instance. The intrapreneur could then sell the completed project for both cash bonuses and intracapital which could be used to develop future projects. Based on the success of some of the early trials of their methods in Sweden they began a school for intrapreneurs and in 1985, they published their first book, *Intrapreneuring*, combining the findings from their research and practical applications .

The first formal academic case study of corporate entrepreneurship or intrapreneurship was published in June 1982, as a Master's in Management thesis, by Howard Edward Haller, on the intrapreneurial creation of PR1ME Leasing within PR1ME Computer Inc. (from 1977 to 1981). *The American Heritage Dictionary of the English Language* included the term 'intrapreneur' in its 3rd 1992 Edition, and also credited Gifford Pinchot III as the originator of the concept. The term "intrapreneurship" was used in the popular media first in February 1985 by *TIME* magazine article "Here come the Intrapreneurs" and then the same year in another major popular publication was in a quote by Steve Jobs, Apple Computer's Chairman, in an interview in the September, 1985, *Newsweek* article, where he shared, "The Macintosh team was what is commonly known as intrapreneurship;only a few years before the term was coined — a group of people going, in essence, back to the garage, but in a large company."

6.4. DEFINITIONS

1. Zahra (1991) has observed that "corporate entrepreneurship may be formal or informal activities aimed at creating new businesses in established companies through product or process innovations and market developments. These activities may take place at the corporate, division(business), functional or project levels,with the unifying objective of improving company's competitive position and financial performance."

2. Guth and Ginsberg (1990) stress that corporate entrepreneurship encompasses two major phenomena: New venture creation within existing organizations and the transformation of organizations through strategic renewal.

3. 1992, *The American Heritage Dictionary* brought intrapreneurism into the main stream by adding intrapreneur to its dictionary, defining it as "a person within a large corporation who takes direct responsibility for turning an idea into a profitable finished product through assertive risk taking and innovation"

4. William D.Guth and Ari Ginsberg have stressed that corporate entrepreneurship encompasses two major phenomena: New venture creation within existing organizations and the transformation of organizations through strategic renewal.

6.4. GENERAL FRAMEWORK FOR UNDERSTANDING CORPORATE ENTREPRENEURSHIP

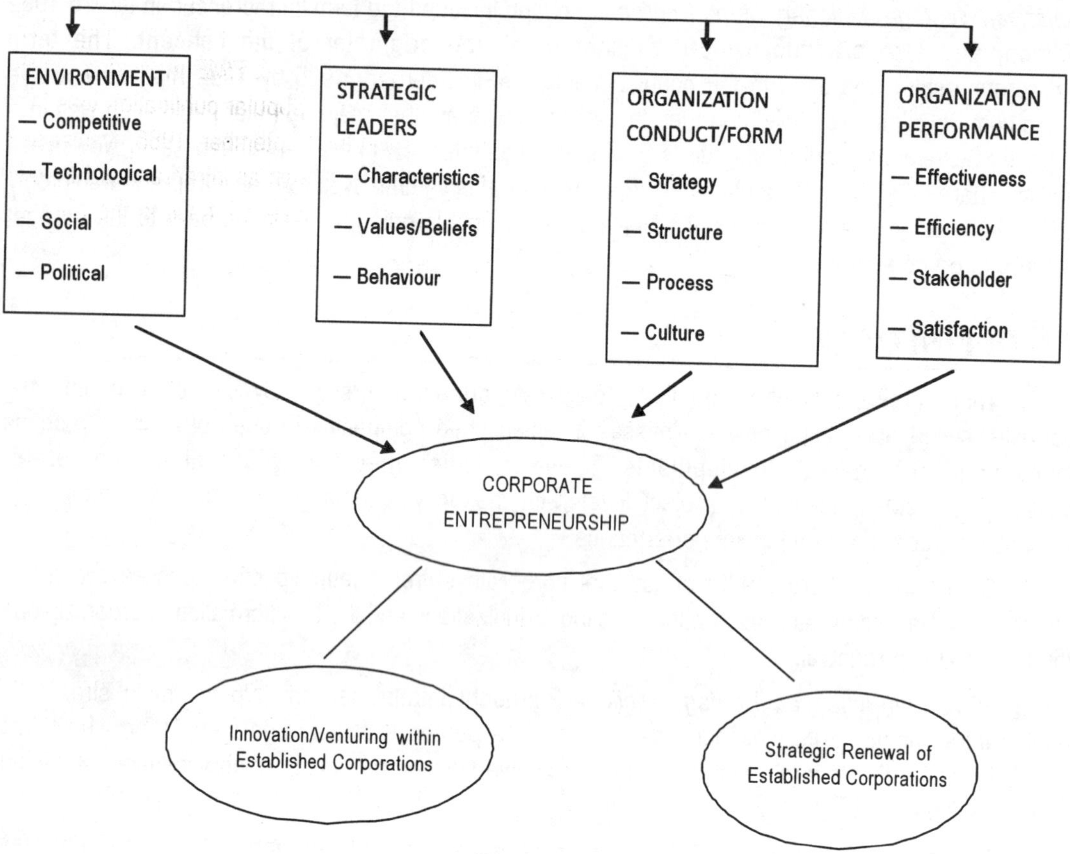

Fig. 6.1.

6.5. NEED FOR CORPORATE ENTREPRENEURING

These days many companies are recognizing the need of corporate entrepreneurship. Some scholars emphasising its analogue to new business creation by individual entrepreneurs, view corporate entrepreneurship as a concept that is limited to new venture creation within existing organisations (Burgelman, 1984). Others argue that the concept of corporate entrepreneurship should encompass the struggle of large firms to renew themselves by carrying out new combinations of resources that alter the relationships between them and their environments (Baumol, 1986; Burgelman, 1983). According to Zahra (1991) corporate entrepreneurship refers to the process of creating new business within established firms to improve organisational profitability and enhance a firm's competitive position or the strategic renewal of existing business.

The need for corporate entrepreneuring has arisen due to the rapid growth of number of new and sophisticated competitors, international competition, desire to improve efficiency and productivity, to meet the needs of customers, to lead the market, etc. But the main reason is to keep the efficient employees within the firm as some of the best and brightest employees with innovative ideas, from the corporations leave their jobs in order to start their own ventures. So, the modern organizations is developing in-house entrepreneuring.

6.6. ACTIVITIES RELATED TO INTRAPRENEURSHIP

1. Opportunity perception
2. Idea generation
3. Designing a new product or another recombination of resources
4. Internal coalition building
5. Persuading management
6. Resource acquisition
7. Planning and organizing.

Key behavioral aspects of intrapreneurship are personal initiative, active information search, out of the box thinking, voicing, championing, taking charge, finding a way, and some degree of risk taking.

6.7. ADVANTAGES AND DISADVANTAGES OF INTRAPRENEURSHIP

Advantages	Disadvantages
Ability to stay in a friendly, well known environment	Reward may not be up to expectation
Practicing your skills within an organization–lower risk	Innovation may not be appreciated accordingly
Using companies resources, good name, knowledge	You can be innovative but to a certain limit
Access to customers, infrastructure	Not provided with adequate resources
Practical innovation is rewarded.	Increase internal competition

6.8. ROLE OF INTRAPRENEURS/CORPORATE ENTRPRENEURS

1. Innovator: Intrapreneurs are innovators. They find new, more efficient ways for production, new products, new markets and some times different type of raw materials will can reduce the cost of organisation. They also save their companies money on overheads the and supplies, keeping their organization's finance healthy.

2. Business Development: The corporate entrepreneur is an individual that exists within an organisation to generate product and process ideas that will create value for the organisation, its stakeholders and its consumers that buy its products. Sustainable business development (SBD) is the art of the societal marketing philosophy which aims to create value for consumers in the long-term by providing superior value to consumers and its stakeholders by the adoption of six sigma and the triple bottom line (Environmental, social and economic) approach. Which pertains to create value superior than its competitors by focusing its resources on sustainable business strategies and activities.The Corporate entrepreneur's role in sustainable business development to create a product or process that under the guidelines of SBD creates a sustainable business strategy that makes the company unique within its market.The allocation of resources in the corporate environment is also important in the growth of SBD, as highly sustainable practices can be expensive to the organisation but creates superior value in the future.

3. Project Manager: Intrapreneurs are expected to develop, implement and lead projects as necessary. They must have the foresight and experience to bring forward the best in the people, redirect their staff's energy when necessary and motivate them toward the project completion.

4. Interpersonal roles: Interpersonal are roles that involve people (subordinates and persons outside the organization) and duties that are ceremonial and symbolic in nature. The three interpersonal roles are.

(*a*) ***Figurehead:*** Symbolic, head; obliged to perform a number of routine duties of a legal or social nature like greeting visitors, signing legal documents.

(*b*) ***Leader:*** Responsible for the motivation of subordinates, responsible for staffing, training and associated duties like performing virtually all activities that involve subordinates.

(*c*) ***Liaison:*** Maintain self developed network of outside contacts and informers who provide favors and information like acknowledging mail, doing external board work, performing other activities that involve outsiders.

5. Informational roles: Informational roles involve receiving, collecting and disseminating information. The three informational roles are

(*a*) ***Monitor:*** Seek and receives wide variety of internal and external information to develop thorough understanding of organization and environment like reading periodicals and reports and maintaining personal contacts.

(*b*) ***Disseminator:*** Transmits information received from outsiders or from subordinates to member of the organization like holding informational meetings, making phone calls to reply information.

(*c*) ***Spokesperson:*** Transmits information to outsiders on organization's plan, policies, actions and results like holding board meetings, giving information to the media.

6. Decisional roles: Decisional roles revolve around making choices. The four decisional roles are.

(*a*) ***Entrepreneur:*** Searches organization and its environment for opportunities and initiates improvement projects" to bring about changes like organizing strategy and review session to develop new programs.

(b) ***Disturbance handler:*** Responsible for corrective action when organization faces important, unexpected disturbance like organizing strategy and review session that involve disturbance and crises.

(c) ***Resource allocator:*** Responsible for allocation of organizational resources of all kinds, making or approving all significant organizational decisions like scheduling, requesting authorization, performing any activity that involves budgeting and the programming of subordinate's work.

(d) ***Negotiator:*** Responsible for representing the organization at major negotiations like participating in union contract negotiations.

7. Development of new markets: Intrapreneurs has important role in the development of B.O.P (Bottom of pyramid) market. With their innovations and out of box thinking intrapreneurs are able to give more ideas regarding the production of new goods at the lesser price which can be easily purchased by the people having low or mid income.

8. Development of economy: With the innovations in the production, process, development of new market or development of new product at lower cost intrapreneurs are able to contribute towards the development of economy.

6.9. ESSENTIALS FOR INTRAPRENEURSHIP

Fradette and Michaud described for main elements essential for the success of intrapreneurship:

1. The structural and strategic environment should be "right" within the organization.The ambience should not stifle innovation and freedom to the employees should be given to make limited changes.

2. An appropriate workforce of enterprising people should be built on which scientific recruitment is made. Talents of the employees are recognized and their key skills are trained.

3. Support system, team working, information sharing and learning are essential for invoking the dormant talents of employees.They should be encouraged to collaborate and network naturally.

4. Successful employees should be suitably rewarded while they should not be panalised for their mistakes to such extent that they are dissuaded from further initiatives.

Other Essentials

1. New ideas enclouraged.
2. Failures allowed
3. Support of Top Management
4. Resources available and accessible
5. Trial and Error encouraged to some extent
6. Appropriate reward system
7. Multidiscipline teamwork approach
8. Encourage open discussion

6.10. RESPONSIBILITIES OF INTRAPRENEURS

1. Intrapreneurs must take the responsibility of his/her actions.
2. They must give their ideas by keeping in mind the availability of the resources like:—raw materials, capital and labour
3. They must check the feasibility of the ideas.
4. It is the responsibility of the Intrapreneurs to check the practical implementation of the ideas given.
5. They must keep in mind that the ideas given must work within the boundaries of law.
6. It is the responsibility of the intrapreneurs that the innovations must not give rise to any type of conflicts within or outside the organization.
7. They must keep the secrecy of the innovative idea from the competitors. So that it must not get leaked out before the actual implementation of the idea.

6.11. SIMILARITIES AND DIFFERENCES BETWEEN ENTREPRENEURSHIP AND INTRAPRENEURSHIP

Unlike the entrepreneur, the intrapreneur acts within an existing organization. "Intrapreneurship refers to employee initiatives in organizations to undertake something new, without being asked to do so." Intrapreneurship is now known as the practice of a corporate management style that integrates risk-taking and innovation approaches, as well as the reward and motivational techniques, that are more traditionally thought of as being the province of entrepreneurship. The intrapreneur is the revolutionary inside the organization, who fights for change and renewal from within the system. This may give rise to conflicts within the organization, so respect is the necessary key in order to channel these conflicts and transform them into positive aspects for the organization. Even though intrapreneurs benefit from using the resources of the organization for the implementation of the emerging opportunities, there are several motives why innovation is more difficult to implement in an existing organization, such as (Malek and Ilbach, 2004):

- *The size*: the bigger the organization the more difficult it is to have an overview of the actions of every employee
- *Lack of communication*: Specialization and separation, help in concentrating on the areas of interest, but hinder communication.
- *Internal competition*: Internal competition amplifies the problem because instead of sharing the knowledge with others it borders the knowledge sharing. Everyone wants to keep the information for themselves.
- *Feedback received in case of success/mistake*: Costs in case of failure are too great and the reward for a successful outcome too small. Intrapreneurs must be allowed to commit mistakes, because such mistakes are an inevitable part of the entrepreneurial process. The recognition

of success is also very rare. No company provides payment in advance for what an entrepreneur might accomplish, but a lot of them like to talk about the concept of intapreneurship and expect their employees to get involved and assume their risk. But finally, when motivated employees get involves and have success their only reward is a small bonus.

- *Dullness*: Many companies are slow and reluctant to change. Many times intrapreneurs has to listen to the well known sentence "We always did it this way", which leaves little or no space to creativity. The willingness to try new things appears only when the company's shortcomings become apparent, but even so they do not give room to an innovative leadership.
- *Hierarchies*: Organizational hierarchies compel employees to ask permission for actions that fall outside their daily duties. The more complex the hierarchy, the more difficult it is to impose change. Hierarchies have also tended to create a short-term thinking. Employees on lower hierarchical levels have a "victim-mentality" due to a reduced area of action and reduced responsibilities. Those who wish to implement innovative ideas should first consider what the best option for them is, as an intrapreneur, as part of an existing organization, or an entrepreneur in a newly established company. In order to give an answer to this question an analysis of the advantages and disadvantages of both concepts is required. The table below helps someone decide what type of business best suits him after confronting him with the advantages and disadvantages that await him.

6.12. SIMILARITIES BETWEEN CORPORATE AND START-UP ENTREPRENEURSHIP

- Both involve opportunity recognition and definition
- Both require a unique business concept that takes the form of a product, service or process.
- Both are driven by an individual champion who works with a team to bring the concept to fruition
- Both require that the entrepreneur be able to balance vision with managerial skill, passion with pragmatism and proactiveness with patience.
- Both involve concepts that are most vulnerable in the formative stages and that require adaption over time.
- Both entail a window of opportunity within which the concept can be successfully capitalized upon.
- Both are predicated on value creation and accountability to a customer.
- Both entail risk and require risk management strategies.

6.13. EXAMPLES OF INTRAPRENEURS

1. Sony Playstation: Intrapreneur: Ken Kutaragi, Company: Sony Computer Entertainment Inc. Year Launched: 1994

Ken Kutaragi was working in Sony's sound labs when he bought his daughter a Nintendo game console. Watching her play, he was dismayed by the system's primitive sound effects. He realized that a digital chip dedicated solely to sound would improve the quality of the games — and the product itself. Keeping his job at Sony, Kutaragi developed the SPC7000 for the next generation of Nintendo machines. Sony execs nearly fired him after discovering his sideline project, but then, CEO Norio Ohga realized the value of his innovation and encouraged Kutaragi's efforts. With Sony's blessing, Kutaragi worked with Nintendo to develop a CD-ROM-based Nintendo. But Nintendo decided not to go forward with it, so Kutaragi helped Sony develop its own gaming system, which became the Play station. The first PlayStation made Sony a major player in the games market, but the PlayStation 2 did even better, becoming the best-selling game console of all time. Kutaragi founded Sony Computer Entertainment, one of the Sony's most profitable divisions.

2. Java Programming Language: Intrapreneurs: Patrick Naughton, James Gosling, Bill Joy, Company: Sun Microsystems, Year Launched: 1995

The circuitous route Java took to market began when Patrick Naughton, a 25-year-old, up-and-coming programmer, told Sun CEO Scott McNealy that he was leaving the company. McNealy asked Naughton to give him an assessment of what Sun was doing wrong, and the programmer responded that Sun, then known for its business workstations, was missing out on the fast-growing PC consumer market. His 12-page e-mail quickly became a rallying cry to change Sun's direction. Naughton stayed, and Sun set up a group dedicated to breaking into the consumer market. Group member James Gosling created an elegant object-oriented programming language called Oak (renamed Java), which Sun initially hoped would be used by Time Warner in its cable set-top boxes. When that deal fell through, it looked like the language would be abandoned. It took Bill Joy, a Sun co-founder, to champion the project. Joy realized that with the explosion of the Web, a programming language like Oak could be used across different platforms — computers, cell phones, PDAs, and more. Joy also understood that the key to making Java a cross-platform linchpin was to give the language and development kit away. By the end of 1996, Java had nearly 100 licensees and had attracted 6,000 developers.

3. ELIXIR Guitar Strings: Intrapreneurs: Dave Myers and John Spencer, Company: W.L. Gore, Year Launched: 1997

W.L. Gore, known primarily as the maker of Gore-Tex rain gear, encourages employees to develop new ideas through its "dabble time" policy: Ten per cent of a work day can be devoted to personal projects. In 1995, the company was experimenting with ePTFE, a chemical cousin to Teflon, to coat push-pull cables for use in animatronics. Dave Myers, an associate in the company's medical unit, thought the coating might be good for guitar strings and recruited both marketing and manufacturing personnel to work on the project. Myers' team originally believed that the coating's appeal would be in making strings more comfortable to use. But extensive market research, piloted by John Spencer, and more than 15,000 guitar-player field tests led the team to realize their real selling point: better sound. The coated strings were only nominally more comfortable than non-coated strings, but they kept their tone longer than conventional guitar strings. W.L. Gore launched them under the brand name ELIXIR Strings, now the No. 1 seller of acoustic guitar strings and the overall No. 2 seller in the guitar string market.

(**Source:** http://www.cbsnews.com/8301-505125_162-51196888/great-intrapreneurs-in-businesshistory/-by Jake Swearingen)

6.14. SUMMARY

"Intrapreneurship refers to employee initiatives in organizations to undertake something new, without being asked to do so." Hence, the *intrapreneur* focuses on innovation and creativity, and transforms an idea into a profitable venture, while operating within the organizational environment. Intrapreneurs/corporate entrepreneurs are very important for the growth of organization and each and every organization must give chance to innovators which exist within the firm, so that they can come up with more and more ideas. These days the concept of corporate entrepreneurship is getting very popular as it leads to development of entrepreneurial spirit within organizational boundaries and thus allow an atmosphere of innovation to prosper. It includes generation, development and implementation of new ideas. To create the right climate for in–house entrepreneurship, the companies must develop—explicit goals, a system of feedback, good communication system, emphasis on individual responsibility, rewards based on results, no punishments for failures and open atmosphere for innovative thinking.

6.15. SELF ASSESSMENT QUESTIONS

1. What do you mean by intrapreneurs/corporate entrepreneurs?
2. What is the importance and need of intrapreneurs?
3. What are the similarities and differences between intrapreneurs and entrepreneurs?
4. With the help of case study explain the input by intrapreneurs which leads the organization to a success.
5. These days number of corporations are working to re-engineer corporate thinking and encourage an innovative environment. What are the various steps that the corporations must take for the same?

7

ENTREPRENEURSHIP: MAINTAINING AND SUSTAINING COMPETITIVE ADVANTAGE

7.1. INTRODUCTION

We live in a time of global entrepreneurial revolution. In virtually every nation, every industry and every market, entrepreneurs are challenging existing assumptions and creating values in novel ways. Today entrepreneurship is an emerging concept and wide open opportunities, therefore, many youngsters are opting it as a career but the role entrepreneurs is changing due to various dilemmas. In order to meet the dilemma situations, entrepreneurs has to sustain competitiveness and has to maintain competitive advantage. In the entrepreneurial age, the rate at which companies must transform themselves is accelerating.

7.2. ENTREPRENEURSHIP AS A CAREER

Entrepreneurs start new businesses and take on the risks and rewards of being an owner. This is the ultimate career in capitalism — putting your idea to work in a competitive economy. Some new ventures generate enormous wealth for the entrepreneur. However, the job of entrepreneur is not for everyone. You need to be hard-working, smart, creative, willing to take risks and good with people. You need to have heart, have motivation and have drive. The lack of opportunities in the formal sectors has driven many young people to strike out on their own. Many youngsters are leaving their their good paying jobs to establish their own small entrepreneurial ventures. This is the sector which is growing the fastest today. The big money in the long run and the freedom to choose their own rainbows are, of course, major guiding factors. Today, the scope and variety of self-generated work is unlimited. Home ventures too offer enormous opportunities for the enterprising. The range of options for self generated work is immense and many of these can even be conducted from home. It can be divided majorly into three activities:

1. Providing service
2. Selling something
3. Manufacturing (making)

Many enterprises combine more than one activities. Deciding which type of entreprise to choose require a great deal of research, because setting up a business is an uncharted area in the conventional career terms.

One of the best things about pursuing a career as an entrepreneur is the wide open possibilities. There is room in many economies throughout the globe for entrepreneurship — such as India, Brazil, Dubai, the U.S. or Kenya. There are many industries where wealth creation is possible be it the Internet and IT, personal services, media, engineering or small local business (e.g., dry cleaning, electronics repair, restaurants). But there is a downside of entrepreneurship too. Your life may lack stability and structure. Your ability to take time off may be highly limited. And you may become stressed as you manage cash flow on the one hand and expansion on the other. Three out of five new businesses in the U.S. fail within 18 months of getting started.

It's important to be savvy and understand what is and is not realistic. Understand that the market is more or less efficient — which means that if a bunch of people know a sure way to be a millionaire then the opportunity has probably already been competed away. On the other hand, look for inefficiencies in markets. Places where a better idea, a little ingenuity or some aggressive marketing could really make a difference. Think about problems that people would pay to have a solution to. It helps to know finance. It's a must to really know your product area well. What do consumers want? What differentiates you from the competition? How do you market this product? A formal business plan is not essential, but is normally a great help in thinking through the case for a new business. You'll be investing more in it than anyone else, so treat yourself like a smart, skeptical investor who needs to be convinced that the maths adds up for the business you propose starting.

The possibilities in entrepreneurship are endless. The rewards can be high. And the risks are undoubtedly high too. But, if you have drive, creativity and the desire to be your own boss, this may very well be the career for you.

7.3. WORK OF ENTREPRENEURS

Variety of self-generated work in unlimited. Providing a service requires the least capital and involves less risk. These services are based on using one's time, skills and possibly any specialized training received. This can cover a large range of activities from freelance writing for magazines and journals to providing beauty care services or providing potted plants for homes or offices. Professionals in law, accountancy, system analysis, or even creative professionals such as copywriters, journalists and so on can be their own bosses while working independently for large organizations.

Selling or Marketing overlaps both manufacturing and providing services. It could involve making something at home and delivering it to some clients or setting up some exibitions for the same. Selling involves more initial organization and business know-how, capital and risk than service venture.

Manufacturing covers anything from making children's clothes to high-tech components for industry. Manufacturing usually requires more skill, capital and risk than service and selling. You may need a physical premises for production.

Most service industry entrepreneurs work from their houses or small offices that they rent. Some of them also go in for freelancing and door-to-door services. This is a major growth area. Other ideas that have generated successful enterprise include the marriage planning service, theme parties, conference and exhibition services, travel services, and food catering service. Enterprising entrepreneurs can also start their own chains for restaurants' delivery services. Computers and information technology industry offers good scope for self-employment. Services like coaching services, software development, graphics designing and website development are the main jobs in this field.

Selling/Marketing is quite popular among entrepreneurs. The sales can be provided directly from homes to other official or residential locations. This may be something like providing complete packed lunch from homes to offices.

Entrepreneurs in manufacturing have to set up their own factories and small-scale industries. The investment in this sector is far more than others. Industries in manufacturing ranges from cottages and villages industries (handicrafts etc.) to very sophisticated industries, which manufacture computer parts, television and other technical units.

Entrepreneurship is becoming an increasingly popular career choice in today's marketplace. While many individuals go on their own internal reasons — a passionate need to be independent, a burning desire to turn a hobby into a profession, or the love of a challenge — others have chosen the entrepreneur route in response to external situations, including layoffs, frustration with their current workplace culture, or a need for greater flexibility in their lives. Owning a business has become the twenty-first century version of the 1950s, American dream of owning a home. But entrepreneurship is not for everyone. It's important to consider whether you have what it takes to start a business and run it successfully. You've probably heard that start-up statistics are grim. The truth is that just 30 percent of business start-ups survive more than five years. Stories of overnight successes and young millionaires are rare. The dot.com era ended two years ago, and venture capital money is increasingly hard to secure. The hard-working, determined, visionary who dedicates long hours and endless energy to his or her business is the more realistic picture of today's entrepreneur. Entrepreneurs face a myriad of internal and external challenges. Within their companies, they need to offer a superior product or service. They need to manage cash flow and maintain profitability and hire and retain the right mix of people. Externally, factors such as access to financing, the economy, government regulations, and technological issues impact entrepreneurs on a regular basis.

Many small businesses fail because of weaknesses in general management, financial management, and marketing (Statistics Canada, "Failing Concerns: Business Bankruptcy in Canada"). Undercapitalization — or insufficient funds — is another common pitfall. Michael Gerber cites the "entrepreneurial seizure" as a primary reason for failure in his book *"The E Myth, Why Most Small Businesses Don't Work, and What To Do About It."* Gerber says many entrepreneurs pursue the dream of being their own boss but fatally assume that an understanding of the technical nature of a business is enough to achieve success.

To avoid becoming a casualty of the start-up craze, it's critical to be aware of the pros and cons of running a business. Sure, you have the potential to earn gobs of money, you can set your own hours and be your own boss. But there are many long hours, substantial risk and lots of dirty work required in the growing stages of any young firm.

7.4. CONCEPTUAL MODEL FOR UNDERSTANDING ENTREPRENEURIAL CAREER

A conceptual model for understanding entrepreneurial career views the career stages as dynamic one, with each stage reflecting and interacting with other stages and events in individuals life – past, present and future. The life cycle approach conceptualizes entrepreneurial career in nine major categories:

(a) Educational environment

(b) The individual's personality

(c) Childhood family environment

(d) Employment history

(e) Adult development history

(f) Adult non work history

(g) Current work situation

(h) Individuals current perspective

(i) Current family situation

All the above said points have positive and negative impact on entrepreneurial careers.

7.5. ENTREPRENEURSHIP AS STYLE OF MANAGEMENT

Globalization and business competition around the globe has made entrepreneurial strategies an important concept in new and well established businesses. Styles of managing an enterprise are determined by enterprise culture, the nature of work, the nature of employee and the personal attributes and skills of the leaders. This means that leadership style is determined by prevailing conditions and permits the leaders to practice different leadership styles as the circumstances may necessitate. Having an entrepreneurial style of managing may be thought of as having the structure and flexibility to assist an organization to succeed. The manager implementing an entrepreneurial style must be flexible in adapting to the rapid changing of the market conditions and ideas which are important factors for developing strategies for a company's growth. Entrepreneurial managers may be thought of as being aggressive, survivalist, creative, passionate, honest, and an innovator of ideas. They often strive to make the vision of the organization a reality. More organizations are beginning to adopt an entrepreneurial structure which often provides an intimate and enthusiastic organization. One in which the company is "malleable and responsive" to the leadership's plan.

By and large, the existing business knows how to manage but needs to learn how to become entrepreneurial and how to innovate. The non-business, public-service institution too faces different problems, has different learning needs, and is prone to making different mistakes.The new venture, on the other hand, needs to learn how to be an entrepreneur and how to innovate and, above all, how to manage. Today's businesses, especially the large ones, are not likely to survive in this period of rapid change and innovation unless they acquire entrepreneurial competence.

This is not only in their self-interest; they also have a social responsibility to do so.

Based on our observations, we have identified a few tendencies that really work well for leaders of small companies or start-ups but could become a problem as the company grows larger. These are:

- ***Loyalty to comrades:*** Leaders tend to be loyal to those few colleagues who were there at the start of the business. However, blind loyalty to these people can become a major liability in managing the organization as it becomes large and complex.
- ***Task orientation:*** Focusing on the job at hand, say,in driving a big product launch, is critical but excessive attention to detail can cause a large organization to lose its focus.
- ***Single-mindedness:*** This is an important attribute in a visionary who wants to unleash a revolutionary product or service. Yet, this quality can turn into tunnel vision, if the leader cannot take a broader view of things as the business grows.
- ***Working in isolation:*** While it is acceptable for a brilliant scientist focused on an ingenious idea to work in isolation, it could be disastrous for a leader whose growing organization must depend on the customers, investors, analysts, media, government officials, and various other stakeholders.

7.6. THE CHANGING ROLE OF THE ENTREPRENEUR: MID CAREER DILEMMAS

Start your own business and you can begin to make your own rules. For example, you can set your work hours, make employee hiring decisions and release new products and services without having to wait for approval from another supervisor or manager. Become an entrepreneur and you'll also face dilemmas that other workers may not have to deal with, dilemmas that may cause you to lose sleep or wonder if you made the right choice when you decided to open your own company.

Entrepreneurs, particularly during the first few years they are in business, can find themselves filling two or more job responsibilities. For example, the owner of a restaurant might order food, operate the cash register, interview and hire employees, market the restaurant, help clean the restaurant, oversee budgets, manage payroll and pay other business expenses. Furthermore, if a business has few employees, entrepreneurs also might perform administrative tasks such as mailing business correspondence, filing paperwork, handling all incoming telephone calls and scheduling client meetings. By wearing multiple hats, entrepreneurs can start to lose sight of the company's mission and sales goals, causing their business to experience lack of growth, an event a successful entrepreneur wants to avoid. After all, as reported in *"Inc's"* September 6, 2012 "The Many Hats of an

Entrepreneur" article, "Growth, and new business, should always be the focus of the entrepreneur, because if the business is not growing, it's slowly dying."

7.6.1. Various Dilemmas

(a) Financial Resources: Even when the economy is strong, entrepreneurs may find it challenging to secure cash to cover start-up costs and everyday expenses such as payroll, utilities and rent for office space. "Entrepreneur" reports in its "How to Better Manage Your Cash Flow" article that, "The lag between the time you have to pay your suppliers and employees and the time you collect from your customers is the problem, and the solution is cash flow management." Should companies start losing profits due to events such as a decline in customer sales or lawsuit, entrepreneurs must find ways to strengthen business cash flows to keep their companies from becoming insolvent. For example, business owners might have to sell equipment, ask vendors to give them extensions on invoice due dates or borrow money from a bank.

(b) Time Away from Work: To meet demands for things such as developing new products, marketing business services and addressing customer complaints, entrepreneurs might work seven days a week. They also might work when they are ill. For example, Angel Wilkes, owner of Children's Party Plus, is reported in *"The Wall Street Journal's"* March 22, 2012 "Personal Time Gets Short Shrift" article as saying, "If I don't work, I don't eat." Taking time off from work may cost entrepreneurs money. For this reason, entrepreneurs might struggle to gain work/life balance. They also might put themselves at risk of becoming burned out or overly stressed due to work obligations.

(c) Succession Planning: Because entrepreneurs may not want to relinquish control of companies they spent years building, they might avoid selecting and training someone to replace them. As the *"Harvard Business Review's"* February 2008 "The Founder's Dilemma" article stated, "Four out of five entrepreneurs are forced to step down from the CEO's post. Most are shocked when investors insist that they relinquish control." Additionally, lack of succession planning can leave businesses at risk of being bought and taken over by competitors, especially if founders die before a successor has been identified and trained.

(d) Others are

The Dilemma of Survival: Can survival issues be identified?

The Dilemma of Ethics: Is honesty important to an entrepreneur?

The Dilemma of Cultural Diversity in the Workforce: Is diversity an issue in a small company?

The Dilemma of Harvest/Exit Strategy: Will I know when?

The Dilemma of Instinctual vs. Analytical Decision Making: How do entrepreneurs make successful decisions?

The Dilemma of Growth: Is growth good or bad and how will I know?

The Dilemma of Experience: Should I keep my day job?

The Dilemma of Partners: Can't live with them, can't live without them

The Dilemma of Money and Control: Owning a little of a lot or a lot of a little?

The Dilemma of Building a Team: Can engineers and scientists coexist with marketers and accountants?

7.7. THE SIX STYLES OF ENTREPRENEURIAL LEADERSHIP

Too much literature preaches "good management" as if it were a generic skill that comes in a plain white box. The reality is that there are all sorts of ways to manage and all of them can work. Entrepreneurs classically will recognize themselves in each of the following styles, or a combination of several styles. The challenge is to match your own style with the needs of the company.

Many entrepreneurs prefer to run their businesses single-handedly, to maximize their' independence. There are three ways to run a company without management assistance: the Classic, the Coordinator, and the Craftsman.

The Classic

This is the traditional entrepreneurial management style. It's also known as the "watch it all yourself" mode of operation. You hire people but you insist on tight, personal monitoring and supervision. And of course, you'll do all of the really critical jobs yourself.

If this is your style, you are probably unwilling to admit it. People criticize entrepreneurs for being unwilling to delegate. Management consultants contemptuously exhort entrepreneurs to reform their evil ways, to cure themselves of the neurotic need to supervise everything personally.

But this is a perfectly legitimate way to run a company — as long as you convince yourself somewhere along the line that it's OK to delegate, and that it's OK not to delegate. It's pretending to delegate that spells sure disaster for these types of leaders.

Because you think you are using team management, these types of leaders let the business become too big and too complex to run alone. So they hire managers to join their team, convinced they are empowering them with authority. Unfortunately, you don't really trust them, and hence, you keep yanking back the reins. Your subordinates quickly become disillusioned and the leader is left thinking "I just can't keep good people."

Confront the problems of this management style head on by deciding whether or not you are a leader who can delegate. If you cannot delegate, then by virtue of your decisions, you must limit the complexity of the business.

The Coordinator

An alternative to the classic style is the coordinator method, whereby leaders can run a fairly good-sized business with just a handful of employees. This type of business structure is sometimes called a "virtual corporation" and the essence of its style is that most of the sub-tasks are jobbed out. The leader does little more than organize the enterprise and verify that everything gets done.

In theory, this type of entrepreneur can job everything out: arrange for the product to be manufactured; get brokers and reps to sell it; hire an accounting firm to handle the books and sell your receivables to someone else to do the collections. In real life, however, even this type of entrepreneur has to do some of the work — so pick the parts you enjoy and sub the rest out.

A coordinator can grow a multi-million-dollar business without a single employee. If you're willing to have a few assistants, you can grow even bigger. So why isn't the coordinator style more popular? Theory has it that it has to do with the conservatism of most leaders — the plain fact that work is cheaper if produced in-house. That, however, is generally false economy.

One cardinal error is calculating costs without accounting for the value of time. It's true that it costs an entrepreneur "nothing" to say, solder circuit boards, but is that the best use of the time available? If you answered "yes" to that, read on.

The Craftsman

Craftsmen are leaders who maximize their control over business by doing everything themselves. Obviously this approach, like the classic approach, limits the size of the business. This style makes sense if the business' biggest concern is the quality of the output. It's an attitude characterized by craft types, although many entrepreneurs in other businesses also adopt this style.

There are advantages to doing everything: everything is done "right" because the expert does it; expenses are minimized; and operating without employees can simplify your life. The only problem with this rosy scenario is that the leader must do the tasks he or she likes, as well as the ones disliked. Advice for the craftsman: streamline your business and job out those tasks you don't like.

Focusing on Management Styles

In the end, all the single-leader styles impose limitations on the business. It cannot grow indefinitely unless a group of people shares in the authority and responsibility. For those leaders who feel most at home in single-style management, stay clear of large, growing businesses. Evaluate how large an operation you want to lead and follow your instincts toward success.

A tip: Most authors warn that entrepreneurs who take on too much tend to make bad decisions. But experience indicates a different symptom: if you take too much you will probably fail to make decisions. Period.

If you find that you are having trouble making up your mind — on business, personal or even trivial issues — chances are, you're suffering from decision overload. Delegate some authority, or simplify your operation. Neither of which is an easy task for this personality type.

Businesses beyond a certain size cannot be managed by a single person; a management team is required. What is the size limit? That depends on the complexity of the business. Manufacturing, particularly if it involves high technology, can be very complicated even on a small-scale.

A complex business needs a top management team in place, with several people, each of whom has decision making authority in a particular sphere. That means you have really delegated, saying in effect, "You make the decisions in this area. I will never overrule you; if I find one of your decisions truly unacceptable, I'll fire you."

The Entrepreneur + Employee Team

This leadership strategy gives the entrepreneur the most control within the big business leadership styles. Authority is delegated to key employees, with the understanding that final authority rests with the entrepreneur. Few start-ups can afford a host of high-level employees, most often leaders find themselves growing from the classic style into this mode of operation. It's company growth that most often forces the change.

That transition, however, is not as easy as it might appear. Don't hesitate to delegate: Do it all at once. This forces the transition, rather than muddling it over a longer period of time where people question your sincerity and are less apt to rise to the occasion. Be firm and explicit. Announce to one and all that the company has grown and is successful, so much so that the old ways of doing things won't work anymore. Point out the opportunities for promotion, and make an effort to promote from within.

The Small Partnership

This once-popular leadership style has all but disappeared among today's modern management techniques. However, it may be on the comeback. Leaders who adopt the small partnership style have considerably less control and autonomy in this type of structure, and they must share tactical decisions with one or more partners.

In compensation for this loss of control, small partners receive a substantial advantage: the assistance of others who, like you, have a real stake in the company and share your motivation to make it succeed in a way no employee can. Like you, they are hungry.

One of the most effective and widespread ways to organize a company around small partnership lines is to make it an "inside-outside" partnership. One partner takes all of the "inside" tasks—operations and management. The other partner handles marketing and sales. But even small partners eventually face the limit of their abilities and must decide to manage a dynamic firm that won't grow any larger—only better—or change.

The Big Team Venture

This style puts the leader right on the back of the tiger. Prepare before you saddle up. In addition to capital, you need a growth-company management team. Make sure the team you shepherd is good. You can't afford to skimp here. Cut corners with these tigers and you'll soon find yourself cutting out employment ads.

Regardless of your current management style, and the leadership style you desire to emulate, if you are considering changing your stripes, look to your past for guidance:

- When you were a kid, did you play sports?
- Are you a perfectionist?
- Do you have a history of trusting other people with good results?
- Did you stay up all night before the Senior Prom to adjust the final decorations after everyone else had called it a night?

Be honest, there are no right or wrong answers to these types of questions — they serve to illustrate your innate leadership style. Accept what you are and make the best of it.

7.8. COMPETITIVE ADVANTAGE[1]

The term competitive advantage is the ability gained through attributes and resources to perform at a higher level than others in the same industry or market (Christensen and Fahey 1984, Kay 1994, Porter 1980 cited by Chacarbaghi and Lynch 1999, p. 45) "A firm is said to have a competitive advantage when it is implementing a value creating strategy not simultaneously being implemented by any current or potential player" (Barney 1991 cited by Clulow, *et al.*, 2003). Successfully implemented strategies will lift a firm to superior performance by facilitating the firm with competitive advantage to outperform current or potential players (Passemard and Calantone 2000, p. 18). To gain competitive advantage a business strategy of a firm manipulates the various resources over which it has direct control and these resources have the ability to generate competitive advantage (Reed and Fillippi,1990, cited by Rijamampianina 2003, p. 362).

Competitive advantage occurs when an organization acquires or develops an attribute or combination of attributes that allows it to outperform its competitors. These attributes can include access to natural resources, such as high grade ores or inexpensive power, or access to highly trained and skilled personnel human resources. New technologies such as robotics and information technology can provide competitive advantage, whether as a part of the product itself, as an advantage to the making of the product, or as a competitive aid in the business process (for example, better identification and understanding of customers). The term competitive advantage is the ability gained through attributes and resources to perform at a higher level than others in the same industry or market (Christensen and Fahey, 1984, Kay 1994, Porter, 1980, cited by Chacarbaghi and Lynch, 1999).

7.9. VARIOUS COMPETITIVE STRATEGIES[2]

(a) Cost Leadership Strategy: The goal of Cost Leadership Strategy is to offer products or services at the lowest cost in the industry. The challenge of this strategy is to earn a suitable profit for the company, rather than operating at a loss and draining profitability from all market players. Companies such as Walmart succeed with this strategy by featuring low prices on key items on which customers are price-aware, while selling other merchandise at less aggressive discounts. Products are to be created at the lowest cost in the industry. An example is to use space in stores for sales and not for storing excess product.

(b) Differentiation Strategy: The goal of Differentiation Strategy is to provide a variety of products, services, or features to consumers that competitors are not yet offering or are unable to offer. This gives a direct advantage to the company which is able to provide a unique product or service that none of its competitors is able to offer. An example is Dell which launched mass-customizations on computers to fit consumers' needs. This allows the company to make its first product to be the star of it's sales.

(c) Innovation Strategy: The goal of Innovation Strategy is to leapfrog other market players via the introduction of completely new or notably better products or services. This strategy is typical of technology start-up companies which often intend to "disrupt" the existing marketplace, obsoleting the current market entries with a breakthrough product offering. It is harder for more established companies to pursue this strategy because their product offering has achieved market acceptance. Apple has been a notable example of using this strategy with its introduction of iPod personal music players, and iPad tablets. Many companies invest heavily in their research and development department to achieve such statuses with their innovations.

(d) Operational Effectiveness Strategy: The goal of Operational Effectiveness as a strategy is to perform internal business activities better than competitors, making the company easier or more pleasurable to do business with than other market choices. It improves the characteristics of the company while lowering the time it takes to get the products on the market with a great start. State Farm Insurance pursues this strategy by promoting their agents as "good neighbors" who actively help customers.

7.10. SUSTAINING COMPETITIVENESS

Sustainable competitive advantage is the focal point of your corporate strategy. It allows the maintenance and improvement of your enterprise's competitive position in the market. It is an advantage that enables business to survive against its competition over a long period of time. It includes how to survive against your competition over a long period of time and succeed in business. Sustainable competitive advantage is the prolonged benefit of implementing some unique value-creating strategy based on unique combination of internal organizational resources and capabilities that cannot be replicated by competitors.

[3]Core competency is also very important in order to have sustainable competitive advantage. A core competency results from a specific set of skills or production techniques that deliver additional value to the customer. Such competences enable an organization to access a wide variety of markets. Executives should estimate the future challenges and opportunities of the business in order to stay on top of the game in varying situations. In an article from 1990, titled "The Core Competence of the Corporation", Prahalad and Hamel illustrate that core competencies lead to the development of core products which further can be used to build many products for end users. Core competencies are developed through the process of continuous improvements over the period of time rather than a single large change. For an organization to be competitive, it needs not only tangible resources but intangible resources like core competences that are difficult and challenging to achieve.

For example, Microsoft has expertise in many IT-based innovations where, for a variety of reasons, it is difficult for competitors to replicate or compete with Microsoft's core competences.

Other examples

***Case in Point:* Warren Buffet's Investment Criteria**

When asked what is the most important thing he looks for when evaluating a company to invest in, without hesitation, Warren Buffet replied, "Sustainable competitive advantage. It is the future growth and prosperity of the company, not its current price, that is most important. A company's prosperity, in turn, is driven by how powerful and enduring its competitive advantages are." Sustainable competitive advantage gives a company the edge that keeps competitors at bay and reap extraordinary growth and profits. "The key to investing is determining the competitive advantage of any given company and, above all, the durability of that advantage. The products or services that have wide, sustainable moats around them are the ones that deliver rewards to investors."

Detail of core competences

1. They should make a disproportional contribution to stakeholder value
2. They should open doors to other opportunities

3. They should represent such a unique blend of tacit and explicit knowledge that it cannot be copied by others

E.g.:- **Amazon.com**

New business model developed by Amazon.com creates value for customers by offering a synergistic combination of the following benefits:

1. Shopping convenience
2. Ease of purchase
3. Speed
4. Decision-enabling information
5. A wide selection
6. Discounted pricing
7. Reliability of order fulfillment

No single aspect of Amazon.com's business model is sufficient to create a sustainable competitive advantage. It is the synergistic combination of all of these information services and logistical processes that creates value for customers and comprise Amazon.com's competitive advantage

E.g.:- **Walt Disney World Parks and Resorts**

Walt Disney World Parks and Resorts has three main core competencies:

- Animatronics and Show Design
- Storytelling, Story Creation and Themed Atmospheric Attractions
- Efficient operation of theme parks

7.11. NEW PATH TO SUSTAINABLE COMPETITIVE ADVANTAGE

How are today's firm reacting to the challenge? The response has been dramatic. A veritable cornucopia of new strategic initiatives have preoccupies executives time over the past decade. These include right sizing, unbundling, focusing on core businesses while divesting others, business process reengineering, total quality management, team work and many more. Meanwhile, major companies have found themselves eliminating millions of jobs, closing plants and moving operations to low-cost countries and attempting to become "Lean and Mean". Yet they continue to struggle.

There are important lessons to be learnt from this. First of all, turbulence in the external environment is causing a fundamental transformation on the internal operations of companies. Or, more simply put, external change forces internal change. Second, there is no simple formula for success in the new competitive environment. It is all about experimentation, as management looks for right structure, approach to control, leadership style and way to reward employees. Thirdly, there is an important upside to external environments as they become more complex, dynamic and hostile. Turbulence also mean opportunity. That is, change in markets, technologies, regulations and other areas. Market fragmentation also means new market segments are appearing, new technologies create new company capabilities, a regulatory change results in some sort of new need and so on. While some companies focus only on defending themselves against treats, other understand that there is a new opportunity to be found behind every threat.

But what is the real quest as managers sort through the various theories, concepts and new techniques and tools? The answer is and always will be sustainable competitive advantage. But the rules have changes here as well. Traditionally, competitive advantage was achieved by having lower cost than the competition, achieving higher quality or product performance, adding a new product feature or delivering better customer service. Unfortunately, this game of" one-upmanship" can no longer produce sustainable advantage. Whatever one firm does in these areas is quickly matched by the other firms. Moreover to be successful in any industry today, firm must continually reduce cost, improve quality, enhance customer service and so forth. Such continuous improvement is a minimal criterion for remaining in the competitive game. Remanining competitive is very different from achieving sustainable competitive advantage. The quest for competitive advantage requires that companies and the managers within them continually reinvent themselves. Specifically, we believe advantage drives from five key company capabilities. These includes:

(a) Adaptability: The ability to adjust on a timely basis to new technologies, cutomer needs, regulatory rules and other changes in conditions without losing focus or causing significant disruption of core operations and commitments.

(b) Flexibility: The ability to design company strategies, processes and operational approaches that can simultaneously meet the diverse and evolving requirements of customers, distributors, suppliers, financers and other stake holders.

(c) Speed: The ability to act quickly on emerging opportunities, to develop new products and services more rapidly and to make critical operational decisions without lengthy deliberations

(d) Aggressiveness: An intense, focused and proactive approach to eliminating competitors, delighting customers and growing employees.

(e) Innovativeness: A continuous priority placed on developing and launching new products, services, processes, markets, technologies and on leading the marketplace.

Firms that are more adaptable,flexible, fast aggressive and innovative are better positioned not only to adjust to a dynamic, threatening and complex external environment, but to create a change in that environment.They do not take external environment as a given, and instead of following them, creating new markets, and rewriting the rules of the competitive game. Entrepreneurship is the core source of sustainable advantage.

7.12. PORTER'S FIVE FORCES MODEL OF COMPETITIVE ADVANTAGE[3]

Michael Eugene Porter is the author of 18 books and numerous articles including *Competitive Strategy*, *Competitive Advantage*, *Competitive Advantage of Nations*, and *On Competition*. Michael Porter's core field is competition and company strategy. He is generally recognized as the father of the modern strategy field.

According to Porter, Competitive advantage occurs when an organization acquires or develops an attribute or combination of attributes that allows it to outperform its competitors. These attributes can include access to natural resources, such as high grade ores or inexpensive power, or access to highly trained and skilled personnel human resources. New technologies such as robotics and information technology can provide competitive advantage, whether as a part of the product itself, as an advantage to the making of the product, or as a competitive aid in the business process (for example, better identification and understanding of customers). Porter five forces analysis is a framework for industry analysis and business strategy development. It draws upon industrial organization (IO) economics to derive five forces that determine the competitive intensity and therefore attractiveness of a market. Attractiveness in this context refers to the overall industry profitability. Three of Porter's five forces refer to competition from external sources. The remainder are internal threats. These are:

1. **Threat of new entrants:** Profitable markets that yield high returns will attract new firms. This results in many new entrants, which eventually will decrease profitability for all firms in the industry. New entrants adds capacity, inflate cost and reduce profitability. Unless the entry of new firms can be blocked by incumbents, the abnormal profit rate will trend towards zero (perfect competition).

- The existence of barriers to entry (patents, rights, etc.) The most attractive segment is one in which entry barriers are high and exit barriers are low. Few new firms can enter and non-performing firms can exit easily.
- Economies of product differences
- Brand equity
- Switching costs or sunk costs
- Capital requirements
- Expected retaliation
- Access to distribution
- Customer loyalty to established brands
- Absolute cost
- Industry profitability; the more profitable the industry, the more attractive it will be to new competitors.

Threat of new entrants, sources. (1) Economies of scale, (2) Product differentiation, (3) Cost disadvantages independent of size, (4) Access to distribution channels, (5) Government policy.

2. Threat of substitute products or services: The existence of products outside of the realm of the common product boundaries increases the propensity of customers to switch to alternatives. For example, tap water might be considered a substitute for Coke, whereas Pepsi is a competitor's similar product. Increased marketing for drinking tap water might "shrink the pie" for both Coke and Pepsi, whereas increased Pepsi advertising would likely "grow the pie" (increase consumption of all soft drinks), albeit while giving Pepsi a larger slice at Coke's expense. Another example is the substitute of traditional phone with VoIP phone.

- Buyer propensity to substitute
- Relative price performance of substitute
- Buyer switching costs
- Perceived level of product differentiation
- Number of substitute products available in the market
- Ease of substitution. Information-based products are more prone to substitution, as online product can easily replace material product.
- Substandard product
- Quality depreciation

3. Bargaining power of customers (buyers) : The bargaining power of customers is also described as the market of outputs: the ability of customers to put the firm under pressure, which also affects the customer's sensitivity to price changes.

- Buyer concentration to firm concentration ratio
- Degree of dependency upon existing channels of distribution
- Bargaining leverage, particularly in industries with high fixed costs
- Buyer switching costs relative to firm switching costs
- Buyer information availability
- Force down prices
- Availability of existing substitute products
- Buyer price sensitivity
- Differential advantage (uniqueness) of industry products
- RFM (customer value) Analysis

4. Bargaining power of suppliers: The bargaining power of suppliers is also described as the market of inputs. Suppliers of raw materials, components, labor, and services (such as expertise) to the firm can be a source of power over the firm, when there are few substitutes. Suppliers may refuse to work with the firm, or, e.g., charge excessively high prices for unique resources.

- Supplier switching costs relative to firm switching costs
- Degree of differentiation of inputs
- Impact of inputs on cost or differentiation
- Presence of substitute inputs
- Strength of distribution channel
- Supplier concentration to firm concentration ratio
- Employee solidarity (e.g., labor unions)
- Supplier competition - ability to forward vertically integrate and cut out the BUYER

E.g. if you are making biscuits and there is only one person who sells flour, you have no alternative but to buy it from him.

5. Intensity of competitive rivalry: For most industries, the intensity of competitive rivalry is the major determinant of the competitiveness of the industry.

- Sustainable competitive advantage through innovation
- Competition between online and offline companies
- Level of advertising expense
- Powerful competitive strategy
- Firm concentration ratio

7.13. CONDITIONS FOR SUSTAINING COMPETITIVENESS

(a) Distinctive Capabilities: Distinctive capabilities are the basis of your competitive advantage. According to the new resource-based view of the company, sustainable competitive advantage is achieved by continuously developing existing and creating new resources and capabilities in response to rapidly changing market conditions. Among these resources and capabilities, in the new economy, knowledge represents the most important value-creating asset.

The opportunity for your company to sustain your competitive advantage is determined by your capabilities of two kinds – distinctive capabilities and reproducible capabilities — and their unique combination you create to achieve synergy. Your distinctive capabilities — the characteristics of your company which cannot be replicated by competitors, or can only be replicated with great difficulty — are the basis of your sustainable competitive advantage. Distinctive capabilities can be of many kinds: patents, exclusive licenses, strong brands, effective leadership, teamwork, or tacit knowledge. Reproducible capabilities are those that can be bought or created by your competitors and thus by themselves cannot be a source of competitive advantage.

(b) Leadership: Leadership is the necessary condition for long-term competitiveness. In particular in the knowledge economy, what is proving to be most effective is "the emerging style of value — based leadership, both as motivation for constant innovation up and down all organization levels and as a source of unity and coherence across fragmented firm boundaries." Harnessing your abilities to lead through the power of intellect, will, persistence, and vision creates synergies that propel successful companies in the quest for, and achievement of, competitive advantage.

(c) Systemic Innovation: Innovation used to be a linear trajectory from new knowledge to new product. Now innovation is neither singular nor linear, but systemic. It arises from complex interactions between many individuals, organizations and environmental factors. Firms which are successful in realizing the full returns from their technologies and innovations are able to match their technological developments with complementary expertise in other areas of their business, such as manufacturing, distribution, human resources, marketing, and customer relationships.

(d) Radical Innovation: Long-term corporate success linked to the ability to innovate. Although corporate investment in improvements to existing products and processes does bring growth, it is new game changing breakthroughs that will launch company into new markets, enable rapid growth, and create high return on investment.

(e) Customers for Life: The two most important words to keep in mind in developing a successful customer base are Positioning and Differentiation. Differentiation refers to your ability to separate yourself and your product or service from that of your competitors. And it is the key to building and maintaining a competitive advantage. This is the advantage that you and your company have over your competitors in the same marketplace – the unique and special benefits that no one else can give your customer.

(f) Corporate Culture as a Fundamental Competitive Advantage: The strength of your organizational culture is one of the most fundamental competitive advantages. If you can build and preserve an innovation-adept culture, a culture of commitment, one where employees passionately pursue your organization's cause and mission, you will be better positioned for success.

(g) Leveraging Opposite Forces: You can find a strategic competitive advantage in an organizational and cultural context by seeking to leverage, rather than diminish, opposite forces. "An important but widely overlooked principle of the business success is that integrating opposites, as opposed to identifying them as inconsistencies and driving them out, unleashes power. This is true on both a personal level and on organizational level as well." To be successful in today's complex, rapidly changing and highly competitive world, you must embrace and manage critical opposites.

(h) Cross-Functional Excellence: Although innovation is driven by technology, required competence extends beyond technical know-how. In the new knowledge economy and knowledge-based enterprises, systemic innovative solutions arise from complex interactions between many individuals, organizations and environmental factors. The boundaries between products and services fade rapidly too. If you wish to be a market leader today, you must be able to integrate in a balanced way different types of know-how that would transform stand-alone technologies, products and services into a seamless, value-rich solution.

7.14. TYPES OF COMPETITIVE ADVANTAGE

There are three parts of competitive advantage:-

(a) Basic competitive advantage: This is like the entry ticket for entrepreneur to the global hyper competition game. It implies product / service with internationally competitive quality, cost and after sale serveice.

(b) Revealed competitive advantage: This is the advantage which is reflected by the market share of the entrepreneur in the market.

(c) Sustainable competitive advantage: This allows the enterprise for the maintenance and improvement of enterprise's competitive position in the market.

7.15. FIVE CRITERIA OF SUSTAINABLE COMPETITIVE ADVANTAGE

1. Unique
2. Difficult to replicate

3. Superior to competition
4. Sustainable
5. Applicable to multiple situations

7.16. MAINTAINING COMPETITIVE ADVANTAGE

1. Balanced approach to business system i.e proper balance between customer, innovation, finance and process and increase stakeholder value.

2. Managing change and moving with speed

3. Competitive and differentiation strategies

4. Visionary and daring growth strategies

5. Wining organization and people.

6. Radical Innovation, it is new game changing breakthroughs that will launch company into new markets, enable rapid growth, and create high return on investment. Radical innovation, concerned with exploration of new technology, is fundamentally different from incremental innovation that is concerned with exploitation of existing technology. "Radical innovation is a product, process, or service with either unprecedented performance features or familiar features that offer potential for significant improvements in performance and cost." It creates such a dramatic change in processes, products, or services that they transform existing markets or industries, or create new ones.

7.17. SKILLS OF EFFECTIVE COMPETITOR

Knowing: the ability to get hard information.

Vision: the ability to foresee the future.

Action: the ability to move or stay where we are.

Positioning: the ability to use the ground to find success

7.18. SUMMARY

Entrepreneurship is the creation of value through the pursuit of opportunity. The ability to seek new ways of doing things and to systematically exploit opportunities is fundamental for management in all forms of organization. Entrepreneurs take risks and are innovative, opportunistic, creative, flexible, dynamic and growth-oriented. Entrepreneurs can also be classified as opportunity-driven or necessity-driven. Individuals who perceive a business idea and pursue it as a career option willingly, are opportunity driven entrepreneurs. However, in some cases, entrepreneurship might stem from the need to be entrepreneurial. Due to the absence of other career options or a lack of satisfactory options, some individuals are forced to become entrepreneurs. These days many young person are opting entrepreneurs as career. Such individuals are called necessity-driven entrepreneurs. Entrepreneurs are known for innovation and creativity and in order to compete they have to maintain and sustain competetiveness through various means.

7.19. SELF ASSESSMENT QUESTIONS

1. Explain Entrepreneurship as career.
2. What do you mean by mid career dilemmas?
3. What are the conditions for Sustaining Competitiveness?

SOURCES/NOTES

1. http://en.wikipedia.org/wiki/Competitive_advantage
2. http://en.wikipedia.org/wiki/Competitive_advantage
3. Prahalad, C.K. and Hamel, G. (1990) The core competence of the corporation, *Harvard Business Review* (v. 68, no. 3) pp. 79–91.

Others

Entreprenurship and Innovation:Satayabir Bhattacharyya,

Competitive Disruption: R. D'Adveni, Author of *Hypercompetition (http://www.1000advices.com/guru/strategy_competition_disruption_adveni.html)*

Passemard; Calantone (2000), *Competitive Advantage: Creating and Sustaining Superior Performance by Michael E. Porter 1980.*

8

ENTREPRENEURSHIP AND INNOVATION: OPPORTUNITY ANALYSIS

8.1. INTRODUCTION

Innovation refers to do new things or to do the things that are already done but in new ways. Innovation involves introduction of new products, creation of new markets, application of new method of production, discovery of new and better sources of raw material and developing a new and better form of industrial organization. It also include the development of new customers value through solutions that meet new needs, inarticulate needs, or old customer and market needs in value adding new ways. This is accomplished through more effective products, processes, services, technologies, or ideas that are readily available to markets, governments, and society. The word innovation derives from the Latin word *innovates*, which is the noun form of *innovare* "to renew or change".

Over the last decades, innovation has become more globalized; therefore, the importance of innovation as a driver of competitive advantage in economies has increasingly grown. Innovation matters because it can deliver better products and services, new and more efficient production processes, and improved business performance. For consumers, innovation means higher quality and better value goods, more efficient services and higher standards of living . For business organizations, it means sustained and improved growth because it delivers higher profits. For employees, innovation has a meaning of new and more interesting work, better skills and higher wages. For the economy as a whole innovation is the key to higher productivity and greater prosperity for all. (DTI, 2003).

8.2. MEANING

To be called an innovation, an idea must be replicable at an economical cost and must satisfy a specific need. Innovation involves deliberate application of information, imagination and initiative in deriving greater or different values from resources, and includes all processes by which new ideas are generated and converted into useful products. In business, innovation often results when ideas are applied by the company in order to further satisfy the needs and expectations of the customers. In a social context, innovation helps create new methods for alliance creation, joint venturing, flexible work hours, and creation of buyers' purchasing power. Innovation has been studied in a variety of contexts, including in relation to technology, commerce, social systems, economic development, and policy construction. Therefore, there is a wide range of approaches to conceptualizing innovation in the scholarly literature. Much of the current business literature associates the concept of innovation with value creation, value extraction and operational execution. In this view, an innovation is not an innovation until someone successfully implements an idea, creates value and makes profit.

Innovations are divided into two broad categories:

1. Evolutionary innovations (continuous or dynamic evolutionary innovation) that are brought about by many incremental advances in technology or processes and
2. Revolutionary innovations (also called discontinuous innovations) which are often disruptive and new.

Innovation is synonymous with risk taking and organizations that create revolutionary products or technologies take on the greatest risk because they create new markets.

8.3. DEFINITIONS OF INNOVATION

A convenient definition of innovation is provided by **Luecke and Katz (2003)**. According to them, innovation is generally understood as the introduction of a new thing or method . . . It is the embodiment, combination, or synthesis of knowledge in original, relevant, valued new products, processes or services.

1. According to John Emmerling "Innovation is creativity with a job to do"

2. According to Braden Kelley, "Innovation transforms the useful seeds of invention into solutions valued above every existing alternative."

3. According to Robert Bastarache, "Value + Creativity + Execution = Innovation."

4. According to Lars Christensen , "Innovation is to dare to challenge mainstream thinking and behaviour pattern."

5. According to Hutch Carpenter, "A change in a product offering, service, business model or operations which meaningfully improves the experience of a large number of stakeholders"

6. According to A Michele Davies, "The creation of new products or services which provide value to my marketplace in one form or another, and which use my existing resources."

Definitions—Innovation and Entrepreneurship

1. According to J. Schumpeter: "An entrepreneur is basically an innovator as he introduces something new in the economy. An entrepreneur in Schumpeter's view is one who carries new combinations of means of production such as:—

(a) The introduction of new goods, that is, one with which consumers are not yet familier, new quality of goods;

(b) The introduction of new method of method of production, that is, one not yet tested by experience in the branch of manufacture concerned, which need by no means be founded upon a discovery significantly new, and also exist in a way of handling in commodity commercially;

(c) The opening of new market, that is market into which that particular branch of manufacture of the company in question has not previously entered ,irrespective of whether or not this market has existed before.

(d) The conquest of a new source of raw materials or half.

8.4. CHARACTERISTICS OF INNOVATION IN ENTREPRENEURSHIP

1. Introduction of new product with which customers are not yet familiar or introduction of new variant of an existing product.
2. Introduction of new method of production that has not yet been tested.
3. Opening of new markets.
4. Discovery of new source of raw material
5. Carrying of new organization.

8.5. TYPES OF INNOVATION[1]

Type	Description	Examples
Invention	Totally new product, service, or process	Wright brothers—airplane Thomas Edison—lightbulb Alexander Graham Bell—telephone
Extension	New use or different application of an already existing product, service or process.	Ray Kroc—McDonald's Nolan Bushnell— Atari Kemmons Wilson—Holiday Inn
Duplication	Creative replication of an existing concept.	Wal-Mart—Department stores Gateway—Personal computers Pizza Hut—Pizza parlor
Synthesis	Combination of existing concepts and factors into a new formulation or use.	Fred Smith—Federal Express Merrill Lynch—Home equity financing

8.6. SOURCES OF INNOVATION

Peter Drucker, one of the greatest management thinkers from the last century, defined in his book *"Innovation and Entrepreneurship"* (1986) 7 classes of "**Opportunities**". He named these the "**Sources of innovation**", namely:

1. The Unexpected Occurrance

Sometimes unexpected success or failure prove to be a major innovation.These happings are normally unplanned. An example of the unexpected is the development of Nutrasweet. A chemist developed a new chemical. Accidentally he got some of it in his mouth. To his surprise it tasted very sweet. This was the start of a development trajectory, that took many years before Nutrasweet was introduced by Searle into the market.

2. Incongruities

Incongruities means conflicts between opposing functions, i.e., difference exists between the expectations and reality. It may be the start of an innovation.

3. Process Needs

An old proverb says that "necessity is the mother of invention". So innovation takes place due to the demand of the situation.

4. Industry and Market Structure

Industry markets and market structure may offer opportunity's for new types of services. Outsourcing of activities such as maintenance of the IT infrastructure is an example. Other examples are the merging of industry's such as for example the merging of the computer industry with consumer electronics or IT with business consulting services. The X box of Microsoft is just one example from many.

5. Demographics

Demographics have long been a major source of innovation creating opportunities for new types of products and services. It includes changes in lifestyle, population, education, etc., helps in innovation.

6. Changes in Perception

An example of changes in perception as source of innovation is the following. In older days health was seen as related to body mass, meaning fatter people were perceived as more healthy. In the last century this perception changed as a result of medical study's that revealed that overweight was a risk factor. Since that time many light products have come to the market. Many substitutes of sugar have been developed such as Nutrasweet. Also substitutes of fat have been developed although these have not been successfully introduced into the market yet.

7. New Knowledge

Last but not least new knowledge has produced many opportunities for new products. The emergence of micro-electronics and new programming methods and tools, biotechnology, nano-technology, etc., have been the main motors of innovation and progress over the last decades.

8.7. INNOVATION VS. INVENTION

Invention means to come up with a unique idea, thought or fabrication; a new object, device or process that no one has seen or heard of before. An **invention** is a unique or novel device, method, composition or process. It may be an improvement upon a machine or product, or a new process for creating an object. On the other hand innovation refers to application of inventions. Innovation differs from invention in that innovation refers to the use of a better and, as a result, novel idea or method, whereas invention refers more directly to the creation of the idea or method itself.

So, invention is conceiving new ideas while innovation means to put these ideas into action. An important distinction is normally made between invention and innovation that Invention is the first occurrence of an idea for a new product or process while innovation is the first attempt to carry it out into practice. Therefore in order to be inventive, one has to be creative and in order to become an innovator, one has to be an entrepreneur.

8.8. BARRIERS TO INNOVATION[2]

1. Lack of self-confidence

Lack of confidence always act as biggest limitation in innovation. A person who is not confident either cannot do any kind of innovation or cannot put forwards his/her innovation (i.e., cannot commercialize the innovation). So only a person who believe in himself/herself can take risk and think something new and innovative.

2. Inadequate funding

Getting the start-up funds for an innovation often means taking money away from an established program. Getting the money at just the right time is also problematic since organizations often work on annual funding cycles that do not match up well with real world opportunities. And many an excellent innovation needs more than seed money to survive and is starved out of existence. But broader thinking on needs and resources can help innovators move their ideas along.

3. Time commitments

Time is a scarce and precious commodity. One of management's jobs is to verify that minutes are productively filled. And while enlightened management will invest some of workers' on-the-job time in education, experimentation, relationships, personal growth and health, it's difficult to prove that such investments pay-off. Even worse, such investments may not pay-off in a timely way (for example, quick enough for returns to be apparent through a quarterly measurement) for a sponsoring organization. But increasing the value, benefits and urgency of an innovation will tend to free up time for work on it.

4. Risk avoidance

Most of us won't run toward risks. We want to maintain our health, wealth and peace of mind. But no progress is made without calculated risk taking. Since people know that innovation is risky, many people run away from it. In fact, some organizations habitually play the game of finding things that could go wrong. Many of the classic responses ("We've never done this before"; "This failed when we tried it before") come up almost as a reflex. Once risks are identified, innovation is often stopped. But a clear-eyed view of risks balanced against benefits can create an environment where innovation is nurtured rather than killed.

5. Siloing

Organizations seek to protect create their identities, get proper credit, sustain themselves and protect themselves. That's why they create boundaries, assign responsibilities and put rules in place. No matter how artificial the divisions and processes are, they are usually defended – even when ignoring them is to everyone's advantage. By nature, innovations tend to cross boundaries and create new categories. It's not unusual to see competing claims of ownership and disputes about authority. Deals break down over who will run things and how imagined profits will be divided. As a result, innovations that might benefit the whole enterprise are killed by organizations that don't benefit themselves.

6. Incorrect measures

For many organizations, revenue, profits and market share are the only measures used. These are easier to quantify than intangibles such as reputation, knowledge, attractiveness to talent, leadership and other assets that make major contributions to the true value of an enterprise. Most innovations that matter are difficult to explain in terms of return on investment (ROI). Even those innovations that have the potential to disrupt or create new markets may suffer by comparison when put up against more pedestrian projects as they grind through a standard budgeting process. But by expanding the view of measures and including decision makers in the process of creating new measures, it's often possible to avoid the ROI trap.

7. Rigidity in Manager's thinking

The most common barrier to innovation in organization is a leader or manager that is not open to new ideas. This negatively impacts the team by discouraging creative thoughts. Employees won't be motivated to come up with new ideas if nobody is going to bother listening to them. There are also managers who listen to ideas but are reluctant to take them any further, resulting in lost opportunities.

8.9. INNOVATION AND ENTREPRENEURSHIP

Innovation is the development of new customers value through solutions that meet new needs, inarticulate needs, or old customer and market needs in value adding new ways. This is accomplished through more effective products, processes, services, technologies, or ideas that are readily available to markets, governments, and society. The word innovation derives from the Latin word *innovates*, which is the noun form of *innovare* "to renew or change,"

To be called an innovation, an idea must be replicable at an economical cost and must satisfy a specific need. Innovation involves deliberate application of information, imagination and initiative in deriving greater or different values from resources, and includes all processes by which new ideas are generated and converted into useful products. In business, innovation often results when ideas are applied by the company in order to further satisfy the needs and expectations of the customers.

In a social context, innovation helps create new methods for alliance creation, joint venturing, flexible work hours, and creation of buyers' purchasing power. Innovations are divided into two broad categories:

(1) Evolutionary innovations (continuous or dynamic evolutionary innovation) that are brought about by many incremental advances in technology or processes and

(2) revolutionary innovations (also called discontinuous innovations) which are often disruptive and new.

Innovation is synonymous with risk-taking and organizations that create revolutionary products or technologies take on the greatest risk because they create new markets.

8.10. INNOVATION AND CREATIVITY[3]

Innovation typically involves creativity; however, it is not only identical to it. It involves proactive proceeding on the creative ideas to make salient and tangible difference in the domain in which the innovation occurs. For example, Amabile, *et al.,* (1996) state that all innovations begin with creative ideas. They define innovation as the successful implementation of creative ideas within an organization. In this view, creativity by individuals and teams is a starting point for innovation; the first is necessary but not sufficient condition for the second. Innovation is defined as a successful exploitation of new ideas. Creativity is the ability to develop new ideas and to discover new ways of looking at problems and opportunities and Innovation is the ability to apply creative solutions to those problems and opportunities to enhance or enrich people's lives. Ideas may be entirely new to the market or involve the application of existing ideas that are new to the innovating organization or often a combination of both. Innovation involves the creation of new designs, concepts and ways of doing things, their commercial exploitation, and subsequent diffusion through the rest of the economy and society (Wickham, 2006). Most innovations are incremental – a succession of individually modest improvements to products or services over their life cycle. However, a few will be dramatic, creating entirely new industries or markets (Brockhoff and Chakrabarti, 1999).

A key challenge in innovation is making the innovation to occur because something more than the generation of a creative idea or insight is required. For this purpose, the insight must be put into action to make a significant difference, resulting for example in new or altered business processes within the organization, or changes in the products and services provided.

8.11. CREATIVITY AND THE BUSINESS IDEA

Creativity is the ability to bring something new into existence. Being creative means solving a problem in a new way, taking risks and ignoring doubt and facing fears. So it is an important attribute of a successful entrepreneur. Creativity can also be defined "as the process of producing something that is both original and worthwhile". Creativity and innovation are considered to be inseparable from entrepreneurship, which is in turn manifested in the act of starting up and running an enterprise. DO IT is a **process** for creativity. DO IT is an acronym that stands for:

D – Define problem

O – Open mind and apply creative techniques

I – Identify best solution

T – Transform

According to Torrance," Creativity is a process of sensing gaps or disturbing, missing elements, forming ideas of hypothesis concerning them, testing these hypothesis, and communicating the results possibly and retesting the hypothesis."

Entrepreneurs implement creative ideas to introduce innovative products or services, or to deliver products or services in a new, more efficient, and hence innovative way.

8.12. STAGES OF CREATIVE PROCESS[4]

Following are steps of the creative process:-

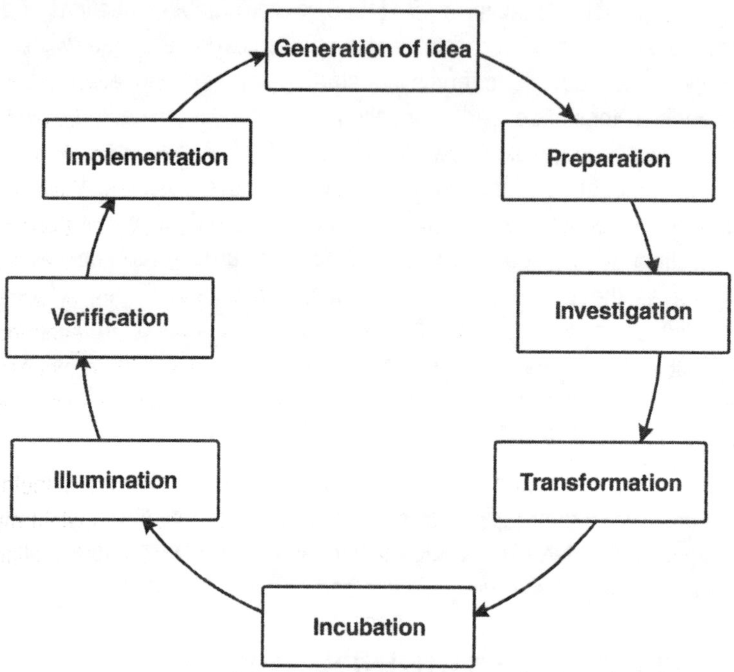

Fig. 8.1

1. Generation of Idea — Generation of idea is the start of any creative process. Ideas can be generated from various sources and most creative ideas come out of individual's interest or curiosity.

2. Preparation — This step involves getting the mind ready for creative thinking.Prepration might includes formal education, on the job training, work experience and taking advantage of other learning opportunities. This training and education provides foundation for creativity and innovation. During the stage of preparation, regulated thought is employed. This is a logical stage of examination and preparation. This is the time for research, fact gathering, assembling materials, gathering needed information before the creative act.

3. Investigation— It is a stage in which the problem is investigated. This step requires one to develop a solid understanding of the problem, situation or decision at hand. To create new ideas and concepts in a particular field, an individual first must study the problem and understand its basic components. Creative thinking comes about when people make careful observations of the world around them and then investigate the way things work.

4. Transformation —Transformation involves viewing the similarities and the differences among the information collected. This phase requires two types of thinking — Convergent and divergent. **Convergent thinking** is the ability to see the similarities and the connections among various and often diverse data and events. **Divergent thinking** is the ability to see the differences among various data and events. E.g.:-Physicist Bruce Middleton used convergent thinking to develop the idea for the award winning Flybar, the highest flying pogo stick in the world.

5. Incubation — It is a stage in which the problem is thought about unconsciously. This is the period of gestation, of letting go so that the mind, the unconscious, intuition, and emotion can mull over the information and put it into its own original perspective. Dreaming and relaxing may be a part of this period. Incubation occurs while the individual is away from the problems,often engaging in some totally unrelated activity.

6. Illumination — It is a stage in which ideas come together to form a possible solution. In the illumination stage, ideas arise from the mind to provide the basis of a creative response. These ideas can be pieces of the whole, i.e. seeing the entire concept or entity all at once. In this stage, all of the previous stages come together to produce the "Eureka Factor" – the creation of the innovative idea. Unlike the other stages, illumination is often very brief, involving a tremendous rush of insights within a few minutes or hours.

7. Verification — For entrepreneurs, validating an idea as accurate and useful may include conducting experiments ,running simulations, test marketing ,building prototypes and engaging in many other activities designed to verify that the new idea will work and practical to implement. It is a stage in which result is evaluated and deemed acceptable. Verification is the development stage. This is often tedious and requires perseverance by an individual committed to finding a way to harvest the practical results of his/ her creation.

8. Implementation — This step transform the idea into reality. Plenty of people come up with creative idea for promising new products or services, but most never take them beyond the idea stage. This helps in the proper implementation of idea and makes them true.

8.13. BUSINESS IDEA

A business idea is a concept which can be used for commercial purposes. It typically centers around a commodity or service that can be sold for money, according to a unique model. There are several methods for developing and testing a business idea. The ability to come up with a business idea can be transformed into a viable business, where ideas supported by feasibility and a business plan can then be sold to interested investors, firms, and interested parties for a lump sum or a management contract, or as agreed. Business ideas are always available through different sources; however, it is the application applied on these ideas, and timing makes all the difference in failure or success.

8.13.1 Sources of Business Idea

1. Consumers: Potential entrepreneurs should continually pay close attention to potential customers as it act as very good source of business idea. There must be proper arrangement so that the consumer must get the opportunity to express their opinion. But care should be taken to ensure that the idea or need represent a large enough market to support a new venture.

2. Existing Product and Services: Potential entrepreneurs should monitor and evaluate competitive product and services in the market. These analysis uncovers ways to improve an offerings that may result in a new product or service that has more market appeal.

3. Distribution Channels: Distribution channel act as very good source of business idea as they are familiar with the needs of the market.These channels frequently give suggestions for completely new product and also help in marketing the entrepreneur's newly developed products.

4. Federal Government: Sometimes new product ideas come in response to government regulation. E.g.:- Restriction on polythene bags by government give new ideas to entrepreneurs to make eco friendly bags or paper bags from sugarcane waste.

5. Research and development: The largest source of new idea is the entrepreneur's own "research and development". The research and development department of the organization continuously work on the generation of new idea , checking the feasibility of the idea and testing the same.

6. Unfulfilled Market demand: Unfulfilled demand of a product will open the door for new products, i.e., need of the market always act as a very good source of business idea.

7. Social and Economic trends: Social and Economic status of people is always dynamic in nature and offer wide opportunities.An entrepreneur should observe such change as it act as very good source for business idea.

8. Environmental scanning: One technique that entrepreneurs can use to generate ideas is environmental scanning, the screening of large amounts of information to detect emerging trends. Here are some "ideas" to stimulate your own idea creation by scanning the world around you: Read your local and other major metropolitan newspapers. Read popular consumer and news magazines; review the fiction and nonfiction best-seller lists; review government and consumer publications; subscribe to relevant trade publications; pay attention to commercials; watch and review top primetime television shows; browse through the magazine section of a bookstore; walk through a local shopping mall to see what's there; and so forth. The challenge of this method is not having too little information to scan; it's having too much. It may seem like a lot of effort and work, but if you're serious about being a successful entrepreneur in action, it's energy well spent.

8.13.2 Methods of Generating Ideas

1. Focus Groups: This is very important method of generating ideas and is used for variety of purposes since 1950. It means group of individuals providing information in a structured format. It includes open indepth discussion. The group of 8-14 participants is stimulated by comments from other group members in developing a new product idea to fulfill a market need.In addition to generating new ideas ,the focus group is an excellent method for initially screening ideas and concept.

2. Brainstorming. This is the most widely used method for generating ideas. Brainstorming is a group or individual creativity technique by which efforts are made to find a conclusion for a specific problem by gathering a list of ideas spontaneously contributed by its member(s). The term was popularized by Alex Faickney Osborn in the 1953, book *Applied Imagination.* Osborn claimed that brainstorming was more effective than individuals working alone in generating ideas, although more recent research has questioned this conclusion. In a brainstorming session, a group of people gets together in a room, preferably one with a relaxed environment, where everyone would be free to stretch their minds and think beyond the ordinary. A group leader states the issue or problem to be addressed and ensures that all participants understand it. Then members contribute as many ideas as they can in a given time by describing them verbally (often shouting them out). Participants are encouraged to come up with as many ideas possible and to build on each others' ideas. In brainstorming sessions, talking is often nonstop as participants suggest ideas. No criticism of ideas is allowed during the brainstorming session. Instead, all ideas, no matter how illogical or crazy, are recorded for later discussion and analysis. The purpose of brainstorming is to be an idea-generating process that opens up as many alternatives as possible as other people's remarks act to stimulate others in a sort of chain reaction of ideas. It can be afrenzied, yet productive way to generate numerous ideas. Today, the term is used as a catch all for all group ideation sessions.

3. Nominal Group Technique. The nominal group technique is a type of brainstorming that encourages all participants to have an equal say in the process. It is also used to generate a ranked list of ideas. Participants are asked to write their ideas anonymously. Then the moderator collects the ideas and the group votes on each idea. The vote can be as simple as a show of hands in favor of a given idea. This process is called distillation. After distillation, the top ranked ideas may be sent back to the group or to subgroups for further brainstorming. For example, one group may work on the color required in a product. Another group may work on the size, and so forth. Each group will come back to the whole group for ranking the listed ideas. Sometimes ideas that were previously dropped may be brought forward again once the group has re-evaluated the ideas

4. Problem Inventory Analysis. It's a method for obtaining new ideas and solutions by focusing on problems. However, instead of generating new ideas themselves, consumers are provided with the list of problems in general product category. Then they are asked to identify and discuss products in this category that have the particular problem. Now company can easily relate known products to suggested problems and arrive at new product idea.

5. Reverse Brainstorming: Its similar to Brainstorming, except that in this criticism is allowed in order reach at end result. In fact, the technique is based on finding fault by asking questions.The process usually involves the identification of everything wrong with an idea, followed by discussion of ways to overcome these problems.

6. Gordon Method: In this method, group members are not known with the exact nature of the problem. In this, entrepreneur starts by mentioning a general concept associated with the problem then the group responds back with number of ideas.Then the actual problem is revealed, enabling the group to make suggestions for final solution.

7. Free Association: This is developing of new idea through chain of word association. First, a word or phrase related to the problem is written then another and another is written with each new word attempting to add something new to ongoing thought. This helps in forming a chain of ideas which help in forming a new product idea.

8. Group Passing Technique: Each person in a circular group writes down one idea, and then passes the piece of paper to the next person, who adds some thoughts. This continues until everybody gets his or her original piece of paper back. By this time, it is likely that the group will have extensively elaborated on each idea.

8.14. IDEA INCUBATION[5]

Idea incubation is a process for bringing ideas into reality. It starts on a very fundamental level, often with a single individual who comes up with a concept he or she thinks should be further explored. This individual brings others in on the idea incubation process, making the idea stronger and more viable. Ultimately, the idea may be turned into a product, assuming that funding can be secured and that the idea is commercially viable.

Many companies foster idea incubation by clustering workers together in collaborative environments. Cooperative groups work best for idea incubation because other members of the group can identify strengths and weaknesses of the idea, resulting in a stronger finished product. Some companies offer their services as professional idea incubators. These companies use a staff of individuals who are trained to think innovatively. Idea incubation firms often provide support for product development all the way through the process from the initial vague concept to commercial production.

Successful idea incubation can result in products ranging from clothespins to computers. Ultimately, strong leadership and executive skills are required along with an entrepreneurial spirit. Once an idea has been incubated, it needs to be developed, prototyped, and commercially presented. Appointing a team leader can encourage this, along with creating a work environment in which all employees are encouraged to make contributions.

Business incubators are programs designed to accelerate the successful development of entrepreneurial companies through an array of business support resources and services, developed and orchestrated by incubator management and offered both in the incubator and through its network of contacts. Incubators vary in the way they deliver their services, in their organizational structure, and in the types of clients they serve. Successful completion of a business incubation program increases the likelihood that a start-up company will stay in business for the long-term: Historically, 87% of incubator graduates stay in business.

The incubation process (Most common incubator services):

- Help with business basics
- Networking activities

- Marketing assistance
- High-speed Internet access
- Help with accounting/financial management
- Access to bank loans, loan funds and guarantee programs
- Help with presentation skills
- Links to higher education resources
- Links to strategic partners
- Access to angel investors or venture capital
- Comprehensive business training programs
- Advisory boards and mentors
- Management team identification
- Help with business etiquette
- Technology commercialization assistance
- Help with regulatory compliance
- Intellectual property management

Entrepreneurs who wish to enter a business incubation program must apply for admission. Acceptance criteria vary from program to program, but in general only those with feasible business ideas and a workable business plan are admitted. It is this factor that makes it difficult to compare the success rates of incubated companies against general business survival statistics. Although most incubators offer their clients office space and shared administrative services, the heart of a true business incubation program is the services it provides to start-up companies. The amount of time a company spends in an incubation program can vary widely depending on a number of factors, including the type of business and the entrepreneur's level of business expertise. Life science and other firms with long research and development cycles require more time in an incubation program than manufacturing or service companies that can immediately produce and bring a product or service to market.

8.15. OPPORTUNITY

The opportunity may be a situation which already exists, or one which we create and which would not otherwise have occurred. An opportunity may be one which we can actually recognise now, or one which will arise in the future.

Opportunity can be defined as an attractive and excellent project idea which, an entrepreneur search for and accept such idea as a basis for his investment decision."

Opportunity is defined as: 'the potential for change, improvement or advantage arising from our action in the circumstances'.

Casson (2003) defined entrepreneurial opportunities as 'those situations in which new goods, services, raw materials and organising methods can be introduced and sold at greater than their cost of production'.

Shane (2003) defined them as 'a situation in which a person can create a new means–end framework for recombining resources that the entrepreneur believes will yield a profit.

Both of these are only definitions of profit opportunities. The pursuit of profit is important but not the sole determinant of entrepreneurial opportunity. Improvements in social, cultural, health and environmental arenas are also important, especially for social entrepreneurs and entrepreneurial managers in public sector organisations, as well as 'mainstream' entrepreneurs. Types of opportunity may include, for example,

- a 'gap in the market' for a product or service
- a mismatch between supply and demand
- a future possibility which can be recognised or created
- a problem that can be solved, for example by applying a solution to a need
- a more effective or efficient business process, system or model
- a new or existing technology or approach which has not yet been applied
- the transfer of something that works in one situation to another, such as a product, process or business concept
- a commodity or experience people would desire or find useful if they knew about it.

8.15.1 Opportunity Recognition A Challenge[6]

A business opportunity represents a possibility for the entrepreneurs to meet enough unsatisfied need and entrepreneurs must have ability to recognize business opportunity. Main factors which helps in recognition of the opportunity are — Education, experience (personal and work), prior knowledge of market and customer problems, entrepreneur alertness and networking. Those entrepreneurs who have ability to recognize meaningful business opportunities are in position to successfully launch new venture.

In a dynamic world, a company's success rests to a very large degree on its ability to pursue new opportunities. Recognizing the importance of the entrepreneurial opportunities, research attention on the phenomenon of entrepreneurial opportunities assumes critical significance (Dutta, 2005).

Eckhardt and Shane define entrepreneurial opportunities as the situations in which new goods, services, raw materials, markets and organizing methods can be introduced through the formation of new means, ends, or means-ends relationships (as cited in Dutta, 2005).

According to Schumpeter, they arise in the economy as an outcome of a self-transformation process, the driving element of which is an innovating "entrepreneur-hero". In other words, he gives cognizance to the importance of the personal traits and motivation of the entrepreneur. Schumpeter suggests that entrepreneurs are the rare breed of individuals motivated intrinsically to utilize the benefits of technological, demographic, and social changes to create upheavals in the current state of equilibrium and to usher new products and services or new ways of working (as cited in Dutta, 2005).

A business opportunity, as a chance to do something differently and better (Wickham, 2006), represents a possibility for the entrepreneur to meet a large enough unsatisfied need that is worthwhile (Hisrich, Peters and Shepherd, 2005). In order to deal with it, entrepreneur has to be able to identify and select the right opportunities by applying important abilities (Ardichvili, Cardozo and Ray, 2003).

The major challenge in opportunity is its recognition. Although an opportunity for entrepreneurial profit might exist, an individual can earn this profit only if he or she recognizes that the opportunity exists and has value (Shane and Venkataraman, 2000). Due to complexity and multidimensionality of this process, entrepreneurs must receive and utilize all the information that they obtain from the external environment to create, shape, and maintain a kind of information asymmetry that allows them to notice new opportunities that are either not seen or are disregarded by the other groups of the population (Stewart, Watson, Carland, and Carland, 1999) (as cited in Dutta, 2005).

The opportunity challenge encourages entrepreneurs to see the world in a new way, more as world full of opportunities and possibilities rather than a world full of problems and obstacles. It motivates them to be always curious and looking for new ways to serve and share their gifts and talents with the world.

Examples:

CRT recycling

The shortage of basic resources, coupled with the need to improve recycling of manufactured materials to reduce waste disposal, is providing various opportunities for environmentally oriented businesses.

In the UK and Europe, strict regulations to restrict the dumping of electrical and electronic equipment have been introduced to prevent land and water pollution. However, as old-style cathode ray tube (CRT) televisions and computer monitors come to the end of their lives and are replaced by flatscreen technology, there will be a need over the next ten years for environmentally sound methods of disposing of millions of glass screens, which contain heavy metals.

Most of these methods are labour intensive and costly. However an entrepreneur realised that a government-funded CRT manufacturing plant had closed, and that this had included an automated recycling facility for defective screens produced during the manufacturing process. Local authorities were keen to find a cost-effective means of disposing of life-expired screens without the additional costs of transporting them to mainland Europe. An upcoming entrepreneur recognised the opportunity to combine this redundant yet efficient facility with the recycling need, and prepared a plan to reopen the plant for a limited lifespan to meet the peak in demand for recycling before the site was redeveloped by its new owner. This would create jobs in an unemployment black spot and produce sand from the recycling process which could be used in golf bunkers and other applications.

Spinning Tale of Innovation

Home video cameras are common today, but there were significant technological challenges to overcome before they became a reality. For example, in their earlier "analogue" format (non-digital), in order to record the amount of information onto videotape that moving pictures require (30 images per second) the tape would have to pass very quickly over the recording heads, thereby requiring an enormous amount of tape. Inventors solved this problem by mounting the recording heads on a spinning drum and having the tape pass by relatively slowly while the drum spins very quickly. The same process made videotape players possible, which started the new electronics revolution. Entrepreneurs quickly spun off innovative businesses such as video rentals. If you peek into the slot in your VCR, you can see this silver drum quite easily. This invention led to a series of yet more innovative spin-offs.

Although it was invented for video, this same process allowed audio engineers to solve a similar problem — how to produce high-fidelity recordings without using vast amounts of tape. By mounting audio heads on the spinning drum, they were able to produce very high quality audio, which you get with hi-fi VHS videocassette decks, for example.

When digital imaging was developed, the pictures it produced were high quality, but required vastly more storage space — as much as a megabyte per image. At thirty images per second, this created a daunting problem. However, digital audiotape had already been invented, which allowed audio signals to be recorded, using a static audio head, in digital format. Designers combined the rotating video recording drum concept with digital audiotape and applied it to digital video recording. As a result, a single small digital audiotape is able to hold a full hour of digital video, the equivalent of 108,000 megabytes (108 gigabytes) of information!

With high quality full-motion digital video now possible, more innovative applications followed. The same tape that can hold an hour of video could also hold more than 600 high quality still images, which meant that digital video cameras could also work as still cameras.

However, innovators were also at work creating ever smaller hard drives for computers, which eventually allowed them to use this technology for image storage in digital cameras. At the same time, memory chips are becoming more powerful as well, making possible.

8.15.2 Opportunity-centred Entrepreneurship Concept

Opportunity-centred Entrepreneurship is a learning process which focuses on four interconnected themes. These themes, shown in Figure 8.2, are essential to exploring and understanding an opportunity by relating it to personal (individual and group) interests and goals, planning to realise it, and acting to make the opportunity happen.

Developing and managing opportunities requires skills of creative thinking, planning, managing human relationships, marketing and selling, and project and resource management. These management skills must be deployed and in many cases learned through experience. We can term these the skills of *entrepreneurial management*. Opportunity-centred Entrepreneurship is an integrative approach which connects with the broader subjects of business and organisational management, creativity, innovation and learning. The learning process of Opportunity-centred Entrepreneurship focuses on

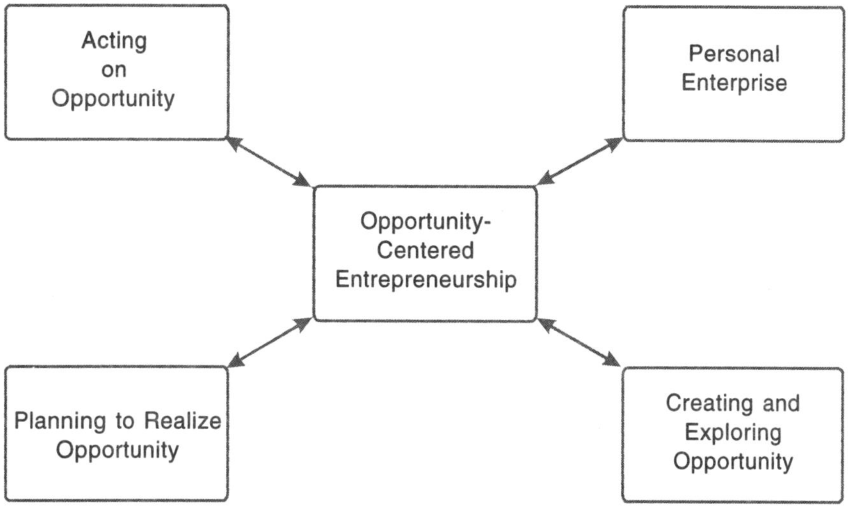

Fig. 8.2. Opportunity-centered Entrepreneurship

the identification, development, planning and implementation of an opportunity, from idea to realisation. In developing the opportunity, we work and learn through four interconnected processes. These are shown in the simple mind-map in Figure 8.2.

Example[7]: Opportunity-centred Entrepreneurship in action: William Chase – Tyrrell's Potato Chips

Personal enterprise

William Chase grew up in rural Herefordshire in a potato-farming family. His mother died while he was young, and William raised the money to buy the family farm from his father. He was keen to be a farmer, but struggled to meet the debt repayments on the farm and the 1992 recession led to his own bankruptcy. As a result of this he evaluated his life, 'grew up', and subsequently bought back the farm a second time from the receiver. He grew potatoes successfully for a few more years, but realised that the major supermarkets were constantly forcing down farmers' prices and profit margins. He concluded that there was no future in growing potatoes as a commodity: 'I had to change direction or go out of business.'

Creating and exploring the opportunity

William needed to consider other options to use the farm and the high-quality potatoes he could grow. He sold potatoes to a crisp manufacturer and realised that the profit margin was around 35 per cent, far higher than on potatoes, with crisps being sold for thousands of pounds per ton. Visiting the United States, he found sales of gourmet hand-produced chips were growing by 15 per cent each year, and discovered that farm-based production was feasible. Assessing the UK snack food market, he concluded that whilst there were potato crisp brands which were perceived as 'premium', there was an opportunity in the market for a genuine top-quality brand of potato chips aimed at premium customers. He decided that making hand-produced chips from potatoes grown on his own farm, aimed at the gourmet end of the market, would be unique and this was where he wanted to be. He knew nothing about making chips but realised from his experience with the supermarkets that 'you have to find a niche.'

Planning to act on the opportunity

Initially he produced and successfully test-marketed batches of crisps using an adapted chip-shop fryer. This, together with market research, proved that demand existed. On the strength of this, William prepared a business plan to invest £1m of a bank loan, a small grant and personal equity in buying chip-manufacturing equipment from the United States, converting a potato storage shed into a production plant and training the farm staff to become chip makers, 'starting off as you mean to go on, with good people and equipment'. Chase also invested in creating the Tyrrell's brand, named after the farm. The identity, packaging and marketing materials are carefully produced to 'sell the story' and convey the 'magic' of the farm-grown, hand-produced chips with a distinctive range of'natural' flavours, and even root vegetable and apple chips. Having experienced downward price pressure from supermarkets, he refused to supply these and instead targeted the product at up-market retailers, independent stores and gastro-pubs, which enabled Tyrrell's to offer a premium-priced product with a good profit margin and avoid the pressure to discount: 'I decided to be the little guy who took the supermarkets on.'

Acting to make the opportunity happen

After starting full production in 2002, Tyrrell's grew rapidly through successful marketing, product innovation and distribution to achieve over £7m turnover by the end of the fourth year. The brand involved customers and retailers closely from the beginning, continually gaining customer feedback and giving excellent support and service to retailers with independent distribution. However, William felt that 'there are no rules, no limit to keeping the magic going' and aimed to grow to be a £50m turnover brand, growing 100 per cent per year and becoming the country's foremost innovative producer and supplier of excellent-quality, farm-produced artisan delicacies for the discerning customer. Chase saw his role as 'doing the thinking, moving the business forward, anticipating issues and responding to potential cracks before they appear'. By visiting trade shows, talking to retailers and observing customers, he predicts international market trends, and has a growing export business: 'I'm learning all the time, gaining ideas from the United States and Spain.' Based on the successful first few years, Chase invested a further £2m to build a new factory on the farm, doubling the production area and potato planting acreage, whilst moving into muesli, oats, fruit and cereal bars, and other healthy and organic products. Chase credits much of the success to the staff: 'a successful business attracts people – you find and develop the best people, who come to work with passion.' The business success was recognised in 2005 when William Chase won National Business Awards for Entrepreneur of the Year and Small Medium Sized Business of the Year.

8.16. STEPS IN IDENTIFICATION OF BUSINESS OPPORTUNITY

1. **Preliminary Evaluation:** It is the first step in identification of business opportunity. An entrepreneur has to analyse and evaluate the investment opportunities against set of specific criteria. It can include the feasibility check on various grounds like:- Compatibility with government rules and regulations, cost of project, availability of raw material etc.
2. Selection of the Product or Service.
3. Market Survey, which include the survey regarding the availability of raw material, equipment, marketing and distribution, Consumer Behaviour etc.
4. Contractual Programmes to collect sufficient information about proposed ventures.
5. Succeeding the market by proving the right product, at right time, at right place, with right and appropriate value in order to satisfying the customer demand.

8.16.1 How to Select the Right Opportunity

Step 1: Identify Your Business and Personal Goals

Step 2: Research Your Favourite Industries

Step 3: Identify Promising Industry Segments

Step 4: Identify Problem Areas and Brainstorm Solutions

Step 5: Compare Possible Solutions with Your Objectives and Opportunities in the Marketplace

Step 6: Focus on the Most Promising Opportunities

8.17. SUMMARY

Entrepreneurship is the cycle of actions an entrepreneurs undertakes to start anew enterprise. It is described at process of handling economic activity, undertaking risk, creating something new and organizing resources. So it's a purposeful activity of an individual or a group of associated individuals undertaken to initiate, maintain or organize a profit oriented business unit. It is an innovative and creative activity which include the search of business idea and opportunity recognisition. But its different from intrapreneurs/corporate entrepreneurs.

The corporate entrepreneur is an individual that exists within an organisation to generate product and process ideas that will create value for the organization.

8.18. SOME CASE STUDIES

Case Study: Innovation in Entrepreneurship – A Case Study on Keen Mobility[8]

Keen Mobility is a story of innovation, invention and entrepreneurship. Innovation is often focused on inventions and new products, but innovation is also a new way of thinking about conventional wisdom.

Keen Mobility was founded by Vail Blackwell Horton and Jerry Carleton. Vail and Jerry were college roommates at the University of Portland (UP). Vail, born without legs, had been using artificial legs to walk but the crutches he needed to use with the artificial legs were destroying his shoulders. He wanted to find a better way to keep walking – for him, and for others. Vail went in search of a way to fulfill this mission.

Vail brought an idea for a new type of crutch – one with shock absorbing technology – to a group of engineering students at UP. He suggested the engineers try to build a working prototype for their senior project. They agreed, and the student engineers went to work. The concept worked! The engineering students successfully built a working prototype, and Vail and Jerry realized their concept could fly. They set off to start a company to build a product that would help Vail stay vertically mobile, and help others do so as well. Jerry and Vail called the UP Center for Entrepreneurship. The UP Center for Entrepreneurship encouraged the team to enter UP's Entrepreneurs Challenge and other business competitions. By April 2002 they had won the $10,000 first prize in the UP competition and third place in Portland Business Journal's business plan competition, winning $35,000 in cash and services. UP sent them to more competitions around the U.S. where they consistently finished in the top three. The team also looked for other sources of funding. They wrote a successful proposal to UP to fund their trade show booth and travel costs. They contacted the National Collegiate Inventors and Innovators Alliance (NCIIA). With support from the Lemelson Foundation, NCIIA awards approximately 2 million dollars in grants annually to college students or recent graduates of member institutions. Keen was awarded a $10,000 NCIIA grant funding prototype development and provisional patent filing costs.

A great partnership, Vail focused on creating the product and the vision for company while Jerry continued fund raising efforts. They partnered with universities where student engineering teams would apply to NCIIA to prototype Keen's new product ideas. A crutch with shock absorbing technology was the company inspiration but ultimately represented only a small market. The team realized they needed a full suite of "world-class products focused on safety, mobility, and comfort for the disabled, elderly and injured." They now focused their efforts on building out their product line.

Keen Mobility today has "over $2.5 million in annual sales, 25 different product lines, more than $1.7 million in capital, and 12 employees. Keen Mobility has also been recognized by the Oregon Entrepreneurs Forum as one of the three most successful growth-stage companies in the state, ranked number 30 on the 100 Fastest Growing Private Companies List, and was placed on the Governor's Honor Role for Employers of People with Disabilities." Keen Mobility has been named in 2008 and in 2009 to *Inc.'s* annual ranking of the fastest-growing private companies in America and to the *Portland Business Journal's* Oregon 100 Fastest Growing Private Companies list three consecutive years. Vail and Jerry were both named to the "Top Forty Under Forty" list by the *Portland Business Journal.*

A Novel Idea for a Bookshop—Beyond Q Bookshop

When customers enter Beyond Q, they are greeted by several kilometres of bookshelves, the smell of freshly-brewed coffee and a frog that croaks hello. Even if they don't realise it, they're experiencing a series of small innovations that have been pieced together over the past few years.

It took over the bookshop with the goal of turning it into a store that customers would feel at home. According to co-owner of Canberra's Beyond Q Bookshop, "One of the first things I noticed was that many customers wanted to stay in the store longer but had partners who weren't interested in books. So, I looked at different ways to get non-readers involved. Over time, we introduced a bar, live music and a café that looks like a bloke's tin shed. It makes for something that passers-by want to come and experience — even those who aren't into books. There's not any one big innovative idea that has shaped who we are. Instead, they are small changes that we have tested and measured every step of the way. For example, a while ago we replaced two aisles of cheap metal bookshelves with wooden shelves. We found that there was a big increase in sales in those areas of the shop. People may say 'well, you've done something different and that's what has attracted people's attention'. However, when you measure the results over six months and find there's been a 20 per cent increase in sales from those shelves, there has to be a reason for it. Our staff members take the time to talk to customers, and not just about what's happening in the bookshop but about what's happening in their lives."He added, "From our experience, it's important that small business owners ask questions when looking to innovate. Ask everybody: other business owners, friends and, most importantly, your customers. Customers are the ones who keep the shop alive and well, and if they know you appreciate them they will become loyal."

8.19. SELF ASSESSMENT QUESTIONS

1. What is the role and importance of innovation in Entrepreneurship?
2. What do you mean by evolutionary and revolutionary innovations? Explain with the help of case study of each.
3. What are the various types of innovations?
4. What are the various sources of innovation?
5. What is the difference between innovation and invention? Explain the importance of creativity in innovation.
6. Opportunity recognition is a challenge, explain it with the help of some entrepreneurs who recognize the opportunity at the right time and turn it as a success.

SOURCES/NOTES

1. www.yahoo.com/typesofinnovation/image results
2. Andrews, Peter. "Enemies of innovation: What they look like, and how not to become one." IBM Executive Business Institute. October 2005 AND http://www935.ibm.com/services/us/index.wss/multipage/imc/executivetech/a1022675/1?cntxt=a1005266
3. http://www.kimep.kz/files/BCB/V.3The_Challenges_of_Entrepreneurship_in_Dynamic_Society.pdf
4. *Essentials of Entrepreneurship and Small Business Management*-5th edition-Thomas W. ZimmererandNorman

5. *Entrepreneurship Development*-Dr. V. Sudharani, Associate Professor, College of Agriculture
6. The challenges of entrepreneurship in dynamic society 1 (1) 34-45 M.N.Shahidi, A.Smagulova Volume I, No. 1, 2008 Central Asia Business, ISSN 1991-0002
7. www.tyrrellspotatochips.co.uk and 1_4039_4175_0_04_cha01.qxd opportunity centered entrepreneurship- chapter1
8. http://www.competingonexecution.com/2010/03/innovation-in-entrepreneurship-%E2%80%93-a-case-study-on-keen-mobility.

9

ENTREPRENEURSHIP DEVELOPMENT PROGRAMMES (EDP)

9.1. INTRODUCTION

Entrepreneur is the person with a vision, with the drive and with the ability to bear risk. He is a pivot around which the entire industry rotates because it his foresight, knowledge, optimism, hard work, persistence and efficient management of the enterprises that brings success to the enterprise. He is the 'spark plug' who transforms the economy of a country. This shows how important an entrepreneur is in the economic system of the country. Hence, it is said that an economy is an effect for which entrepreneurship is the cause. Entrepreneurship Development (ED) has, therefore, become a matter of great concern in all developing and under developed countries all over the world. It refers to the process of enhancing entrepreneurial skills and knowledge through structured training and institution-building programmes.

Entrepreneurial development means to help a person in inculcating and strengthening his entrepreneurial skills, abilities and capabilities , so that they can achieve their entrepreneurial goals more efficiently and effectively. Entrepreneurial development is a prerequisite for an overall economic development of a county. An entrepreneur is one who always looks for a change, reacts to it and exploit it as an opportunity .Entrepreneur development is an act of human resource development in which qualities like motivation, knowledge, opportunity creation, etc., can be injected to entrepreneurs through proper training programmes.

9.2. DEFINITIONS

According to Joseph E.Schumpeter, "Intelligence, motivation, knowledge and opportunity are the prerequisites of entrepreneurial development".

Joseph E.Schumpeter (1934), for the first time, put the human agent at the centre of process of economic development and assigned a critical role to the entrepreneurship in his theory of economic development.

According to C.B. Gupta and N.P Srinivasan, "Development of an entrepreneur means inculcating entrepreneurial traits into person, imparting the required knowledge, developing the technical, financial marketing and managerial skills, and building the entrepreneurial attitude".

It has been found out that **'n Ach'** factor developed by **David McClelland,** the behavioural scientist, is the most important quality for entrepreneurial development. In order to prove that the need for achievement could be induced, he conducted an experiment in collaboration with the erstwhile Small Industries Extension and Training Institute (SIET) of Hyderabad at Kakinada, Andhra Pradesh. Young persons were selected and put through rigorous training for a period of three months to guide them to set new goals. The achievement motivation has a positive impact upon their task performance.

9.3. CONCEPT OF ENTREPRENEURSHIP DEVELOPMENT

Entrepreneurial competencies and talent can be raised by conducting various entrepreneurship development programmes (EDP). EDP means programme designed to help a person in strengthening his entrepreneurial motive and in acquiring skill and capabilities necessary for playing his entrepreneurial role effectively. In other words, EDP is primarily concerned with developing and motivating entrepreneurial talent and growing him to be an effective entrepreneur. Entrepreneurial development has been conceived by successive government as a programme of activities to enhance the knowledge, skill, behaviour and attitudes of individual and groups to assume the role of entrepreneurs.

EDP helps in inculcating entrepreneurial traits into a person, imparting the required knowledge, developing technical, financial, marketing and managerial skills and building the entrepreneurial attitude. EDP has been recognised as an effective human resource development tool. It is primarily for developing the first-generation entrepreneurs who on their own cannot become successful entrepreneurs. EDP through its continuous process of training and motivation help them to set up their own profitable enterprise and become successful entrepreneurs in their own right. An entrepreneurship development programme should help aspiring entrepreneurs to recognize and design unique, innovative business opportunities, based on an analysis of local conditions and their own special skills. The programme can help the entrepreneur to diversify based on his/her basic knowledge of a product or skill in a certain sector without distorting the local markets. In a truly entrepreneurial approach, innovative capacity matters more than the size of the market.

It is not merely a training programme, rather it is a comprehensive programme involving the following process:

(i) It is a process which enhances the knowledge, skill and motivation of the potential entrepreneur.

(ii) It is a process which instills entrepreneurial behaviour in the minds of entrepreneur in their day to day activities, and

(iii) It is a process through which the potential entrepreneurs can develop and set up their own enterprise.

EDP by itself therefore, aims at achieving the specific objectives of the programmes through continuous training and motivation.

9.4. NEED FOR ENTREPRENEURIAL DEVELOPMENT PROGRAMME

The EDP programme is innovative in that it identifies persons with entrepreneurship abilities and trains them systematically to strengthen their self-confidence, seize a business opportunity and initiate an enterprise. So it helps in following achievements:-

(i) Helps in Removing Poverty and Unemployment: EDPs are in a massive scale undertaken in backward and rural areas which are confronted with chronic problem of poverty and unemployment. EDPs help the people in getting self- employment. It helps in creating employment opportunities for the unemployed there by increasing the standard of living.The government of India has initiated various schemes like Nehru Rozgar Yojna, National Rural Employment, etc., in order to eliminate poverty and generate gainful employment opportunities for the unemployed.

(ii) Prevents Industrial Slums: EDPs help in removing the industrial slums which are created in highly congested industrial areas. The entrepreneurs through EDPs are able to set up their enterprises in different places best suited to their product. They learn through EDPs about various schemes, incentives, facilities, infrastructural requirements etc. for their enterprise. This helps in the dispersal of industrial units which ultimately prevents growth of industrial slums and industrial pollution.

(iii) Helps in Achieving Balanced Regional Development: The need for EDPs arise in order to solve the problem of regional imbalances which is an important feature of underdeveloped nations. EDPs are basically provided to establish small scale industrial units in remote areas with little financial resources (mostly backward and underdeveloped areas) in order to accelerate the pace of industrialization. It helps in the reduction of concentration of economic power, thus leads towards achievement of balanced regional development.

(iv) Uses Locally Available Resources: EDPs help the entrepreneurs in harnessing the available local resources for creating a healthy base for sound economic growth and rapid industrialization. It help in channelizing on right lines the talent and energies of unemployed youth. It thus helps in easing social tension.

(v) Capital Formation: Adequate funds are essential to start a new enterprise. Entrepreneur mobilize the idle savings of the public in productive use because he act as an organizer of facts of production by employing his own and borrowed resources. Various public and private banks and state financial corporation's provide financial help to new entrepreneurs through various agencies involved in EDP.

(vi) Improvement in Standard of Living: EDP provides necessary support to entrepreneurs by educating them about new and latest innovations and market trends. This enables to ensure easy availability of quality products at lower prices to consumers which result in improvement in standard of living of the people.

9.5. OBJECTIVES OF ENTREPRENEURIAL DEVELOPMENT PROGRAMME

1. To identify and train the potential entrepreneurs .
2. To develop necessary knowledge and skills among the participants in EDPs.
3. To impart basis managerial knowledge and understanding;
4. To provide post-training assistance;
5. To develop and strengthen entrepreneurial quality and motivation;
6. To analyze the environmental issues related to the proposed project;
7. To help in selecting the right type of project and products;
8. To formulate the effective and profitable project;
9. To enlarge the supply of entrepreneurs for rapid industrial development;
10. To develop small and medium enterprises sector which is necessary for employment generation and wider dispersal of industrial ownership;
11. To industrialize rural and backward regions;
12. To provide gainful self-employment to educated young men and women;
13. To diversity the source of entrepreneurship;
14. To provide knowledge and information about the source of help, incentives and subsidies available from government to set up the project;
15. To impart information about the process, procedure and rules and regulations for setting up a new projects.

9.6. PHASES OF ENTREPRENEURIAL DEVELOPMENT PROGRAMME

There are three different phases of EDP like in Fig. 9.1:

- Pre-training phase
- Training phase
- Follow-up phase

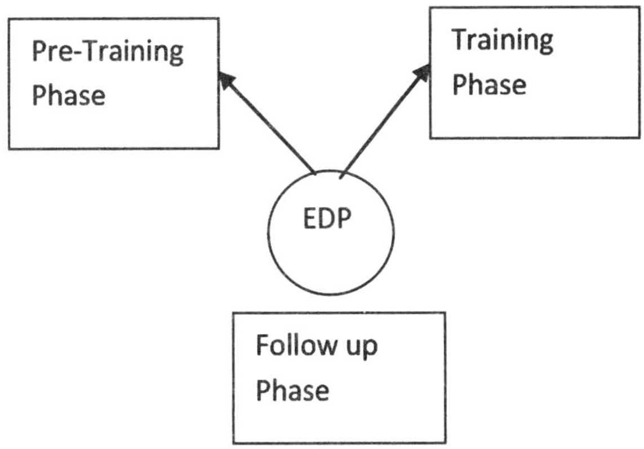

Fig. 9.1

(i) Pre-training phase: Pre-training phase consists of all activities and preparation to launch training programme. It is also called as initial phase.Pre-training phase is divided into two phases i.e promotional activities and selection of trainees. Promotional activities primarily aim at getting maximum cooperation from local support systems and maximum response from potential entrepreneurs. These activities involve understanding the local economy and society, establishing rapport with local population, leaders and organizations and establishing credibility of the organizations undertaking EDP training. After this phase, applications are invited from potential entrepreneurs, and some are selected for training after a written test and personal interview. Other activities of EDP under Pre-training phase are :

- Identification of operationally-promising area, normally a district.
- Selection of entrepreneurs for the training programme.
- Arrangements of infrastructure are for the programme like selection of place of training.
- Deciding guest faculty for the programme from education industry and banks.
- Taking necessary steps for inauguration of programme.
- Formation of selection committee to select trainees from the programme.
- Making provision with regard to publicity and campaigning for the programme.
- Selection of a project leader/course coordinator to coordinate the programme
- Establishing contacts with business personalities, NGOs and related agencies which can contribute to the programme both directly and indirectly
- Getting the application forms printed and making them available at different centers along with instructions

(ii) Training Phase: The primary objective of training programme is to develop motivation and skill or competency amongst the potential entrepreneurs. Care should be taken to impart both theoretical and practical knowledge to various trainees. Training potential entrepreneurs are providing them proper guidance for setting up enterprise constitutes the cornerstone of EDP. The training consists of initial opportunity inputs(during which the trainees are helped, through interactions and discussions in selecting product) as well as three training modules, namely, achievement motivation (AMT), business opportunity guidance and technical training (if needed) and management inputs. Most of the Entrepreneurship Development Institutes generally conduct training programmes of 4-6 weeks duration on full time basis. The training phase of EDP will be so designed that it will answer the following questions:

(a) Whether the attitude of the entrepreneur has been tuned towards the proposed project or no?

(b) Whether the trainee has been motivated to accept entrepreneurship as a career?

(c) Does the trainee behaves like an entrepreneur?

(d) Whether the trainee has sufficient knowledge on resources and technology or not?

(e) What kind of entrepreneurial traits he lacks and what steps should be taken to set it?

Training Phase: Programme Design

Objectives	Focus	Inputs
Motivation and reinforcement of entrepreneurial traits, confidence building.	Entrepreneur.	Behavioral inputs.
Facilitating decision making process to set up a new venture.	Enterprise establishment.	Business opportunity guidance, information and project planning inputs, technical inputs
Successful and profitable operation of enterprise. Industrial exposure.	Enterprise management,first-hand knowledge of factory layout, business sites. etc.	Management inputs, plant visit/in-plant training.

Fig. 9.2

(iii) Follow-up Phase: Follow-up phase of EDP has been termed as post-training phase. During this phase, post-training support services are rendered to the participants who have successfully completed the Entrepreneurship Development Programme (EDP). This is because of the fact that, very often, the potential entrepreneur after undergoing the training confronts a number of problems while implementing the action plan for grounding the project. So during this phase, the training organization helps the entrepreneur in sorting out the problems through counseling support. A committee is formed consisting of members generally drafted from the leading bank of the district, State Financial Corporation, training organization and above all, the District Industries Centre to help the entrepreneurs with the following objectives during the follow-up:

(i) To provide a meaningful direction to the trainees in grounding their enterprise

(ii) To review the progress made by the trainees in implementation of the project

(iii) To review the post-training approach

(iv) To provide escort services to the trainees by involving financial institutions and promotional agencies

The ultimate objective is to develop competent entrepreneurs, so that they can start their project. Post-training phase is a review phase of training programme. It consists of reviewing of work in the following manner:

- Review of pre-training work
- Review of actual training programme
- Review of post-training programme so that cost effectiveness of the present programme can be evaluated.

9.7. EDP STRATEGY FOR INDUSTRIALIZATION AND ECONOMIC DIVERSIFICATION[1]

It will be useful to divide the ventures that could be promoted under EDPs into two broad types –

1. Ventures with low level of investment, technology and income – which can be described as self-employment ventures (under rural self-employment institutes, Ministry of rural development)
2. Ventures with higher level of investment and skills– which can be described as entrepreneurial ventures

The former ventures could be either related to primary needs of a village (such as flour mills, cycle repair shop, grocery shop, repairs of agricultural implements, etc.) or to certain need based or resource based manufacturing and trading activities for the local market in and around the village (such as carpentry, country-tile manufacturing, tailoring, pottery, etc.). Such ventures could be promoted in any village of a minimum size even in backward and remote areas without bothering much about forward and backward linkages. The latter types of ventures need relatively high skills and productivity, higher investments, good infrastructural support and strong linkages with the local economy. Such ventures could be promoted in clusters to diversify and to industrialize the regional economy. The nature of the EDPs conducted for these two types of ventures would also be different in some ways. While the three stages of EDP would remain the same, the contents of each would need to differ. Standard behavioural test can be replaced by interviews for the self-employment ventures. The post-training follow-up also needs to be intensive and personal for a relatively longer period to ensure the establishment of an enterprise, in the case of second type of ventures.

9.8. PROBLEMS FACED IN CONDUCT OF EDPs

The low level of performance is usually attributed to the following problems involved in organizing and conducting EDP trainings:

(a) Shortage of adequate number of specialized and committed organizations

(b) Insufficient trainer motivators to motivate people for undergoing EDPs and to impart training

(c) Identification and selection of wrong projects

(d) Lack of entrepreneurial culture

(e) Apathetic attitude of the support agencies like banks and financial institutions to support entrepreneurs

(f) Lack of forward and backward linkages

(g) Selection of wrong person for training

(h) Improper identification of projects

(i) Inadequate counseling support after training

(j) Lack of continuous follow-up action or post-training support services for grounding the projects

(k) Improper targeting of potential entrepreneurs

9.9. CRITERIA FOR ASSESSMENT OR EVALUATION OF EDPs

Following criteria are being used by the behavioral scientists to assess the effectiveness of EDPs in the country.

(i) New enterprise creation

(ii) Employment generation in quantifiable terms

(iii) Creation of job opportunities both directly and indirectly

(iv) Increase in sales and profit

(v) Enterprise expansion

(vi) Enterprise transformation

(vii) Improvement in quality of product or services

(viii) Repayment of loans

9.10. SUGGESTIONS TO MAKE EDPs SUCCESSFUL

1. Emphasis on stimulating, supporting and sustaining activities

There should be balance between stimulating, supporting and sustaining activities for making EDPs successful. It includes Entrepreneurial education, publicity of Entrepreneurial facilities, training and assistance in the identification of viable projects, creating a common platform for entrepreneurs where they can share their problems, experience and success. Under supporting activities come various forms of support that can be extended to the potential entrepreneurs for setting up and running of their units. Supporting activities include registration, funds mobilization, license, taw, relief and incentives and management consultancy services. Sustaining activity include expansion, diversification, modernization and quality control and how to sustain in the competitive environment. EDPs normally is more emphasis on stimulating and supporting activities and neglect sustaining activities. This results in imbalance which will adversely affect entrepreneurial development and the credibility of EDPs will be eroded.

2. Behavioural trait

One of the primary ingredients of successful EDP program is identification of 'potential entrepreneur'. Only certain types of personalities are fit to undergo EDP programs and benefit from them. The EDP programs have evolved over last 40 years, but at the heart of EDP programme is McClelland's 'achievement need' theory, which highlights importance of entrepreneurial traits and believes that right EDP trainees can be identified through psychological and behavioral tests, and can be trained to become full-fledged entrepreneurs. Even if conduct of tests is not feasible in rural areas, the interviews should screen the candidates for entrepreneurship traits. Certain standard questions can be asked during the interview to assess entrepreneurship traits.

3. Focus on achievement motivation

In order to create right import on potential entrepreneurs it is essential to develop achievement motivation amongst them through proper training and conducive their dream into reality. A successful entrepreneur will serve as a role model for others and they will like to follow him.

4. Designing of viable projects

A project is known as viable which seems to feasible in term of availability of resource and market potentials. A viable man has the requisite aptitude and competence to initiate a project. The EDP organizers should prepare the projects keeping in mind available resources, funding, training requirements and assessing the feasibility of the same. The entrepreneurial development agencies should select right person, impact right training and entrust viable projects to them for making EDPs successful.

5. Training trainers

Success of EDPs depends on the trainers. They should be committed, competent and qualified. Trainers must be fully aware with whatever is latest in their respective fields.

6. Organizing part-time programmes

Most of the trainees of EDP are already working or studying. So, part-time EDPs can definitely suit them who are working (or) studying somewhere else. These EDPs can be conducted during weekends (or) in the evening. By providing part-time EDPs, we can provide opportunity to those who cannot joint any regular EDP.

7. Duration of EDPs

There are no short cuts for entrepreneurial development. Under EDPs an attempt is make to provide self employment to unemployed through a series of activities involving identification of potential entrepreneurs, providing them with the requisite training, developing achievement motivation amongst them and helping them in various ways for making them a successful entrepreneur. Since it is a lengthy process and as such the duration of EDPs should be increased to 6 months, so that these may remain relevant and serve the purpose for which we are conducting these programmes.

9.11. SUCCESS RATE OF EDP TRAININGS AND TIME LAG IN ESTABLISHING AN ENTERPRISE[2]

Success rate of EDP trainings, An evaluation study by North Eastern Council (1990) showed that overall success rate of EDPs organized during the 7th Five Year Plan (1985-90) was 20.88 per cent.

During April 1990 to March 1996 North Eastern Council, Industrial Development Bank of India and Small Industrial Development bank of India together sponsored 212 EDPs in the North east in which 5375 participants participated. Only 25.2 per cent of the participants trained could set up their enterprises as quoted by Mali (2001) in his study on entrepreneurship development in North east. Beena and Sushma (2003) conducted a study on motivational perspective of women entrepreneurs managing petty business and revealed that 73 per cent of the entrepreneurs were very successful followed by 24 per cent were successful and 3 per cent were moderately successful.

9.12. SUMMARY

Entrepreneurs play a predominant role in accelerating the socio-economic development of a country. They are regarded as the nation builders and wealth creators. They are the change agents who initiate economic activities to create wealth. They undertake the business initiative, employ themselves in that business and open up employment avenues for others. Therefore, the role of entrepreneur is of fundamental importance to a country like India where the twin problems of poverty and unemployment coexist. Considering the importance of Entrepreneurship in employment creation and economic development, the Government of India envisaged promotional packages to facilitate setting up of new enterprises. In order to bring about entrepreneurial growth, the policy mailers and financial institutions started thinking in terms of imbibing entrepreneurship culture through training interventions. Thus, Entrepreneurship Development Programmes (EDPs) conducted for a selective group of energetic and potential entrepreneurs who had the willingness and desire to achieve the goal set by them.

9.13. SELF ASSESSMENT QUESTIONS

1. Define EDP and what are its objectives.
2. What is the importance of Entrepreneurship Development?
3. What are the different phases of EDPs?
4. Describe the role of financial institutes in the entrepreneurship development.
5. Discuss the major problems faced in conducting EDP.
6. What is Entrepreneurial Development? Explain the role and relevance of EDPs.

SOURCE/NOTES

1. http://www.aajeevika.gov.in/Best-Practices/Strategies-for-improving-rural-EDP-through-RSETI.pdf
2. An Analysis of Entrepreneurship Development In Women Through EDP Trainings - By SUSHMA K. C.

Others:

Entrepreneurship : Robert D Hisrich (McGraw-Hill Co.)

Entrepreneurship and Small Business: Purnima Sehga I and Manjinder Singh.

10

ENTREPRENEUR DEVELOPMENT PROGRAMMES AND ROLE OF GOVERNMENT

10.1. INTRODUCTION

Entrepreneurship development is the prerequisite for the overall economic development of economy. A worldwide consensus on the critical role of competitive markets and entrepreneurs in economic development has emerged in the last decade. In developing countries, the primary barrier to economic growth is often not so much a scarcity of capital, labour or land as it is a scarcity of both the dynamic entrepreneurs that can bring these together and the markets and mechanisms that can facilitate them in this task. So the development of the country depends upon its entrepreneurs. So Government of India has been taking number of steps and policies through various ministries to promote entrepreneurship. The Government has provided an impressive and effective policy framework for financial and technological support to entrepreneurs.

The Ministry of small-scale industries, designs and implements policies and programmes through its field organizations and attached offices for promotion and growth of entrepreneurship and small industries.

10.2 MEANING OF ENTREPRENEURSHIP DEVELOPMENT

Entrepreneurship Development (ED) refers to the process of enhancing entrepreneurial skills and knowledge through structured training and institution-building programmes. Entrepreneurship

Development aims to enlarge the base of entrepreneurs in order to hasten the pace at which new ventures are created. This accelerates employment generation and economic development. Entrepreneurship development focuses on the *individual* who wishes to start or expand a business. It concentrates on growth potential and innovation.

10.3. ROLE OF ENTREPRENEURSHIP IN ECONOMIC DEVELOPMENT

Entrepreneurship is the practice of starting new organizations or revitalizing mature organizations, particularly new businesses generally in response to identified opportunities. It plays an important role in the economic development of the country. It creates wealth for the nation. It provides employment and act as source of livelihood, also benefit through indirect opportunities more over it helps in the improvement of standard of living. In this way economic development and entrepreneurial activity are dependent upon each other. Entrepreneurship can help economic development in following ways:

1. Improvement in Standard of Living: The growth of entrepreneurship has enabled an improvement in standard of living of people. Entrepreneurship means innovation of new ideas. Moreover entrepreneur tries to make goods at cheaper rate so that it can be easily affordable which increases the standard of living. The growth of entrepreneurship increases production which will increase consumption and more consumption means better standard of living.

2. Develop New Markets: Under the modern concept of marketing, markets are people who are willing and able to satisfy their needs. In Economics, this is called effective demand. Entrepreneurs are resourceful and creative. They can create customers or buyers. This makes entrepreneurs different from ordinary businessmen who only perform traditional functions of management like planning, organization, and coordination and more markets means more economic development.

3. Promotes Capital Formation: Entrepreneurs promote capital formation by mobilising the idle savings of public. They employ their own as well as borrowed resources for setting up their enterprises. Such type of entrepreneurial activities lead to value addition and creation of wealth, which is very essential for the industrial and economic development of the country.

4. Creates Large-scale Employment Opportunities: Entrepreneurs provide immediate large-scale employment to the unemployed which is a chronic problem of underdeveloped nations. With the setting up of more and more units by entrepreneurs, both on small and large-scale numerous job opportunities are created for others. As time passes, these enterprises grow, providing direct and indirect employment opportunities to many more. In this way, entrepreneurs play an effective role in reducing the problem of unemployment in the country which in turn clears the path towards economic development of the nation.

5. Promotes Balanced Regional Development : Entrepreneurs help to remove regional disparities through setting up of industries in less developed and backward areas. The growth of industries and business in these areas lead to a large number of public benefits like road transport, health, education, entertainment, etc. Setting up of more industries lead to more development of backward regions and thereby, promotes balanced regional development.

6. Reduces Concentration of Economic Power : Economic power is the natural outcome of industrial and business activity. Industrial development normally lead to concentration of economic power in the hands of a few individuals which results in the growth of monopolies. In order to redress this problem a large number of entrepreneurs need to be developed, which will help reduce the concentration of economic power amongst the population.

7. Wealth Creation and Distribution : It stimulates equitable redistribution of wealth and income in the interest of the country to more people and geographic areas, thus giving benefit to larger sections of the society. Entrepreneurial activities also generate more activities and give a multiplier effect in the economy.

8. Increasing Gross National Product and Per Capita Income: Entrepreneurs are always on the look out for opportunities. They explore and exploit opportunities, encourage effective resource mobilisation of capital and skill, bring in new products and services and develops markets for growth of the economy. In this way, they help increasing gross national product as well as per capita income of the people in a country. Increase in gross national product and per capita income of the people in a country, is a sign of economic growth.

9. Promotes Country's Export Trade: Entrepreneurs help in promoting a country's export-trade, which is an important ingredient of economic development. They produce goods and services in large scale for the purpose earning huge amount of foreign exchange from export in order to combat the import dues requirement. Hence, import substitution and export promotion ensure economic independence and development.

10. Induces Backward and Forward Linkages: Entrepreneurs like to work in an environment of change and try to maximise profits by innovation. When an enterprise is established in accordance with the changing technology, it induces backward and forward linkages which stimulate the process of economic development in the country.

10.4. ROLE OF CENTRAL GOVERNMENT IN ENTREPRENEURSHIP DEVELOPMENT

The Micro, Small and Medium Enterprises (MSME) sector has been recognised as engine of growth all over the world. Many countries of the world have established a SME Development Agency as the nodal agency to coordinate and oversee all Government interventions in respect of the development of this sector. In the case of India, also Medium establishment has for the first time been defined in terms of separate Act, governing promotion and development of Micro, Small and Medium Enterprises (MSME), i.e., Micro, Small and Medium Enterprises (MSME) Development Act, 2006 (which has come into force from 02nd Oct, 2006) the Office of Development Commissioner (Micro, Small and Medium Enterprises) functions as the nodal Development Agency under the Ministry of Micro, Small and Medium Enterprises (MSME). Earlier it was known as Small Industrial Development Organisation (SIDO) which was set up in 1954. Office of the Development Commissioner (MSME) provides a wide spectrum of services to the Micro, Small and Medium Industrial sector. These include facilities for testing, toolmenting, training for entrepreneurship development, preparation of project and product profiles, technical and managerial consultancy, assistance for exports, pollution and energy audits etc. Office of the Development Commissioner (MSME) provides economic information services and advises Government in policy formulation for the promotion and development of SSIs.

The field offices also work as effective links between the Central and the State Governments. Micro, Small and Medium-sized Enterprises (MSMEs) in market economies are the engine of economic development. Owing to their private ownership, entrepreneurial spirit, their flexibility and adaptability as well as their potential to react to challenges and changing environments, SMEs contribute to sustainable growth and employment generation in a significant manner. SMEs have strategic importance for each national economy due a wide range of reasons. Logically, the government shows such an interest in supporting entrepreneurship and SMEs. There is no simpler way to create new job positions, increasing GDP and rising standard of population than supporting entrepreneurship and encouraging and supporting people who dare to start their own business. Every surviving and successful business means new jobs and growth of GDP.

Therefore, designing a comprehensive, coherent and consistent approach of Council of Ministers and entity governments to entrepreneurship and SMEs in the form of government support strategy to entrepreneurship is an absolute priority. A comprehensive government approach to entrepreneurship and SMEs would provide for a full coordination of activities of numerous governmental institutions (chambers of commerce, employment bureaus, etc.) and NGOs dealing with entrepreneurship and SMEs. With no pretension of defining the role of government in supporting entrepreneurship and SMEs, we believe that apart from designing a comprehensive entrepreneurship and SMEs strategy, the development of national SME support institutions and networks is one of key condition for success. So the government has created different types of support institutes for the development of entrepreneurship. These are as under —

(a) Training: Basic training differs from product to product but will necessary involve sharpening of entrepreneurial skills. Need based technical training is provided by the Govt. and State Govt. technical Institutions.

There are a number of Government organisations as well as NGOs who conduct EDPs and MDPs. These EDPs and MDPs and are conducted by MSME's, NIESBUD, NSIC, IIE, NISIET, Entrepreneurship Development Institutes and other state government developmental agencies.

(b) Entrepreneurship Development Programmes(EDPs): Entrepreneurship Development Programmes are being organized regularly to nurture the talent of youth by enlightening them on various aspects of industrial activity required for setting up MSEs. These EDPs are generally conducted in ITIs, Polytechnics and other technical institutions, where skill is available to motivate them towards self-employment. The course contents of such Entrepreneurship Development Programmes are designed to provide useful information on product/process design, manufacturing practices involved, testing and quality control, selection and usage of appropriate machinery and equipments, project profile preparation, marketing avenues/techniques, product/service pricing, export opportunities, infrastructure facilities available, financial and financial institutions, cash flow, etc

(c) Marketing Assistance: There are Governmental and non-governmental specialised agencies which provide marketing assistance. Besides promotion of MSME products through exhibitions, NSIC directly market the MSME produce in the domestic and overseas market. NSIC also manages a single point registration scheme for manufacturers for Govt. purchase. Units registered under this scheme get the benefits of free tender documents and exemption from earnest money deposit and performance guarantee.

(d) Promotional Schemes: Government accords the highest preference to development of MSME by framing and implementing suitable policies and promotional schemes. Besides providing developed land and sheds to the entrepreneurs on actual cost basis with appropriate infrastructure, special schemes have been designed for specific purposes like quality upgradation, common facilities, entrepreneurship development and consultancy services at nominal charges.

(e) Concession on Excise Duty: MSME units with a turnover of ₹ 1 crore or less per year have been exempted from payment of Excise Duty. Moreover there is a general scheme of excise exemption for MSME brought out by the Ministry of Finance which covers most of the items. Under this, units having turnover of less than ₹ 3 crores are eligible for concessional rate of Excise Duty. Moreover, there is an exemption from Excise Duty for MSME units producing branded goods in rural areas

(f) Credit Facility To MSME: Credit to micro, small and medium scale sector has been covered under priority sector lending by banks. Small Industries Development Bank of India (SIDBI) has been established as the apex institution for financing the MSME. Specific schemes have been designed for implementation through SIDBI, SFCs, Scheduled Banks, SIDCs and NSIC etc. Loans upto ₹ 5 lakhs are made available by the banks without insisting on collaterals. Further Credit Guarantee Fund for micro, small and medium enterprises has been set up to provide guarantee for loans to MSME up to ₹ 25 lakhs extended by Commercial Banks and some Regional Rural Bank.

10.4.1 Government Policies and Support Measures: Brief History

The evolution of the policy framework and support measures of the Government can be broadly grouped into the following three periods:

1948-1991: In all the Policy Resolutions from 1948 to 1991, recognition was given to the micro and small enterprises, termed as an effective tool to expand employment opportunities, help ensure equitable distribution of the national income and facilitate effective mobilization of private sector resources of capital and skills. The Micro, Small and Medium Enterprise Development Organisation [earlier known as Small Industries Development Organization (SIDO)] was set up in 1954, as an apex body for sustained and organised growth of micro, small and medium enterprises. Within next two years, the National Small Industries Corporation, the Khadi and Village Industries Commission and the Coir Board were also set up. The era provided the supportive measures that were required to nurture MSEs, in the form of reservation of items for their exclusive manufacture, access to bank credit on priority through the Priority Sector Lending Programme of commercial banks, excise exemption, reservation under the Government Purchase Programme and 15% price preference in purchases, infrastructure development and establishment of institutes for entrepreneurial and skill development. MSME – Development Institutes [earlier known as Small Industries Service Institute (SISI)] were set up all over India to train youth in skills/entrepreneurship. Tool Rooms were established with German and Danish assistance for providing technical services essential to MSEs as also for skill-training. At the State level, District Industries Centres were set up all over the country.

1991-1999: The new Policy for Small, Tiny and Village Enterprises of August, 1991, laid the framework for government support in the context of liberalisation, which sought to replace protection with competitiveness to infuse more vitality and growthto MSEs in the face of foreign competition and open market. Supportive measures concentrated on improving infrastructure, technology and quality.

Testing Centres were set up for quality certification and new Tool Rooms as well as Subcontracting Exchanges were established. The Small Industries Development Bank of India (SIDBI) and a Technology Development and Modernisation Fund were created to accelerate finance and technical services to the sector. A Delayed Payment Act was enacted to facilitate prompt payment of dues to MSEs and an Industrial Infrastructure Development (IID) scheme was launched to set mini industrial estates for small industries.

1999 onwards: The Ministry of MSME [earlier known as Ministry of Small-scale Industries and Agro and Rural Industries (SSI and ARI)] came into being from 1999, to provide focused attention to the development and promotion of the sector. The new Policy Package announced in August, 2000, sought to address the persisting problems relating to credit, infrastructure, technology and marketing more effectively. A Credit Linked Capital Subsidy Scheme was launched to encourage technology upgradation in the MSE sector and a Credit Guarantee Scheme was started to provide collateral-free loans to micro and small entrepreneurs, particularly the first generation entrepreneurs. The exemption limit for relief from payment of Central Excise duty was raised to ₹1 crore ($0.25 million) and a Market Development Assistance Scheme for MSEs was introduced. At the same time, consultations were held with stakeholders and the list of products reserved for production in the MSE sector was gradually reduced each year. In 2006, the long-awaited enactment for this sector finally became a reality with the passage of the Micro, Small and Medium Enterprises Act. In March, 2007, a third Package for the Promotion of Micro and Small Enterprises was announced which comprises the proposals/schemes having direct impact on the promotion and development of the micro and small enterprises, particularly in view of the fast changing economic environment, wherein to be competitive is the key of success.

10.4.2. Role of MSME in Entrepreneurship Development

(a) Organisational Structure of MSME: The Ministry of Micro, Small and Medium Enterprises (M/o MSME) is the administrative Ministry in the Government of India for all matters relating to Micro, Small and Medium Enterprises. It designs and implements policies and programmes through its field organisations and attached offices for promotion and growth of MSME sector.

The Office of the Development Commissioner (MSME) is an attached office of the Ministry of MSME, and is the apex body to advise, coordinate and formulate policies and programmes for the development and promotion of the MSME Sector. The office also maintains liaison with Central Ministries and other Central/State Government agencies/organisations financial institutions.

(b) Institutional Network of MSME: The Development Commissioner (MSME) have a network of 30 MSME-Development Institute(MSME-DI), 28 Br. MSME-Development Institute(Br. MSME-DI), 4 MSME-Testing Centres (MSME-TCs), 7 MSME-Testing Stations (MSME-TSs), 21 Autonomous bodies which include 10 Tool Rooms (TRs) and Tool Design Institutes (TDI), 4 MSME-Technology Development Center(MSME-TDC), 2 MSME-Technology Development Center-Footwear(MSME-TDC), 1 Electronics Service and Training Centre (ESTC), 1 Institute for Design of Electrical Measuring Instruments (IDEMI) 2 National Level Training Institutes, and 1 Departmental Training Institute and one Production Center. These are:-

(a) MSME-Testing Center (MSME-TC) (Formerly Regional Testing Centers(RTCs)

- Provide Testing facilities for quality upgradation
- Training/constancy in testing, quality control, quality management
- Process quality control systems, etc.

Product specific testing facilities are provided by MSME-Testing Stations(MSME-TSs)

(b) Autonomous Bodies

(i) Tool Rooms/Tool Design Institutes (TRs/TDI)

- To assist MSMEs in technical up gradation, provide good quality tooling by designing and producing tools, moulds, jigs and fixtures, components, etc.
- Provide Training and consultancy for tool and die markers.

(ii) MSME-Technology Development Center(MSME-TDC) (Formerly Product-cum-Process Development Centers (PPDCs) These are product specific Centers to:

- look into their specific problems and render technical service
- develop and upgrade technologies
- manpower development and training

(iii) MSME-Technology Development Center-Footwear(MSME-TDC) (Formerly Central Footwear Training Institutes (CFTIs)

- Develop footwear designing to promote exports
- Training for manpower in Footwear Industry.

(iv) Training Institutes

There are three National Level Training Institutes. These are:

- National Institute of Micro, Small and Medium Industry Extension Training (NIMSMIET), Hyderabad,
- National Institute for Entrepreneurship and Small Business Development (NIESBUD), New Delhi, which conducts national and international level training programmes in different fields and disciplines.
- Indian Institue of Entrepreneuship (IIE), Guwahati. The main objective of the institute is to act as a catalyst for entrepreneurship development with its focus on the North East.

(c) Other Associated Agencies

- National Small Industries Corporation (NSIC) for technology and marketing support
- Small Industries Development Bank of India (SIDBI) an apex bank set up to provide direct/ indirect financial assistance under different schemes to meet credit needs of the small-scale sector and to coordinate the functions of other institutions in similar activities.

- Khadi and Village Industries Commission (KVIC) assists the development and promotion and disbursal of rural and traditional industries in rural and town areas.

(d) State Level Institutional Support

- State Government executes different promotional and developmental projects/schemes and provide a number of supporting incentives for development and promotion of MSME sector in their respective States.
- These are executed through State Directorate of Industries, who have District Industries Centers (DICs) under them to implement Central/State Level schemes.
- The State Industrial Development and Financial Institutions and State Financial Corporations also look after the needs of the MSME sector.

10.5. VARIOUS SCHEMES AND INCENTIVES BY CENTRAL GOVERNMENT

The Micro, Small and Medium Enterprises Development (MSMED) Act, 2006, seeks to facilitate the development of these enterprises as also enhance their competitiveness. It provides the first-ever legal framework for recognition of the concept of "enterprise" which comprises both manufacturing and service entities. It defines medium enterprises for the first time and seeks to integrate the three tiers of these enterprises, namely, micro, small and medium. The Act also provides for a statutory consultative mechanism at the national level with balanced representation of all sections of stakeholders, particularly the three classes of enterprises; and with a wide range of advisory functions. It also provides various schemes and incentives. Some schemes and incentives offered by central government are as under:-

1. National Manufacturing Competitiveness Programme (NMCP) Schemes Under XI Plan: The Government has announced formulation of National Competitiveness Programme in 2005 with an objective to support the Small and Medium Enterprises (SMEs) in their endeavor to become competitive and adjust the competitive pressure caused by liberalization and moderation of tariff rates. The scheme will be called the "Manufacturing Competitiveness Programme". The design of the scheme will be worked out by the National Manufacturing Competitiveness Council (NMCC) in consultation with the industry.

2. Micro and Small Enterprises Cluster Development Programme (MSE-CDP): DC(MSME) launched MSE-CDP for holistic development of selected MSEs clusters through value chain and supply chain management on co-operative basis.

Objectives of the Scheme:

1. To support the sustainability and growth of MSEs by addressing common issues such as improvement of technology, skills and quality, market access, access to capital, etc.
2. To build capacity of MSEs for common supportive action through formation of self help groups, consortia, upgradation of associations, etc.

3. To create/upgrade infrastructural facilities in the new/existing industrial areas/ clusters of MSEs.
4. To set up common facility centres (for testing, training centre, raw material depot, effluent treatment, complementing production processes, etc).

3. Credit Linked Capital Subsidy Scheme for Technology Upgradation: The Scheme was launched in October, 2000 and revised *w.e.f.* 29.09.2005. The revised scheme aims at facilitating Technology Upgradation of Micro and Small Enterprises by providing 15% capital subsidy (12% prior to 2005) on institutional finance availed by them for induction of well established and improved technology in approved subsectors/products. The admissible capital subsidy under the revised scheme is calculated with reference to purchase price of Plant and Machinery. Maximum limit of eligible loan for calculation of subsidy under the revised scheme is also been raised ₹ 40 lakhs to ₹ 100 lakh *w.e.f.* 29-09.2005. The scheme has been continues 10th Five Year Plan to 11th Five Year Plan. Under the scheme approximately 7396 units have availed subsidy of ₹ 315.21 crore upto August, 2009.

4. Credit Guarantee Scheme: To ensure better flow of credit to micro and small enterprises by minimizing the risk perception of banks/financial institutions in lending without collateral security, the Government launched Credit Guarantee Fund Scheme for Micro and Small Enterprises in August 2000 and is operational with effect from 1st January 2000. The Credit Guarantee Fund Scheme for Micro and Small Enterprises (CGMSE) was launched by the Government of India to make available collateral-free credit to the micro and small enterprise sector. Both the existing and the new enterprises are eligible to be covered under the scheme. The scheme covers collateral-free credit facility extended by eligible lending institutions to new and existing micro and small enterprises for loans up to ₹100 lakh ($250,000) per borrowing unit. The guarantee cover is up to 75 per cent of the credit sanctioned [85% in respect of loans up to ₹ 5 lakh ($12,500) and 80% for loans provided to MSEs owned/ operated by women and all loans in the North-East Region]The Ministry of Micro, Small and Medium Enterprises and Small Industries Development Bank of India (SIDBI), established a Trust named Credit Guarantee Fund Trust for Micro and Small Enterprises (CGTMSE) to implement the Credit Guarantee Fund Scheme for Micro and Small Enterprises.. The corpus of CGTMSE is being contributed by the Government and SIDBI in the ratio of 4:1 respectively and has contributed ₹1906.55 crore to the corpus of the Trust up to March 31, 2010. As announced in the Package for MSEs, the corpus is to be raised to ₹ 2500 crore by the end of 11th Plan.

5. Performance and Credit Rating Scheme: The Performance and Credit Rating Scheme for manufacturing MSEs was launched in April, 2005 with the objective of assisting the MSEs in obtaining performance-cum-credit rating which would help them in improving performance and also accessing bank credit on better terms if the rating is high. Under the scheme (implemented by the National Small Industries Corporation in conjunction with reputed rating agencies), 75% of the fee charged by the rating agency is reimbursed by the Government subject to a maximum of ₹ 40,000 ($1,000).

6. ISO 9000/ISO 14001 Certification Reimbursement Scheme: To enhance the competitive strength of the MSEs, the Government introduced a scheme for technological upgradation, quality improvement and better environment management by the MSEs. The scheme reimburses 75% of the fees, subject to a maximum of ₹ 75,000 ($2000), for acquiring Quality Management System (QMS)/

ISO 9000 certification and/or Environment Management System (EMS)/ISO 14001 certification by the MSEs.The Scheme shall provide one time reimbursement only against a Entrepreneurship Memorandum Number. It means the total entitlement of reimbursement of acquiring one or more than on certifications shall be up to the maximum limit of ₹ 75,000/- only. In case a unit has received reimbursement/subsidy/grant from Central Govt./State Govt./Financial Institution against any one of the certifications for an amount less than maximum limit of ₹ 75,000/-, the unit shall be eligible to receive the balance amount only.

7. MSME MDA: The scheme offers funding upto 75% in respect of to and fro air fare for participation by MSME Entrepreneurs in overseas fairs/trade delegations. The scheme also provide for funding for producing publicity material (upto 25% of costs) Sector specific studies (upto ₹ 2 lakhs) and for contesting anti-dumping cases (50% upto ₹ 1 lakh)-for individual MSMEs and Associations.

Participation in the International Exhibitions/Fairs: For registered Small and Micro manufacturing enterprises with DI/DIC.

Financial Assistance for using Global Standards (GS1) in Barcoding: Recognized the importance of bar coding and avail financial assistance through Office of DC(MSME). In order to enhance the marketing competitiveness of MSEs in domestic as well as international market, Office of Development Commissioner (MSME), Ministry of MSME, provides the financial assistance for reimbursement of 75% of one-time registration fee (Under SSI-MDA Scheme) *w.e.f.* 1st January,2002 and 75% of annual recurring fee for first three years (Under NMCP Scheme) *w.e.f.* 1st June,2007 paid by MSEs to GS1 India for using of Bar Coding. The work of reimbursement has been decentralised and transferred to field offices, *i.e.,* MSME-DIs *w.e.f.* 1st April, 2009 with a view to ensure speedy and timely and extensive implementation of the scheme.

8. Purchase and Price Preference Policy: This is administered through the Single Point Registration Scheme of NSIC. Under this, 358 items are reserved for exclusive purchase from MSME by Central Government. Other facilities include tender documents free of cost, exemption from earnest money and security deposit and 15% price preference in Central Government purchases- ***for individual MSMEs***. E.g.: Castor Oil, Boxes Leather, Boxes made of metal, Cleaning Powder, Clinical Thermometers etc.

9. Marketing assistance and technology upgradation scheme: Assistance under the scheme will be available for the benefits of micro, small and medium enterprises in the manufacturing segments as per the definition of the Micro, Small and Medium Enterprises Development Act, 2006 (MSMED Act).

10. Prime Minister's Employment Generation Programme (PMEGP): Government of India has approved the introduction of a new credit linked subsidy programme called Prime Minister's Employment Generation Programme (PMEGP) by merging the two schemes that were in operation till 31.03.2008 namely Prime Minister's Rojgar Yojana (PMRY) and Rural Employment Generation Programme (REGP) for generation of employment opportunities through establishment of micro enterprises in rural as well as urban areas. PMEGP will be a central sector scheme to be administered by the Ministry of Micro, Small and Medium Enterprises (MoMSME). The Scheme will be implemented by Khadi and Village Industries Commission (KVIC), a statutory organization under the administrative control of the

Ministry of MSME as the single nodal agency at the National level. At the State level, the Scheme will be implemented through State KVIC Directorates, State Khadi and Village Industries Boards (KVIBs) and District Industries Centres (DICs) and banks. The Government subsidy under the Scheme will be routed by KVIC through the identified Banks for eventual distribution to the beneficiaries / entrepreneurs in their Bank accounts.

Eligibility Conditions of Beneficiaries

(i) Any individual, above 18 years of age

(ii) There will be no income ceiling for assistance for setting up projects under PMEGP.

(iii) For setting up of project costing above ₹ 10 lakh in the manufacturing sector and above ₹ 5 lakh in the business /service sector, the beneficiaries should possess at least VIII standard pass educational qualification.

(iv) Assistance under the Scheme is available only for new projects sanctioned specifically under the PMEGP.

(v) Self Help Groups (including those belonging to BPL provided that they have not availed benefits under any other Scheme) are also eligible for assistance under PMEGP.

(vi) Institutions registered under Societies Registration Act,1860;

(vii) Production Cooperative Societies, and

(viii) Charitable Trusts.

(ix) Existing Units (under PMRY, REGP or any other scheme of Government of India or State Government) and the units that have already availed Government Subsidy under any other scheme of Government of India or State Government are not eligible.

11. Scheme of National Award: The Micro, Small and Medium Enterprises (MSMEs) in India have seen a vast development in the last five decades. The MSMEs have registered tremendous growth as also progress in terms of quality production, exports, innovation, product development and import substitution, very much beyond the expected objectives of setting up MSMEs by the planners of industrial production base in the country. The ministry of Micro, Small and Medium Enterprises with a view to recognizing the efforts and contribution of MSMEs gives National Award annually to selected entrepreneurs and enterprises under the scheme of National Award. It includes: — To encourage and appreciate the outstanding efforts of MSMEs in three categories (i) Entrepreneurship, (ii) Quality Upgradation and (iii) Research and Development.

- First National Award: ₹ 1,000,000/- cash prize, a Trophy and a Certificate.
- Second National Award: ₹ 75,000/- cash prize, a Trophy and a Certificate.
- Third National Award: ₹ 50,000/- cash prize, a Trophy and a Certificate.
- Special National Award to Woman Entrepreneur: ₹ 1,00,000/- cash prize, a Trophy and a Certificate.
- Special National Award for SC/ST Entrepreneur: ₹ 1,00,000/- cash prize, a Trophy and a Certificate.

- Special National Award to Outstanding Entrepreneur from NER: ₹ 1,00,000/- cash prize, a Trophy and a Certificate.
- Special Recognition Award to MSMEs Scoring Marks above 80% (50% in case of NER) : ₹ 20,000/- cash prize, a Trophy and a Certificate each.

12. Rajiv Gandhi Udyami Mitra Yojana: The objective of Rajiv Gandhi Udyami Mitra Yojana (RGUMY) is to provide handholding support and assistance to the potential first generation entrepreneurs, who have already successfully completed EDP/SDP/ESDP or vocational training from ITIs, through the selected lead agencies, i.e., 'Udyami Mitras', in the establishment and management of the new enterprise, in dealing with various procedural and legal hurdles and in completion of various formalities required for setting up and running of the enterprise.It includes:-

- To provide handholding support to potential first generation entrepreneurs.
- Financial assistance @ ₹ 4,000/- per trainee for service enterprises and @ ₹ 6,000/- per trainee for manufacturing enterprises would be provided to Udyami Mitras as handholding charges.
- For the beneficiaries from NER the beneficiary's contribution of ₹ 1,000/- shall also be provided as grant.
- For empanelment as Udyami Mitra the interested institution to apply on prescribed format through the Director of Industries

13. Scheme of Fund for Regeneration of Traditional Industries (SFURTI): Government has recently launched the Scheme of Fund for Regeneration of Traditional Industries (SFURTI) under which 100 traditional industry clusters (of khadi, village industry and coir) would be taken up for comprehensive development over 5 year. The KVIC and the Coir Board are the nodal agencies for the Scheme, which will be the first comprehensive initiative for regeneration of the khadi and village industries sector, based on the cluster development methodology. The guidelines for the SFURTI have been issued on 3.10.2005. Main objectives of this schemes are as under:-

(a) To develop clusters of traditional industries in various parts of the country

(b) To create sustained employment opportunities in traditional industries.

14. Scheme for Assistance to Training Institutions: The Scheme envisages financial assistance for establishment of new institutions (EDIs), strengthening the infrastructure of the existing EDIs and for supporting entrepreneurship and skill development activities. The main objectives of the scheme are development of indigenous entrepreneurship from all walks of life for developing new micro and small enterprises, enlarging the entrepreneurial base and encouraging self-employment in rural as well as urban areas, by providing training to first generation entrepreneurs and assisting them in setting up of enterprises. The assistance shall be provided to these training institutes in the form of capital grant for creation of infrastructure.

15. Scheme To Support 5 Selected Universities/Colleges to run 1200 Entrepreneurship Clubs: The scheme is to support 5 universities to run Entrepreneurship Clubs (one each from Northern, Western, Eastern, Southern and North East region). Each university will have to run 240 clubs per year and each club may have a membership of 50 entrepreneurs. In a period of 5 years, 3 lakh entrepreneurs are to be benefited in all.

Objectives: The scheme has been devised to encourage entrepreneurs to run self-employment ventures of Micro or Small Enterprises. Moreover, this will be a very important scheme bringing the entrepreneurs, universities and MSME-Development Institutes (MSME-DI) together. In addition, this will create a base to entrepreneurs for coming together to solve their common problems a shift from Lobbying Mode to Facilitation Mode, giving hard intervention in the form of technology and soft intervention like arranging workshops, seminars, guidelines to obtain ISO certification, ISI Marks, participation in Trade Fairs, implementation of Quality Management Tools.

10.6. ROLE OF STATE GOVERNMENT

In order to encourage setting up of industrial units in states, State Governments provide various schemes and incentives to entrepreneurs and micro and small scale industries. All the State Governments provide technical and other support services to small units through their Directorates of Industries, and District Industries Centres. Although the details of the scheme vary from state to state, the following are the common areas of support.

1. Development and management of industrial estates
2. Suspension/deferment of Sales Tax
3. Power subsidies
4. Capital investment subsidies for new units set up in a particular district
5. Seed Capital/Margin Money Assistance Scheme
6. Priority in allotment of power connection, water connection.
7. Consultancy and technical support

10.6.1. Various Incentives and Schemes are as under

1. State Capital Investment Subsidy:- In order to encourage setting up of various industrial units, state governments provides state capital investment subsidy to priority sector industries. This facility is available in Uttar Pradesh, Jammu and Kashmir, Sikkim, Andaman and Nicobar islands, Karnataka, Maghalaya, Himachal Pradesh, Gujarat, Punjab, Andhra Pradesh, Kerala, Maharashtra, Tripura and Manipur in order to encourage setting up of industrial units in their states.

2. Mini Tool Rooms: In order to meet the growing demand of Tools and dies in the country, particularly in the MSME sector, Govt. of India have decided to assist the State Govts to set up Mini Tool Room and Training Centres. The Central assistance will be in the form of one time grant-in-aid equal to 90% of the cost of machinery/equipment (restricted to ₹ 9.00 crores ineach case) in the case of a new Mini Tool Room, and 75% of the cost of machinery/equipment (restricted to ₹ 7.50 crores) in case of an existing Mini Tool Room to be upgraded/modernised. The balance cost of machinery/ equipment, the cost of land and buildings and the recurring costs would be met by the States/State Agencies. The scheme will be implemented as a Centrally sponsored Scheme, for which approval of the Planning Commission has been obtained.

Assistance to Entrepreneurship Development Institutes: For strengthening training infrastructure in EDIs, assistance upto 50% or ₹ 50 lakhs whichever is less is provided .

3. Madhya Pradesh Financial Corporation: It is the premier institution in the State of Madhya Pradesh engaged in providing financial assistance to small and medium industries. This assistance has been extended in the form of a wide range of fund and non fund based services/ schemes. The fund-based schemes are available for setting up of business ventures within the State, whereas, non fund-based schemes are available throughout the country.

The fund-based schemes include:

- Term Loan
- Equipment Finance
- Asset Credit
- Short-term Loan
- Working Capital
- Loan Replenishment
- Finance for Market Activities
- Composite Loan
- Credit Linked Capital Subsidy for SSI

The non-fund-based schemes include:-

- Public Issue Appraisal
- Credit Syndication
- Corporate Advisory Services

4. Kerala Financial Corporation (KFC): It is incorporated under the State Financial Corporations Act of 1951 and is a trend setter in the field of industrial finance. It has been playing a major role in the development and industrialisation of Kerala by extending financial assistance well-suited for the requirements of the entrepreneurs. Its main objective is to extend term loan assistance for establishing new industrial units or to extend credit assistance for meeting expansion/diversification/modernisation costs of the existing units, in small-scale or medium sectors. Some of its major schemes include:

lGeneral Scheme For SSI Units

- General Scheme for SME Units
- National Equity Fund (NEF) Scheme
- Working Capital Finance
- Scheme for Assistance to Information Technology and Software Development Sector
- Financial Assistance for Infrastructure Projects

5. Industrial Promotion Subsidy Scheme: Govt. of Maharashtra is one of the first States implementing Package Scheme of Incentives for decentralization of industries. Scheme is proven as most effective for industrial decentralization. Govt. involves the the Chamber of Commerce and

Industries, Indl. Organizations while framing the policies. Govt. has simplified the procedural Rule and Regulations while framing the policy and classified whole State in 6 categories like A, B, C, D, D+ . Nanded dist. is categorized as D+zone and eligible up to 50% and 30% subsidy against the total fixed capital investment, done by the Micro/Small and Medium/Large Scale units respectively. Besides this, other incentives like Stamp duty/Electricity duty exemption, Royalty refund, Interest subsidy for Textiles. Special incentives for quality up gradation are also admissible.

6. Revised Seed Money Scheme: To encourage self employment venture amongst unemployed youths, Govt. has specially announced New Seed Money Scheme *w.e.f.*18.5.07 increasing project cost limit from ₹ 10 lakhs to 25 lakhs, reducing rate of interest on seed capital from 10% to 6%. A special rebate of 3% is admissible for regular repayment of seed capital.Eligible educated unemployed gets 15% soft loan from D.I.C @ 6% as seed money lcan for the project cost upto ₹ 25 lakhs and the upper limit of seed money ₹ 3.75 lakhs. In the interest of social justice, for all backward categories and handicapped youths, 20% seed money loan is eligible for the project cost upto ₹ 10 lakhs.

Eligibility :

1. Age limit - 18 to 50 years.
2. Minimum 7th Std. pass.
3. Domicile of Maharashtra State.

7. District Award to Small-scale Entrepreneurs. Directorate of Industries has introduced in 1985 a scheme of District Awards for promoting entrepreneurship and recognizing the achievements of successful entrepreneurs in the sector of small scale industries. First Award is of ₹ 15,000/- in cash and Silver Plated Mementos and Shawl Second Award is of ₹ 10,000/- in cash and Silver Plated Mementos and Shawl. The awards will be granted in each calendar year.

Eligibility : The SSI units permanently registered before 3 years of that calendar year and in continuous production at least 2 years and not defaulter of the Financial institutions. Units that have already been awarded National Awards are not entitled to this award.

8. Quality Marking Centres: The Department of Industries, Punjab, has also set up Quality Marking Industrial Development Centres in the State for providing facilities of testing, marking and all types of services to the manufacturers. Quality control helps to secure uniformity of products. These centres facilitate constant improvement of processing in manufacturing. The uniformity in specifications also facilitates the inter-changeability in the products. Moreover, production cost can be reduced through continuous processing

9. The Punjab Financial Corporation, Chandigarh: It was established in 1953 under the State Financial Corporation Act, 1951, with the object of providing medium and long-term loans to the industrial concerns located in the State of Punjab. It was reconstituted under the Punjab Reorganization Act, 1966, on 1 April 1967. It generally grants term loans for creation/acquisition of fixed assets like land, building, plant and machinery, provides guarantee against deferred payments for the purchase of capital goods and offers underwriting facility on issue of stocks and shares to companies. The corporation also provides financial assistance for setting up of hotels, nursing homes/small hospitals, development of industrial estates, purchase of transport vehicles, etc.

10. Exemption from stamp duty and local taxes: State Governments exempt stamp duty in respect of land allotment by the government to the new industrial units. Machinery, equipments, raw materials and packing materials of new units are exempted from payment of octroi duty and other local taxes. The facilities are available in Jammu and Kashmir, Sikkim, Daman, Karnataka, Meghalaya, Gujarat, Nagaland, Rajasthan, Haryana, Maharashtra and Manipur.

11. Special facilities for export-oriented units: State Governments provide special package of incentives and better infrastructural facilities for export oriented units. State Governments reimburse costs incurred by SSI units for shipment of export samples from the nearest port/container depot to the port of destination. The facilities are available in U.P, Himachal Pradesh, Karnataka, Punjab, Rajasthan and Tripura.

12. Land, Building and water at concessional rates: State governments acquire land and development industrial plots, sheds and industrial estates. State Government allot land and industrial sheds to new units at nominal rates in their respective states. Moreover state governments and the local governments are providing water to small-scale units at a concessional rate to encourage setting up of such units .(Note:- There are many more schemes by different state governments so students can check it from various state government sites or business.gov.in)

10.7. VARIOUS INCENTIVES AND SCHEMES FOR EXPORT–ORIENTED UNITS

The Export-oriented Units (EOUs) scheme, introduced in early 1981, is complementary to the SEZ (Special Economic Zone) scheme. It adopts the same production regime but offers a wide option in locations with reference to factors like source of raw materials, ports of export, hinterland facilities, availability of technological skills, existence of an industrial base and the need for a larger area of land for the project. As on 31st December 2005, 1924 units are in operation under the EOU scheme. The main objectives of the EOU scheme is to increase exports, earn foreign exchange to the country, transfer of latest technologies stimulate direct foreign investment and to generate additional employment. Major Sectors in EOUs: Granite, Textile/Garments, Food Processing, Chemicals, Computer etc. To set up an EOU for the following sectors, an EOU owner needs a special license:

- Arms and ammunition,
- Explosives and allied items of defense equipment,
- Defense aircraft and warships,
- Atomic substances,
- Narcotics and psychotropic substances and hazardous chemicals,
- Distillation and brewing of alcoholic drinks,
- Cigarettes/cigars and manufactured tobacco substitutes.

In the above mention cases, EOU owner are required to submit the application form to the Development Commissioner who will then put them up to the Board of Approvals (BOA).

The EOUs are required to achieve the minimum NFEP (Net Foreign Exchange Earning as a Percentage of Exports) and the minimum EP (Export Performance) as per the provisions of EXIM Policy which vary from sector to sector. As for instance, the units with investment in plant and machinery of ₹ 5 crore and above are required to achieve positive NFEP and export US$ 3.5 million or 3 times the CIF value of imported capital goods, whichever is higher, for 5 years. For electronics hardware sector, minimum NFEP has to be 'positive' and minimum EP for 5 years is US$ 1 million or 3 times the CIF value of imported capital goods, whichever is higher. NFEP is calculated cumulatively for a period of 5 years from the commencement of commercial production according to a prescribed formula.

Some incentives given to EOUs

- No import licences are required by the EOU units and import of all industrial inputs exempt from customs duty.
- Supplies from the DTA to EOUs are regarded as deemed exports and are hence exempt from payment of excise duty which means that high quality inputs are available at lower costs.
- On fulfillment of certain conditions, EOUs are exempted from payment of corporate income tax for a block of 5 years in the first 8 years of operation. Export earnings continue to be exempt from tax even after the tax holiday is over.
- Industrial plots and standard design factories are available to EOUs at concessional rates.
- Single window clearance for EOU. For example, the State Government of Kerala as well of Karnataka has constituted single window clearance mechanisms such as District Single Window Clearance Board (in Kerala) and Karnataka Udyog Mitra (in Karnataka) for the purpose of speedy issue of various licences, clearances.
- Private bonded warehouses in the 7 EPZs can be set up for
    - Import and sale of goods including in the DTA, subject to payment of applicable duties at the time of sale.
    - Trading including re-export after repacking/labeling.
    - Re-export after repair, reconditioning or re-engineering
- EOUs and EPZs are permitted to subcontract part of their production processes for job work to units in the DTA on a case by case basis.
- Supplies to the DTA under international competitive bidding against payment in foreign exchange to other EOUs and EPZ units and against import licenses are considered towards fulfillment at the export obligation.
- The FOB value of exports of EOUs and EPZ units can be clubbed with that of parent companies located in the DTA for the purpose of obtaining a Trading or Export House status.
- EOUs and EPZ units may export goods through Trading and Export Houses or other EOU and EPZ Units.

- Exchange Earners Foreign Currency (EEFC) Account-Facility to retain 100% foreign exchange proceeds in EEFC AccountandFacility to realize and repatriate export proceeds within twelve months.

Fiscal Incentives available to 100% EOUs

- I Exemption from Customs and Central Excise duties on import/local procurement of capital goods, raw materials, consumables, spares, packing material etc.
- Reimbursement of Central Sales Tax (CST) on purchases made from Domestic Tariff Area (DTA)
- Reimbursement of duty paid on fuels procured from domestic oil companies as per the rate of Drawback notified by the DGFT from time to time.

Special Package of Incentives for Star Export House EOUs (Fast Track Clearance)

- Permissions and Customs clearances for both Imports and Exports on self declaration basis.
- Fixation of Input-Output norms on priority within 60 days.
- Exemption from compulsory negotiation of documents through Banks.
- 100% retention of foreign exchange in EEFC account.
- Exemption from furnishing of Bank Guarantee in Schemes under this policy.
- Exemption from examination of Import Cargo
- Install one Fax machine and Two computers in their Administrative/Registered Office on prior intiation only.
- Remove their Capital goods (or) part thereof for repairs under prior intimation to the jurisdictional Asst./Deputy Commissioner of Customs and Central Excise authority .
- DTA clearance of rejects on priority basis
- Personal carriage of samples of Gems and Jewellery without a need for prior permission
- DTA sale of finished products on prior intimation only
- Participation in exhibition for export promotion on prior intimation only.

10.7.1. Some Other Schemes and Incentives

1. Export Promotion Capital Goods Scheme: The scheme allows import of capital goods for pre production, production and post production (including CKD/SKD thereof as well as computer software systems) at 5% Customs duty subject to an export obligation equivalent to 8 times of duty saved on capital goods imported under EPCG scheme to be fulfilled over a period of 8 years reckoned from the date of issuance of licence. Capital goods would be allowed at 0% duty for exports of agricultural products and their value added variants. The capital goods shall include spares (including refurbished/ reconditioned spares), tools, jigs, fixtures, dies and moulds. EPCG licence may also be issued for import of components of such capital goods required for assembly or manufacturer of capital goods by the licence holder.

2. Incentives available from Government of Andhra Pradesh:

- 100% reimbursement of stamp duty and transfer duty paid by the industry
- 100% reimbursement of stamp duty for lease of land, shed or building
- 100% reimbursement of stamp duty and transfer duty paid by the industry on financial deeds and mortgages etc.
- Reimbursement of 25% of the cost of land purchased in the Industrial Development Areas of AP Industrial Infrastructure Corporation Ltd., subject to a limit of ₹ 5 lakhs
- Infrastructure assistance to stand alone units by contribution of 50% of the cost of infrastructure from Industrial Infrastructure Development Fund with a ceiling of ₹ 1 Crore
- Provision of a Corpus fund matching the contribution made by consortium industries in Industrial estates subject to a limit of ₹ 25 lakhs
- 15% investment subsidy on fixed capital investment to Small-scale Industry (SSI) and Tiny Industrial Units subject to a limit of ₹ 15 lakhs
- 25% of the tax paid during one financial year will be ploughed back to all eligible industries as a grant by the Government towards the payment of tax during next year
- 3% interest rebate on the prime-lending rate (PLR) on term loans taken by new tiny/SSI units subject to a limit of ₹ 5 lakh per year
- This will be 5% if SC and ST entrepreneurs promote the units
- An additional investment subsidy of 5% subject to a maximum of ₹ 5 lakhs will be provided to women entrepreneurs. They will be also given a 5% interest rebate on PLR
- Projects with an investment of ₹ 100 crores and above are eligible for all the incentives available to large and medium-scale industries
- The Government will also extend tailor-made benefits to suit to particular investments on case-to-case basis

3. Incentives available from Government of Chattisgarh

- EOUS will get infrastructure support to the extent of 25% of infrastructure cost subject to a maximum limit of ₹ 1 crore
- Mega projects (₹ 100 crores and above) will be eligible for infrastructure support outside Industrial Estates upto 25% of the infrastructure cost subject to a maximum limit of 5 Years for Mega Units
- Electricity duty exempted for a period of 10 years and 15 years for Mega Units
- SSI units enjoy interest subsidy @ 5% per annum for 5 years upto ₹ 5 lakhs
- Entry Tax and Stamp Duty exempted

4. Incentives available from Government of Karnataka: The Government of Karnataka has announced a State Policy for Special Economic Zones-2009 to support and encourage development of SEZs in the State. These are:

- Exemption of Sales Tax, VAT, Entry Tax and Special Entry Tax on all purchases (excluding petroleum products) from DTA.
- Exemption of Stamp Duty and Registration fees for Registration of Land and Loan/Credit Documents.
- **For Developers and Co-developers,** exemption of Electricity Duty or Taxes on sale, of self generated or purchased electric power for use in the processing area of SEZ.
- Capital subsidy to Common Effluent Treatment Plant:One time Capital subsidy up to 50% of the cost incurred by the Developer/Co-developer for setting up of Common Effluent Treatment Plant is available subject to a ceiling of ₹ 100.00 lakhs per CETP/SEZ.

10.8. SUMMARY

Government accords the highest preference to development of MSME by framing and implementing suitable policies and promotional schemes like- providing incentives for quality upgradation, concession on excise duty and provides technical supportive services. Thus Government play supportive role in developing entrepreneurs. These include facilities for testing, tool menting, training for entrepreneurship development, preparation of project and product profiles, technical and managerial consultancy, assistance for exports, pollution and energy audits etc. There are various incentives and schemes from central as well as state governments and special schemes for export oriented units. Different schemes are provided by different states in order to encourage the development of entrepreneurship and new industries in their respective states.

10.9. SELF ASSESSMENT QUESTIONS

1. What is the need and role of Central Government in entrepreneurship development?
2. What are the various schemes and incentives provided by central government for the promotion of entrepreneurship?
3. Discuss the schemes and incentives provided by State Government for the development of industries in their respective states.
4. What do you mean by MSME Act and how does it helps in the promotion of entrepreneurship?
5. What are the various schemes and incentives for the export-oriented units?

SOURCES/NOTES

1. http://www.dcmsme.gov.in/ssiindia/MSME_OVERVIEW09.pdf
2. www.dcmsme.gov.in and www.sezindia.nic.in
3. infodriveindia.com-eximguru.com
4. Ministry of commerce and industry-dgft.govt.in

11

ROLE OF VARIOUS AGENCIES IN ENTREPRENEURSHIP DEVELOPMENT

11.1 INTRODUCTION

Government has recognized the important role of entrepreneurs in the industrial development of the country, especially through the small-scale industries (SSIs).SSIs are essential for Indian economy in terms of employment generation, foreign exchange earnings, its share in industrial output, and contribution to national income. The Government of India and State Governments are taking various steps for entrepreneurship development. In spite of financial assistance and concessions provided by Government (Discussed in previous lessons) the small industries in the rural areas were not developing much due to lack of infrastructure facilities. In view of this central and state government institutes have come to support small entrepreneurs by providing them various types of assistance and facilities. Various institutes and agencies has been evolved for the promotion of entrepreneurship in the country and the institution network is classified into Central Level, State Level and District Level.

11.2 DISTRICT INDUSTRIES CENTRES (DICs)

The District Industries Centers programme was launched in 1978 for effective promotion of cottage and small-scale industries widely dispersed in rural areas and small towns. These centers are the focal points providing all the services and support required by small-scale and village entrepreneurs under one roof. These serves as an integrated administrative framework at the district level for industrial development. The District Industries Centers (DIC's) programme was started with a view to provide integrated administrative framework at the district level for promotion of small-scale industries in rural areas. The DIC's are envisaged as a single window interacting agency at the district level providing service and support to small entrepreneurs under a single roof. DICs are the implementing arm of the central and state governments of the various schemes and programmes. Registration of small industries is done at the district industries centre and PMRY (Pradhan Mantri Rojgar Yojana) is also implemented by DIC. The organizational structure of DICs consists of General Manager, Functional Managers and Project Managers to provide technical services in the areas relevant to the needs of the district concerned. Management of DIC is done by the state government.

11.2.1. Structure of DIC

DIC consists of

(a) One General Manager,

(b) Four functional managers of whom three would be in the area of economic investigation, credit, and village industries. Fourth Manager may be entrusted with responsibility in any of area like raw materials/marketing/training, etc., depending upon the specific requirements of each district.

(c) Three Project Managers to provide technical service in the area relevant to needs of the district concerned. Their role is to facilitate modernization and upgradation of technology in small sector.

11.2.2. Functions and Role of DICs

DICs role is mainly promotional and development and to provide all support and services to smalland village industries. The main functions of DICs are as follows:

(a) It **conducts surveys** to know industrial potential of a district keeping in view the availability of raw material, human skills, infrastructure, demand, etc. It also provides investment advice to entrepreneurs based on these assessments.

(b) It **prepares an action plan** for industrial development that can be effectively implemented in the concerned district on the basis of possibilities and endowments.

(c) It **appraises** the various **investment proposals** received from entrepreneurs.

(d) It **guides and assists** entrepreneurs in buying appropriate machinery ,equipment and raw material. It also interact with various authorities for the supply of scarce and critical raw materials

(e) It suggests appropriate **marketing strategies** to entrepreneurs.

(f) It maintains links with research and development institutions for upgradation of technology, quality improvement, industrial training, etc.

(g) It conducts **artisans training programmes.** It also function as the technical arms of DRDA in administering IRD and TRYSEM programmes, designing and implementing training programmes and identifying appropriate opportunities and projects for the beneficiaries.

(h) It has been assigned operation responsibility for special schemes to provide self-employment to educated unemployed youths.

(i) To prepare and keep model project profiles for reference of the entrepreneurs.

(j) To undertake industrial potential survey and to identify the types of feasible ventures which can be taken up in ISB sector, i.e., industrial sector, service sector and business sector.

(k) To assist entrepreneurs for availing land and shed, equipment and tools, furniture and fixtures.

(l) To appraise the worthness of the project-proposals received from entrepreneurs.

(m) To help the entrepreneurs in obtaining required licenses/permits/clearance.

(n) To assist the entrepreneurs in marketing their products and assess the possibilities of ancillarization.

(o) To help the entrepreneurs in clarifying their doubts about the matters of operation of bank accounts, submission of monthly, quarterly and annual returns to government departments.

(p) To act as the nodal agency for the district for implementing PMRY (Prime Minister Rojgar Yojana).

(q) To help the specialized training organizations to conduct Entrepreneur development programmes.

(r) The DICs have launched a scheme to assist the educated unemployed youth by providing them facilities for self employment. The youth should be in the age group 18- 35 years with minimum qualification of Metric or Middle with I.T.I in Engineering or Technical Trade. Technocrats and women are given preference.

In fine DICs function as the torch-bearer to the beneficiaries/entrepreneurs in setting up and running the business enterprise right from the concept to commissioning. So the role of DICs in enterprise building and developing small-scale sector is of much significance.

11.2.3. Funding of DICs

The DICs are funded by the State concerned and the centre jointly. The Government has provided substantial assistance to the DICs which can be spent by the DIC s on the construction of an office building, expenditure on furniture, fixtures, equipment, vehicles and other expenses.

11.3. SMALL INDUSTRIES SERVICE INSTITUTES (SISI)

The small industries service institutes have been set up in state capitals and other places all over the country to provide consultancy and training to small entrepreneurs both existing and prospective. These are operational throughout the country and the office of DC(SSI) oversees their respective performances. They occupy a pivotal place in the central networks. These institutes employ regular staff for imparting training. The activities of SISIs are coordinated by the Industrial Management, Training Division of DCSSI's office. The activities of SISIs are supervised by a Director at the headquarter. The training is imparted in the following areas:—

(a) Industrial Management

(b) Marketing Management

(c) Personnel Management

(d) Financial Management

(e) Production Management

11.3.1. Functions of SISI

1. To serve as interface between Central and State government.
2. To render technical support services and consultancy services.
3. To conduct entrepreneurship development programmes.
4. To initiate promotional programmes.
5. To promote export promotion and liaison activities.

The SISIs also render assistance in the following areas:

1. Economic consultancy/information/EDP consultancy.
2. Trade and market information.
3. Project profiles.
4. State industrial potential surveys.
5. District industrial potential surveys.
6. Modernization and in plant studies.
7. Workshop facilities.
8. Training in various trade/activities.
9. Identify the potential for ancillary development through subcontract exchanges.
10. Conduct economic and technical surveys and prepare techno-economic feasible reports for selected areas and industries.

Reports prepared by SISIs have been emphasizing the implementation of programmes on modernization, energy conservation, quality control/ upgradation and pollution control for the benefit of entrepreneurs. The Small Industries Service Institutes have been generally organizing the following types of EDPs on specialized courses for different target groups like energy conservation, pollution control, Technology upgradation, Quality improvement, Material handling, Management technique, etc., as mentioned earlier.

11.3.2. Subcontract Exchanges (SCXs) at SISI

Sixteen subcontract exchanges have been established in the major SISIs in the country with the objective of promoting ancillarisation.

The activities of these exchanges are to

1. register spare capacities available in SSI and tiny units.
2. identify the items required by large units on a regular basis and match this with spare capacity available.

3. promote interaction between small and large units.
4. organise vendor development programmes, exhibitions and promotional programmes.
5. establish networking linkages with other SCXs in the country for flow of information

11.4. ENTREPRENEURSHIP DEVELOPMENT INSTITUTE OF INDIA(EDII)

The Entrepreneurship Development Institute of India (EDII), an autonomous body and not-for-profit institution, set up in 1983, is sponsored by apex financial institutions, namely the IDBI Bank Ltd, IFCI Ltd., ICICI Ltd., and State Bank of India (SBI). The Institute is registered under the Societies Registration Act, 1860 and the Public Trust Act, 1950. The Government of Gujarat pledged twenty-three acres of land on which stands the majestic and sprawling EDII campus. EDII has helped set up twelve state-level exclusive entrepreneurship development centres and institutes. Entrepreneurship has been taken to schools, colleges, science and technology institutions and management schools by including entrepreneurship in their curricula. The University Grants Commission appointed the EDII as an expert agency to develop a curriculum on Entrepreneurship. The EDII has been selected as a member of the Economic and Social Commission for Asia and the Pacific (ESCAP) network of Centres of Excellence for HRD Research and Training. EDII as a member of the Network will have interactive access to information on other 123 member institutions via Internet. The main mission of the EDII is committed to entrepreneurship education, training and research. The institute strives to provide innovative training techniques, competent faculty support, consultancy and quality teaching and training material.

11.4.1. Mission of EDII

- Creating a multiplier effect on opportunities for self-employment
- Augmenting the supply of competent entrepreneurs through training
- Augmenting the supply of entrepreneur trainer-motivators
- Participating in institution building efforts
- Inculcating the spirit of 'Entrepreneurship' in youth
- Promoting microenterprises at rural level
- Developing and disseminating new knowledge and insights in entrepreneurial theory and practice through research
- Facilitating corporate excellence through creating intrapreneurs (entrepreneurial managers),
- Improving managerial capabilities of small-scale industries
- Sensitizing the support system to facilitate potential and existing entrepreneurs establish and manage their enterprises
- Collaborating with similar organizations in India and other developing countries to accomplish the above objectives

In the international arena, the development of entrepreneurship by sharing resources and organising training programmes, have helped the EDI earn support from the World Bank, Commonwealth Secretariat, UNIDO, ILO, British Council, Ford Foundation, European Union and other agencies. EDII has been superheading an entrepreneurship movement throughout the nation in the belief that entrepreneurs need not necessarily be born, they can be developed through well conceived and well directed activities.

11.4.2. Training Programmes of EDII

1. Entrepreneurship in Education
2. Microfinance and microenterprise development
3. Performance and growth of existing entrepreneurs
4. Performance improvement of Entrepreneur development institute and Entrepreneur development programmes .

EDII has designed and successfully implemented several national and international training programmes and workshops for the academic community and for youth. EDII organises training programmes on Informal Microcredit Delivery System(IMCDS) and management for strengthening the participating NGOs in the area of informal credit. To strengthen NGOs through building their managerial capabilities, the EDII has launched a programme on the sustainability of NGOs through better management. EDII has supported the creation of centres for entrepreneurship development and institutes of entrepreneurship development in various states to achieve institutionalization of ED activities.

11.5. NATIONAL INSTITUTE OF ENTREPRENEURSHIP AND SMALL BUSINESS DEVELOPMENT (NIESBUD)

NIESBUD is an Apex Institute in the area of Entrepreneurship and Small Business Development under the **Ministry of Micro, Small and Medium Enterprises** Government of India. The basic objects for which the Institute has been established are: Promotion and Development of Micro, Small and Medium Enterprises including Enhancement of their Competitiveness through Various Activities. The Institute has Conducted a total of 5023 Training Programmes covering 1,33,863 Participants which includes 151 International Training Programmes with 2,285 Participants from more than 125 Countries till 31st October 2012.

The National Institute for Entrepreneurship and Small Business Development (NIESBUD) was established as an apex body for coordinating and overseeing the activities of various institutions/ agencies engaged in Entrepreneurship Development particularly in the area of small industry and small business. NIESBUD was set up in 1983, by the then Ministry of Industry [now Ministry of Micro, Small and Medium Enterprises (MSMEs)], Government of India. The Institute which is registered as a Society under Societies Registration Act, 1860 (XXI of 1860), started functioning from 6th July, 1983. The policy, direction and guidance to the Institute is provided by its Governing Council whose Chairman is the Minister of MSME. The Executive Committee consisting of Secretary (Micro, Small and Medium Enterprises) as its Chairman and Director General of the Institute as its Member-Secretary, executes the policies and decisions of the Governing Council through its whole-time Director General.

11.5.1 Objectives of NIESBUD

- To evolve standardised materials and processes for selection, training, support and sustenance of entrepreneurs, potential and existing.
- To help/support and affiliate institutions/organisations in carrying out training and other entrepreneurship development related activities.
- To serve as an apex national level resource institute for accelerating the process of entrepreneurship development ensuring its impact across the country and among all strata of the society.
- To provide vital information and support to trainers, promoters and entrepreneurs by organising research and documentation relevant to entrepreneurship development
- To train trainers, promoters and consultants in various areas of entrepreneurship development. To provide national/international forums for interaction and exchange of experiences helpful for policy formulation and modification at various levels.
- To offer consultancy nationally/internationally for promotion of entrepreneurship and small business development. To share internationally experience and expertise in entrepreneurship development.
- To share experience and expertise in entrepreneurship development across national frontiers.

11.5.2. Activities of NIESBUD

(a) Assisting/Supporting EDPs

- Evolving standardized materials, research, publications.
- Formulation of standardised procedures of identification and selection of potential entrepreneurs.
- Preparation of Training Aids Materials:—
  - — Manuals
  - — Handbooks
  - — Lesson Plans
  - — Learning Text
  - — Case Studies
  - — EMT Kits etc.

(b) Research and Publications

- Research on topics related to entrepreneurship and allied areas widely disseminates the findings. The Status Analysis Study on Entrepreneurship in India; Potential of Women Entrepreneurship in India; Successful Women Entrepreneurs: Their identity; Expectations and Problems and Directory of EDP Institutions in India are some of the notable research publications by the Institute.

- Information materials for entrepreneurs like Handbooks on Industrial Laws; Commercial Laws; Ready Reckoner for Product Selection, etc., have been prepared.
- Directory of Experts.
- Newsletter covering Schemes; News; Views; Forthcoming Activities; Agency Profile; Entrepreneurial Profile, etc.,

(c) Creation and Capacity Building Of EDP Institutions

The Institute provides support and guidance in establishing EDP institutions. The assistance covers developing programmes and faculty, providing training,library facilities and sharing experiences of conducting programmes at the initial stage(s).

(d) Small Business in Focus

The Institute focuses its attention on small business development by encouraging and supporting arrangements in remote and backward areas. The number and percentage of small business among small entrepreneurs is very large. The Institute concentrates its efforts on evolving methodology for training, supporting and sustaining this Group.

(e) National/International Forum for Exchange of Ideas and Experiences

- The Institute organises National as well as International Meets for sharing experiences with a view to enhance success in implementation of entrepreneurship development programmes.
- Organises Workshops and Seminars on comtemporary topics/issues such as sustaining entrepreneurship, emerging entrepreneurial opportunities, etc.
- Encourages foreign delegations for mutual exchange of experiences.

(f) Developing Entrepreneurial Culture

- The Institute strives to create a climate conducive to emergence of entrepreneurs from all strata of society.
- Conducts awareness campaigns for students of school and college and Institutions of higher learnings.
- Produces and distributes material for use by mass media like TV, AIR, etc.
- Organises group discussions representing a variety of cross-sections of the society.

(g) Services to Affiliate Members

- The Institute affiliates individuals/ institutions/ organisations engaged in entrepreneurship development and related activities such as Ordinary, Associate and Corporate Members. The Institute offers the following services to the Members:—
- Be some Member of the Society and thus, contribute towards discussing strategy for propogating entrepreneurship.
- Provision of Consessional Facilities.
- Free Services(Library, Documentation, etc.)
- Free Academic Advice/Guidance.

(h) Sustaining Entrepreneurship

Sustaining existing entrepreneurs is an important activity. In this direction, the Institute organises Continuing Education Programmes for SSI Entrepreneurs besides providing counselling and consultancy. Short duration training programmes on Working Capital Management, Marketing, Project Identification and Selection, Accounting, etc., are conducted on campus while counselling/consultancy is provided on and off campus.

11.5.3. Functions of NIESBUD

- It act as an Apex Institute.
- It organize the various training programmes.
- It helps in setting up of self employment ventures.
- It publishes literatures for furtherance of entrepreneurship and small business development.
- It conducts various examinations, tests and confer certificates to trainers.
- It also coordinates the training activities of various institutes and organization in country providing training in entrepreneurship.
- It also provides national and international forms for interaction and exchange of views with agencies engaged in various aspect of entrepreneurship.

11.6. NATIONAL ENTREPRENEURSHIP DEVELOPMENT BOARD (NEDB)

The National Entrepreneurship Development Board (NEDB) is the body for entrepreneurship development in the country. It devises and recommends to the Government, schemes for promotion of entrepreneurship for encouraging self-employment in small-scale industries and small business. The Board also recommends suitable facilities and incentives for entrepreneurship training. The Board may appoint committees for specific purposes and also invite persons to the meeting of the Board, as and when necessary.

11.6.1. Objectives of NEDB

1. To seek to evolve a ten years perspective plan of resource development and support services, required by micro, tiny, small and medium scale entrepreneurs to lead a national drive by the concerned governmental agencies both Central and State Government, R&D institutions, entrepreneurship promoting institutions and all others interested in supporting the cause of entrepreneurship and entrepreneurial ventures.

2. To articulate priorities and design and monitor the implementation of Action Plans thereby helping the area to cope with the business environment of 21st Century.

3. To identify and remove entry barriers for potential entrepreneurs (first generation and new entrepreneurs).

4. To focus on existing entrepreneurs in micro, tiny and small sector and identify and remove constraints to survival, growth and continuously improve performance.

5. To facilitate the consolidation, growth and diversification of existing entrepreneurial venture in all possible ways.

6. To support skill upgradation and renewal of learning processes among practising entrepreneurs and managers of micro, tiny, small and medium enterprises.

7. To sensitise to support agencies in the area of entrepreneurship about the current requirement of growth.

8. To act as catalyst to institutionalise entrepreneurship development by supporting and strengthening state level institutions for entrepreneurship development as most entrepreneurship-related activities take place at the grass roots level and removing various constraints to their effective functioning.

Under NEDB, funds are provided for entrepreneurship development, training, studies, etc., to meet the above mentioned objectives.

11.6.2. Eligibility

Any institution seeking the financial assistance for the activities mentioned above relating to entrepreneurship development under the NEDB Scheme may send their application giving details including objective, activities proposed to be covered, cost break-up, funding arrangements, details of the organization including audited accounts of last 3 years, etc., to Joint Secretary, Ministry of Small-scale Industries,

11.6.3. Entrepreneurship and Business Development Centres (EBDCs)

In addition to the above activities, a new component of Entrepreneurship and Business Development Centres (EBDCs) to be established in selected Colleges/Universities/Organisations has been included in the NEDB Scheme to motivate students to take up entrepreneurship as a career option with the objective to promote self-employment through creation of small, micro and tiny enterprises in the country which would not only provide self-employment opportunities but are also expected to create additional job opportunities in these enterprises. The Scheme will be implemented through selected Universities/Colleges, Regional Engineering Colleges and other Institutions/ Organisations. The Host Institution could be a university / a premier college (preferably autonomous)/ organisation of repute; offering courses in management, liberal arts, social sciences, commerce, science or agriculture, engineering and technology etc., or associated with the industrial sector and should:

(i) Be in existence for at least five (5) years.

(ii) Have qualified and experienced faculty in the various related disciplines.

(iii) Be in a position to spare or provide adequate space for establishing the Centre (at least two rooms) with lecture theatres/classrooms equipped with modern teaching aids (like overhead projector, VCR/Video, etc.), adequate computer facilities and other infrastructure and willing to commit for the use of the EBDC as and when required.

(iv) Have good library facilities.

(v) Preferably, have some experience in entrepreneurship development.

(vi) Ideally, have access to industries nearby and preferably should have good networking with local industries.

During Tenth Plan a minimum of 5 EBDCs, one each in East, West, South, North and North-Eastern region of the country are to be set up under the Scheme. The financial assistance/grant will be provided to the EBDCs under the scheme initially for a period of 2 years and extendable by another 2 years depending on the performance. After 4 years it would be responsible of the host institution to continue the EBDCs and arrange funds for the same. The EBDCs are expected to organize fee based training programme and EDP courses. Each EBDC will be provided a one time capital grant of ₹ 5 lakhs for setting up of the Centre,(for procurement of office equipments, furniture, computers, etc). A block grant/recurring grant of ₹10 lakhs (@ ₹ 5 lakhs per annum over a period of 2 years will be provided for expenditure including special incentive, books, stationaries, grant for conducting entrepreneurship/thematic programmes, travel, contingencies, trainers' training, etc.

The EBDCs will maintain a separate bank account in a scheduled public sector bank, which will be jointly operated by the Head/Director of the EBDC and Head of the Host Institution. All financial receipts/funds received by the Centre will be credited to this account. Efforts should be made to make the EBDC financially viable at the earliest. All payments by the EBDC should be authorised jointly by the Head of the Host Institution and Head/Director of the EBDC.

11.7. NATIONAL SCIENCE AND TECHNOLOGY ENTREPRENEURSHIP DEVELOPMENT BOARD (NSTEDB)

The National Science and Technology Entrepreneurship Development Board (NSTEDB), established in 1982 by the Government of India under the aegis of Department of Science and Technology, is an institutional mechanism to help promote knowledge driven and technology intensive enterprises. The Board, having representations from socio-economic and scientific Ministries/ Departments, aims to convert "job-seekers" into "job-generators" through Science and Technology (S&T) interventions.

11.7.1 Objectives of NSTEDB

1. To promote and develop high-end entrepreneurship for S&T manpower as well as self-employment by utilizing S&T infrastructure and by using S&T methods.

2. To facilitate and conduct various informational services relating to promotion of entrepreneurship.

3. To network agencies of the support system, academic institutions and Research and Development (R&D) organisations to foster entrepreneurship and self-employing using S&T with special focus on backward areas as well.

4. To act as a policy advisory body with regard to entrepreneurship.

11.8. BIRLA INSTITUTE OF TECHNOLOGY - SCIENCE AND TECHNOLOGY ENTREPRENEURS' PARK (BIT-STEP)

(Earlier *Small Industries Research and Development Organization*) at Birla Institute of Technology, Mesra, Ranchi is the first Science and Technology Entrepreneurs' Park approved and established by

National Science and Technology Entrepreneurship Development Board (NSTEBD), Department of Science and Technology, Government of India. The Science and Technology Entrepreneurs' Park (STEP) programme was initiated to provide a reorientation in approach to innovation and entrepreneurship involving education, training, research, finance, and management.

11.8.1. Objectives of BIT-STEP

BIT-STEP's aims have to be considered within the overall goals of BIT - which themselves were formulated in the context of State industrial development. BIT-STEP aims:

- To forge a close linkage between university, academic and R&D institutions on the one hand and industry on the other
- To promote entrepreneurship among science and technology persons and
- To provide R&D support to small-scale industries mostly through interaction with research institutions.

11.9. TECHNICAL CONSULTANCY ORGANIZATIONS (TCOs)

All India financial institutions and state governments have set a net work of technical consultancy organizations. The functions of the TCOs include, conducting surveys on industrial potential, preparing project profiles, undertaking techno-economic appraisal of projects, carrying out market research, providing technical and managerial assistance to entrepreneurs, assistance in modernisation, technology upgradations and rehabilitation programmes and organizing information cell and Data Bank concerning industrial and economic activities and provide these to entrepreneurs.

TCO identify potential entrepreneurs,train them and provide post training counseling and guidance in selecting projects, preparing profiles and establishing their own units

11.10. KERALA INDUSTRIAL AND TECHNICAL CONSULTANCY ORGANIZATION

KITCO Limited (formerly Kerala Industrial and Technical Consultancy Organisation Ltd.), India's first TCO (Technical Consultancy Organisation), was established in 1972 by Industrial Development Bank of India (IDBI) and Govt. of Kerala along with Public Sector Banks for aiding in Industrialization of the state of Kerala. The aim of this initiative, which had the blessing of Govt. of India and the Reserve Bank of India, was to provide professional technical consultancy assistance to banks by appraisal of projects for priority sector lending and to entrepreneurs in the SME Sector by way of preparation of Project Reports and Market Studies and by conducting training programmes for entrepreneurship development. Subsequently similar TCOs were set up in almost all the states with one of the National Financial Institution (IDBI, IFCI or ICICI) as the prime shareholder.

Today, 49% shares of the company are held by Small Industries Development Bank of India. Other shareholders are Govt. of Kerala, Kerala State Industrial Development Corporation, Kerala Financial Corporation, 7 Govt. sector banks, Industrial Finance Corporation of India and ICICI Bank.

Moreover according to *Economic Times* news[1] dated 12 July,2013 KSEB(Kerala State Electricity Board) Chairman M Sivasankar and Start-up Village chairman Sanjay Vijayakumar are to sign the one-year agreement obligating both the sides to partner the venture, which will be a landmark in the development of an innovation ecosystem in the country. An Electrical Open Innovation Zone(EOIZ), coming up on 2500 sq ft, will train people in the skills required to launch businesses in and around the energy sector. Apart from the operational funding, KSEB will also extend technical and non-technical support while Startup Village will develop, own and execute the programme. Startup Village will offer incubation support to selected participants through its Mentor Panel and Partner Network. The innovation zone will work in line with the National Electrical Mobility Mission 2020.

Start-up Village, the first public-private partnership incubator in the telecom sector of the country, has already an innovation zone set up by Blackberry (RIM). Many other global leaders are also in talks with Startup Village to set up similar zones that will provide better eco-system for innovations.

11.11. INSTITUTES OF ENTREPRENEURSHIP DEVELOPMENT (IED)

IDBI had announced the proposal to set up Institutes for Entrepreneurship Development in association with other financial institutions, banks and State Government as part of strategy of giving special attention to entrepreneurship development needs of more backward states. IEDs set-up in U.P, Bihar, Orissa are in operation.

11.12. NATIONAL PRODUCTIVITY COUNCIL (NPC)

NPC is an autonomous institute functioning under the overall supervision of the Ministry of Industry, Government of India. The primary objective of NPC is to act as a catalyst in enhancing the productivity of all sectors of the economy. NPC is active in the field of consultancy and training and has number of specialized divisions to provide tailor made solutions to agriculture and industry.

These divisions, manned by trained consultant ,deal with issues related to industrial engineering, plant engineering energy management etc. NPC is a member of Asian Productivity Organisation (APO) and has number of Entrepreneurship Development Programmes which is designed to identify persons with entrepreneurial abilities and to train them to set up new small/ tiny industries.

11.13. SUMMARY

Keeping in view the contribution of small business to employment generation, balanced regional development of the country, and promotion of exports, the Government of India's policy thrust has been on establishing, promoting and developing the small business sector, particularly the rural industries and the cottage and village industries in backward areas. Governments both at the central and state level have been actively participating in promoting self employment opportunities in rural areas by providing assistance in respect of infrastructure, finance, technology, training, raw-materials, and marketing. The various policies and schemes of Government assistance for the development of rural industries insist on the utilisation of local resources and raw materials and locally available manpower. These are translated into action through various agencies, departments, corporations, etc., all coming under the purview of the industries department. All these are primarily concerned with the promotion of small and rural industries.There are various agencies at center and state level like;— EDII, NIESBUD, NEDB, etc.

11.14. SELF ASSESSMENT QUESTIONS

1. What do you mean by EDII and what is the mission behind it?
2. What do you mean by NIESBUD ? What are the objectives and activities of NIESBUD?
3. Give detailed description of various agencies which help in the promotion of entrepreneurship.
4. What do you mean by SISI, NEDB, NIESBUD,EDII and DIC?

SOURCES/NOTES

Entrepreneurship and Small Business-Rajesh Marwaha

Entrepreneurship Development Small Business Enterprises- Poornima MCharantimath

http://www.dcmsme.gov.in/ssiindia/MSME_OVERVIEW09.pdf

http://economictimes.indiatimes.com/news/emerging-businesses/startups/KSEB-to-open-innovation-zone-at-Startup-Village)

12

INTRODUCTION TO PROJECT

12.1. INTRODUCTION

To become globally competitive, Indian industry has to strive hard to induct new technologies and focus on producing cost effective, best quality, energy efficient and environmental friendly products. As India aspires to emerge as one of the top five economies of the world within next two decades, there is need to leverage new technology for the innovative and sustainable products and services. For this Indian Entrepreneurs has to take up more and more new projects and complete them within the time constraints and expected quality standards. This is the only means for the economic development. Because of this great need the role of project and its planning has assumed greater significance. The success and failure of an enterprise is largely dependent upon the project

12.2. PROJECT – MEANING AND DEFINITION

The word project is derived from Latin where *"pro"* means "forward" and *"jacere"* means "throw". Thus the original meaning of project is something that in a figurative sense has been thrown forward, a proposal. The meaning has gradually been extended to include the process of realizing the proposal and the people who perform the realization.

When the English language initially adopted the word, it referred to a plan of something. So according to dictionary meaning, project is known as -a scheme of something to be done.

In each and every enterprise there is a need of undertaking of different types of projects and for that an entrepreneur has to identify the need of the market and has to take necessary steps to meet the need of the market by starting different projects. For that an entrepreneur has to identify the suitable project. There is no set rules and regulations for the identification of the project but the success of the project greatly depend upon the selection of the right type of project. A project can be considered to be series of activities and tasks that have a specific objectives to be completed within certain specifications.

A project is defined as one shot, time bound, goal oriented activity which require the commitment of various resources and skills. It is also known as combination of human and non human resources which work together in a temporary organization to achieve set objectives. It can be considered as a proposal involving capital investment for the purpose of developing facilities. A project involve allocation and consumption of resources on one hand and generation of resources, goods and services on the other as in Fig. 12.1.

INPUT (ALLOCATIONS AND CONSUMPTION OF RESOURCES)	PROJECT	OUTPUT (GENERATION OF RESOURCES, GOODS AND SERVICES

Fig. 12.1

A project is a productive activity which can be analyzed, appraised and monitored independently. It is defined as scientifically evolved work plan devised to achieve a specific objectives with a specific period of time. Three basic attributes of a project are:-

(a) course of action

(b) specific objectives

(c) definite time perspective

So, a project is an organized unit dedicated to the attainment of a goal and the successful completion of a project means the attainment of objectives, within budget, in time and in conformance with pre-determined programme specifications. A project can be a new plant, structure, process, system or software, the replacement, renewal or removal of an existing utility. It is simply a one off investment. In business area there are large number of projects like Construction projects IT projects, Product development projects, RD projects, Organisation development projects, Logistics projects, Marketing projects, Community projects and Cultural projects.

12.3. DEFINITIONS

1. According to F.L Harrison, "A project can be defined as a non-routine, non-repetitive, one off undertaking normally with discrete time, finance and technical performance goals."

2. According to Project Management Institute, USA: "A project is one shot, time limited goal directed, major undertaking, requiring the commitment of varied skills and resources. It also described project as a combination of human and non-human resources pooled together in a temporary organization to achieve a specific purpose. The objective and set of activities differ from one project to another project."

3. According to World Bank, "A project is an approval for a capital investment to develop facilities to provide goods and services."

4. According to Mintzberg, "A project is an organizational unit that solves a unique and complex task."

5. According to APM(Association for Project Management), "Project is unique, transient endeavour undertaken to achieve desired outcome."

6. The Report of Economic Commission for Asia and Far East(ECAFE) describes that "Project is a smallest unit of investment activity to be considered in the case of programming. It will, as a rule, be a technically coherent undertaking which has to be carried out technically speaking, independently of other projects."

7. According to Gillinger, " Project is the whole complex of activities involved in using resources to gain benefits."

8. According to Newman, "a project typically has a distinct mission that it is designed to achieve and a clear termination point, the achievement of the mission."

So according to above definitions a project is an action oriented undertaking. It is one shot, time tested, goal directed, major undertaking requiring the commitment of varied skills and resources (Fig. 12.2). A project is a temporary entity established to deliver specific (often tangible) outputs in line with predefined time, cost and quality constraints. A project should always be defined and executed and evaluated relative to an (Executive) approved business case which balances the costs, benefits and risks of the project. The project business case should be managed under change control.

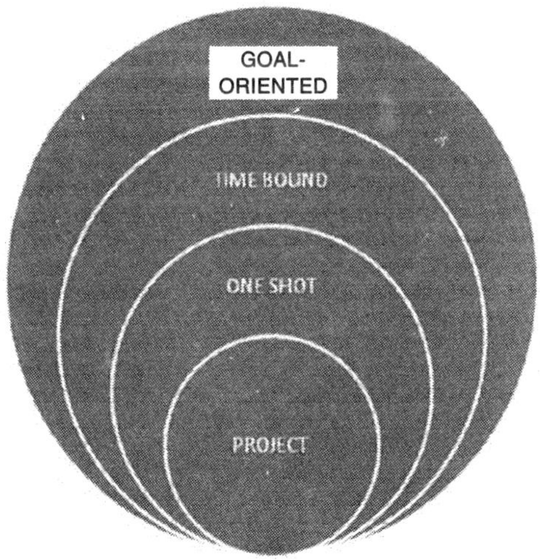

Fig. 12.2

12.4. BASIC ATTRIBUTES OF PROJECT

Basic attributes of project are :-

1. Input of Resources
2. Output of product
3. Social Benefit

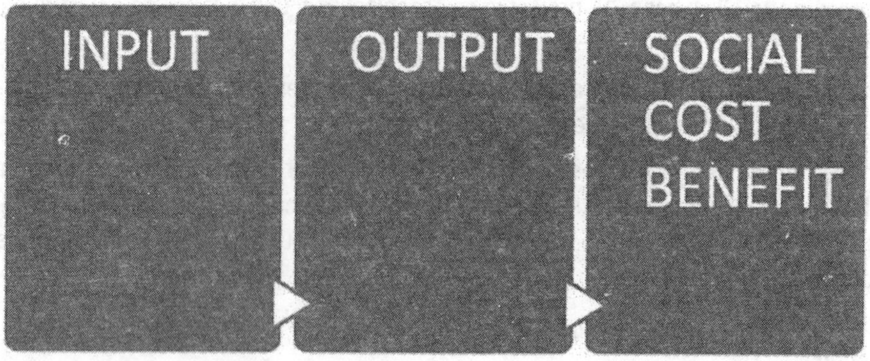

Fig. 12.3

12.5. DIFFERENCE BETWEEN PROJECT AND PROGRAMME

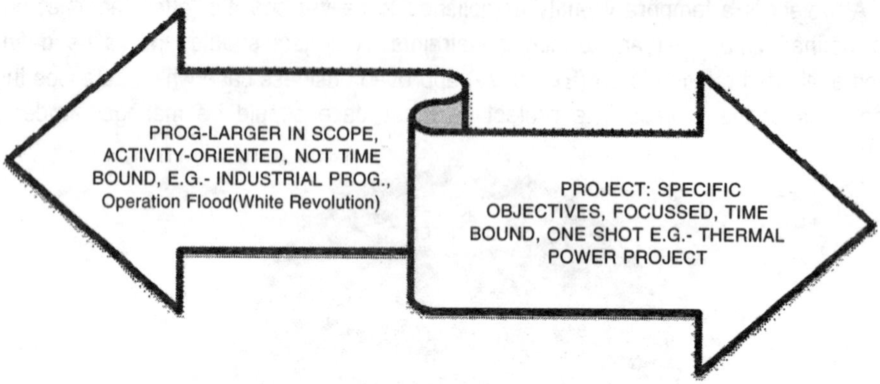

Fig. 12.4

A project is more or less temporary in nature that is undertaken to get specified results in given time along with constraints of cost and quality.

A program is a portfolio comprised of multiple projects that are managed and coordinated as one unit with the objective of achieving (often intangible) outcomes and benefits for the organization.

Though they look similar, there are many points of difference that are as follows.

First major difference pertains to the objective of a project in comparison to the objective of a program. In a project, the manager knows the output he has to achieve; they are tangible, and can be described easily in words. One can measure the progress of a project, which is why the outputs are referred to as objectives. On the other hand, there are outcomes, and not outputs in case of a program, and even these are subjective and hard to quantify. Scope is vaguely defined in case of program, and can change as per the whims of managers during implementation of the program. On the other hand, the scope of a project is clear cut and demarcated, and cannot be changed during the life of the project.

The following Table 12.1 summarizes the main areas of difference between a project and a program.

Table 12.1

	Project	Program
Objectives	Outputs – tangible; relatively easy to describe, define and measure; tending towards objective.	Outcomes – often intangible; difficult to quantify; benefits often based on changes to organizational culture and behaviors; introducing new capabilities into the organization; tending towards subjective.
Scope	Strictly limited; tightly defined; not likely to be subject to material change during the life of the project.	Not tightly defined or bounded; likely to change during the life cycle of the program.
Duration	Relatively short-term; typically three to six months and are pursued in a planned manner	Relatively long-term typically eighteen months to three years.
Risk profile	Project risk is relatively easy to identify and manage. The project failure would result in relatively limited impact on the organization relative to program risk.	Program risk is more complex and potentially the impact on the organization if a risk materializes will be greater relative to project risk. Programme failure could result in material financial, reputational or operational loss.
Nature of the problem	Clearly defined.	Ill-defined; often disagreement between key stakeholders on the nature and definition of the problem
Nature of the solution	A relatively limited number of potential solutions.	A significant number of potential solutions with often with disagreement between stakeholders as to the preferred solution.
Stakeholders	A relatively limited number of stakeholders.	A significant number of diverse stakeholders; probable disagreement between them as to the definition of the problem and the preferred solution.
Relationship to environment	Environment within which the project takes place is understood and relatively stable.	Environment is dynamic; and programme objectives need to be managed in the context of the changing environment within which the organization operates.
Resources	Resources to deliver the project can be reasonably estimated in advance.	Resources are constrained and limited; there is competition for resources between projects.

12.6. CHARACTERISTICS OF A PROJECT

1. Projects have a purpose: Projects have clearly-defined aims and set out to produce clearly-defined results. Their purpose is to solve a "problem", and this involves analysing needs beforehand. Once these aims/objectives are achieved the project ceases to exist.

2. Set objectives: A project has fixed set of objectives to be achieved. Once these objectives are achieved it means the project is completed and it will exit from the organizational pyramid.

3. Projects are realistic: Their aims must be achievable, and this means taking account both of requirements and of the financial and human resources available.

4. Projects are time bound: They have a beginning and an end and are implemented in (a) specific place(s) and context. A project cannot continue indefinitely. It is either executed, terminated or dead. Every project is invariably time bound and the time limits are well defined through schedules.

5. Projects are complex: A project is not contingent to single factor hermitic. Projects call on various planning and implementation skills and involve various partners and players.It is a *mélange* of various partners, i.e., natural and man made,which traces a complex interrelationship among things, people and environment. This 'unity in diversity' is a global concept for any kind of project.

6. Projects are collective/teamwork: Projects are the product of collective endeavours. They involve teamwork and various partners and cater for the needs of others. So it encourages team spirit among the group of people who participate in it and are instrumental in achieving its goals. The team consists of different individuals from varied disciplines who bestow their knowledge, experience and credence towards a total performance.

7. Projects are unique: Projects are as unique as 'fingerprints' of individuals. No two projects are same/alike in execution even if the plans are duplicates of each other. Projects stem from new ideas. They provide a specific response to a need (problem) in a specific context. They are innovative and no two projects are exactly same because the location, infrastructure, aim, people make the project unique and moreover the deployment and performance of the resources will vary even if the two projects conform to same standards and quality.

8. Projects can be assessed: Projects are planned and broken down into measurable aims, which must be open to evaluation.

9. Projects involve risk: Risk, uncertainty and projects are correlated, i.e., every project involves the element of risk and uncertainty. The degree of risk depends upon how project has passed from different stages of its life cycle. A well -conceived project may have a lesser degree of risk and uncertainty whereas an ill-defined one will be susceptible to high degree of risk and uncertainty.

10. Customer Specific: Projects are not ready-made articles, rather they are made ready. A project is always customer specific and considers constraints on the demand side of economics more often than on the credits of the supply side. But all are secondary concern except the 'customer requirement', so project is executed to fulfill some specific customers needs only.

11. Unity in diversity: Every project has the characteristic feature of unity in diversity. As a project is a complex set of number of different activities which remain interrelated with each other.

Although these activities differ in terms of requirement of resources like;-materials , machines, technology, people etc but these are essentially inter-related during stages of a project life span.

12. Team spirit: Every project encourages team spirit as a project is a team activity. Team consists of different individuals from varied disciplines who give their knowledge, experience and credence towards total performance. So project encourage team spirit in order to achieve the goals.

12.7. PROJECT CLASSIFICATION

Project classification is a natural corollary to the study of project idea. Different authorities have classified projects differently. Following are the major classifications of projects:

1. Quantification Basis: Quantifiable and Non-quantifiable Projects: Projects for which a plausible quantitative assessment of benefits can be made are called 'quantifiable projects.' Projects concerned with industrial development, power generation, mineral development fall in this category. On the contrary, non-quantifiable projects are those in which a plausible quantitative assessment cannot be made. Projects involving health education and defense are the examples of non-quantifiable projects.

2. Techo-Economic Projects: Projects classification based on techno-economic characteristics fall in this category, i.e., technological and economic factors prevailing in the country. This types of classification following:—

(a) **Factor Intensity-oriented Classification:** Based on factor intensity classification, projects may be classified as capital intensive or labor intensive. If large investment is made in plant and machinery, the projects will be termed as 'capital intensive'. On the contrary, projects involving large number of human resources will be termed as 'labor intensive'.

(b) **Causation-oriented Classification:** Where causation is used as a basis of classification, projects may be classified as demand based or raw material based projects. The very existence of demand for certain goods or services makes the project demand-based and the availability of certain raw materials, skills or other inputs makes the project raw material-based.

(c) **Magnitude-oriented Classification:** In case of magnitude oriented classification, based on the size of investment involved in the projects, the projects are classified into large-scale, medium-scale or small-scale projects.

3. Sectoral Projects: Indian Planning Commission has been following the sectoral basis for the classification of projects.

(i) Agriculture and Allied Sector

(ii) Irrigation and Power Sector

(iii) Industry and Mining Sector

(iv) Transport and Communication Sector

(v) Social Services Sector

(vi) Miscellaneous Sector.

The project classification based on economic sectors is found useful in resource allocation more especially at macro levels

4. Purpose-oriented Projects: Following are the projects which are classified on the basis of purpose for which they are sought—

(a) Rehabilitation of Sick Units Project: According to RBI, a sick unit is one which has incurred cash losses for one year and in the judgment of the financial bank, is likely to incur cash losses for the current as well as following year and/or there is imbalance in the unit's financial structure, that is, current ratio is less then 1:1 and debt/equity ratio is worsening. The purpose of rehabilitation project is to rejuvenate the sick unit. These projects are generally undertaken by the financially sound investing groups to revive sick or worn-off projects. In fact, reorganisation of these units is a rare activity for the new investor because of high risk involvement but sometimes well known companies may fall sick due some reasons ,so other big business houses take these projects as challenge. In fact, reorganization of poorly fed or so-called dead industrial projects is a rare activity because of high-risk involvement. Some of the financial institutions which help such projects are IRBI and SFC.

(b) Maintenance Projects: Maintenance projects are those projects whose main aim is to upkeep the existence plant and machinery .These projects involve overhauling the machinery, repairs and patching up activities at more than regular interval. These projects are often met through 'in-house budgetary provisions'. In other words, when the scope of normal maintenance task gets enlarged seeking additional coordination from other department, then it is identified as a 'maintenance project'.

(c) Modernisation Projects: Under modernisation projects there is switch–over from the old machines to latest tools and techniques. In order to cope up with the dynamic environment and customer need the change is always needed. The existing firm will feel an urge for modernisation, when the total 'industry' experiences the changes or there is fear of becoming obsolete. So these projects are always needed after certain time interval. In total, it means shifting from existing process to a new process that brings new economies of scale.

(d) Diversification Projects: Diversification refers to the expansion of existing operations to either different lines of business or the same line of business. These projects come into existence due to tapping of additional potential of the market. The main reason for the diversification project is that either the current products are not able to meet the growth or there will be more profit in diversifying .Sometimes the available market, unforeseen opportunity occurs which result in increase in profitability and development through R&D operations may lead to diversification. E.g.:-Tata's diversifying from steel to chemicals, salt, motors, jewellery, etc., or Ambani's diversifying from textiles to petrochemicals, telecom, jewellery, etc.

In Diversification Projects, the direction of the project has to be decided in advance. It either can be vertical or horizontal:

(i) Vertical integration(diversification) : This kind of diversification is opted when an entrepreneur wishes to control the source of supply for a project. This is a kind of defensive mechanism where input supply of the product is controlled in order to reap the benefits of specialization.

This is also known as backward integration. This helps in generating competition among the manufacturers in the industry by timely delivery of the products with all the benefits such as reduced overheads, prompt delivery of raw materials, minimum cost of production etc. E.g.:- Reliance Industries under textile unit established a PFY(polyester filament yarn) manufacturing plant which is a basic input to its textile plants.

(ii) **Horizontal diversification:** This a kind of offensive mechanism where the movement of expansion is vertically downward and coves the areas such as distribution, marketing, advertisement etc. It helps in cutting down the cost of marketing and distribution and helps in reducing the cost price of the product.It also helps in discouraging the middle man which result in reduction of the price of the product. Eg.:-Titan watches establish their own sales and after sales service centres, Reliance trends selling their own products under one roof.

5. Other classification: There are four major classifications of project type. The type depends on how much is known about what needs to be done, and how much is known about how to do it.

Every project has a set of objectives to meet. These relate to how quickly the project needs to be completed, how much it should cost, and what quality level will be achieved. The project manager is responsible for these once he or she accepts the project.

Before accepting responsibility for a project, the project manager may need to negotiate for resources. Knowing the type of project is the key to this, and the four types of project (Fig.12.5) are described here:-

(*i*) **Painting by Numbers:** This is the most straightforward type of project. The stakeholders all know exactly what needs to be done, and they also how it needs to be done. This type of project tends to move along steadily, and the problems that may arise are usually quite predictable.

An example of "Painting by Numbers" is building a house, where the project manager and his employer have experience in this trade.

The project manager has the least negotiating options with this type of project.

(*ii*) **Going on a Quest:** This type of project is characterized by the stakeholders knowing what they want to achieve, but are not so clear as to how to achieve it. There are typically several strands of the project happening at the same time, which come together to meet certain deadlines. This type of project is common in Research and Development.

For example, NASA was given a brief to put a man on the moon by the end of 1969. When they were asked to do this at first, there was no known way to do it. Separate teams were set up to deal with the rocket, nutrition for the astronauts, and so on.

The project manager can negotiate for resources based on the large number of unknowns.

(*iii*) **Making a Movie:** In this type of project, the methods to be used are known, but the end result is not so clear. This is quite often the case with creative projects, where the final result could be a masterpiece or a flop, hence the title "making a movie". With this type of project, the person with ultimate responsibility needs to be aware of how the end result may not be well liked, even though a standard process has been followed.

(*iv*) **Walking in the Fog:** This is the most difficult type of project. The main stakeholders are not only unclear about how things need to be done, but are also not totally sure about what the end result should be. An example of this type of project is the introduction of a new Business Excellence program such as Six Sigma or Lean Manufacturing.

This type of project needs a strong leader, and he must ensure that the project has the complete commitment and support of the senior stakeholders.

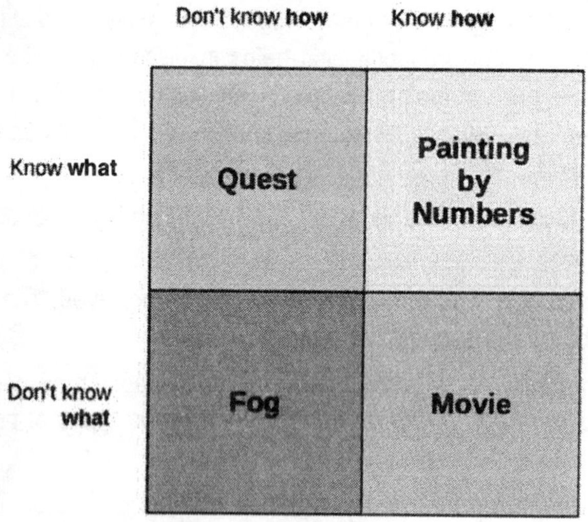

Fig. 12.5

12.8. SMART PROJECT TASKS

Since project tasks can be virtually anything and have possibly multiple relationships with other tasks it is important to try and be consistent and work at a level of detail that ensures all significant tasks are captured. The following guide to project tasks is intended to help project managers select an appropriate level of detail and use that consistently for project planning. Project tasks should be SMART:

1. Specific - a single, well defined, discrete activity
2. Measurable - it should be an activity that can be measured such as a deliverable produced, an elapsed period of time or number of iterations
3. Achievable - it should be something that can be done as a single task and can be defined as being completed or done such as a document being produced
4. Result-oriented - some deliverable or output is produced by the activity
5. Time bound - defined period of time for task to be done

12.9. PROJECT MANAGEMENT

Project management is the discipline of planning, organizing, motivating, and controlling resources to achieve specific goals. The primary challenge of project management is to achieve all of the project goals. The secondary — challenge is to optimize the allocation of necessary inputs and integrate them to meet pre-defined objectives.

It is involved in executing the projects. Project management as a discipline is one of the richest sources of proven techniques for accomplishment of the goals, allowing organizations to reduce the need for strict control and heavy rigidity. Project management in the recent past was recognized as a management philosophy in addition to that of a discipline. It is a proven technique for the accomplishment of the goals. It provides techniques for making trade-offs between conflicting goals and enterprise priorities. It also helps in reducing developmental time, lowering cost, better coordination and better control. According to Project Management Institute, the processes are guided through five stages:

(a) initiation (b) planning (c) executing (d) controlling and (e) closing.

12.10. BENEFITS OF PROJECT MANAGEMENT TECHNIQUES:

Project management provides techniques which helps in better control and co-ordination. It also helps in reducing developmental time, lowering cost and producing higher order results. Other benefits are as under:-

(i) Project management techniques helps in clear description of the work to be performed which further helps in minimization of surprises and conflicts;

(ii) Project Management helps in identifying responsibilities and assignment of specific activities;

(iii) It helps in reduction of continuous reporting;

(iv) It specifies the time for the completion of task;

(v) It enabled the measurement of accomplishment against the set plans;

(vi) It simplified the tracking of functional responsibilities to ensure that all activities are accounted forregardless of personal turnover;

(vii) It helps in explosion of problems in advance and allows corrective action.

12.11. IMPORTANCE OF PROJECT

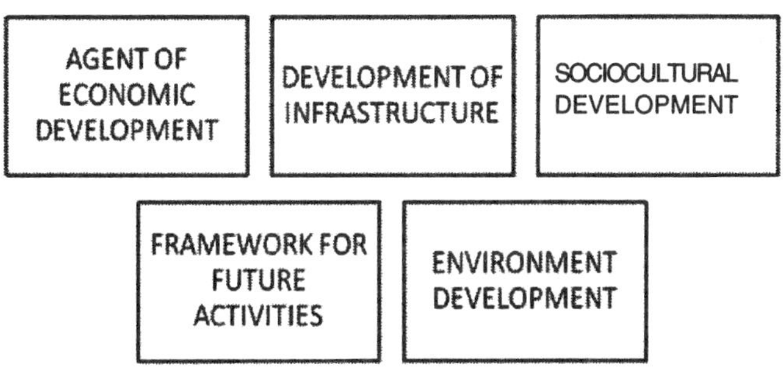

Fig. 12.6

1. Agent of Economic Development: Project are very important agents of economic development. More and more projects means more and more development of the country through employment generation, utilization of resources etc. More and more projects means more and more employment, increase in forex earnings, increase in per capita income balanced regional growth etc.

2. Development of Infrastructure: Infrastructure is basic physical and organizational structures needed for the operation of a society or enterprise, or the services and facilities necessary for an economy to function. It can be generally defined as the set of interconnected structural elements that provide framework supporting an entire structure of development. It is an important term for judging a country or region's development. The term typically refers to the technical structures that support a society, such as roads, bridges, water supply, sewers, electrical grids, telecommunications, and so forth, and can be defined as "the physical components of interrelated systems providing commodities and services essential to enable, sustain, or enhance societal living conditions." These are all done because of projects. Projects facilitate the development of basic infrastructure and environment.

3. Socio-cultural Development: Project is a team work activity where human and non human resources come together to complete one common task. And here project leaders, managers and other humans come from different areas, different cultures and backgrounds but they work together as a team to attain the set mission which helps in sociocultural development.

4. Framework for Future Activities: Projects provide framework for future activities of the enterprise and also determines the nature of future pattern of services. It is done through project planning where the projects are decided in advance for future.

5. Environment Development: Projects help in the overall development of the environment. Different projects are planned for according to different social or environmental needs.

12.12. THE PROJECT LIFE CYCLE

Project is an undertaking or venture that demands resources to accomplish an objective. Despite the dissimilarities between various projects, these projects undergo similar phases as the project matures from conception to completion. Some managers find it useful to use the project life cycle as the cornerstone for managing projects. The Project Life Cycle refers to a logical sequence of activities to accomplish the project's goals or objectives. Regardless of scope or complexity, any project goes through a series of stages during its life. There is first an Initiation or Birth phase, in which the outputs and critical success factors are defined, followed by a Planning phase, characterized by breaking down the project into smaller parts/tasks, an Execution phase, in which the project plan is executed, and lastly a Closure or Exit phase, that marks the completion of the project.

The life cycle recognizes that projects have a limited life span and that the project lifecycle typically passes sequentially through five stages:

Project conception, i.e., identification, Project definition., i.e., formulation, Project planning, Project implementation, Project completion and audit. These are:

1. Project Conception(Identification): This is the first stage in the life cycle of a project.It is primarily concerned with germination of project idea. The idea can come from various sources i.e:- customers, employees, problem faced like non or under utilization of resources. We initiate a project by defining its reason, business goals, and scope. The reason for initiating it, and the propose solution to be implemented. We will also put together a project team, define early milestones, and early budget proposal. With the above information we can move on and perform an end of Phase study in order to get a GO No GO decision. If the idea seems to be feasible only then the project life cycle moves to its next stage.Here the project is identified and after identification pre-screening takes place.

2. Project Definition Phase: During this phase of life cycle, project idea is developed into an investment proposition. During this phase detailed feasibility takes place and documents are prepared with provide sufficient details covering all the necessary aspects needed by the financial institutes to make up their mind about the project idea. Under this phase all the aspects of the projects are taken into consideration like the availability of raw material, labour, location, plant and machinery, avalibility of finance, training of manpower etc.

3. Project Planning Phase: Once we define the project and assemble the project team, we are ready to enter the in depth Project Planning phase. In this phase the entrepreneur prepares project execution plan and deals with areas such as project infrastructure ,system design and basic engineering package, licensing, budget etc. It includes the definition of project specifications, establishment of project objectives and its scope. In this phase teams are formed and major responsibilities are assigned. This involves creating the "PMP", Project Management Plan, in order to guide the team during the project development and after. We will define the Required Skills of Development Team. Define Non-labor Resources, Risks plan, detailed action items and milestones.

4. Project Implementation Phase: With a comprehensible characterization of the project and the full and detailed PMP, we are now ready to enter the Execution phase of the project. This is the stage in which the requirements are actually built and programmed. This stage entails lot of mental andas well as physical project work. The physical product like a bridge, a report and a software programe is the outcome of the implementation of work. Proper monitoring and control measures also take care of at this stage of project. After the QA process the product will be presented to the customer for acceptance and full implementation. If the customer has accepted the final product, the project is complete and ready for closure.

5. Project Closure: Project Closure involves releasing the final product to the customer, handing over project documentation, Manuals, Source code, and Network layouts. Last remaining step is to undertake a Post Implementation Review to identify the level of project success and note down any lessons learned. This stage includes two activities:— delivering the product to customer, and redeploying project resources. This stage also known as project cleanup phase where project accounts are closed, materials reconciliations are carried out, outstanding payments are made and outstanding dues are collected.

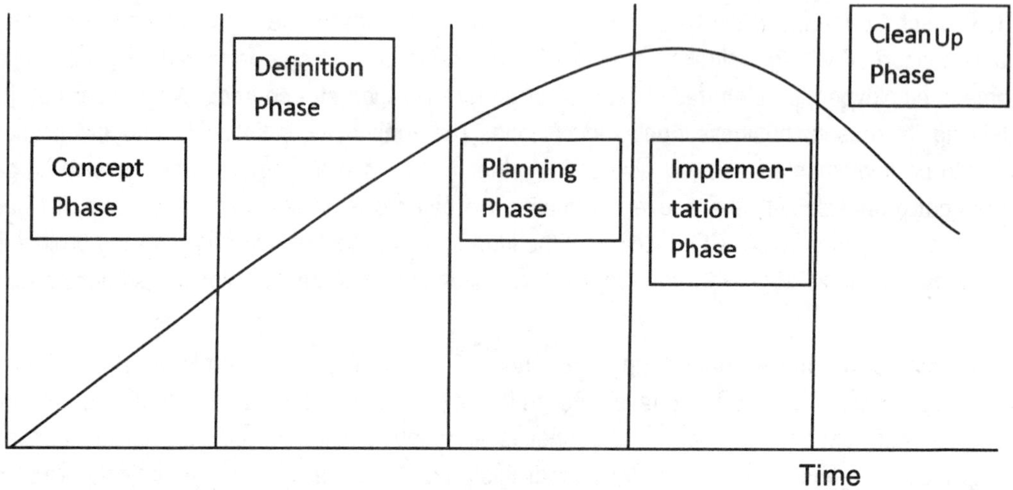

Fig. 12.7

In practice, the project life cycle is used by some project groups to depict the timings of major task over the life of the project.

Another type of project life cycle:

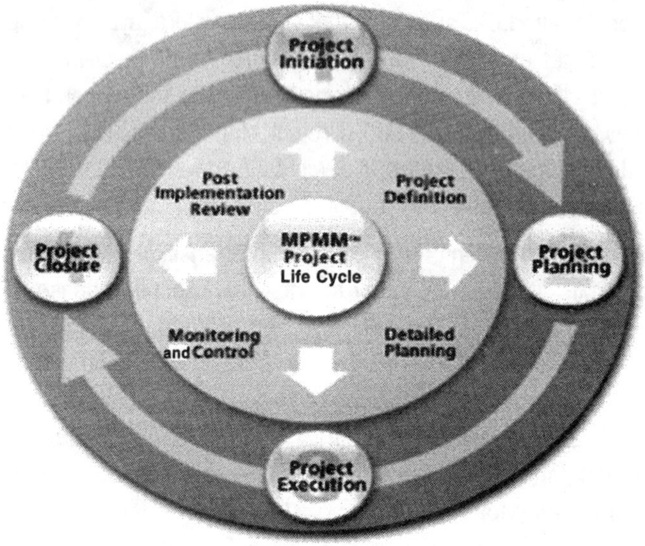

Fig. 12.8

12.13 WHAT ARE THE STEPS OF IMPLEMENTING A PROJECT

One of the biggest factors contributing to the success of a project is how effectively the project manager carries out the steps of implementing project. Managing a project is an orderly process that, if properly executed, will maximize project resources, enable effective communication among project personnel and the project's clients, and allow for the unexpected bumps along the way.

For the inexperienced project manager, it is essential that there be in place an implementation plan outlining the tasks needed to complete a project. The following is a brief guide to the basic steps of implementing a project. Project managers should keep in mind that all projects regardless of industry and scope will follow the same basic structure:-

1. Inexperienced Project Managers Should Seek Counsel: First-time project managers to should seek out someone who can help them through the process of completing the project. Ideally, this person should be someone within the company since such an individual may also benefit from the project and thus be more motivated to help. Where this is not possible, the manager should look for counsel from any individual who is experienced in project management in general. But this consultant should at least be familiar with the industry and/or type of project.

2. Inexperienced Project Managers can also try Self-education and Guidance by Reading Informative Articles or Attending a Webinar: New project managers should equip themselves with tools and software. Project managers should try to build-up a supporting project infrastructure. This includes: communications devices and software, computer hardware, and any software specific to project management, such as time management or project tracking tools.

3. A New Project Manager Must Clarify the Details of the Project: One of the first tasks a project manager must take care of is the creation of a project proposal. The project proposal should include the following information:

1. A description of the project goals
2. The project time frame
3. The project budget
4. A breakdown of the project team members and assigned tasks
5. The methods used to complete the project
6. How project uncertainties will be accounted and dealt with.

4. Project Managers Must Assign Job Responsibilities to Project Team Members: When a team of people is assigned to complete the project, then all members should be aware of their individual roles and duties. This job assignment plan is referred to as the work breakdown structure. Project managers should also establish a system of communication to ensure that project team members are updated regularly throughout the project schedule.

5. Monitoring Progress and Documenting Project Information: The project manager should have a system in place to measure the project's progress and efficiency. By doing so, the project manager will be able to determine whether additional information or resources are needed to complete the project, whether resource should be shifted around, and occasionally whether a new approach to the project should be taken. Project managers should focus on performance

12.14. CONSTRAINTS OF A PROJECT

There are internal and external constraints of a project which hinders its performance. These are:

(i) Internal Constraints: Internal constraints arise on account of the limitations of the management system, which will eventually be responsible for the implementation of a project. In India, the internal constraints for the entrepreneurs while venturing the projects comprise inputs, resources and outputs.

Internal project constraints would typically be resource-related. For example, if project team members are committed to supporting more than one project, they have some limitation on the number of hours that they can support your project. Also, your project may utilize an operations factory, laboratory, or equipment resource that is shared by the organization. The Project Manager must work within the constraints of the availability of that resource. These are narrated as under:-

1. Rely on outside consultants: Entrepreneurs, while implementing the projects, rely more on outside consultants for preparation of feasibility reports in the formulation of their projects. The limitation of the part of entrepreneurs to provide inbuilt project services in the form of preparing feasibility reports is an important internal constraint in the early implementation of the project.

2. Limited budget and time schedule: For early implementation of projects within the budgeted cost and time schedule, all the entrepreneurs cannot develop independent project management system, organization structure, network analysis and other elements. In such a situation, the entrepreneurs' inherent internal constraints are developing well equipped project management strategies and tools while implementing them.

3. Unrealistic objective: Project goals and objectives lay down the main purpose for which an organization exists. Practically, project management team is not much involved with the determination of project objectives. Certainly this will be another internal; constrain for the project objectives the unrealistic objectives, which is decided by the top management personnel of the business.

4. Non-availability of resources:- The availability of the necessary internal project elements and resources are physical and non-physical resources. The physical resources include finance, personnel, inventories and facilities. The non-physical resources are patents, secret processes, unique experience and skills. Both the physical and non-physical resources are the important constraints for the entrepreneurs to make available at a time when the project implementation is in progress.

5. Selection of technology: The main problem faced by an entrepreneur is in the matter of selection of appropriate technology for his enterprise. Modern technology developed in the highly industrialized countries may not be suitable for adoption in the developing countries as the conditions prevalent differ from country to country. For example, the optimal size of plants recommended for a highly industrialized country may be too big for acceptance in a developing country owing to the factors such as limited market for the products and limit availability of capital and skilled labor. Hence, the entrepreneur has to examine the project idea thoroughly as regards its design, production, and marketing after sales service, etc.

(ii) External constraints: External constraints also restricts in project implementation. The external constraints include restrictions in the project environment which comprises people and situation outside the project. These are:

1. Non-conformity to socio-economic environment: The external environmental factors like;— nature, size, location and extent of projects can limit the entrepreneurs when the project does not conform to the socio-economic objectives of society or project is not feasible from social point of view.

2. Government policies and regulation: Sometimes the government regulations act as an external constraint to the project. Delay in getting government approval, licencing, foreign exchange permit etc delay the project and act as very big hurdle in the execution of the project.

3. Arrangement of external finance: Financial institutes and banks are very important source of external finance but the long procedures, paper work and formalities act as biggest external constraint. Due to time consuming formalities entrepreneurs do not get the finance on time and unnecessarily the project got delayed.

4. Influence of external economics: The problem relates to the absence or non-availability of external economics. No project can function in isolation in any economy. It has to depend on other industries for the supply of raw materials, power tools spare parts etc., or on ancillary enterprise which can provide technical, financial, and managerial services or a complex network of communication and transport facilities or an intricate system of business practices. The entrepreneur in developing countries is, therefore to consider not only the basic costs of the project but also the ancillary costs, which in industrially advance countries would have been contributed by the external economics.

5. Knowledge about government regulations: Besides these problems the entrepreneur has to comprehend number of Government directives. Import and export policies, price controls, etc. The difficulty is to be familiar with all these regulations, for they are not available in a consolidated and detailed form in most of the developing countries. However, in India, a compendium entitled 'Guidelines for Industries has been published by the Ministry of Industrial Development. It provides information

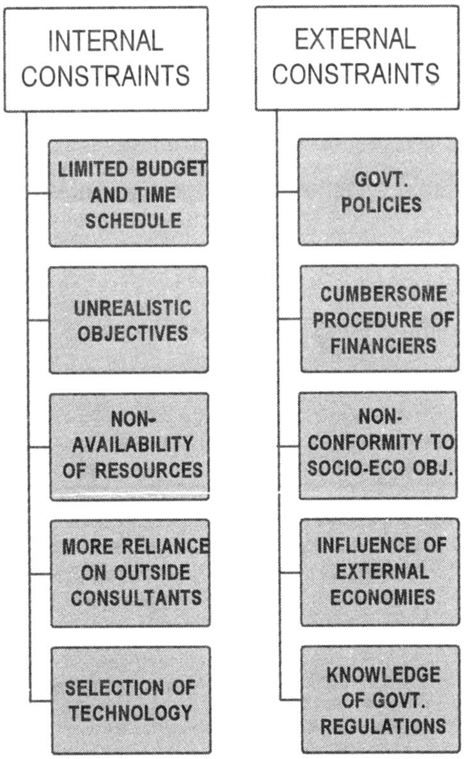

Fig. 2.9

regarding the industrial regarding the present status of capacities and possibilities of future development in various industrial fields capacities and possibilities of future development in various industrial fields like metallurgical industries, electronics equipment industries,transportation industries and the like.These problems make the entrepreneur to undergo a lot of harassment, disappointment and despair. However a project formulation exercise undertaken at the right time mitigates the severity as well as magnitude of these problems

12.15. SUMMARY

A project is a temporary venture to accomplish a need or desire.It can be defined as any venture that is a set of interrelated, independent as well as precedence relationship activities for the accomplishment of some objectives demanding dedicated commitment of resources and time. The project activity helps in fulfilling one's need or desire by changing the current state of the activity. Projects normally begin with a scratch definition of the mission, generate activities around the defined limit intergrating resources, machines, materials and money, that are directed towards the fulfillment of the stated mission or goal.

12.16. SELF ASSESSMENT QUESTIONS

1. What do you mean by project and how is it different from project management?
2. Is project management a bane or a boon?
3. Define Project and describe briefly the silent features of projects.
4. "A project is influenced by the participating teams and their interrelationships." Discuss the above statement in the light of roles and responsibilities played by the people involved in a project.
5. What is the importance of a project and explain the different phases of a project?
6. What are the basic attributes of a project?. Explain it with the help of live example.
7. What do you mean by programme and how is it different from a project?
8. Classify the project and explain each with examples.
9. What are the internal and external constraints of a project?

SOURCE/NOTES

1. http://www.independent-consulting-bootcamp.com/
2. *Project Management* — Vasant Desai
3. *Project Management and Control* — P.C.K.Rao

13

PROJECT IDENTIFICATION

13.1. INTRODUCTION

There is an old saying that success lies in getting a robust business opportunity. Hence, getting a promising idea is the first step towards successful business venture. And getting a promising idea demands creativity, imaginations, sensitivity to changing environment and objective analysis of quantifiable factors. Thinking beyond imaginations can bring limitless possibilities for good business idea. So getting a new idea is a very crucial decision as the ultimate success of the venture greatly depends upon the selection of the right type of project idea, i.e., the identification of right project.

13.2. MEANING

Project identification means identification of a suitable project for the enterprise. Project identification is concerned with the collection, compilation and analysis of economic data for the purpose of locating possible opportunities for investment. There are various opportunities available to an entrepreneurs but he has to select the right opportunity with care and according the availability of resources and skills. An entrepreneur has a vast choice of investment opportunities. The ability to identify an Investment Opportunity which can be converted into a viable business proposition (after careful and systematic consideration) ensures entrepreneurial success.

Some projects are aimed at development of the society such as 'education and health' some are aimed at increasing employment opportunities for youth, some aimed at increasing the standard of living of society by providing civic faciiities, some are oriented towards commercial and industrial development etc. So opportunities are galore and the means to attack are equally abundant. Only the right vision and direction are needed to snapshot the idea and nurture it towards success. So, project identification is concerned with the collection, compilation and analysis of economic data for the eventual purpose of locating possible opportunities for investment and with the development of the characteristics of such opportunities.

An entrepreneur is said to be an opportunity seeker. For a potential entrepreneur, his main job is to identify, explore and then select an attractive business opportunity. So, "Opportunity can be defined as an attractive and excellent project idea which, an entrepreneur search for and accepts such idea as a basis for his investment decision."

13.3. TYPES OF OPPORTUNITIES BY PETER DRUCKER

Opportunities, according Drucker (1955), are of four kinds—Incremental, additive, complementary and breakthrough.

1. Incremental Innovation: Incremental innovation includes doing more of the same thing, i.e., change and additions in the things which were already done so that better results can be achieved.

2. Additive Opportunities: Additive opportunities are those opportunities, which enable the decision maker to better utilize the existing resources without in any way involving a change in the character of business. Additive opportunities involve the least amount of disturbance to the existing state of affairs and hence the least amount of risk. It includes, fully exploiting already existing resources, such as product lines extensions. These opportunities should rarely be treated as high priority efforts.

3. Complementary Opportunities: Complementary opportunities involve the introduction of new ideas and as such do lead to a certain amount of change in the existing structure .

4. Breakthrough Opportunities: Breakthrough opportunities on the other hand, involve fundamental changes in both the structure and character of business, i.e., creating a new industry and new avenues for extensive wealth creation.

Element of risk is more in complementary and breakthrough opportunities. When the element of risk increases, it becomes more important to precisely define the scope and nature of project idea, to develop alternative solutions for achieving the project objectives and to select the best possible approach so as to minimize both resource consumption and risks and to optimize the return or gains. Project identification cannot be complete without identifying the characteristics of a project.

13.4. DIMENSIONS OF PROJECT

Every project has three basic dimensions—inputs, outputs and social costs and benefits. The input characteristics define what the project will consume in terms of raw materials, energy, manpower, finance and organizational set up. The nature and magnitude of each of these inputs must be determined in order to make the input characteristic explicit. The output characteristics of a project define what the project will generate in the form of goods and services, employment, revenue, etc., the quantity and quality of all these outputs should be clearly specified.

In addition to inputs and outputs every project has an impact on the society. It inevitably affects the current equilibriums of the demand and supply in the economy. It is necessary to evaluate carefully the sacrifice, which the society will be required to make, and the benefits that will accrue to the society from a given project. Project do not emerge themselves. The inputs to set up a project can come from different sources such as Government agencies, credit and financial institutions, non-governmental organization like chambers of commerce and industry, inter-institutional groups, technical consultancy organizations and international collaborations. Once the venture ideas have been developed by entrepreneurs by following on or combination of sources explained, these have to be screened and evaluated in a preliminary fashion on the basis of internal and external constraints prior to being put to additional tests of pre-feasibility. This project identification comes to an end by laying down specific project objectives clearly and concisely and without any ambiguity so that these convey one and the same meaning to all concerned.

13.5. IDENTIFICATION OF INVESTMENT OPPORTUNITIES

The identification of the project is the most difficult frame of work. It is more and more dependent upon the economy of the country or the present status of the industry. The more the economy or industry is prone to change, the more will be the opportunities for identifying for identifying promising projects. There are a number of sources from which an entrepreneur can gain knowledge about Project ideas and one of them is the thorough knowledge of governmental and competitive stigmas and opportunities in the specified area may help in identifying new and innovative projects. Any decision to embark on a project after considering only the obvious or immediately available opportunities may lead to a lost opportunity. It would be advisable to scout for new ideas from the sources which can either be internal sources or external sources. Various sources are as under:

(a) A study of the performance of existing units in an industry with particular reference to profitability of units and capacity utilisation would allow an entrepreneur to identify relatively risk-free opportunities. This kind of analysis helps in checking the present performance of the industry. For example: If a majority of the hotels in a town enjoy 80% occupancy rate, it indicates that there is still a need for lodging facilities.

(b) A study of projects being encouraged by financial institutions ensures that the areas of these projects are deemed highly viable. This is because the financial institutions back projects after careful and thorough analysis.

(c) A study of economic trends and consumption patterns of individuals will help in the identification of project Ideas.

  For example: The increasing affluence of the middle class and larger expenditure on tourism, travel and leisure indicates a vast potential for Travel Agencies.

(d) An enquiry into Social and Cultural Trends may provide valuable insights.

  For example: The search for an Indian identity has caused a boom in the sales of ethnic fashion wear in India.

(e) An enquiry into business practices in foreign countries may also provide valuable clues for business opportunities.

  For example: Adventure sports as a part of tourism has been essentially borrowed from foreign countries.

(f) An investigation into locally available resources and, raw materials and skills may indicate-the availability of business opportunities.

For example: The Kondapalli Toys made in Kondapally, Andhra Pradesh enjoy a worldwide market and opportunities still exist for their marketing within the country.

(g) A study of developments in technology may also provide new product ideas. Often, new technologies allow a better utilisation of locally available raw materials as witnessed in the Coir Industry.

(h) A constant search for unfulfilled needs of the market allows identification of a series of business opportunities. A constant surge in the taste and preference of the customers forces the investor to perform well by producing as per the need of the market. It initiates the development of any product and service which satisfies a human need which was earlier not catered. This phenomenon can be seen in the quick success of Fast Foods, Pre-school Nurseries and labour saving devices in the kitchen.

(i) Today, government regulations are more dynamic than in past. Changes in the government regulations ultimately affect new and old projects. In a country like India where the Government plays a positive role in the economic development of the nation as a regulatory and promotional agency, the policies of the Government must be taken into consideration while scouting for new ideas.

(j) The imports statics in the past years can be used as a trend in the changing climate of imports and exports of various commodities. It provides various opportunities to the investor.

(k) Sometimes the financial institutes help the prospective investors by guiding them towards promising ventures and provide them with sufficient funds to meet their project needs.These list of suggestions act as major source of new ideas.

13.6. STEPS IN IDENTIFICATION OF BUSINESS OPPORTUNITIES

The Process of Identifying, Evaluating and Selecting a Business opportunity involves the following steps:

— Identify the needs and wants of customers.

— Scanning (examining) the environment and evaluating of self (Entrepreneur) and the community.

— Screening (Process of evaluating) of business opportunities.

— Selecting a business opportunity

— Preparing a business plan.

1. Identify the needs and wants of the customer: Human needs and wants includes:

— A need is something that is basic in life, for example we need food, clothing and shelter.

— But as human we also have wants that is, there is a desire or craving something that is far better than basic items.

Wants are shaped by :

— Our lifestyle

— Level of education

— Purchasing power

— Personality of the person

So human needs and wants are unlimited and are of all types and sometimes society affluence lead to increase to human wants and needs. Thus, entrepreneurs must take this opportunity to provide products and services. Moreover, entrepreneurs must be sensitive to changes in customers' needs and wants in order to be aware of new business opportunities.

2. Scanning the environment and evaluating of self and the community—Environmental Scanning (ES), can lead to an idea that can be converted into a business opportunity.The two approaches are used to scan the environment *i.e.*, scan the environment by micro and macro perspective. Another approach of scanning the environment is by looking at the following factors:

— Structure of the population, income and tastes.

— Examine the import and export information of a country.

— Study and examine types of local resources and technological breakthrough.

— Examine the Industrial linkages.

— Examine the development projects by the public and private sectors.

— Newspaper and magazines – local and foreign as a source of business opportunities

Another approach of scanning the environment is by looking at the following factors:

— Examine what the local issues and social problems

— Examine what new government policies and regulation have impact on small business.

Besides Environmental scanning one is to do a self evaluation to identify what skills, experience is available in an entrepreneur that can be used in business development and engagement. Because, according to the Arkansas Small Business Development Center, most small businesses fail because of poor management and the owner's inability to manage resources. Before you even start researching the feasibility of your idea and the market you plan on entering, evaluate your own talents, desires and goals. Consider your willingness to take risks as well as the amount of time and energy you'll need to make the business a success. Review your financial, personnel and marketing skills as well to ensure you have the necessary background to make a success of your new venture

— Skill competency, experience, knowledge that match the business opportunities.

— Experience

— Knowledge and competency skills

— Financial status and situation

— Interest – likes and dislikes

— Networking – circle of friends and associates

— Cultural values and norms of the community.

3. Screening (process of evaluating) of business opportunities: In the preceding stage, the primary objective was to ensure that no worthwhile idea would be ignored by the entrepreneur. It would be impossible for us to submit a large number of proposals to such an exercise. Hence, the need arises for a preliminary screening of ideas to eliminate project ideas which are not *prima facie* promising. The following factors may be used as screening devices to eliminate such alternatives:

(a) **Organisation Strengths and Weaknesses:** Project ideas must be compatible with the organisation. The projects are identified primarily on the basis of the knowledge of the surroundings and the internal SWOT analysis. A project idea which falls in the area of an organisation's strength can be converted into an effective project. A project idea, however profitable basically, which falls in the area of a company's weaknesses cannot be converted into a successful project.

(b) **Matching with Chieftain's Profile:** According to Murphy, three important equations to be considered are:

 (i) The entrepreneur 's personality should match the necessities of the project, i.e., he should be skillful, able and trained in the areas of the project and preferably have a proven track record of a successful project initiator;

 (ii) the project teams and resources should be easily accessible to him;

 (iii) The project should show promising signs of being an investment and a prospective competitor with a high rate of return.

(c) **Compatible with Rules and Regulation of the Government:** Entrepreneur must carefully consider all the related rules and regulations of the government regarding investment, license, clearance, reservation category etc.

(d) **Adequate Market:** Every Business organisation requires a minimum level of business. Where the market is restricted and cannot allow the organisation to reach the breakeven point in the near future, the prospects of success are rather limited. So idea to be select must be screened from the point of view of markets.

(e) **Availability of Infrastructure:** No business venture can succeed in the absence of basic services like transportation, electricity, water supply, etc. In most of the cases, the business organisation cannot create these services independently. So the projects are dependent on other organizations for these services and in order to screen the idea there must be check on the availability of infrastructure.

(f) **Availability of Essential Inputs and Labour:** A project can only be converted into reality only if the necessary raw materials or basic inputs are easily available.The entrepreneur must consider whether there is a regular and assured supply of essential inputs and labour to ensure regularity of operations essential for success of the venture. Moreover, the project location should be accessible of basic inputs.In the economically backward countries ,there is serious deficiency of certain key inputs like–power supply, raw material, foreign exchange, etc. India is one of such developing countries that suffer from chronic shortage of power, fuel etc and is unable to exploit its natural resources. However the recent economic reforms have made it possible to steer the growth through various schemes like– generating power by successful collaboration between public and private sector etc.

(g) Cost Constraints: The cost structure of a proposal must enable it to realize an acceptable profit with a competitive price. If the estimated cost of producing the product/service is comparatively very high in view of factors like high material costs or labour costs or any related reasons, the project idea should be eliminated.

So the following aspects should be examined-

(i) Cost of the raw materials and other inputs(direct and indirect)

(ii) Factory cost

(iii) Labour cost

(iv) Selling and distribution cost

(v) Service and maintenance cost

(vi) Economies of scale

(h) Risk Consideration: Risk levels associated with various projects differ on the basis of factors like changes in technology, changes in fashion, and vulnerability to trade cycles. So the idea must be screened critically by taking into consideration the risk involved in the selected idea. While assessing the risk, the following factors should be considered:

(i) Trade cycles

(ii) Technological changes

(iii) Change in demand

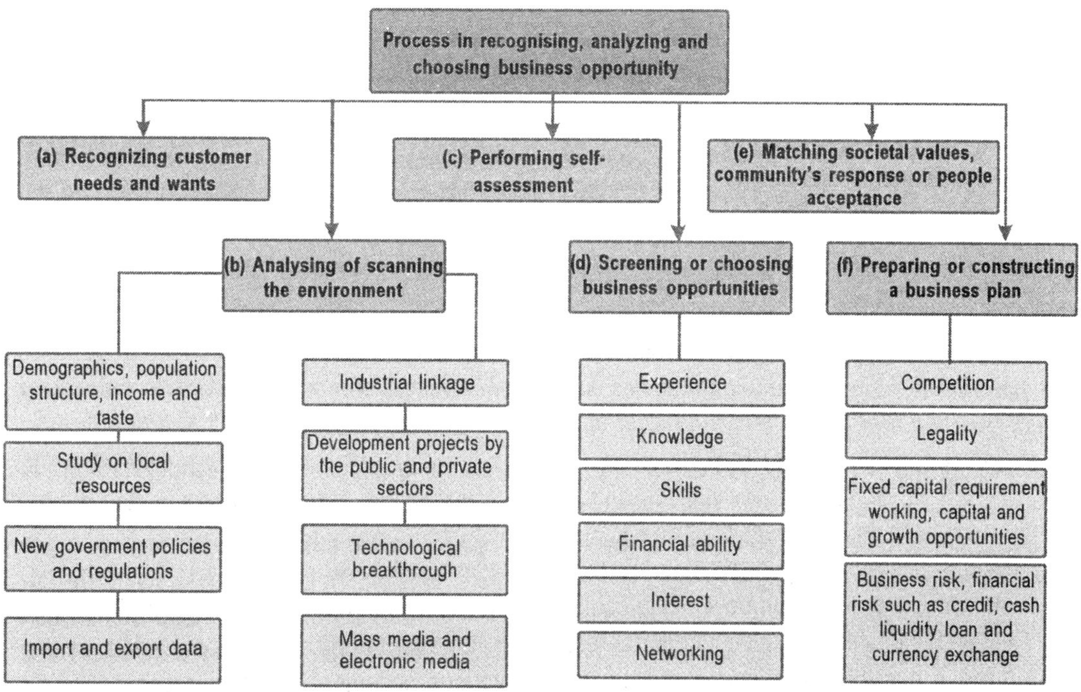

Fig. 13.1

(iv) Competition

(v) Government regulations

4. Selecting a business opportunity and conducting a market research: Entrepreneur should select the product which he wishes to manufacture considering the above points.To thoroughly understand what you're getting into, perform an extensive market research project to determine the feasibility of your business. In addition to gleaning statistics of trends and current customer buying patterns, entrepreneur must know about the customers, where they are located and what kind of competition exists in your area. It also includes matching societal values, community's response or people's acceptance for the product.

5. Preparing a business plan: Last but not the least, entrepreneur has to prepare a business plan keeping in view various legal formalities, rules and regulation of the government, fixed capital requirement, working capital requirement and various kinds of risks attachments with the business .

13.7. TOOLS FOR IDENTIFICATION OF INVESTMENT OPPORTUNITIES

There are several tools that are helpful in identifying investment opportunities. The popular ones are Porter Model, life cycle approach and experience curve.

1. Porter Model: Profit Potential of Industries : Michael Porter has argued that the profit potential of an industry depends on the combined strength of the five basic competitive forces as discussed in Chapter 7 (7.9).The basic competitive forces are:

(i) Threat of new entrants

(ii) Rivalry among existing firms

(iii) Pressure from substitute products

(iv) Bargaining power of buyers

(v) Bargaining power of sellers.

All the above forces are already discussed in Chapter 7 and all these forces provide different investment opportunities.

2. Life Cycle Approach : There is life cycle of the product which mostly has four stages and each stage presents investment opportunities that exhibits different characteristics.Different stages of product are:

(i) Pioneering Stage: This is the starting stage and during this stage, the technology and the product is relatively new. This stage is characterized by low growth rate of sales as the product is newly launched in the market. Monopoly can be created, depending upon the efficiency and need of the product to the customers. Investment in this stage, may have low return and negativeNPV. The stage has the following characteristics: (1) Low competition (2) Firm mostly incurs losses and not profit. This low competition attracts new investors and provide various investment opportunities.

(ii) Growth Stage: In the growth stage, the firm seeks to build brand preference and increase market share. Growth comes with the acceptance of the innovation in the market and profit starts to flow. If the monopoly exists, companies can experiment with new ideas and innovation in order to maintain the sales growth. This stage is the best time to introduce new effective products in the market thus creating an image in the product class in the presence of its competitors who try to copy or improve the product and present it as a substitute.

(iii) Maturity Stage: At maturity, the strong growth in sales diminishes. Competition may appear with similar products. The primary objective at this point is to defend market share while maximizing profit. In the maturity stage, the end of stage of the growth rate and sales slowdown as the product has already achieved acceptance in the market. New firms start experimenting in order to compete by innovating new models of the product. With many companies in the market, competition for customers becomes fierce, despite the increase in growth rate of sales at the initial part of this stage. Aggressive competition in the market results in profits decreasing at the end of the growth stage thus beginning the maturity stage. In addition to this, the maturity stage of the development process is the most vital. In the maturity stage, the end of stage of the growth rate and sales slowdown as the product has already achieved acceptance in the market. New firms start experimenting in order to compete by innovating new models of the product. With many companies in the market, competition for customers becomes fierce, despite the increase in growth rate of sales at the initial part of this stage. Aggressive competition in the market results in profits decreasing at the end of the growth stage thus beginning the maturity stage. In addition to this, the maturity stage of the development process is the most vital.

(iv) Decline Stage: The decline stage is where most of the product class usually dies due to low growth rate in sales. A number of companies share the same market, making it difficult for all entrants to maintain sustainable sales levels. Not only is the efficiency of the company an important factor in the decline, but also the product category itself becomes a factor, as the market may perceive the product as "old" and may not be in demand. It is not always necessary that a product should go through these stages. it depends on the type of product, its competitors, scope of the product, etc. As sales decline, the firm has several options:

- Maintain the product, possibly rejuvenating it by adding new features and finding new uses.
- Harvest the product - reduce costs and continue to offer it, possibly to a loyal niche segment.
- Discontinue the product, liquidating remaining inventory or selling it to another firm that is willing to continue the product.

The marketing mix decisions in the decline phase will depend on the selected strategy. For example, the product may be changed if it is being rejuvenated, or left unchanged if it is being harvested or liquidated. The price may be maintained if the product is harvested, or reduced drastically if liquidated.

Each stage presents investment opportunities. Investment in pioneering stage generate low returns but may possibly create options for participating in the growth stage. Investment in the growth stage is likely to earn a high return and generate positive NPV and the investment in the maturity stage may earn average return and the NPV is neutral. Finally, investment in the decline stage may earn meager returns and produce negative NPV.

3. The Experiment Curve: For the long term profits and survival, it is essential for the investments to aim at reduction of cost and the experience curve is a useful tool for planning such investments. The experience curve shows how the cost per unit behaves with respect to the accumulated volume of production and the accumulated volume of production is the total number of units produced cumulatively from the very beginning but its not annual rate of production. There are various factors which contribute to decline in unit cost with respect to accumulated volume of production. Some of these are:

(i) learning effects – Learning makes the man perfect as with more and more production, labour skills improves and the productivity increases which lead to lowering of the cost.

(ii) technological improvements – Increased production lead to deployment of improved technology which result in lowering of the cost.

(iii) economies of scale – When the production increases, the cost per unit decreases and it's done due to economies of scale

13.8. PROJECT SELECTION

Project selection starts from where project identification ends. After having some project ideas, these are analyzed in the light of existing economic conditions, the government policy and so on. A tool generally used for this purpose is, what is called in the managerial jargon, SWOT analysis. The intending entrepreneur analyses his/her strengths and weaknesses as well as opportunities/competitive advantages and threats/challenges offered by each of the project ideas. On the basis of this analysis, the most suitable idea is finally selected to convert it into an enterprise. The process involved in selecting a project out of some projects is also described as the "zeroing in process".

What follows from above analysis is that there is a time interval involved in between project identification and project selection. But, in some cases, there may be almost no time gap between the two. Normally, there are following criteria's in project selection:-

(a) Specific Criteria

(b) General Criteria

Under specific criteria the development of a country is focused while in general criteria the firm or the promoters interest and many other unspecified factors play a dominant role.

Under the specific criteria the following factors are considered:

1. Factor Intensity : There are some countries which are labour intensive and some are capital intensive.The countries like – India, South Africa and many other developing countries are labour intensive as there are large number of labour force which is unemployed so this unemployed labour always wanted the projects which will use labour intensive methods of production so the unemployed labour can get some work and by this firm can also get the advantage of cheap labour.

So the projects which are started/executed in order to utilize the unutilized resources which are available in abundance like – labour comes under specific criteria.

2. Foreign Exchange Benefit : The projects that can derive foreign exchange benefits fall under this criteria. The countries with poor foreign exchange reserves and devalued currency are always interested in these types of projects. These kinds of projects also gets the subsidies from the government. There are some established norms through which the costs and benefits of such emphasis on foreign exchange benefit scheme are measured and then the viability of such projects will be observed.

3. National Economic Profitability: It includes the measurement of approximately rate of return to the national economy on an investment in a project, taking into account all major measurable economic costs and benefits but it avoids the inclusion of economic costs or benefits which by nature are not measurable and also those non-economic costs or benefits which require value judgement.

An imaginary case can illustrate it:

Two friends Sohan and Mohan were traveling from Guwahati to Delhi by North East Express. Their train stopped at Allahabad. Some teenagers with pears baskets crowded the compartment. Almost every passenger purchased pears. So did Sohan and Mohan also. They started eating pears. Mohan told to Sohan: "The pears are really delicious". Sohan nodded. They reached Delhi by evening and parted company. While Mohan went to his home, Sohan took Bramputra Mail to Allahabad. He contacted shopkeepers in Allahabad who were selling pears. He finalized a business deal for them to send a packet of 1500 kgs of pears daily to Delhi. Thus, Sohan's business started from the third day when he was selling pears in Delhi. Here on pertinent question for us is how did this idea make its headway into a business opportunity for Sohan? In its answer, what can we mention is that Sohan must have turned questions in his mind like:

(i) Who will buy his pears?

(ii) What will be the size of the packet and what will be its price?

(iii) How much will be the cost of per kg.

Project identification and selection is half done in the process of establishing an enterprise. The entrepreneur needs to analyze other related aspects also like raw material, potential market, labor, capital, location, forms of ownership etc. It is necessary to mention that each of these aspects has to be evaluated independently and in relation to each other. Project ideas identified earlier are screened on the basis of their technical, economic and financial soundness. After screening the ideas are translated into project profiles.

A project profile consists of the following broad items.

1. Economic size
2. Status of industry or scope
3. Raw material availability
4. Cost of production
5. Capital cost

6. Utility requirements
7. Infrastructure facilities needed
8. Profitability
9. Government policy

After gathering a large number of project profiles, the entrepreneur is faced with the problem of selecting the most appropriate project. The following criteria may be used for this purpose:

1. Investment size: Investment size depends upon the entrepreneur's capacity to raise resources and his attitude towards economies of scale. If the project is to be financed through all-India institutions with lesser promoter's contribution, the project cost should be at least ₹ 3 to ₹ 5 crores and if it is self-financed then it has to according to the finances available.

2. Location: Location plays very important role in project selection.A new entrepreneur should as far as possible locate his project in and around a state headquarters. Such a location helps to attract competent managers and facilitates liaison with the State Industrial Development Corporation, the State Electricity Board and various other agencies.

3. Technology: It is better for a new entrepreneur to go in for a project with proven technology, which is indigenously available. It avoids the problems of foreign technical collaboration and makes life easier but sometime technological superiority enables a firm to enjoy excellent returns by superseding the market. E.g.: IBM and Intel earned superior returns due to technological edge they had over their rivals.

4. Equipment: While selecting the equipment the advice of experienced technical consultants should be obtained. Some entrepreneurs enter into some sort of a deal with the equipment manufacturers for a 'kick-back' and in the process sacrifice quality. This is shortsightedness and no compromise on quality should be made.

5. Marketing: It is advisable to go in for a product with a limited number of industrial customers. A new entrepreneur should not go into a project having cut-throat competition.

6. Power and water: The entrepreneur should ensure abundant supply of these two inputs. If possible, power-intensive and water-intensive projects should be avoided.

7. Others' performance: A new entrepreneur should judge how well the existing units in the industry are doing. It is not advisable to enter into industries in which seasoned entrepreneurs fear to tread. As a rule, one should get into a line in which others are doing reasonable well.

8. Working capital requirements: The entrepreneur should avoid projects with very long operating cycle and requiring huge working capital. The lending policies of banks are unpredictable and, therefore, good margin money should be provided for. This is particularly necessary when the entrepreneur has to buy from any government agency (advance payments) or to sell to a government agency (delayed settlement of bills).

9. Labor component: A shrewd entrepreneur should minimize unskilled and semi-skilled labor. Material handling labor can be reduced through automatic handling devices and proper buying policies.

10. Economic viability: The project should break-even on a cash basis in the first 6-8 months. It should generate profits in the first year of operations.

After evaluating alternative projects on a multipoint scale, the project with maximum points should be selected for further analysis. A detailed project report may be commissioned with the help of well-known consultants in the field.

13.9. IMPORTANCE OF PROJET IDENTIFICATION

1. Well identified projects comes for processing and become the agent of economic development.
2. It provide the long term benefits.
3. It result in the development of basic infrastructure.
4. It helps in the overall development of the economy in terms of employment and income generation.
5. It act as framework for future activities

13.10. SUMMARY

A project is a temporary venture to accomplish a need or desire .The need can be economic , social, political or environmental. For the project, identification is the initial stage which starts with recognition of a need, problem, opportunities and possibilities. Identification of promising investment opportunity requires imagination, sensitivity to environmental changes, and a realistic assessment of what the firm can do.There are various techniques to identify the project but an entrepreneur has to select the appropriate technique.To stimulate the flow of investment ideas SWOT analysis, clear articulation of objectives and conductive climate is helpful. Good project ideas are key to success, so a wide variety of sources should be tapped to identify them.

13.11. SELF ASSESSMENT QUESTIONS

1. Discuss the role of project as a agent of change from existing state to the desired state.
2. What are the various sources of project identification?
3. Elaborate any two projects of national importance.
4. What are the various tools of project identification?
5. What can a firm do to stimulate the flow of project ideas?
6. What are the various opportunities by Peter Drucker? Explain with the help of examples.

SOURCES/NOTES

1. *Project Management and Control* — P.C.K. Rao
2. *Projects* — Prasanna Chandra

14

PROJECT FEASIBILITY ANALYSIS

14.1. INTRODUCTION

Feasibility analysis is the process of evaluating the future of a project idea within the limitations of the project implementing body and the constraints imposed on the project situation by the environment. The analysis is undertaken to determine the desirability of investing in further development of project idea. When a project is taken up for development three alternatives can arise. First, the project many appear to be positive and in such a case the project assessing body can proceed to invest further resources in pre-investment studies and design development. Secondly, the project may turn out to be not feasible and, therefore, further investment in the project may turn out to be not feasible and, therefore, further investment in the project idea is ruled out. Thirdly, the data is not adequate for arriving at a decision about the feasibility of the project. In such a situation, additional information must be collected and the investment decision is deferred till the final decision. It is the first stage in project formulation and examination is done to see whether to go in for a detailed investment proposal or not.

Generally, the exercise in project feasibility analysis is carried out dividing it formally into three stages, *viz.*, pre-feasibility study, feasibility study and project report.

14.2. PRE-FEASIBILITY ANALYSIS

In the screening of the project idea several indepth investigation is done and in order to scrutinize further two options are available to R&D department are:

(a) Pre-feasibility study

(b) Feasibility study

The project idea must be elaborated in a more detailed study. However, formulation of a techno-economic feasibility study that enables a definite to be made on the project is a costly and time consuming task. Therefore, before assigning funds for such a study, a preliminary assessment of the project idea must be made in a pre-feasibility study. The principal objectives of such a study are to determine whether

(a) The investment opportunity is so promising that an investment decision can be taken on the basis of information elaborated at the pre-feasibility stage,

(b) the project concept justifies a detailed analysis by a pre-feasibility study

(c) any aspects of the project are critical to its feasibility and necessitate in-depth investigation through functional or support studies such as market surveys, laboratory tests, pilot plant tests;

(d) the information is adequate to decide that the project is not either a viable proposition or attractive enough for a particular investor or investor group.

A pre-feasibility study differs from a detailed feasibility study primarily with regard to the detail of the information obtained. If the project is big then both the above step follow one after the other and if after careful observation, it is noticed that a complete feasibility study would be timeconsuming and expensive then only the process of pre–feasibility can be opted. The pre-feasibility study can be viewed as a series of steps culminating in a document which permits determination of whether or not a complete detailed feasibility study should be made. In this study the main emphasis is depended upon the nature of product/service and the target market.

Thus pre-feasibility study is something that falls between the conception of an idea stage and detailed feasibility study and the difference is the degree of detail of information. The main objective of the pre-feasibility study are to determine whether the project is promising or not, i.e., whether the investment decision can be taken on the basis of pre-feasibility analysis.

14.3. ELEMENTS OF PRE-FEASIBILITY STUDY

Even at the pre-feasibility stage it is necessary to examine, perhaps broadly, the economic alternatives of (a) market and plant capacity demand and market study, sales and marketing, production programme and plant capacity; (b) material input; (c) location and site; (d) project engineering; technologies and equipment and civil engineering works; (e) overheads; factory, administration and sales; (f) manpower; labor and staff; (g) project implementation; (h) financial analysis-investment costs, project financing, production costs and commercial profitability. These are:

(i) Project Description: This includes the nature and detail of the project which describes the input and output of the project and all the advantages and disadvantages of the project.

(ii) Market Description and Potential: It study present potential of the market and it study the market demand through an application of appropriate tool. It also includes proximity of the project location to the market.

(iii) Availability of factor of production: It includes the study of availability of raw material, labour, plant and machinery, location of the plant, power, fuel, water etc.

(iv) Technology: It studies the various technologies available for the manufacturing and developing of the project. It also helps in the comparison of the various alternatives available in the market.

(v) Cost estimates: It study the cost of all the factors involved in the project. In this realistic estimates are made to reflect on all relevant investment and operational cost of the project.

(vi) Profit: In this the estimation of the profit is made by comparing all the other projects which are in competition. It also includes the market share which will be enjoyed by our project so that the estimation can be made about the future profits.

Example: The steps of a pre-feasibility of a project on waste water treatment and disposal are as under:

Preliminary recompilation of data, mainly:

- General geography of the region (maps 1:50,000).
- Climate (temperatures, winds, rain, evaporation).
- General socio-economic level of the population.
- Preliminary estimate of flow quantity and quality, and projections.
- Existing sewage network and treatment facilities.
- Availability of land to construct the treatment plant and land cost.
- Availability of energy and energy cost.
- Propose the potential limits of the project (physical limits and design horizon in time).
- Identify potential alternatives for the disposal of the treated effluents.
- Propose sewage treatment technologies that may be used.
- Perform a preliminary estimate of project cost.
- Identify lacking information which will be necessary for the *Feasibility Study*.
- Identify potential financial sources for the project.
- Prepare the TOR to contract the *Feasibility Study* (if the conclusion of the *Pre-Feasibility Study* is that the project is *feasible*).

14.4. MEANING OF FEASIBILITY ANALYSIS

A **feasibility study** is an evaluation and analysis of the potential of the proposed project which is based on extensive investigation and research to support the process of decision making. Feasibility studies aim to objectively and rationally uncover the strengths and weaknesses of an existing business or proposed venture, opportunities and threats present in the environment, the resources required to carry through, and ultimately the prospects for success. a well-designed feasibility study should provide a historical background of the business or project, description of the product or service, accounting statements, details of the operations and management, marketing research and policies, financial data, legal requirements and tax obligations. Generally, feasibility studies precede technical development and project implementation.

Projects identified are normally analyzed in order to establish their viability from different angles such as technical, marketing, technical and their considerations are studied and then findings, with the supporting data, are resented in a systematic form.

Feasibility study, therefore, may be defined as " a formal investigation of the blue-chip opportunity leading to rational decision making to commit investment".

14.5. IMPORTANCE OF FEASIBILITY STUDY

It is the most important part of project analysis, for it provides answers to questions in detail on different aspects relating to a project. In practice this means investigating the project from six different aspects economic, technical, managerial, organizational, commercial and financial. The relative importance of these different aspects varies considerably according to the type of project involved. For example, in the analysis of public sector projects more importance is usually given to wider social benefits than to narrow financial profitability. It will define and analyze the critical elements that relate to the production of a given product together with alternative approaches to such production. Such a study should also provide a project of a defined production capacity at a selected location using a particular technology or technologies in relation to defined materials and inputs, at identified investment and production costs, and sales revenue yielding a defined return on investment.

The feasibility study is an iterative process covering all aspects of an investment project such as possible alternative solutions for production programmes, locations, technology, organizational set up, etc. if the resulting data show a non-viable project, several parameters and the production programmes, materials inputs or technology should be adjusted in an attempt to present a well defined viable project. The feasibility study should describe this optimization process, justify the assumptions made and the solutions selected and define the scope of the project as the integration of the selected partial alternatives. If, however, the project is not viable despite all alterations reviewed, this should be stated and justified in the study

Most of feasibility studies have the same or similar coverage, though there may be considerable difference in orientation and emphasis depending on such factors as the nature of the industry, the magnitude and complexity of the production unit contemplated, investment and other costs involved. By and large, however, a satisfactory feasibility study must analyze all the basic components and implications of an industrial project and any shortfall in this regard will limit the utility of the study.

14.6. DIFFERENCE BETWEEN PRE-FEASIBILITY STUDIES AND FEASIBILITIY STUDIES

1. Objective: The objective of the pre-feasibility study is to determine whether or not the project idea needs further investigation but the objective of feasibility study is to determine the true profitability of the project and decide to go ahead or not.

2. Type of Research: In the pre-feasibility study the primary and secondary research methods are used and in most of the cases and in order to reduce the cost mostly the secondary type of research is done but in the feasibility study, all types of research methods are applied and most of the cases primary research is done in order to get proper information about the project.

3. Time involved in study: Pre-feasibility study takes less time as compared to Feasibility study but in most of the cases time is depended upon the type of the project. In pre feasibility study normally the time taken ranges from 3 to 6 months and in feasibility study time taken ranges from one to two years.

4. Cost: Cost always depend upon the work done and the time spent on the research so its clear that the cost of pre feasibility study is lesser than the feasibility study and the minimum cost involved in the study of pre-feasibility ranges between 0.25% to 1.5% of the project cost and the cost involved in the feasibility ranges from 1.5 -3%.

14.7. MEANING OF FEASIBILITY REPORT

The details gathered from feasibility studies and presented in various tables, reports and statements are consolidated into feasibility report. This report also contains some background information about the industry to which the project belongs, and the enterprise submitting the report. The main purpose of the report is to provide information that is required for the project appraisal. In the case of public sector projects this report would also enable the concerned authorities to take an objective decision on the project. In addition, this report would enable the financing agencies to purposefully evaluate the project before extending financial assistance.

14.8. FEATURES OF FEASIBILITY REPORT

The main purpose of the feasibility report is to provide basic guidelines on technical, economical and commercial issues of the project. Some of the features of project feasibility study are:

1. Feasibility report describes the nature and scope of the project
2. It provides the general view on investment range of the project
3. It highlights the scope of operations
4. It helps in selecting the right technology for the project at right cost
5. It helps in the selection of the right location for the project
6. It prescribes the appropriate environmental conditions for the project
7. It always provide a chance to revise the actions and rectify the mistakes before they are taken for granted.
8. It helps in the verification of various alternatives available regarding equipment, capacity, technology, financing etc.

14.9. GENERAL FORMAT ON SCOPE OF FEASIBILITY REPORT

1. Introduction.
2. Summary and Recommendations.
3. Product Capacity, Chemistry of the Product Specifications, Properties Applications and Uses.
4. **Market potential:** Existing installed capacity and actual production for the last five years. New capacities under consideration/implementation, Demand pattern with specific reference to requirements in various regions based on desk research and field survey.
5. **Process and know-how:** Description of different processes available. Selection of the process for the project and the reason for the same. Selection of suitable know-how for the said project based on technical and economic evaluation from available data. Prospective collaborator and terms of collaborations.
6. **Plant and machinery:** List of imported/indigenous machinery. Broad specifications of the machinery. List of manufacturers of machinery. Critical items of the machinery.
7. **Location:** Actual site selection survey. Availability of raw material, electricity, water, and other infrastructural facilities. Plot plan and building, Overall plot plan along with building plan.
8. **Raw materials:** Raw material requirements and their specifications.
9. **Utilities:** Requirements of power, water and others including fuel, steam, gas, etc., as their specifications.
10. **Effluents:** Nature and type of effluent/specifications and quality of effluent organizational Structure.
11. **Capital cost:** Project cost giving break-up details (based on budgetary estimates) Margin money for working capital in the project cost.
12. **Working capital:** Details of requirement of working capital and norms
13. **Mode of finance:** Based on the debt-equity ratio and other financing norms followed by financial institutions.
14. **Manufacturing cost:** Unit cost of production Projected. cost of production for 10 years.
15. **Financial analysis:** Profitability statement for 10 years. Break-even and sensitivity analysis, Payback period, projected balance sheet for 10 years.
16. **Implementation schedule:** Time schedule for the implementation of the project.

14.10. GUIDELINES FOR FEASIBILITY REPORT

The feasibility report lies in between the project formulation stage and the appraisal and sanction stage. The project formulation stage involves the identification of investment options by the entrepreneur in consultation with the administrative ministry, the planning commission and other concerned authorities.

1. General Information: The feasibility report should include as analysis of the industry to which the project belongs. It should deal with the past performance of the industry. The description of the type of industry should also be given, i.e, the priority of the industry, increase in production, role of the public sector, allocation of investment of funds, choice of technique, etc., This should contain information about the enterprise submitting the feasibility report. It should also includes the scope of the study.

2. Verification of alternatives: This is one of the crucial step in the project feasibility study.This should contain present data on the gap between demand and supply for the outputs which are to be produced, data on the capacity that would be available from projects that are in production or under implementation at the time the report is prepared, a complete list of all existing plants in the industry, giving their capacity and their level of production actually attained, a list of all projects. All options that are technically feasible should be considered at this preliminary stage. The location of the project and its implications should also be looked into. An account of the foreign exchange requirement should be taken. The profitability of different options should also be looked into. An account of the foreign exchange requirement should be taken. The profitability of different options should also be given. The rate of return on investment should be calculated and presented in the report. Alternative cost calculations vis-à-vis return should be presented.

3. Project description: The feasibility report should provide a brief description of the technology/ process chosen for the project. Information relevant for determining the optimality of the location chosen should also be included. To assist in the assessment of the environmental effects of a project every feasibility report must present the information on specific points, i.e., population, water, land, air, flora, fauna, effects arising out of the project's pollution. Other environmental disruption, etc. The report should contain a list of important items of capital equipment and also the list of the operational requirements of the plant, requirements of water and power, requirements of personnel, organizational structure envisaged, transport costs, activity wise phasing of construction and factors affecting it.

4. Marketing plan: It should contain the following items: Data on the marketing plan. Demand and prospective supply in each of the areas to be served. The methods and the data used for making estimates of domestic supply and selection of the market areas should be presented. Estimates of the degree of price sensitivity should be presented. It should contain an analysis of past trends in prices.

5. Capital requirement and costs: The spending for the project deleiverables are always in term of 'costs', irrespective of their nature such as material costs, research costs, labour costs, overhead costs etc. It may be in form of depreciation, loss on sale of fixed assets, etc.The estimates should be reasonably complete and properly estimated. Information on all items of costs should be carefully collected and presented.

6. Operating requirements and costs: Operating costs are essentially those costs, which are incurred after the commencement of commercial production. Information about all items of operating costs should be collected. Operating costs relate to cost of raw materials and intermediaries, fuel, utilities, labor, repair and maintenance, selling expenses and other expenses

7. Financial analysis: The purpose of this analysis is to present some measures to assess the financial viability of the project. A pro forma balance sheet for the project data should be presented.

Depreciation should be allowed for on the basis specified by the Bureau of Pubic Enterprises. Foreign exchange requirements should be cleared by the Department of Economic Affairs. The feasibility report should take into account income tax rebates for priority industries, incentives for backward areas, accelerated depreciation, etc. The sensitivity of the rate of return on the level and pattern of product price

8. Economic analysis: Social profitability analysis need some adjustments in the data relating to the costs and return to the enterprise. One important type of adjustment involves a correction in input and cost, to reflect the true value of foreign exchange, labor and capital. The enterprises should try to assess the impact of its operations on foreign trade. Indirect costs and benefits should also be included in the report. If they cannot be quantified they should be analyzed and their importance emphasized

14.11. CHECKLIST FOR FEASIBILITY REPORT

1. Examination of public policy with respect to the industry.
2. Broad specifications of outputs and alternative techniques of production.
3. Listing and description of alternative locations.
4. Preliminary analysis of profitability for different alternatives.
5. Preliminary estimates of sales revenue, capital costs, and operatingcosts of different alternatives.
6. Marketing analysis
7. Specification of product pattern and product prices
8. Raw material investigation and specification of sources of raw material supply
9. Estimation of material, energy flow balance and input prices
10. Listing of major equipment by type, size and cost.
11. Listing of auxiliary equipment by type, size and cost.
12. Specification of sources of supply for equipment and process know-how.
13. Specification of site and completion of necessary investigation.
14. Listing of buildings, structure and yard facilities by type, size and cost.
15. Specification of supply sources, connection costs and other costs for transportation services, water supply and power.
16. Preparation of layout.
17. Specification of skill-wise labor requirements and labor costs.
18. Estimation of working capital requirements.
19. Phasing of activities and expenditures during construction
20. Analysis of profitability.

21. Determination of measures of combating environmental problems.
22. Analysis of the past performance of the enterprise responsible for implementing and running the project with respect to project completion, capacity utilization, profitability, etc.
23. State of preparedness to implement the project rapidly.

14.12. EXAMPLE

How to Write a Feasibility Report on Starting a Small-scale Fish Farm[1]

Fish farming or aquaculture is a growing industry full of opportunities due to the increased demand for fish as a source of important nutrients for healthy living. A small scale fish farm is relatively easy to establish since the requirements are minimal and the start-up costs are not overwhelming. A feasibility report analyzes an intended project in terms of its viability, start-up costs and profitability. An ideal small scale fish farming feasibility report should include the following steps.

Step 1 :Introduction: The introduction part of the feasibility report should outline the importance and the advantages of small scale fish farming. Explain your project fully in this section. Outline briefly how the project will be rolled out, how you plan to benefit from the project and the processes that will be involved. Basically it is a summary of the small-scale fish farming project.

Step 2: Description of the project: In this section, clearly outline the project's location, the environment surrounding it and the availability of the resources required to start a small scale fish farm. Highlight the project's mission and vision. Business goals and the objectives should also be included. Also include a brief history of the project and what motivated you to start the fish farm.

Step 3: Market description: Describe the type of industry you will be operating in, whether you will be selling your products as a wholesaler or a retailer. Identify your target market and how you plan to penetrate that market. Outline the marketing strategies you will employ to market your fish.

Step 4: Description of your products: Highlight different species of fish that you will be rearing. Describe how you selected those species. Explain the pricing of your products and the competitive edge your fish products have over other products in the market.

Step 5: Organization plan: Outline the legal structure under which the small scale fish farm will operate, whether it will be a sole proprietorship, partnership or a limited liability company. Identify the type of permits and licenses that will be required for the project. Explain the number of staff and their qualifications that will be necessary to successfully run the fish farm. Outline how they will be organized in terms of duties and responsibilities.

Step 6: Marketing plan: Illustrate how you plan to conduct your market research to identify how you will segment your market and how you plan to satisfy each market segment. Market segmentation entails identifying the different portions of the market that are different from one another in terms of lifestyle, income levels, location and spending habits. Explain the strategies that will be used in the sale and distribution of your fish to each market segment to satisfy their unique needs. Also include the strategies you will employ to effectively compete with your competitors in the market

Step 7 : Financial management: Identify the intended sources of capital for your fish farm and how you plan to use this capital in your venture. Outline how the profits will be used to enhance the fish farm and the measures that will be put in place to prevent or reduce losses. In this step you should also be able to show the projected cash flow statement, income statement and the balance sheet statement for the next 12 months.

Step 8 : Conclusion : Give your recommendations and conclusion in this section on the viability of the small-scale fish farm.

14.13. SUMMARY

Feasibility check is the very important aspect of the project as it includes the screening of the project .Screening of the project has either to go through pre-feasibility study or feasibility study. Both differentiate on the basis of the size, scope and availability of finance for the project and if the project is tiny and non complicated then pre-feasibility study is acceptable and if the project is big and needs in depth investigation then feasibility study is needed. Every project should be technically sound, financially feasible economically beneficial, commercially dependable and organizationally adequate so feasibility study applies certain tools in order to evaluate the project from different aspects. Furthermore, its said that feasibility is associated with more of investigation procedure and identification of a viable alternatives from multiple angles.

14.14. SELF ASSESSMENT QUESTIONS

1. What do you mean by pre-feasibility study? What are its objectives?
2. Give an outline of a pre-feasibility study report of any dummy project as presented by a project manager.
3. What do you mean by feasibility study? Describe the sailent features of feasibility report.
4. Outline the steps involved in preparing a project feasibility report.
5. Explain the difference between pre-feasibility study and feasibility study

SOURCE/NOTES

1. www.smallbusiness.chron.com

Others

(a) *Project Management and Control* — P.C.K Rao

(b) *Projects* — Prasanna Chandra

15

FEASIBILITY REPORTS

15.1. INTRODUCTION

As discussed in last chapter, feasibility study is an evaluation and analysis of the potential of the proposed project which is based on extensive investigation and research to support the process of decision making. Feasibility studies aim to objectively and rationally uncover the strengths and weaknesses of an existing business or proposed venture, opportunities and threats present in the environment, the resources required to carry through, and ultimately the prospects for success. In its simplest terms, the two criteria to judge feasibility are cost required and value to be attained. As such, a well-designed feasibility study should provide a historical background of the business or project, description of the product or service, accounting statements, details of the operations and management, marketing research and policies, financial data, legal requirements and tax obligations. Generally, feasibility studies precede technical development and project implementation.

15.2. OBJECTIVE OF FEASIBILITY STUDY

Developing any new business venture is difficult. Taking a project from the initial idea through the operational stage is a complex and time consuming effort. Before the potential members invest in a proposed business project, they must determine if it can be economically viable and then decide if investment advantages outweigh the risks involved. Often construction project operations involve risks with which the members are unfamiliar. The feasibility study allows groups to preview potential project outcomes and to decide if they should continue. It is an integral part in developing a construction project. The purpose of the feasibility study is to explore the project in enough detail for the interested parties and stake holders to make a commitment to proceed with the development of the project. Feasibility studies are useful and valid for many kinds of projects. An evaluation of a new business venture both for new groups and established businesses, is the most common, but not the only usage. Studies can help groups to expand existing services, build or remodel facilities, change methods of operation, add new products, or even merge with another business. A feasibility study assists decision makers whenever they need to consider alternative development opportunities.

Feasibility study permits planners to outline their ideas on paper before implementing them. This can reveal errors in project design, before their implementation negatively affects the project. Applying the lessons gained from a feasibility report can significantly lower the project costs.The study also presents the risks and returns associated with the project so the prospective members can evaluate them. There is no correct rate of return a project needs to obtain before a group decides to proceed. The acceptable level of return and appropriate risk rate will vary for individual members depending on their personal situation.

A feasibility study evaluates the project's potential for success; therefore, the perceived objectivity is an important factor in the credibility to be placed on the study by potential investors and lending institutions. It must therefore be conducted with an objective, unbiased approach to provide information upon which decisions can be based.

15.3. FEASIBILITY REPORT

The feasibility report represents the last step for evaluating a construction process for "go-no-go" decision and financing purposes. It presents a holistic view of the entire project. The principle parameters for a feasibility report are based on sound and complete engineering and design work. Although all studies must start with certain assumptions, they are closer to reality to give a value to the study. A feasibility study presents the environment where the project will occur and describe its scope. The description also includes the need for the project and how the group can accomplish the goals. The scope also includes the key elements of all aspects of the project. Potential reaction by competitors should be included in the study.

Feasibility report consist of tables, reports and details of information gathered during the feasibility check. As already discussed in Chapter 14(14.7 para), the very purpose of a feasibility report is to provide a basic guideline on technical, economical and commercial parameters of a project. It helps in defining and analyzing the problem and alternative approaches to production processes and outcomes. It focuses attention on the material input and various other techno-economic variables. The operational (will it work?), economical (costs and benefits) and technical (can it be built?) aspects are part of the study. Feasibility study is part of the systems development life cycle which aims to determine whether it is sensible to develop some system. The most popular model of feasibility study is "TELOS", standing for Technical, Economic, Legal, Operational, Schedule. These are:-

(a) Technology and system feasibility: Does the technology exist to implement the proposed system? Is it a practical proposition?

(b) Economic Feasibility: Is the system cost-effective? Do benefits outweigh costs?

(c) Legal Feasibility: is there any conflict between the proposed system and legal requirements, e.g., the Data Protection Act?

(d) Operational Feasibility: Are the current work practices and procedures adequate to support the new system?

(e) Schedule Feasibility: Can the system be developed in time?

15.4. SAMPLE OF FEASIBILITY REPORT

Sample contents of a completed Feasibility Study

1. Title Page

2. Table of Contents

3. Executive Summary: This is the summarised version of the feasibility study. It must adequately cover the major points of the feasibility study on one or two pages.

4. Introduction

— Justification

— Study objective

— Scope of study

5. Product/Service Description

Describe your product/service here

6. The Promoter

— Name

— Address

— Telephone number/Email address

— Qualifications

— Work history and background in brief

— Status of promoter – whether company, or individual

— More detailed information on qualifications and career history can be included in the appendices.

7. Market Assessment: In this section you provide an assessment of the market demand for your product or service. The analysis reveals who will buy how much of your product and what they are willing to pay for it. It consists of identifying your markets, determining market factors that create demand for your product, and forecasting the potential demand for your product. It should identify opportunities or threats facing the proposed business. Describe the market research technique that you used to find answers to the questions below. The techniques can include telephone surveys, personal interviews, sales figures on existing products, statistical and published information in your target area, informed opinion of knowledgeable people and test marketing.

Questions to answer in the market assessment

- What is the size of the market?
- What is the sales volume?
- What is the production volume?
- Who is buying the product or service, i.e., who is your target market?

- How many customers are there? Who are they?
- Where are they currently buying the product or service?
- Are the customers satisfied?
- How is your market segmented currently?
- What are the major trends affecting your market?
- What is the growth rate of the market?
- What would the buyers like to see changed about the products they are now buying?
- What are the market trends for your product?
- How is your target group changing?
- Are other groups starting to use your product?
- How do factors such as age, gender, family income, brand loyalty, lifestyle, etc., affect your product?
- How do customers view warranties and packaging of the products? What is the price structure on your product?
- How has the price changed in the last year? Last five years?
- What determines price on your product – quality, size, demand, tourist trade?
- What promotional methods are most effective in reaching your target customers?
- What is your conclusion about your expected market share?
- Are there any legal, environmental or economic factors, which may impact on the business?

8. Competition Analysis

- Who are your major competitors?
- What are the major strengths of each?
- What are the major weaknesses of each?
- What are their production capabilities?
- Are you familiar with the following factors concerning your competitors:
- Price structure?
- Product lines (quality, breadth, width)?
- Location?
- Promotional activities?
- Sources of supply?
- Image from a consumer's viewpoint?
- Do you know of any new competitors?
- Do you know of any competitor's plans for expansion?

- Have any firms of your type gone out of business lately?
- If so, why?
- Do you know the sales and market share of each competitor?
- Do you know whether the sales and market share of each competitor are increasing, decreasing, or stable?
- Do you know the profit levels of each competitor?
- Are your competitors' profits increasing, decreasing, or stable?
- Can you compete with your competition?

9. Marketing Strategy

Note: Depending on the outcome of the feasibility study your business plan will include a detailed marketing strategy. For the feasibility study a briefer outline of your strategy will suffice.

- How will the market be accessed? What distribution methods will you use?
- What is the competitive advantage of your product or the benefits of your product in relation to the competition?
- What will attract customers to your product?
- How is your product differentiated from the competition?
- What pricing methods will you probably use?
- What promotional methods will you use (i.e tradeshows, advertising, etc.)?
- Outline any commitments you have received from customers already.
- Outline export potential, if any.

10. Technical or Production Analysis: This portion should be based on verifiable data and contain sufficient information and analysis so that a determination may be made on the technical feasibility of achieving the levels of income or production that are projected in the financial statements. Depending on your particular business idea it may include the following considerations:

- Determine the suitability of the production site including site environmental impact analysis (provided by architect, engineer or person with the necessary expertise to make the determination).
- Does the site have the desired characteristics and available utilities and transportation facilities, etc.?
- What are the technology needs for the proposed business?
- What are the equipment/resource requirements?
- When and where can the technology/equipment be obtained?
- What does the technology or equipment cost?
- What are the production costs (to be included in the finance section).

- Will the technology achieve the intended production levels?
- What will the production process be?
- What are the product storage requirements etc.?
- Is there availability of local labour?
- Are there any legal or environmental factors or other developments which may impact on the business?

11. Prototype or sample product: If you need to develop a sample product or prototype as part of the feasibility a description should be given here.

12. Management capability: Describe the requirements for the management positions and responsibilities for those personnel.

Describe the skills/expertise you will need to bring to the business.

Describe existing capabilities within the business (related to qualifications and experience of promoter).

13. Financial analysis: Include preliminary financial projections (with a clear understanding of assumptions) and an estimation of all variable and fixed (overhead) costs will be necessary to estimate the profitability of the proposed venture. The accuracy of your revenue projections and costs will be dependent on the reliability of the marketing predictions and production information.

Important considerations to determine profitability include:

- Are you sure that you have considered all costs, variable and fixed, that should be allocated to the new enterprise?
- Do you have enough information to prepare projected statements for the next three or more years, i.e., cash flow forecast, profit and loss, balance sheet?
- Have you done a "sensitivity" analysis to predict the impact that possible variations in costs and revenues will have on profitability?
- When will the enterprise reach the break-even point?
- When will the business become profitable?
- Is there enough profit to allow for growth of the business?

14. Required financing: Required funding to enter this market and feasibility of raising capital (if necessary).

15. Economic impact: Show the potential economic impact of the proposed venture e.g. job creation, salaries of employees, sourcing local suppliers, etc.

Limits and constraints.

16. Conclusions and recommendations: A suggestion as to the feasibility of the project.

17. Appendices: Include any supporting documentation including references here.

15.5. TECHNICAL AND SYSTEM FEASIBILITY

Technical appraisal is an in-depth study to ensure that a project is (i) soundly designed, (ii) appropriately engineered and (iii) follows accepted standards. These considerations differ from project to project. But, in any case, the emphasis is on the inputs needed for the project and the resulting outputs of goods and services. Technical feasibility is an attempt to determine how well the technical requirements of the industry can be met. Technical feasibility studies are aimed at ensuring that all the physical facilities required for successful implementation of the project are available and the best of the alternative facilities are selected for the project. The assessment is based on an outline design of system requirements, to determine whether the company has the technical expertise to handle completion of the project. The technical feasibility assessment is focused on gaining an understanding of the present technical resources of the organization and their applicability to the expected needs of the proposed system. It is an evaluation of the hardware and software and how it meets the need of the proposed system. When writing a feasibility report, the following should be taken to consideration:—

- Proper location of the enterprise,
- Selection of appropriate technology, plant and machinery,
- Availability of raw materials, resources and other inputs,
- Establishing the schedule of project implementation

Basically it includes all the following factors:

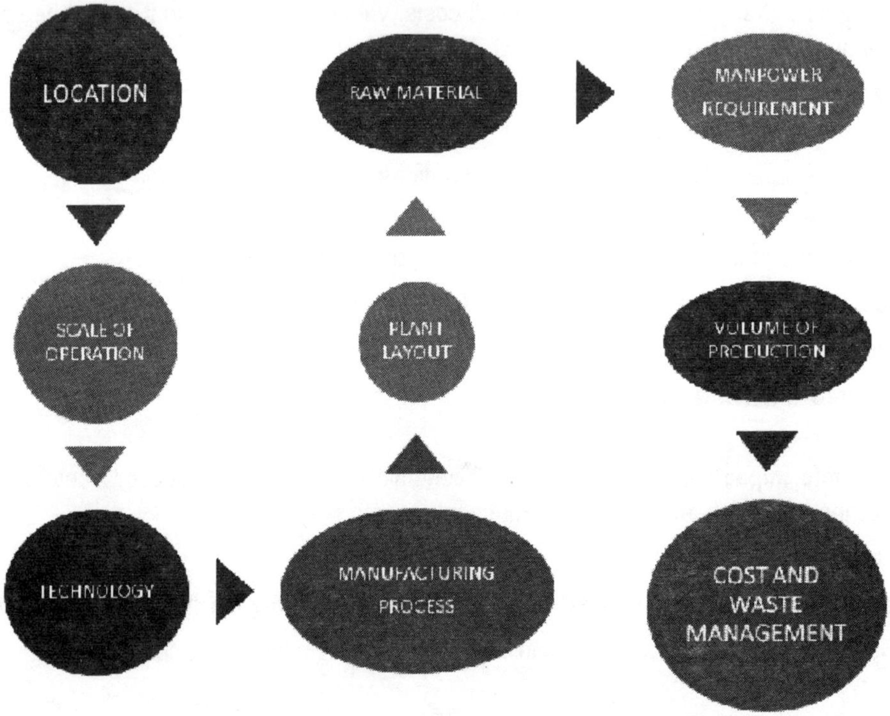

Fig. 15.1. Factors considered for Technical Feasibility

At this level, the concern is whether the proposal is both technically and legally feasible (assuming moderate cost).

(i) Proper location of the enterprise

Proper location of the enterprise is a sine qua non for success. Technical feasibility is an attempt to determine the technical requirements of the industry and the selection of most advantageous location from the industrial point of view. The word Location refers to the general location of the enterprise, whereas the word site refers to a specific area within the location. Location should selected keeping in view the operational advantages, financial advantages and government policies. According to Bethel, Atwater and Smith enterprise location involves three main steps: (i) selection of the region or general area (ii) selection of the particular commodity (iii) selection of the exact plant site.

Selection of location sometimes determined by the role of government policies or policies by the state government. However, since location is an extremely important aspect for ensuring commercial success of an enterprise, location is appraised in relation to availability of raw material, power, labour, fuel and other infrastructure needs.

Important factors that must be kept in mind while selecting the location and site are:

(a) The availability of land, the cost of land and presence of approach roads.

(b) Availability of raw material and labour.

(c) Suitability of climate

(d) The proximity to markets.

(e) Meterological conditions and topography

(f) The availability of transportation and communication facilities.

(g) Availability of finance and research facilities

(h) Availability of water and other fighting facilities

(i) Political stability

(j) Price of land and expansion potential

(k) Availability of amenities

(l) Availability of technology and technological know-how

(j) Attitude of local people and state assistance

All the above factors are taken into consideration while the selection of location and site and optimum site is selected on the basis of the comparative economic survey of the alternative sites in question.Some others are discussed below:-

(a) OPERATIONAL ADVANTAGES

(1) Nearness to raw materials

- Wood processing woods
- Cement plant requiring shale and gypsum

- Sugar mills to be in the crop area

(2) Nearness to market

- Auto-parts (motor assembly plants)
- Services (hotel, banks, training institutes)

(3) Availability of personnel

- Software developers should be in an area with lots of computer universities.
- Engineering goods in areas where skilled workers are concentrated (Lahore and Gujranwala)
- Labor intensive projects like jute and textile mills in those areas where cheap labor is available.

(4) Infrastructure

- Suitability of water and waste disposal– Cloth printing/Paper Plants/Tanneries
- Social amenities

(5) Pleasant climatic conditions for:

- Tourist complex/Health resorts
- Ecological requirements for mineral water.

(b) FINANCIAL ADVANTAGES

- Taxes, subsidies, grants and allowances offered by the Government
- Availability of cheaper credit by banks through Central Bank support.
- Reduced rates for utilities

(c) PUBLIC POLICIES

- Location policy - negative areas - where no industry can be established
- Incentives for unattractive areas
- Establishment of public sector project like steel mills, petrochemical leading to feeder or downstream projects.
- Development of infrastructure.

For example : Let us take the example of a **Water Sports** complex being planned at **Goa** whose target market is tourists from the country and out of the country. So in order to select the particular site following has to take up in mind:

- The location of such a venture must be close to or easily accessible from an airport.
- The site must fit within limits of finance.
- As the project is water sports so the easy availability of utilities like water, power, fuel, etc., must be there.

The presence of other enterprises which would form effective backward linkages and forward linkages.

Alfred Weber's Theory of Industrial Location

Alfred Weber (30 July 1868 – 2 May 1958) was a German economist, geographer, sociologist and theoretician of culture whose work was influential in the development of modern economic geography.

A model of industrial location proposed by A. Weber (1909, trans. 1929), assumes that industrialists choose a least-cost location for the development of new industry. The theory is based on a number of assumptions, among them that markets are fixed at certain specific points, that transport costs are proportional to the weight of the goods and the distance covered by a raw material or a finished product, that perfect competition exists, and that decisions are made by economic man.

Weber postulated that raw materials and markets would exert a 'pull' on the location of an industry through transport costs. Industries with a high material index would be pulled towards the raw material. Industries with a low material index would be pulled towards the market. He singled out two special cases. In one the weight of the final product is less than the weight of the raw material going into making the product. This is the weight losing case. In the other the final product is heavier than the raw material that require transport. Usually this is a case of some ubiquitous (everywhere available) raw material such as water being incorporated into the product. This is called the weight-gaining case.

Once a least-cost location has been established, Weber goes on to consider the deflecting effect of labour costs. To determine whether the savings provided by moving to a location of cheaper or more efficient labour would more than offset the increase in transport costs, isodapanes (isodapanes is a line joining up places of equal total transport costs for industrial production and delivery between the points where the raw materials are located and the markets) are constructed around the point of production at the point of minimum transport costs. The extra price of the wage bill is calculated for the point of production. If the source of cheap labour lies within the isodapane which has the value of the higher wages differential (the critical isodapane), it would be more profitable to choose the site with low labour costs rather than the least transport costs location.

(ii) Plant Size

Size of the plant is very important for the success of a project but its determination is very critical. As the plant entails lot of sunk cost. Plant capacity (referred as production capacity).Plant capacity may be defined in two ways:

(a) Feasible normal capacity

(b) Nominal maximum capacity.

Feasible normal capacity means capacity attainable under normal working conditions and nominal maximum capacity is the capacity which is technically attainable and this often corresponds to the installed capacity guaranteed by the supplier of the plant .

If the plant capacity is not optimum or is under utilization of its capacity then it will result in reduction of profits and it has maximum ill effects in the initial/ early years of the project set up. So, to be on the safer side it is therefore better to be on the lower side and to build a plant having a having a capacity which will be fully utilized. Size of the plant also take into consideration the availability of raw material, technology, equipment, availability of finance etc and the best possible size of the plant and equipment has to select after analyzing the availability, economics, viability and practicability of different size options available.

(iii) Selection of Appropriate Technology, Plant and Machinery

It ensure efficient and economical operations. Technology must be chosen based on the **specific requirements** of the enterprise. It checks the state of existing and available technology(domestic and foreign). A very important decision in the area of plant and machinery refers to the size or capacity of the facilities to be created. This decision must be taken after a careful consideration of demand and fluctuations in demand. Selection of technology also keep a check on the training needs of the personnel with respect to present technology and new technology as well.Technology must be chosen where there will be minimization of wastage as well. So the choice of technology is influenced by following factors:-

1. Principal inputs available for the project, i.e., raw materials available influence the technology chosen.
2. The relationship between the capacity and Investment cost is very important. Typically, the investment cost per unit of capacity decreases as the plant capacity increases.
3. While selecting an appropriate technology, local conditions should be kept in like heat, dust, rain or cold.
4. Also related other factors be considered such as power interruptions and low literacy and skills. In case of low-literacy, semi-automatic process should be introduced.
5. Capacity of the organization to adapt the technology
6. Timely availability of manpower with necessary skills for installation,operation and maintenance.
7. Availability of R&D facilities.

(iv) Network Analysis

A network is a set of symbols connected with each other with a sequential relationship with each step making the completion of a project/event. As discussed earlier, a business plan or project involves various activities to be undertaken to convert it into an enterprise. Delays in the completion of activities cause, among other things, cost overruns. Hence, there is a need for deciding the sequential order' of all activities of the project so as to accomplish the project economically in the minimum available time with the limited resources. This is also called "project scheduling". A number of network techniques have been developed for project scheduling. Some of them are: (a) Programme Evaluation and Review Technique (PERT). (b) Critical Path Method (CPM). (c) Graphical Evaluation and Review Technique (GERT). (d) Line of Balance (LOB).

(a) Programme Evaluation and Review Technique (PERT): PERT was first developed as a Management Aid for completing Polaris Ballistic Missile Project in USA in October 1958. It worked well in expediting the completion of the project from 7 years to 5 years. Since then, PERT has become very popular technique used for project planning and control. In nutshell, it schedules the sequence of activities to be completed in order to accomplish the project within a short period of time. It helps reduce both the time and cost of the project.

Steps Involved in PERT: The following steps are involved in PERT technique:

1. The activities involved in the project are drawn up in a sequential relationship to show what activity follows what.
2. The time required for completing each activity of the project is estimated and noted on network.
3. The critical activities of the project are determined.
4. The variability of the project duration and probability of the project completion in a given time period are calculated.

Advantages of PERT: PERT technique bears the following advantages:

1. It determines the expected time required for completing activity.
2. It helps complete the project within a given period of time.
3. It helps management handle uncertainties involved in the project and thus, reduce the 'risk element in the project.
4. It enables management to make optimum allocation of limited resources
5. It presses for the right action, at the right point and at the right time in the organization.

Limitations of PERT: PERT suffers from the following limitations:

1. PERT network is mainly based on time estimates required for each activity. On account of wrong time estimates, the network is bound to become highly unrealistic.
2. This technique also does not consider the resources required at different stages of the project.
3. For effective control of a project by using PERT technique requires frequent updating and revising the PERT calculations. But, this prove squite a costly affair for the organization.

(b) Critical Path Method (CPM): The Critical Path Method (CPM) was first developed in USA by the E.I.Dupont Nemours & Co. in 1956 for doing periodic overhauling and maintenance of a chemical plant. It resulted in reducing the shut down period from 130 hours to 90 hours and saving the company $ 1 million. The CPM differentiates between planning and scheduling of the project. While planning refers to determination of activities to be accomplished scheduling refers to the introduction of time schedule for each activity of the project. The duration of different activities in CPM are deterministic. There is a precise known time that each activity in the project will take.

Advantages of CPM: The important advantages of CPM technique are:

1. It helps in ascertaining the time schedule of activities having sequential relationship.
2. It makes control easier for the management.

3. It identifies the most critical elements in the project. Thus, the management is kept alert and prepared to pay due attention to the critical activities of the project.
4. It makes better and detailed planning possible.

Limitations of CPM: The main limitations of the CPM are:

1. CPM operates on the assumption that there is a precise known time that each activity in the project will take. But, it may not be true in real practice.
2. CPM time estimates are not based on statistical analysis.
3. It cannot be used, as a controlling device for the simple reason that any change introduced will change the entire structure of network. In other words, CPM cannot be used as a dynamic controlling device

(c) Graphical Evaluation and Review Technique (GERT): Graphical Evaluation and Review Technique, commonly known as GERT, is a network analysis technique used in project management that allows probabilistic treatment of both network logic and estimation of activity duration. The technique was first described in 1966 by Dr. Alan B. Pritsker of Purdue University and WW Happ. Compared to other techniques, GERT is only rarely used in complex systems. Nevertheless, the GERT approach addresses the majority of the limitations associated with PERT/CPM technique. GERT allows loops between tasks. The fundamental drawback associated with the GERT technique is the complex programme (Monte Carlo simulation) required to model the GERT system. Development in GERT includes Q-GERTS - allowing the user to consider queuing within the system. It is a procedure for the study of stochastic networks composed of EXCLUSIVE-OR, INCLUSIVE-OR, and AND nodes (vertices) and multiparameter branches (transmittances or edges). The total concept of stochastic networks, the transformation, and the evaluation method is labeled GERT. Examples show the general applicability of the technique; it is viewed as a starting place for many other avenues of research.

(d) Line of Balance (LOB): The Line of Balance (LOB) process is employed when a repetitive process exists within the contract's work scope. The manufacturing of parts and the assembly of units in the factory are two candidates for the use of LOB. Line of Balance (LOB) is a management control process for collecting, measuring and presenting facts relating to time, cost and accomplishment — all measured against a specific plan. It shows the process, status, background, timing and phasing of the project activities, thus, providing management with measuring tools that help:

1. Comparing actual progress with a formal objective plan.
2. Examining only the deviations from established plans, and gauging their degree of severity with respect to the remainder of the project.
3. Receiving timely information concerning trouble areas and indicating areas where appropriate corrective action is required.
4. Forecasting future performance.

The "Line of Balance" itself is a graphic device that enables a manager to see at a single glance which of many activities comprising a complex operation are "in balance" - i.e., whether those which should have been completed at the time of the review actually are completed and whether any activities scheduled for future completion are lagging behind schedule. The Line of Balance chart comprises only one feature of the whole philosophy which includes numerous danger signal controls for all the various levels of management concerned.

(v) Availability of Raw Materials and Other Inputs

For manufacturing of desired products, a number of raw materials can be used which bring equally good results. Therefore, it should be studied which of the raw materials is economically available in the area and machinery selection be made accordingly. The requirement of various inputs like raw materials and labour must be estimated on the basis of estimated turnover. The availability of inputs of the right quantity and the right quality on a regular and continuous basis is essential for continuity of operations. For example:

- Crystal sugar can be manufactured from sugarcane, beet and sweet potato. Similarly, liquid sugar can be extracted from rice, corn or fruits.
- Paper and board can be manufactured using wood, bagasse, rice husk, wheat straw and cotton stick
- Quality of limestone determines whether the cement process should be wet or dry.

Wherever necessary, the enterprise must enter into supply contracts to ensure availability of essential inputs. The enterprise may also create its own sources of supply. For example:- Iron and steel mills are usually located near the ore deposits and sugar mills in sugar cultivating region

(vi) Establishing the Schedule of Project Implementation

It ensures that the project is completed within the planned time and commences commercial production on schedule. Timing is very crucial. Project coming into operation before time do not find any market. While those coming after time have an obsolete product which no body would buy even offered at low price. Delays in the implementation of project quite often create cost over-runs and may effect the profitability of the enterprise. E.g.:- A project for producing polyethylene shopping bags came into production when homemade waste-paper bags were available at 10% of the price of plastic bag. So plastic bags were out priced and plant had to be closed down after one year of unsuccessful operation. In the case of large and complex project, Advanced scheduling techniques like Programme Evaluation and Review Technique (PERT) are utilized and appraisal in view of the increasing environmental concern and Governmental regulations in this regard, the technical feasibility study must also outline the systems for safe and non-polluting disposal of effluents like solid and liquid wastes. Use of non conventional energy resources like renewable energy from Sun, windmills, etc., must also be taken account of.

(vii) Operational Feasibility

Operational feasibility is a measure of how well a proposed system solves the problems, and takes advantage of the opportunities identified during scope definition and how it satisfies the requirements identified in the requirements analysis phase of system development. The operational feasibility assessment focuses on the degree to which the proposed development projects fits in with the existing business environment and objectives with regard to development schedule, delivery date, corporate culture, and existing business processes.

To ensure success, desired operational outcomes must be imparted during design and development. These include such design-dependent parameters such as reliability, maintainability, supportability, usability, producibility, disposability, sustainability, affordability and others. These parameters are required to be considered at the early stages of design if desired operational behaviors are to be realized. A system design and development requires appropriate and timely application of engineering and management efforts to meet the previously mentioned parameters. A system may serve its intended purpose most effectively when its technical and operating characteristics are engineered into the design. Therefore operational feasibility is a critical aspect of systems engineering that needs to be an integral part of the early design phases.

(viii) Schedule Feasibility

A project will fail if it takes too long to be completed before it is useful. Typically, this means estimating how long the system will take to develop, and if it can be completed in a given time period using some methods like payback period. Schedule feasibility is a measure of how reasonable the project timetable is. Given our technical expertise, are the project deadlines reasonable? Some projects are initiated with specific deadlines. You need to determine whether the deadlines are mandatory or desirable.

15.5.1 Sample of a Technical Report of Expansion of Company's Existing Weaving Facility:

The Project: The project envisages the expansion of the company's existing weaving facilities through the addition of 30 Picanol/Toyoda air jet looms along with allied equipment. It would be completed at a cost of ₹ 500 million and would have a capacity to produce grey cloth of 7 million square meters.

Location: The project pertains to expansion in the existing textile weaving facilities located at Multan Road, Lahore. The site is well developed and connected by roads. All the infrastructure facilities and manpower are available.

Building: An additional 9,680 sq. metres of covered area would be required to house the looms shed, beam store, warping and sizing sections and yarn godown as well as the service bay.

Raw Material: Cotton, the raw material is abundantly available in the area.

Utilities: No difficulty is foreseen in getting the required quantity of water. The requirements of 1,000 KW would be met through own private power plants arrangement exist.

Manpower and Technical Know-how: Suitable qualified and experienced technical staff is available. Labor is estimated at 57 skilled workers while 38 semi-skilled workers would also be inducted. No difficulty is foreseen regarding labour availability.

Environment Consideration: The proposed project would not pose any environmental hazards.

Construction Schedule: It would take about one year to complete the project.

15.6. FINANCIAL FESIBILITY REPORT

The financial feasibility study (FFS) is the web that ties the economics of the project together. On the one end there is revenue stream and on the other end the operating and development costs. The FFS is like the compass on a ship or a GPS in the car. It tells you where you're heading. And if you're heading in the wrong direction, what to do about it. FFS can also be used as a valuation tool. A financial feasibility study is an assessment of the financial aspects of project. If this case, for starting and running a business. It considers many things including start-up capital, expenses, revenues, and investor income and disbursements. Other portions of a complete feasibility study will also contribute data to your basic financial study. Experts carry out economic analysis for evaluating the effectiveness of a proposed solution against the existing solution and all other available options, giving due consideration to limitations and constraints. In other words it provide a snapshot of cost/ benefits analysis. It determines the immediate and projected benefits and savings that are expected from a proposed system and compare them with the immediate and the projected costs. Financial feasibility studies aim to ensure the entrepreneur that: The project can meet the burden of debt i.e., the project can ensure sufficient revenues to pay the interest cost of borrowed funds and meet the schedules for repayment of loans. The project can earn sufficient revenues to satisfy the expectation of the owners .

However, for the purpose of establishing a business or attracting investors, it includes following key things in comprehensive financial feasibility study:

- Start-up Capital Requirements,
- Start-up Capital Sources

(a) Start-up Capital Requirements: Start-up capital is simply how much cash you need to start your business and keep it running until it is self-sustaining. It include enough capital funds (cash, or access to cash) to run the business for one to two years.

(b) Finding Start-up Capital Funding Sources: There are many ways to raise capital for the business, investors are more likely to invest, banks are more likely to approve loans, and large corporations are more likely to give contracts, if you have personally invested into the business.

It covers the following important aspects:

1. Project Cost Determination,
2. Sources of Finance,
3. Profitability Estimates,
4. Cash Flow Estimates,
5. Projected Financial Position and Flows

In case of a new project, financial viability can be judged on the following parameters:

- Total estimated cost of the project
- Financing of the project in terms of its capital structure, debt equity ratio and promoter's share of total cost

- Existing investment by the promoter in any other business
- Projected cash flow and profitability

The financial viability of a project should provide the following information:

- Full details of the assets to be financed and how liquid those assets are.
- Rate of conversion to cash-liquidity (i.e., how easily can the various assets be converted to cash?).
- Project's funding potential and repayment terms.
- Sensitivity in the repayments capability to the following factors:
  - Time delays.
  - Mild slowing of sales.
  - Acute reduction/slowing of sales.
  - Small increase in cost.
  - Large increase in cost.
  - Adverse economic conditions.

15.6.1 Criteria for Financial Feasibility

In order to evaluate the financial feasibility of an investment project, relevant measurements or criteria need to be specified. Remer and Nieto (1995) categorize the evaluation methods into five basic types:

1. Net present value methods;
2. Rate of return methods;
3. Ratio methods;
4. Payback methods;
5. Accounting methods

As seen, financial feasibility can be measured on the basis of accounting profits (from financial statements) or the projected cash flows of the project. Financial statements are records of actual financial activities of a business and are therefore not available for prospective projects, but projections of statements can be used to gain a better understanding of a project's finances. The cash flows of the project can also be projected and used to analyze the performance of the prospective project. The cash flow method is preferred over the accounting profits method, as the cash flow method considers the time value of money but accounting profits does not. Also, cash flows are always calculated in the same way but accounting profits can be calculated in several different ways, e.g. using different depreciation methods or inventory listings, which give different profit results. Hence, the cash flow method is considered more appropriate for evaluating the financial feasibility of investment projects.

There are several different cash flow based methods that can be used to measure the financial feasibility of investment projects, such as the Net Present Value (NPV), Internal Rate of Return (IRR), Annual Equivalent Worth (AE) and Benefit-Cost Ratio (B/C). These measures will be studied further below, as well as the Modified Internal Rate of Return (MIRR), which is a relatively new and still infrequently used criterion. Investors use these quantitative measures to help them decide whether to undertake an investment or not, based on their return requirements. The payback period is another method that is sometimes used in financial feasibility analysis. The method determines when the project will break even, i.e., how long it takes for revenues to pay investment outlays. However, the method does not measure profitability, as it only measures the time it takes to recover the initial investment outlay but not the profit that is made after paying back the initial investment. The method ignores all revenues and cost after the payback period and does therefore not allow for the possible advantages of a project with a longer economic life. Also, the method does not recognize the time value of money, though that can be remedied by using the discounted payback method. Due to these drawbacks, the payback method is not suitable for measuring financial feasibility, and will therefore not be considered further in this thesis (Park, 2002). Finally, financial ratios can be of use when analyzing financial feasibility. Financial ratios are calculated from the financial statements of a company and are generally only used for companies in operation. However, the projected financial statements can be used to calculate the relevant ratios in order to gain a better understanding of the performance of the project. Nevertheless, projected financial ratios should not be used independently as an analytical tool, but only in addition to the cash flow analysis.

(a) Net Present Value: Net Present Value (NPV) is the difference between the present value of all cash inflows and cash outflows associated with an investment project. The NPV establishes whether or not the investment project is an acceptable investment, given the return the investor requires from the investment. Remer and Nieto (1995) claim that maximizing or minimizing the NPV of a project, depending upon the situation, will provide the most efficiency, and as a result, the most profitability.

In order to calculate the NPV, the interest rate used for discounting the cash flows needs to be determined. The interest rate is often referred to as Minimum Attractive Rate of Return (MARR) and it represents the rate at which the investor can alternatively invest his money, i.e. the return of the most preferable alternative investment. The planning horizon of the project also needs to be determined, and the cash flows for each period of the planning horizon projected (Park, 2002).

Formula is:

$$NPV(i) = \frac{A_0}{(1+i)^0} + \frac{A_1}{(1+i)^1} + \dots\dots\dots \frac{A_n}{(1+i)^n}$$

where

A_n = Net cash flow at the end of period n;

i = MARR;

N = Service life of the project

If the NPV(i) is positive for a single project, the project should be accepted, since a positive NPV means that the project has greater equivalent value of inflows than outflows and therefore makes a profit (Park, 2002).

According to Park, 2002 the decision rule for NPV is:-

If NPV (i) > 0, accept the investment;

If NPV (i) = 0, remain indifferent to the investment;

If NPV (i) < 0, reject the investment

(b) Annual Equivalent Worth: The Annual Equivalent Worth (AE) method is a variation of the NPV method. Instead of discounting all cash flows to present value, the AE method converts all cash flows to a series of equal cash flows over a specified time (Remer and Nieto, 1995). Usually the AE determines equal payments on an annual basis, and by that provides a basis for measuring investment worth.

The AE method has several advantages. When comparing mutually exclusive projects, the AE method does not require the projects to have the same service life, i.e., the projects do not have to be compared over equal time period as with the NPV method. The method also delivers simple and easily understood results, as it can be easier for some people to understand the prospects of a project by examining yearly costs/benefits per dollar, instead of examining one cash flow resolved to the present date (Remer and Nieto, 1995). In some situations the AE analysis is even preferred over the NPV analysis, such as when unit cost/profit is needed, when project lives are unequal or when consistency is needed in report formats (Park, 2002). When comparing mutually exclusive projects the same applies for the AE analysis as for the NPV analysis, i.e., the project with the greatest positive AE is selected (Sullivan *et al.*, 2006)

(c) Benefit-Cost Ratio: The benefit-cost method is often used for public projects. The method compares project benefits to the cost of the project, and for the project to be viable, the benefits have to be greater than the cost. By definition, project benefits are the favorable consequences of the project to the public, and project cost is the monetary disbursement required of the government (Sullivan *et al.*, 2006). Park (2002) describes benefit-cost analysis as "a decision-making tool used to systematically develop useful information about the desirable and undesirable effects of public projects". He defines three types of benefit-cost analysis problems:

1. Maximizing the benefits for any given set of cost;
2. Maximizing the net benefits when both benefits and costs vary;
3. Minimizing cost to achieve any given level of benefits.

The worthiness of a public project can be expressed by comparing the benefits (B) of the project to the cost (C) of the project by taking the ratio B/C, *i.e.*, the Benefit-Cost ratio.

(d) Internal Rate of Return: Internal Rate of Return (IRR) is a concept based on the return on invested capital in terms of a project investment, or as Park (2002) defines it: "IRR is the interest rate charged on the unrecovered project balance of the investment such that, when the project terminates, the unrecovered project balance will be zero" (p. 400). In other words, the investment has zero NPV at this rate of return, noted as i*. Therefore, i* serves as a benchmark interest rate, making investors able to accept or reject decision consistent with the NPV analysis. For simple investments, i.e. investments with only one sign change in cash flows, the IRR is the same as the i*(Park, 2002).

(e) Modified Internal Rate of Return: Over the past years there has been some criticism on the lack of robustness in the NPV and IRR methods, as these two measures can rank projects differently and assume reinvestment is always possible atthe discount rate or IRR. The Modified Internal Rate of Return (MIRR), also referred to as External Rate of Return, is a measure that avoids these problems and provides a different and more accurate measure of financial feasibility (Kierulff, 2008). The MIRR method is almost identical to the IRR method, except that the MIRR does not assume that all cash flows are reinvested at the calculated IRR, but instead assumes that all cash flows are reinvested at another rate, i.e. an external rate of return (Remer and Nieto, 1995). The MIRR has not gained the same attention as NPV and IRR, and it is not commonly used for financial feasibility analysis within the industry. This might partly be explained by lack of academic support, but also some find it difficult to understand and compute. The MIRR may be challenging in practice because the user is required to specify both a return on investment that takes account of the risk of the investment, and a reinvestment rate given the risk associated with the future investments of the cash flows (Kierulff, 2008)

Fabozzi and Peterson (2003, p. 433) have listed the following steps involved in MIRR calculations:

1. Calculate the present value of all cash outflows, using a reinvestment rate as the discount rate;
2. Calculate the future value of all cash inflows reinvested at some rate;
3. Solve for rate – the MIRR – that causes future value of cash inflows to equal present value of outflows.

They also define the decision rule for MIRR as:-

If MIRR > Cost of capital, accept the project;

If MIRR= Cost of capital, remain indifferent;

If MIRR < Cost of capital, reject the proposal.

(f) Financial Ratios: Financial statements are records of actual financial activities of a business entity and are therefore not available for prospective projects. However, by forecasting the revenues and costs of the entity, financial statements can be projected and analyzed to gain a better understanding of the performance of the entity. A decision on whether or not to invest in a new, unproven investment project should nevertheless not be based solely on the outcome of this analysis.

One way to analyze financial statements is to use the numbers from the statements to calculate financial ratios. By analyzing a series of financial ratios a clear picture is achieved of the entity's financial condition and performance. Financial ratios can be used to compare two business entities within the same industry and also to compare an entity's present ratios with that same entity's past and expected ratios, which will indicate whether the entity's financial condition has improved or deteriorated (Lee *et al.*, 2009). Financial ratios can be divided into five categories; liquidity ratios, asset management ratios, profitability ratios, market trend ratios and debt management ratios (Park, 2002). Only ratios that are appropriate and of use for prospective investment projects will be studied in this thesis. Ratios from four categories will be studied; liquidity ratios, profitability ratios, market trend ratios, and debt management ratio.

15.6.2 Purpose of Financial Feasibility Analysis

For investors to engage in a new investment project, the project has to be financially viable. Invested capital must show the potential to generate an economic return to investors at least equal to that available from other similarly risky investments, i.e., the return on investment needs to be equal or higher. For example, an investor expects a manufacturing facility to generate sufficient cash flows from operation to pay for the construction of the facility and ongoing operating expenses and, additionally, have an attractive interest rate of return.

Estimates of the cost of operating and maintaining a manufacturing plant, as well as expected income generated, are therefore essential in determining the financial feasibility of the facility (Bennet, 2003). Financial feasibility analysis is an analytical tool used to evaluate the economical viability of an investment. It consists of evaluating the financial condition and operating performance of the investment and forecasting its future condition and performance. A financial decision is dependent on two specific factors, expected return and expected risk, and a financial feasibility analysis is a means for examining those two factors (Fabozzi and Peterson, 2003). Hofstrand and Holz-Clause, (2009b, p. 3) put forward a number of reasons to conduct a financial feasibility study:

- Gives focus to the project and outline alternatives;
- Narrows business alternatives;
- Identifies new opportunities through the investigative process;
- Identifies reasons not to proceed with the project;
- Enhances the probability of success by addressing and mitigating factors early on that could affect the project;
- Provides quality information for decision making;
- Provides documentation that the business venture was thoroughly investigated;
- Helps in securing funding from lending institutions and other monetary sources;
- Helps to attract equity investment

Feasibility studies should be conducted before proceeding with the development of a business idea, and that also applies for financial feasibility analysis.

Determining early that a business idea is not financially feasible can prevent loss of money and waste of valuable time. The results from the feasibility study should outline the various scenarios examined and the implications, strengths and weaknesses of each (Hofstrand and Holz-Clause, 2009b). Financial feasibility analysis is usually done during the project planning process and the results indicate how the project will perform under a specific set of assumptions regarding technology, market conditions and financial aspects. The study is the first time in a project development process that these assumptions are studied to see if together they create a technically and economically feasible concept. It also illustrates the sensitivity of the business to changes in these basic assumptions (Matson, 2000). Knowing which assumptions are sensitive to changes can help the analysts to decide which parts of the analysis might need to be examined in more detail in order to get the best estimate on the financial feasibility as possible. Helfert (2001, p. 10) has defined four key business areas where financial analysis can be necessary. These key areas are shown in a pyramid in Figure 1. The first level of the pyramid includes general decisions and planning of daily operations, and as the levels get higher the analyses become more advanced and extensive. Each area contains challenges and issues in the practice of analysis and decision-making that must be addressed. The area covered in this thesis is the Investment Analysis on the second level of the pyramid

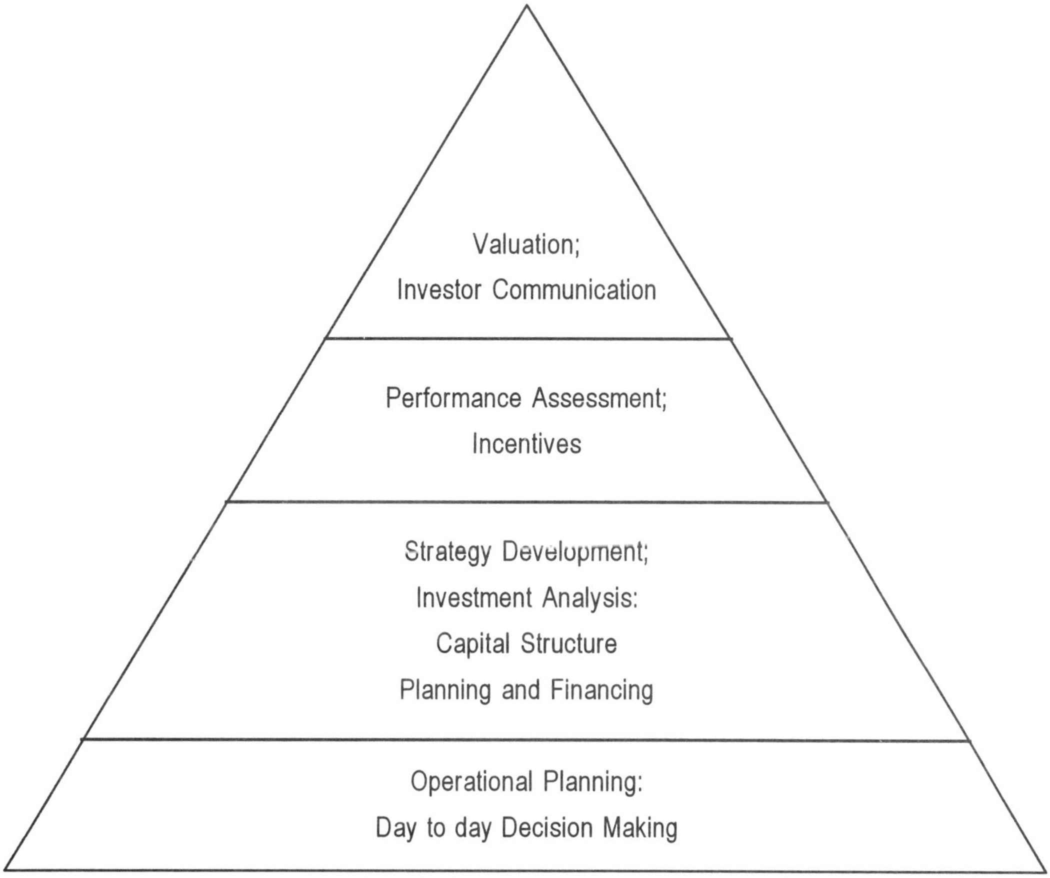

Figure 15.2. Areas where financial analysis can be necessary

15.7. MARKETING FEASIBILITY REPORT

A market feasibility study is an important exercise for all start-ups, small and medium sized enterprises to determine if a sustainable market exists for a product or service. It involves analyzing existing market demand, the competition and future market projections. This is one of the most important sections of the feasibility study as it examines the marketability of the product or services and convinces readers that there is a potential market for the product or services. If a significant market for the product or services cannot be established, then there is no project. Typically, market studies will assess the potential sales of the product, absorption and market capture rates and the project's timing .Once you have determined there is a market for the product or service you are planning to supply, you need to conduct some more research which should include the following:

(a) Stakeholder In-depth Interviews (IDIs) – It is found through past studies, beginning the market research by talking with key stakeholders is a perfect starting point. It helps all groups buy into ownership of the process and support the market research. It also helps the market research team familiarize itself with the project and its goals in a qualitative and open-discussion format. This is a mutually beneficial first step for both parties. These stakeholders can range from key personnel in the organization, outside the organization, those involved in the local economy or any other stakeholders who may offer credible feedback and play a role in your business' plans.

(b) Demographic Assessment and Trend Analysis – This involves secondary research and analyzing the market. This also creates your pool or population that will be used for your demand modeling and estimates. Information is collected for the market with regards to population trends, age, consumer expenditures, education and any other relevant demographic statistics that would impact the feasibility of the project. It also uses secondary research to find existing industry trends and ancillary data that is worth noting. This can easily be collected through the Internet with our team of professional Googlers.

(c) Quantitative Survey – This is the portion of the market research project where primary data is collected among end-users. The questions are focused on current usage and predicted usage and understanding the impact the new business idea will have on the market. This is the most integral part of the market research feasibility study and many of the questions asked in the survey will serve as the foundation for the demand model and estimates.

(d) Competitive Assessment – The competitive assessment takes a look at like-competitors in the market area that will impact your new business. It creates an expansive profile of each competitor and uses mystery shopping calls and visits to collect the non-publically available information, which isn't available on the website. By analyzing competitors, it also helps our clients understand service or product gaps in which they can market themselves in.

(e) Demand Model/Estimates with Recommendations – The final step to a quality market research feasibility study is putting together the first four components and using the findings from each to create a demand model. The demand model will estimate/predict the likelihood and habits of end-users for the new business you are testing. The demand estimates use predictive modeling to offer a rough figure based on the combination of known factors and assumptions. Here you determine the type of demand that exists for your product or service (e.g.: consumer, distributor), and establish the size of the market and its growth capacity. The executive summary also serves as a nice and short snapshot of findings, which works well for upper management if they do not have the time to read through a 100-plus page report. Finally, any good market research firm will be objective in their analysis and provide its client with a "go" or "no go" recommendation.

15.7.1 Market Feasibility Study Template[3]

(MARKET FEASIBILITY STUDY-by SMART prosperity now program)

This template is intended to serve as a guide in preparing the Study Outline and the Proposal. These will be the key elements that the SMART Reviewers will be examining to determine whether or not to approve the Assessment Funding Request.

Applicant Name: Phone:

Company: Email:

Address:

I. **Company Information**
1. Company summary.
2. Product summary.
3. Describe product benefits and differentiation.
4. Describe your current target market.
5. Cost of Study.
6. Time frame for study completion.

II. **International Market Structure**
1. Who are, and who will be, the major competitors for your product?
2. How strong is the current and potential competition?
3. Who are the customers of these competitors? What industries do they serve? Where are the market gaps for product to exploit?
4. What products are offered by the competition? How do competitive products compare with your product on quality, price, packaging and features? How do the services of the competitors compare with those potentially offered by your product?
5. How can you best position your product in the market relative to your competition?
6. What percentage of the total market does each of your competitors hold?
7. What are the major sales drivers in each potential target market industry? (e.g. automotive, aerospace, medical instrument, machinery)
8. What level of sales growth is anticipated in each target market industry over the next three years?

III. SWOT Analysis (Include both and in-depth Internal and External analysis)
1. Internal Analysis–Indicate the strengths of your company that places it at an advantage over the competition. (i.e. patents, financial resources, reputation, etc.)
2. External Analysis–Provide a review of the weaknesses of your company impacting its ability compete. (i.e. economic environment, regulatory affairs, new competitors, etc.)
3. OpportunitiesIdentify your company's largest opportunities as it relates to the export market.
4. Threat–sIdentify your company's threats as it relates to the export market.

IV. Describe potential barriers to enter export market.

V. What are your sales drivers?

VI. Describe your product strategy for the International Market.
1. List your distribution channels.
2. What is your pricing policy?
3. Describe your marketing and promotion strategy for entering the export markets.
4. What are your projected sales and volumes for the first year entering a new market?
5. What is your projected market share and profitability?
6. RisksIdentify your company's largest risks as it relates to the export market.

VII. Recommendation
What is the Consultant's recommendation for pursuing the export market?

15.8. OTHER FEASIBILITY FACTORS

(a) Resource feasibility: This involves questions such as how much time is available to build the new system, when it can be built, whether it interferes with normal business operations, type and amount of resources required, dependencies,

(b) Cultural feasibility: In this stage, the project's alternatives are evaluated for their impact on the local and general culture. For example, environmental factors need to be considered and these factors are to be well known. Further an enterprise's own culture can clash with the results of the project.

15.9. SUMMARY

A feasibility study is designed to discover if a business or project is "feasible" or if it is not.feasibility study is a relatively inexpensive way to safeguard any wastage of further investment.If a project is seen to be feasible from the results of the study, the next logical step is to commission a full business plan. Be sure you know what you want and what to expect when pursuing a new venture, business or project. A lot of time, resources and money can be saved in knowing what to do and the order in which to do it. A good rule of thumb is to never commission a business plan until a feasibility study has been completed first.

15.10. SELF ASSESSMENT QUESTIONS

1. What do you mean by feasibility check?
2. What is the importance and objective of feasibility check?
3. What do you mean by technical and system feasibility and what is its importance?
4. What are the various elements of technical feasibility report? Explain it with the help of one imaginary technical report.
5. What do you mean by network analysis? Differentiate between PERT and CPM.
6. What do you mean by financial Feasibility report? What is the purpose and criteria of financial feasibility analysis?
7. What do you mean by market feasibility report? Explain its importance and elements .

SOURCE/NOTES

1. http://hafeezrm.hubpages.com/hub/Technical-Appraisal-of-an-industrial-project
2. http://www.axiomblair.com/awbprojs/dlid/bnsproj/DLID_FINAL_Financial_Report_28AUG03.pdf
3. Prosperity now program-SMART PROGRAMME-Administered by Canadian manufacturer and exporters.

16

PROJECT FORMULATION AND PROJECT REPORT

16.1. INTRODUCTION

Project formulation is the systematic development of a project idea for the eventual objective of arriving at an investment decision. It has the built-in mechanism of ringing the danger bell at the earliest possible stage of resource utilization. Project formulation involves a step-by-step investigation and development of project idea. And it provides a controlled mechanism for restricting expenditure on project development and when project formulation is done. It is just like feasibility check of different aspects /elements of the project.

Project formulation helps in the comparative analysis from the point of view resource allocation. Project formulation evaluates the sum total effect which the project will have on society and immediate environment.

16.2. MEANING

Project formulation is a concise, exact statement of a project to set the boundaries or limits of work to be performed by the project. It is defined as taking a first look carefully and critically on a project ideas by an entrepreneur to build up an all-round beneficial to project after carefully weighting its various components. It is a formal document that gives a distinctive identity of the project and precise meaning of project work to prevent conflict, confusion, or overlap. It is a process where the entrepreneur makes an objective and independent assessment of various aspects of project idea. In this the idea is analysed from point of view of inputs and outputs. It is a process involving the joint efforts of a team of experts, i.e., specialists. Each member of the team should be familiar with the broad strategy, objectives and other ingredients of the project.

It is assessment of the feasibility of a proposal or a scheme based on the examination of factors like the capacity of the unit to produce, assets and liabilities, the repaying capacity, etc. A well-formulated feasibility report provides a medium, which cuts across scientific, social and positional prejudices and provides a common meeting ground for all those who have a contribution to make in successful implementation of a project. Project team should consist of experts in major substantive fields of the project. Depending on the situation any large project should comprise the various team members like: One industrial economist, One market analysist, One mechanical and/or industrial engineer, One management accounting expert and one or more technologist/engineer specializing in the appropriate industry.

16.3. SIGNIFICANCE OF PROJECT FORMULATION

A well-formulated project is the best passport for obtaining the required assistance from financial institutions. When there is a situation of resource constraint and the available resources are allocated to various projects based on their importance and viability a well-formulated project formulation is the best way of selling a project idea to a financing agency. Project formulation will also be of great assistance for obtaining necessary government clearances. It will pinpoint the matters for which Government sanctions have to be obtained and also provide an independent assessment of the feasibility of obtaining these sanctions based on the existing Government policies. The project report submitted by the entrepreneur will establish his bonafides in the eyes of the bureaucracy and obtain the due Government sanction without much difficulty.

Project formulation can be also defined as one of the stages in the lifecycle of a project. The formulation stage is also called Initiation, Conceptualization, Definition, Pre-Project. This stage aims to:

- Carefully identify and weight various components of project work
- Analyze project feasibility and cost-effectiveness
- Examine and approve project inputs and outputs
- Identify stakeholders and their involvement and contribution
- Define benefits and expectations
- Estimate resources needed
- Perform a preliminary analysis of risks
- Make an outline of project schedule

16.4. COMMON ERRORS IN PROJECT FORMULATION

Project formulation is as important is not so easy. However, the entrepreneurs often make errors while formulating project reports and business plans. Here, we are highlighting the errors widely noticed in project formulation:

1. Product Selection – It is noticed that some entrepreneurs commit mistakes by selecting a wrong product for their enterprises. They select the product without giving due attention to product related other aspects such as size of the product markets, its future demand, competitive position, lifecycle, availability of required labor, raw material and technology. Hence, when you are selecting a product, take a comprehensive view.

2. Capacity Utilization Estimates – The entrepreneurs usually makeover-optimistic estimates of capacity utilization. Their estimates are based on a completely false premise. The estimates are made in complete disregard of present-enterprise performance, prevailing market conditions, competitive atmosphere, the technical snags, etc. A business plan formulated as such falls prey to financial jugglery. Hence, avoid such temptations while estimating capacity utilization for your enterprise.

3. Market Study – Product production is ultimately meant for eventual sale. Hence, market study of the product assumes importance. Market study continues to be a grey area. But, there are some entrepreneurs who pass by this component of their business plan completely. Based on their nebulous ideas and scanty and scattered information on demand and supply of their proposed product, they conclude that market is just there waiting to be tapped. This is a wrong attitudinal block. Avoid it.

4. Technology Selection – The requirement for technology differs from product to product depending upon the nature of products. Swayed by profit margins, the entrepreneurs sometimes plan for a technology not possible to set up within limited financial resources. Thus, in the absence of technological feasibility, enterprise is foredoomed to failure. Hence, make sure your technological feasibility.

5. Location Selection – The entrepreneur often makes two types of errors while selecting location for their enterprises.

First, they are completely swayed by the Government offer of financial incentives and concessions to establish industries in a particular location. This becomes their sole and overriding concern completely disregarding other factors like market proximity, availability of raw materials, manpower and infrastructural facilities.

Second, the entrepreneurs select a location for their enterprises merely because it is their hometown or they own ancestral land there, which is, however, not an appropriate location. Make sure you do not fall prey to such temptations.

6. Selection of Ownership Form – Many enterprises fail merely because the ownership form of enterprises is not suitable. Hence, select a suitable form of ownership taking a comprehensive view of the factors affecting the selection of a form of ownership

16.5. MEANING OF PROJECT REPORT

In simple words, project report or business plan is a written statement of what an entrepreneur proposes to take up. Normally project report is prepared before an investment is undertaken. The project report assesses the demand of the proposed product to be produced, works out the cost of investment and thus estimates the expected profitability of the proposed investment. It is a kind of guide frost or course of action what the entrepreneur hopes to achieve in his business and how is he going to achieve it. In other words, project report serves like a kind of big road map to reach the destination determined by the entrepreneur. Thus, a project report can best be defined as a well-evolved course of action devised to achieve the specified objective within a specified period of time. So to say, it is an operating document which contains relevant data in respect of a project serves as a guide to management and records merits and demerits in allocating resources to production of specific goods or services.

16.6. SIGNIFICANCE OF PROJECT REPORT

The preparation of a project report is of great significance for an entrepreneur. The project report serves the two essential functions:

(1) First and most important, the project report is like a road map. It describes the direction the enterprise is going in, what its goals are, where it wants to be, and how it is going to get there. It also enables an entrepreneur to know that he is proceeding in the right direction.

(2) The second function of the project report is to attract lenders and investors. Although, it is not mandatory for the small enterprises to prepare project reports, yet it is useful and beneficial for them to prepare the project reports for various reasons. The preparation of project report is beneficial for those small enterprises, which apply for financial assistance from the financial institutions and the commercial banks. It is on the basis of project report that the financial institutions make appraisal if the enterprise requires financial assistance or not If yes, how much.

Similarly, other organizations which provide various assistance such as raw material, seed/ margin money, etc., are equally interested in knowing the economic soundness of the proposal. In most cases, the quality of the firm's project report weighs heavily in the decision to lend or invest funds.

16.7. CONTENTS OF A PROJECT REPORT

Having gone through the significance of project report, it is now clear that there is no substitute for a well-prepared business plan or project report and also there are no short-cuts to preparing it. The more concrete and complete the business plan, the more likely to earn their support in making and running an enterprise. Therefore, the project report needs to be prepared with great care and consideration. A good project report should contain the following contents:

1. General Information: Information on product profile and product details.
2. Promoter:His/her educational qualification, work experience, project related experience.
3. Location: Exact location of the project, lease or freehold, locational advantages.
4. Land and Building: Land area, construction area, type of construction, cost of construction, detailed plan and estimate along with plant layout
5. Plant and Machinery: Details of machinery required, capacity, suppliers, cost, various alternatives available, cost of miscellaneous assets.
6. Production Process: Description of production process, process chart, technical know how, technology alternatives available, production programme.

7. Utilities: Water, power, steam, compressed air requirements, cost estimates, sources of utilities.
8. Transport and Communication: Mode, possibility of getting, costs.
9. Raw Material: List of raw material required by quality and quantity, sources of procurement, cost of raw material, tie-up arrangements, if any, for procurement of raw material, alternative raw material, if any.
10. Manpower: Manpower requirement by skilled and semi-skilled, sources of manpower supply cost of procurement, requirement for training and its cost.
11. Products: Product mix, estimated sales, distribution channels, competitions and their capacities, product standard, input-output ratio, product substitude
12. Market: End-users of product, distribution of market as local, national, international, trade practices, sales promotion devices, proposed market research.
13. Requirement of Working Capital: Working capital required, sources of working capital need for collateral security, nature and extent of credit facilities offered and available.
14. Requirement of Funds: Break-up of project cost in terms of costs of land, building, machinery, miscellaneous assets, preliminary expenses, contingencies and margin money for working capital arrangements for Meeting the cost of setting up of a project.
15. Cost of Production and Profitability of first ten years.
16. Break-Even Analysis
17. Schedule of Implementation

16.8. DIFFERENCE BETWEEN DETAIL PROJECT REPORT AND FEASIBILITY REPORT

The difference between pre-investment report and preparation of the detailed project report should be clearly understood. Feasibility analysis is an investigating process, which precedes investment decisions. Its purpose is to present relevant facts before the decision makes to enable them to accept or reject the project. Therefore, the project idea is examined from the viewpoint of overall objectives, financial viability, technical feasibility and social impact. On the other hand, detailed project report preparation is a post-investment decision. It involves the preparation of detailed specifications and design, engineering drawings, site investigation, foundations design and process design as well as time schedules for project implementation. Detailed project report (DPR) serves as the work plan for the implementation of a project whereas feasibility report and pre-investment report (PIR) is the basis on which the investment decision is taken. Thus, project formulation always precedes detailed project report.

16.9. FORMULATION OF A PROJECT REPORT

Normally, small-scale enterprises do not include sophisticated technique, which is used for preparing project reports of large-scale enterprises. What and how much information will be given in the project report depends upon the size of the unit as well as nature of the production. A general set of information given in any project report is listed below. Project formulation divides the process of project development into eight distinct and sequential stages. These stages are:

1. General Information, 2. Project Description, 3. Market Potential, 4. Capital Costs and Sources of Finance, 5. Assessment of Working Capital Requirements, 6. Other Financial Aspects, 7. Economic and Social Variables, 8. Project Implementation. The nature of information to be collected under each one of these stages has been given below:

1. General Information

The information of general nature given in the project report include the following:

Bio-data of Promoter;

Name and address of entrepreneur;

the qualifications, experience and other capabilities of the entrepreneur;

if these are partners, state these characteristics of all the partners individually.

2. Industry Profile

A reference of analysis of industry to which the project belongs, e.g., past performance; present status, its organization, its problems etc.

3. Constitution and Organization

The constitution and organizational structure of the enterprise; in case of partnership firm, its registration with the Registrar of Firms; application for getting Registration Certificate from the Directorate of Industries/District Industry Centre.

4. Product Details

Product utility, product range; product design; advantages to be offered by the product over its substitutes, if any.

5. Project Description

A brief description of the project covering the following aspects is given in the project report.

6. Location

Location of enterprise; owned or leasehold land; industrial area; No Objection Certificate from the Municipal Authorities if the enterprise location falls in the residential area.

7. Physical Infrastructure

Availability of the, following items of infra structure should be mentioned in the project report

(i) Raw Material : Requirement of raw material, whether inland or imported, sources of raw material supply.

(ii) Skilled Labor : Availability of skilled labor in the area,arrangements for training laborers in various skills.

(iii) Utilities: These include:

(a) *Power* : Requirement for power, load sanctioned, availability of power.

(b) *Fuel*: Requirement for fuel items such as coal, coke, oil or gas, state of their availability.

(c) *Water* : The sources and quality of water should be clearly stated in the project report.

(iv) Pollution Control: The aspects like scope of dumps; sewage system and sewage treatment plant should be clearly stated in case of industries producing emissions.

(v) Communication System: Availability of communication facilities, e.g.,telephone, telex, etc. should be stated in the project report.

(vi) Transport Facilities: Requirements for transport, mode of transport, potential means of transport, distances to be covered, bottlenecks etc., should be stated in the business plan.

(vii) Other Common Facilities: Availability of common facilities like machine shops, welding shops and electrical repair shops etc. should be stated in the report.

(viii) Production Process: A mention should be made for process involved in production and period of conversion from raw material into finished goods.

(ix) Machinery and Equipment: A complete list of items of machinery and equipments required indicating their size, type, cost and sources of their supply should be enclosed with the project report.

(x) Capacity of the Plant: The installed licensed capacity of the plant along with the shifts should also be mentioned in the project report.

(xi) Technology Selected: The selection of technology, arrangements made for acquiring it should be mentioned in the business plan.

(xii) Research and Development: A mention should be made in the project report regarding proposed research and development activities to be undertaken in future.

(xiii) Market Potential: While preparing a project report, the following aspects relating to market potential of the product should be stated in the report:

(a) *Demand and Supply Position*: State the total expected demand for the product and present supply position. This should also be mentioned how much of the gap will be filled up by the proposed unit.

(b) *Expected Price*: An expected price of the product to be realized should be mentioned in the project report.

(c) *Marketing Strategy*: Arrangements made for selling the product should be clearly stated in the project report.

(d) *After Sales Service*: Depending upon the nature of the product, provisions made for after-sales service should normally be stated in the project report

(e) *Transportation*: Requirement for transportation means indicating whether public transport or entrepreneur's own transport should be mentioned in the project report.

8. Capital Costs and Sources of Finance

An estimate of the various components of capital items like land and buildings, plant and machinery, installation costs, preliminary expenses, margin for working capital should be given in the project report. The present probable sources of finance should also be stated in the project report. The sources should indicate the owner's funds together with funds raised from financial institutions and banks.

(i) Assessment of Working Capital Requirements: The requirement for working capital and its sources of supply should be carefully and clearly mentioned in the project report. It is always better to prepare working capital requirements in the prescribed formats designed by limits of requirement. It will minimize objections from the banker's side.

(ii) Other Financial Aspects: In order to adjudge the profitability of the project to be set up, a projected Profit and Loss Account indicating likely sales revenue, cost of production, allied cost and profit should be prepared. A projected Balance Sheet and Cash Flow Statement should also be prepared to indicate the financial position and requirements at various stages of the project

In addition to above, the Break-Even Analysis should also be presented inthe project report. Break-even point is the level of production/sales wherethe industrial enterprise shall earn neither profit nor incur loss. In fact, it will just break even. Break-even level indicates the gestation period and thelikely moratorium required for repayment of loans. BEP is calculated as follows:

$$BEP = F/(S-V) \times 100$$

Where, F = Fixed cost

S = Sales Projected

V = Variable costs.

9. Economic and Social Variables

In view of the social responsibility of business, the abatement costs, i.e.,the costs for controlling the environmental damage should be stated In the project. Arrangement made for treating the effluents and emissions should also be mentioned in the report. Besides, the socio-economic benefits expected to accrue from the project should also be stated in the report itself. Following are the examples of socio-economic benefits.

(i) Employment Generation.

(ii) Import Substitution.

(iii) Ancillarisation.

(iv) Exports.

(v) Local Resource Utilization.

(vi) Development of the Area.

16.10. PLANNING COMMISSION'S GUIDELINES FOR FORMULATING A PROJECT REPORT

In order to process investment proposals and arrive at investment decisions, the Planning Commission of India has also issued some guidelines for preparing/ formulating realistic industrial projects. So far as feasibility report is concerned, it lies in between the project formulating stage and the appraisal and sanction stage. The project formulation stage involves the identification of investment options by the enterprise and in consultation with the Administrative Ministry, the Planning Commission and other concerned authorities.

Realizing the usefulness of these guidelines, we are now presenting these guidelines in a summarized manner.

1.General Information

The feasibility report should include an analysis of the industry to which the project belongs. It should deal with the past performance of the industry. The description of the type of industry should also be given, i.e., the priority of the industry, increase in Production, role of the public sector, allocation of investment of funds, choice of technique, etc. This should also contain information about the enterprise submitting the feasibility report.

2. Preliminary Analysis of Alternatives

This should contain present data on the gap between demand and supply for the outputs which are to be produced, data on the capacity that would be available from the projects that are in production or under implementation at the time the report is prepared, a complete list of all existing plants in the industry, giving their capacity and level of production actually attained, a list of all projects for which letters of intents/licenses have been issued and a list of proposed projects. All options that are technically feasible should be considered at this preliminary stage. The location of the project as well as its implications should also be looked into. An account of the foreign exchange requirement should also be taken. The profitability of different options should also be given. The rate of return on investment should be calculated and presented in the report. Alternative cost calculations *vis-à-vis* return should be presented.

3. Project Description

The feasibility should provide a brief description of the technology and process chosen for the project. Information relevant to determining optimality of the locations chosen should also be included. To assist in the assessment of the environmental effects of a project, every feasibility report must present the information on specific points, i.e., population, water, air, land, flora and fauna, effects arising out of project's pollution, other environmental discretions etc. The report should contain a list of the operational requirements of the plant, requirements of water and power, requirements of personnel, organizational structure envisaged, transport costs, activity wise phasing of construction and factors affecting it.

4. Marketing Plan

It should contain the following items:

- Data on the marketing plan.
- Demand and prospective supply in each of the areas to be served.
- The method and data used for main estimates of domestic supply and selection of the market areas should be presented.
- Estimates of the degree of price sensitivity should be presented.
- It should contain an analysis of past trends in prices

5. Capital Requirements and Costs

The estimates should be reasonably complete and properly estimated. Information on all items of costs should be carefully collected and presented.

6. Operating Requirements and Costs

Operating costs are essentially those costs, which are incurred after the commencement of commercial production. Information about all items of operating cost should be collected; operating costs relate to the cost of raw materials and intermediates, fuel, utilities, labor, repair and maintenance, selling expenses and other expenses.

7. Financial Analysis

The purpose of this analysis is to present some measures to assess the financial viability of the project. A pro forma Balance Sheet for the project data should be presented. Depreciation should be allowed for on the basis of specified by the Bureau of Public Enterprises. Foreign exchange requirements should be cleared by the Department of Economic Affairs. The feasibility report should take into account income tax rebates for priority industries, incentives for backward areas, accelerated depreciation, etc. The sensitivity analysis should also be presented. The report must analyze the sensitivity of the rate of return of change in the level' and pattern of product prices.

8. Economic Analysis

Social profitability analysis needs some adjustment in the data relating to the costs and returns to the enterprise. One important type of investment involves a correction in input and costs, to reflect the true value of foreign exchange, labor and capital. The enterprise should try to assess the impact of its operations' on foreign trade. Indirect costs and benefits should also be included in the report. If they cannot be quantified, they should be analyzed and their importance emphasized.

9. Miscellaneous Aspects

The preceding three areas are deemed appropriate to almost every new small enterprise. Notwithstanding, depending upon the size of the operation and peculiarities of a particular project, other items may be considered important to be applied out in the project report. To mention, probable use of minicomputers or other electronic data processing services, cash flow statements, method of accounting etc., may be of great use in some small enterprises

16.11. PROJECT FORMULATION VS. DETAILED PROJECT REPORT

The difference between project formulation and preparation of the detailed project report should be clearly understood. Project formulation is an investigating process, which precedes investment decisions. Its purpose is to present relevant facts before the decision makes to enable them to accept or reject the project. Therefore, the project idea is examined from the viewpoint of overall objectives, financial viability, technical feasibility and social impact. On the other hand, detailed project report preparation is a post-investment decision. It involves the preparation of detailed specifications and design, engineering drawings, site investigation, foundations design and process design as well as time schedules for project implementation. Detailed project report (DPR) serves as the work plan for the implementation of a project whereas project formulation and pre-investment report (PIR) is the basis on which the investment decision is taken. Thus, project formulation always precedes detailed project report.

16.12. SAMPLE PROJECT REPORT[1]

ALUVA PLASTIC CONSORTIUM PVT. LTD.

ERNAKULAM DISTRICT

KERALA

PROPOSAL FOR SETTING UP OF A COMMON FACILITY CENTRE UNDER SMALL INDUSTRIES CLUSTER DEVELOPMENT PROGRAMME SCHEME OF OFFICE OF DC (SSI)

UNDER THE TECHNICAL GUIDANCE OF NTTF TECHNICAL TRAINING CENTRE, NETTUR P.O, TELLICHERRY.

CONTENTS

CONTENTS

LIST OF ANNEXURES

EXECUTIVE SUMMARY

(a) Industrial Department of Kerala State Government has identified the plastic cluster at Ernakulam under cluster development programme and approved as SIDO cluster. There are 108 tiny and small scale plastic industrial units functioning in Ernakulam district under SSI sector. In this Cluster Development Programme presently 11 small scale plastic based industries in Ernakulam District have formed a consortium under the name and style of M/S. ALUVA PLASTIC CONSORTIUM PVT. LTD. The remaining plastic industrial units will become a member of this consortium immediately. The Diagnostic Study conducted on this Cluster will found some major issues and recommend certain solutions. The immediate requirements of this cluster is a common facility centre for mould making, mould repairing, machinery repairing, machinery spare parts manufacturing, injection moulding etc. which will benefit the units by way of improving the quality of the products, product differentiation, production cost reduction etc. Thus this CFC will improve the performance of this plastic cluster in total.

(b) As per the direction of small industries service institute, Ayyanthole P.O., Thrissur, Kerala the consortium approached NTTF technical training centre, Tellicherry which is the competent organisation in die and mould engineering. This report is prepared under the technical guidance of NTTF.

(c) The total project cost is estimated to be ₹ 460 lakhs of which 70% of fixed capital ₹ 315 lakhs can be obtained as grant from Government of India under 'Small Industries Cluster Development Programme' scheme, ₹ 92 lakhs from govt of Kerala and balance ₹ 53 lakhs is to be shared by the beneficiaries and stakeholders. The projected performance of this common facility centre for the first eight years of operation is appended. The unit will generate profit from the first year of operation. The project is technically feasible and overall economics of the project is very attractive.

(d) The active support for the project from the industrial department of Kerala in the form of implementing agency will benefit the plastic based industries at Ernakulam District and especially those in consortium.

(e) The consortium will provide the necessary land and building for setting up this common facility centre as their contribution and execute necessary agreements and undertakings with the implementing agency-Industrial Department of Kerala.

(f) The day to day operating expense of the common facility centre in terms of electricity charges, labour charges, etc., will be borne by the consortium and the required periodic maintenance, modernisation, etc., will be met by the corpus fund raised from the profit of the common facility centre.

(g) The consortium will appoint necessary technical experts and skilled labours for running the common facility centre.

SECTION-I : INTRODUCTION

Background

Industry Status

There are 108 tiny and small-scale plastic industrial units functioning in Ernakulam district under SSI sector. The capital investment of these industries vary from 5 to 350 lakhs. Total turnover per annum is about ₹ 380 Crores. Plastic industry in Ernakulam District is creating employment opportunities directly to 1500 persons and indirectly to 700 persons. The power requirement per each unit is around 30 to 150 HP.

Presently around eleven small scale plastic based industries have formed a consortium under the name and style of 'Aluva Plastic Consortium Pvt. Ltd.' The remaining units will become the members of this consortium immediately.

Major Issues and Immediate Solution

Dies are moulds are fabricated to give desired shape to molten mass. Most of the units in this cluster are using moulds for making products. Moulds are necessary for making new products. Production mould are usually made from steel for the usual high pressure moulding that requires heating or cooling channels, strength to resist the forming forces, and wear resistance to withstand the wear of plastics, particularly that which has glass or other abrasive fillers. Now these units are making moulds out side Kerala. Besides the mould makers are duplicating these moulds and there-by, their interests are not protected. More than that the lead-time required for mould making is very high and time required for mould repair is also very high. For encountering these difficulties it is better to start a common centre for making and repairing moulds.

Presently there is no facility for repairing machinery and supporting equipments in this cluster. The units have to spend huge amount and time for repairing machineries. Most of the spare parts are brought from North India at higher cost because of middle men. The lead time required for getting spare parts such as screw barrel, nozzles, die clamp, cylinders, gear boxes, etc., are very high. There by the machineries have to be shut down for more days and production of the unit is suffered. By providing a common facility centre the cost and time required for maintenance of machineries can be reduced drastically.

Most of the member industries in the consortium group are small and tiny. They are not in a position to install latest micro processor control injection moulding machine suitable for meeting big orders. By installing a micro processor controlled injection moulding machine these units can meet big orders.

In this context the consortium decided to establish a centralised common facility centre to over come above problems.

Benefits for members

The consortium members can utilise this common facility centre for making moulds and there by they can produce fresh items in their units and this will help to increase their market potential. This will also help to compete with manufacturers of other states such as Maharashtra, Gujarat, Delhi etc.

The injection moulding machine installed in the common facility centre can be utilized by the members in order to cater bulk orders. This common facility centre render the services on the basis of engineering hours.

This common facility centre will ultimately help the plastic industries in Ernakulam District to increase it s productivity, improve quality, improve capacity utilisation, improve marketing etc. In other words these small-scale industries can produce bulk quality products at competitive rate.

Modus of operant

The common facility centre provide mold making, mould repair, machinery maintenance, and injection moulding services to members on hourly basis. It charge a nominal amount for meeting operational expenses and making corpus fund for future modernisation, up gradation and sustenance of the plant. If there is any additional spare time available in the centre can be offered to other industrial clusters such as rubber cluster, plywood cluster, rice cluster etc. Thus maximum capacity utilisation can be achieved.

The raw material required for making moulds, repairing moulds, repairing machineries etc. will be provided by the individual units. So there is no need of heavy working capital for maintaining inventory.

The technical experts in the common facility centre will give the technical specification of the material is to be purchased for making moulds and repairing machineries. They also give the details of quality raw material suppliers.

The micro processor controlled injection moulding machine installed in the CFC will help the member units for meeting orders (Export orders) which requires high quality and good appearance.

SECTION-II : TECHNICAL ASPECTS

The word "tooling" refers to hard ware necessary to produce a particular product. A considerable amount of tooling is the result of work performed by the tool designer. Tooling, as viewed by the tool designer, consist of a vast array of cutting devices, jigs, fixtures dies, gauges, etc., used in normal production. The type of production will determine to a large extent the type of tooling. The most common classification of types of tooling is as follows:

1. Cutting tools, such as drills, reamers, milling cutters, broachers, and taps.
2. Jigs and fixtures for guiding the tool and holding the work piece.
3. Gauges and measuring instruments.
4. Sheet-metal press working dies for all types of sheet-metal fabrication.
5. Dies for plastic moulding die casting, permanent moulding, and investment casting.
6. Forging dies for hot and cold forging, upsetting, extrusion, and cold finishing.

A competent mould designer must have a thorough knowledge of the principles of mould making as the design of the various parts of the mould depends on the technique adopted for this manufacture.

The majority of moulds are manufactured by the use of conventional machine tools found in most modern tool rooms. From the manufacturing viewpoint we classify the mould into two parts (i) the cavity and core, and (ii) the remainder of the mould. The later part is commonly referred to as bolster work.

The work on the cavity and core is by far the most important as it is from these members that the plastics moulding takes its form.

The moulding parts for the simple form are produced on such machine tools as the lathe and the milling machine, where as the more complex form requires the use of some kind of copying machine.

Machine Tools

The purpose of any machine tool is to remove metal. Each machine tool removes metal in a different way. Which machine tool is to be used for a particular job depends to a large extent upon the type of machining required.

The machine tools which will be found in the modern tool room are as follows:

(i) Lathes for turning, boring and screw cutting, etc.

(ii) Cylindrical grinding machines for the production of precision cylindrical surfaces.

(iii) Shaping and planning machines for the reduction of steel blocks and plates to the required thickness and for squiring up these plates.

(iv) Surface grinding machines for the production of precision flat surfaces.

(v) Milling machines for the rapid removal of metal, for machining slots, recesses, boring holes, machining splints, etc.

(vi) Tracer-controlled milling machines for the accurate reproduction of complex cavity and core forms.

In addition to the above list of major machine tools there is, of course,ancillary equipment without which no tool room would be complete. This includes power saws, drilling machines, tool post grinders, hardening and polishing facilities, etc.

Lathe

The primary purpose of the lathe is to machine cylindrical forms. Rotating the work with respect to a single-point cutting tool generates the contour. For machining the outside surface, the cutter is moved parallel to the axis of rotation. This operation is called turning. Alternatively, metal may be removed from the inside of the work in which case the operation is called boring. When the tool is moved across the face of the work it is called facing. The lathe is extremely versatile and is used for making a large variety of mould parts. For example, guide pillars, guide bushes, circular support blocks, ejector rods, ejector rod bushes, push back pins, etc, are all manufactured on the lathe. In addition to this bolster work the cavity and core are also produced on a lathe if the moulding form is cylindrical. Turning is a relatively fast machining operation and for this reason moulds for circular components are cheaper to produce than corresponding moulds for components of any other form.

Internal and external thread forms are also easily generated. In these cases it is necessary to make some allowance for the plastic material shrinkage on the mould thread pitch (i.e. the mould thread pitch must be machined slightly larger than required to allow for the material shrinkage on cooling).

Cylindrical Grinding Machine

This machine tool is use for precision grinding cylindrical mould parts. Metal is removed by the action of a rotating abrasive grinding wheel, which is brought into contact with a contra-rotating work piece. The axes of both the grinding wheel and the work piece are parallel for normal operation.

An important feature of the grinding machine is that it can cut hardened metal. This characteristic, together with the close tolerances and the high surface finish obtainable, makes this machine tool an essential piece of tool room equipment.

In normal grinding of cylindrical parts, the wheel slide is adjusted forward until the rotating grinding wheel just contact the contra rotating work piece. Further forward movement of the wheel slide sets the depth of cut. The table is then caused to reciprocate, thereby grinding the outside surface of the work piece over a preset distance. This operation is repeated and the depth of cut progressively increased until the required diameter on the work piece is obtained.

Shaping and Planing Machines

A mould normally includes a number of steel plates suitably secured together. Each of these plates must have parallel faces and, ideally, the four sides should be square. Now, as the primary purpose of a shaping machine is to produce flat surfaces, this machine tool is used in the initial preparation of mould blocks.

Surface Grinding machine

The surface-grinding machine performs a similar function for flat surfaces, and grinding normally follows the shaping or planning operation. An excellent surface finish combined with accuracy can be achieved on hard or soft steel with this machine tool.

Milling Machine

Milling is a metal is removed from a work piece by a rotating milling cutter. The work piece can be moved in three directions at right angles to each other, with respect to the cutter. The three directions are longitudinal, transverse and vertical respectively. There are two basic types of milling machine. In one the axis of the cutter is perpendicular to the surface of the work piece and this is called a horizontal milling machine. Both types are used extensively in the manufacture of various parts of the mould.

Spark Machine

This is one of the more recent additions to mould making methods and strictly speaking, it should come under the machine tool section. However, as the principle of operation is different from that of all other basic machine tools it is preferable to discuss this technique separately.

Spark machining is a process in which steel, or other metals, can be machined by the application of an electrical discharge spark. The spark is localized and metal is progressively removed in small quantities over a period of time.

Hardened steel can be machined by this technique so that intricately shaped hardened cavities (which might be impracticable by conventional machine-tool methods because of possible distortion during hardening) can be formed.

Spark machine finds many applications in the repairing and modifications of hardened cavities and core. For instance, a small pocket can be machined in to the mould plate and a suitable insert fitted, which saves the necessity of softening the mould plate with the possibility of distortion, etc.

The major limitation of the process is that several tools are required to produce one cavity. If the cavity form is complex, the cost of machining these tools may make the use of this technique uneconomic.

Bench Fitting

Irrespective of the tool or technique used to manufacture the various parts of mould, the final responsibility for the finishing of the individual parts and for fitting them together lies with the bench fitter. The mould finishing and assembly procedure adopted by the bench fitter varies from tool room to tool room and quite often between individual toolmakers working in the same tool room; it is there for impossible to set down a standard pattern for the work. The various stages in the bench fitting involved manufacture of a simple mould.

Stage 1: Finishing the Impression

When the mould plates are received from the machine tool section, the impression form (on both plates) is in the rough machined state. Cutter marks, burrs, etc., are varying apparent on the surface. The bench fitters first job is to produce a cavity and core free of machine marks and to the shape and dimensions specified on the mould detail drawing.

Basic hand tools, such as files, scrapers and chisels, are used for this operation, various sizes, grades and shapes being used as and when applicable. In addition, where ever possible, power driven flexible shaft equipment is used to speed up this operation. This equipment incorporates various heads, which accommodate special needle files or scrapers. The heads can have a rotary or a reciprocating motion.

Once the cavity (or core) is free of machine marks the next stage is to remove the marks left by the final and the scraper. This is achieved by one or more of several techniques depending on the shape of the cavity.

Stage 2: Aligning Cavity and Core

Once the cavity and core have been semi-finished, the next operation is to align the two parts with respect to each other so that the moulding produced will have the correct wall section. This is achieved by using packing pieces between the cavity and core. The two mould plates are clamped together and returned to the milling or jig-boring machine to have guide holes bored through both plates. When this operation is complete, the clamps are removed, the mould plates separated and the guide pillars and guide bushes fitted. The two mould plates are again brought together and checked to ensure that the core is an alignment with the cavity. A dummy moulding is often made at this stage, using wax, so that the wall section of the product can be checked. Any slight inaccuracies need to be corrected, of course.

Stage 3: Bedding Down

The next stage is to bed down the two mould halves. This is the process of „marrying the two opposing mould halves together to prevent the plastic material escaping between the two surfaces when the material is injected into the impression. Basically the process of bedding-down is simple. One surface is given a very fine coating of toolmakers blue. The two plates are then momentarily brought together and where there are high spot on the second mould plate blue will be picked up. Scraping and filing remove these high spots. This procedure is repeated until an even film of blue is transferred from one plate to other.

Stage 4: Water Cooling Circuit

The holes drilled for the water circulation in the mould plate are tapped and plugs, baffles, or connectors fitted as appropriate. The circuit is checked to ensure that the flow is unidirectional and that no leakage occurs.

Stage 5: Fitting Ejector System

(a) The holes to accommodate the ejector pins and push back pins are markedout on the mould plate and subsequently bored and reamed.

(b) The retaining plate is normally clamped in position below the mould plate.The ejector holes, etc, are spotted through to this plate.

(c) The remaining plate is drilled and counter board to accommodate the ejector pins and push-back pins. The ejector plate and retaining plate are marked out, drilled, counter board, and tapped where appropriate to permit the two plates to be held rigidly together by socket-headed screws. Assembled the ejector plate assembly.

(d) The ejection half of mould consisting of the mould plate, support blocks and back plate are marked out according to the mould detail drawing, drilled, counter bored and tapped where specified. The entire moving half of the mould isassembled.

Stage 6: Fitting Square Bush and Register Ring

Turning to the fixed mould half, the square bush and the register ring are located and fitted. Clamping holes are marked out drilled and tapped.

Stage 7: Polishing, Hardening and Try-out

The mould is disassembled and the cavity and core form polished. All parts which require heat treatment are sent for hardening. When this operation is complete the mould is reassembled and the cavity and core form given a final polish. The mould is then sent for try-out on an injection machine to produce a sample moulding. This is checked and, if necessary adjustments are made. The mould is ready for production.

SECTION-III : LAND AND BUILDING

Land :

The common facility centre is proposed to set up in 75 Cents of land in survey number 177/1Pt Aluva East Village, Aluva Taluk, Ernakulam District. The cost of Land for common facility centre is ₹ 7.50 Lakhs including land developments.

Technical Civil Work :

The proposed factory and office building have a total plinth area of 900 Sq.Mtrs. required for common facility centre. All the heavy machineries are installed in the ground floor and the designing centre, office, stores etc are established in the first floor. The total construction cost of the proposed technical civil work is ₹ 37.50 lakhs.

The ground floor is divided in to two sections

1. Engineering Section
2. Injection Moulding Section

The consortium will provide this land and building as their contribution. The consortium will execute necessary agreements and undertakings with the implementing agency.

SECTION-IV : PLANT AND MACHINERY

A plant is a place where men, material, money, equipment, machineries etc. are brought together for manufacturing products. Today in modern industry equipment and machineries are very important part of the total production effort than the case years ago.

The following machineries are required.

1. High speed precision lathe straight bed,with center height minimum250mm
2. All graded heavy duty precision lathe(Centre ht 400 mm).
3. Radial drilling machine, Drilling cap. 50 mm dia
4. Pillar type drilling machine, Drilling cap.40 mm.
5. Heavy duty vertical milling machine, 1600x300 (1 No)
6. Turret milling machine with DRO 250x1200
7. Surface grinding machine, Surface capacity 700 x 1020
8. Surface grinding machine 250 x 500
9. Cylindrical grinding machine with Center height 150 mm
10. Air Conditioner split type 1.5 ton capacity –Total 4 Nos.
11. Heavy Duty Air Compressor
12. Electrically operated Staker
13. CAD, CAM Software- Master CAM/Solid worked /AutoCAD
14. Gas Cutting Set
15. EOT Crane –2 Nos.
16. Horizontal Metal Cutting Band Saw-175 mm round
17. EDM Tank Capacity 1750 x 650
18. CNC Wire Cut Machine work piece size 730 x 500 x 300
19. CNC Heavy Duty Vertical Milling M/c (1600x810x700)
20. CNC Heavy Duty Vertical Milling M/c 1000x 510x610
21. Injection Moulding Machine 730 ton Capacity 1 No. (Including Chiller, Hopper & Drier)
22. Measuring Instruments and Tools.
23. Diesel Generator Set
24. Electrification-

The details are shown in Annexure II.

Supporting Equipment

The common facility center is in need of office equipment and computers. The total proposed investment required for office furnishing and automations is shown in Annexure III.

SECTION-V : MANPOWER REQUIREMENTS

The consortium will arrange necessary technical experts and skilled operators for running this common facility centre. The continuity of professionals and skilled workers are ensured by the consortium by conducting training programmes.

According to organisational structure envisaged for the common facility centre, General Managers will be in charge of functions of the unit. He looks after the production, and finance. There will be two Design Engineer, 30 machine operators, 5 tool makers, 3 maintenance staff, 5 skilled workers and 6 unskilled workers reporting to General Manager.

There will be 2 accountant in helping Managers in matters like accounting, book keeping, banking and other finance related affairs. There will be 3 Office Staff in charge of office matters.

In total there will be 57 persons including Manager employed in the unit. The monthly salary and benefits will come to ₹ 4,91,050/- shown in Annexure-VI.

SECTION-VI : OTHER PROJECT DETAILS

A. Utilities :

1. Power : Required power is available from Kerala State Electricity Board. The total connected load for common facility centre is 229.35K.W. The annual electric charge is ₹ 31.44 lakhs at fully capacity utilisation. Details are given in Annexure-IV. The consortium will pay this amount from the service charge obtained from its members.

B. Miscellaneous Expenses :

These items includes repair and maintenance of building, plant and machineries, postage charges, cost of printing and stationary items, insurance charges. An amount of ₹ 14.73 lakhs per annum has to be incurred towards for the smooth operation of the unit. The details of estimation are given in Annexure-VIII.

C. Preliminary and Pre-operative Expenses :

These items include company registration, project report preparation, building design and drawing, technical consultancy fee etc. Thus the preliminary and pre operative expense required for implementing the proposed project is approximately ₹ 9.71 lakhs. The details of estimation are given in Annexure-IV.

SECTION-VII : PROJECT PARTICULARS

Plant Capacity and Capacity Utilisation

The common facility centre will provide around 20 hours service per day. Around 6000 engineering service hours are available from this tool room annually. Because of down time and other various reasons, the capacity may not be releasable and it is assumed that 65% of the capacity utilisation will be achieved during first year and 75% during second year 80% during third year and 85% capacity utilisation will be achieved, fourth year onwards.

	Particulars	*Qty in Hours*	*Rate ₹*
1.	Service Charge from High speed precision lathe straight bed,with center height minimum250 mm	5200	200
2.	Service Charge from All graded heavy duty precision lathe	2500	150
3.	Service Charge from Radial drilling machine, Drilling cap. 50 mm dia	3500	150
4.	Service Charge from Pillar type drilling machine, Drilling cap.40 mm.	5000	300
5.	Service Charge from Heavy duty vertical milling machine, 1600x300 (1 No)	4000	300
6.	Service Charge from Turret milling machine with DRO 250x1200	4000	300
7.	Service Charge from Surface grinding machine Surface capacity 700 x 1020	4500	350
8.	Service Charge from Surface grinding machine 250 x 500	3500	200
9.	Service Charge from Cylindrical grinding machine with Center height 150 mm	3000	350
10.	Service Charge from Horizontal Metal Cutting Band Saw-175 mm round	3000	250
11.	Service Charge from EDM Tank Capacity 1750 x 650	3500	350
12.	Service Charge from CNC Wire Cut Machine work piece	3000	1500

13.	Service Charge from CNC Heavy Duty Vertical Milling M/c (1600x810x700)	3000	2200
14.	Service Charge from CNC Heavy Duty Vertical Milling M/c 1000x 510x610	4200	1200
15.	Service Charge fromDesign Software	3000	264
16.	Service Charge from Injection moulding machine	4500	1200

The details are shown in Annexure IX.

The individual units will bring mild steel, alloy steel etc. to the common facility centre. This proposed common facility centre will charge on hourly basis.

Cluster members can utilise this common facility centre for repair and maintenance of their existing moulds and machine parts.

Presently around 2500 moulds of worth ₹ 2000 Lakhs are used by the cluster members. Around 10 to 15 percentage of cost of mould is required every year for their maintenance and making of new moulds. That means this cluster all together spend around ₹ 300 lakhs for purchase of new moulds and for repair and maintenance of existing moulds and machine parts. Now this cluster depends common facility centre in Mumbai and Pune for this work. By setting up a common facility centre the entire mould work of the cluster can be done. The injection moulding machine also can be utilized by the consortium members on hourly basis. So consortium members can meet bulk orders by using this common facility centre.

SECTION-VIII : FINANCIAL ASPECTS

The estimated capital outlay of the project is ₹ 460 lakhs as shown in Annexure-X. The capital expenditure is proposed to be raised as the contribution of consortium to the extent of ₹ 53 lakhs in terms of land and building and the Grant from DCSSI under small industries cluster development programme for setting common facility centre is expected to ₹ 315.00 lakhs and from govt of Kerala is ₹ 92.00 lakhs.

I. Viability of the Project

Assumption to Profitability Estimates :

The projected profitability of the unit is shown in Annexure XIII and are based upon the following assumptions.

1. The unit will be 20 engineering hours per day and the unit will work for 300 days in year.
2. The installed capacity of the unit is 6000 engineering service hours per year.
3. The capacity utilisation is at 65% first year, 75% during second year, 80% third year and 85% fourth year onwards.
4. The main utilities is power. The total power requirement is 229.35 K.W. The power charge is calculated considering the tariff fixed by KSEB.

5. Repairs and Maintenance is provided @ 2% on building and 3% on Plant and Machinery.
6. Details of computation of depreciation is attached as Annexure-XI and XII. Straight line method of depreciation is applied for project purpose. However, for income tax purpose, written down value method is applied for.
7. Administrative expenses is provided in the profitability estimate. It includes rates and taxes travelling expenses, postage telephone and telegram, printing and stationery, other office expenses etc.
8. Income tax is provided considering the rates applicable to private limited company. Computation of income tax is attached as Annexure-XIV.
9. A corpus fund is raised from the profit of the common facility centre.

Profitability estimates are furnished in Annexure-XIII According to this statement there is a profit of ₹ 36.12 lakhs in the first year of operation. The viability of the scheme is worked out taking into account, the operating results of the first eight years of operation. The projected cash flow statement is appended as Annexure-XV. As per cash flow statement there is cash surplus adequate to meet all the probable payments and debt servicing.

The internal rate of return of the project is 11% after tax which is computed in Annexure-XVIII.

Break even level of operation is computed in Annexure-XVIII. Operating BEP works out to 39.11% of the installed capacity and the cash BEP works out to 13.75% of installed capacity.

II. Implementation Period

Phase I : Collection of all information, data, preparation of drawings and inviting quotations etc. A detailed schedule in terms of bar charts is prepared for implementing the project. This will be carried out within a period of three months.

Phase II : Actual implementation of the project. This will take at least 15 months as a supply period of the machines will take 10 to 11 months. Besides it will take around 6 to 7 months for land development and building construction. The tentative date of trial production will be August 2006 and commercial operation will be carried out within 30 days from the date of trial production.

SECTION-IX: CONCLUSION AND RECOMMENDATION

M/s. Aluva Plastic Consortium Pvt. Ltd, Erumathala Post, Aluva, is planning to set up a common facility centre for mould making, mould repairing, machinery repairing, machinery spare parts manufacturing, injection moulding etc. under Small Industries Cluster Development Programme scheme. Presently about 11 industrial units in Ernakulam District have joined the consortium and remaining industries will join immediately. The proposed annual capacity of the unit is 6000 Engineering service hours for mould making and repair per year. The required technical knowhow for production is indigenously available.

The implementation agency for the proposed common facility centre is Government of Kerala (Industrial Department).

This common facility centre will be set up under the technical guidance of NTTF Technical Training Centre, Nettur, Tellicherry.

This common facility centre will not create any atmospheric pollution.

The estimated capital outlay of the project is ₹ 460 lakhs as is proposed to be financed as follows :

	(₹ in Lakhs)
Contribution from consortium members	53.00
Grand from Govt of India	315.00
Grant from Govt of Kerala	92.00
	460.00

The projected profitability estimated of the unit for first 8 years are satisfactory. The unit is expected to make an average operating profit of 48.12 lakhs per annum for the first 8 years. The project is technically feasible and commercially viable.

K. SAJIL KUMAR, M.Tech A.M.I.E., C.E.

CHARTERED ENGINEER & CONSULTANT

A2, ASHOK APARTMENT, NEAR CIVIL SATATION

KAKKANAD, ERNAKULAM, KERALA–682 030

16.13. SUMMARY

A project is an idea or plan that is intended to be carried out. The dictionary meaning of a project is that it is a scheme, design; a proposal of something intended or devised to be achieved. Project formulation is the systematic development of a project idea for the eventual objective of arriving at an investment decision. It has the built-in mechanism of ringing the danger bell at the earliest possible stage of resource utilization. Project formulation is a process involving the joint efforts of a team of experts. Project formulation involves a step-by-step investigation and development of project idea. And it provides a controlled mechanism for restricting expenditure on project development.

Project report or business plan is a written statement of what an entrepreneur proposes to take up. It is a kind of guide frost or course of action what the entrepreneur hopes to achieve in his business and how is he going to achieve it.It contains relevant data , on the basis of which the project has been appraised and found relevant to the entrepreneur. Project report is prepared by the experts after the detailed study and analysis of the various aspects of a project. The objective of the project report is to identify the requirement of the resources (technical, financial, commercial, managerial and operational) and to facilitates financial appraisal of the project by financial institutes, banks, insurance companies, etc.

16.14. SELF ASSESSMENT QUESTIONS

1. What do you mean by project formulation?
2. What is the difference between project formulation and feasibility study?
3. What do you mean by project report and what is its significance?
4. Explain the difference between a project report and project feasibility study.
5. Prepare an imaginary project report .

SOURCE/NOTE

1. http://www.dcmsme.gov.in

17

PROJECT FINANCING AND FINANCIAL SCHEMES

17.1. INTRODUCTION

Finance is one of the basic requirement of any organization/ project. It is the prerequisite to start an enterprise. Finance is the key input of production, distribution and development. Availability of finance enables an entrepreneur to bring together various resources like:land, labour, machinery and raw material in order to produce the product. Therefore, finance is known as lifeblood of enterprise as no business activity is possible without finance. The need of finance starts rightly from the start of the enterprise and continue till the business remain in existence and even the smooth running, expansion and growth of enterprise basically depends upon the proper management of finance.

17.2. MEANING

An entrepreneur needs capital to start the business and needs financial assistance at every stage of the project. For this assistance , development banks and commercial banks plays an important role .They not only provide the finance for the start up but also for development at various stages.Types of industrial finance can be:

(a) **Short-term:** In this the funds are required for less than one year and the important sources for the short term finance can be borrowings from friends, relatives, banks, trade credit and customer advances.

(b) **Medium-term:** In this the funds are required for the period from one to five years. Medium-term finance is usually required for working capital, small expansion, modifications etc. Various sources of medium-term finance can be: issue of shares, ploughing back of profits, borrowings from the bank, etc.

(c) **Long-term:** In this funds are required for the longer period, i.e., more than 5 years. It is required for the permanent fixed capital, procuring of fixed assets, for the establishment of new business etc. Various sources of long-term capital can by issue of shares, debentures and loans from the financial institutions.

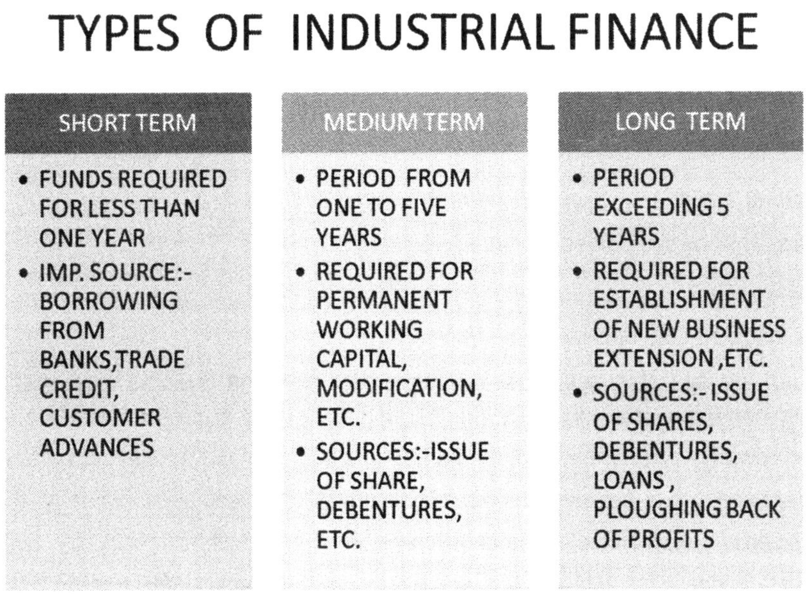

Fig 17.1.

17.4 PROJECT FINANCING

Financing is one of the most essential parts of all projects. The financing structure can be very different between projects and it often depends on the type of the investment, the risk level of the investment, and the credit rating of the project owner. According to Fabozzi and Peterson (2003), the decision on how to finance a project is a very important managerial decision, since the different methods of financing obligate the project in different ways. Project finance is a method of financing an economically capable project on the basis of the expected cash flows generated by the project. It is usually restricted to capital intensive projects and often involves a high proportion of debt finance. The cash flows of the project are segregated from the sponsoring organization, as the project is a separate entity. Project financing provides certain advantages over conventional financing, such as sharing of risk, reduced agency cost of debt and free cash flow, and expansion of sponsor's debt capacity (Vishwanath, 2007). Finnerty (1996) stresses that project financing should be distinguished from conventional financing, i.e., financing on a firm's general credit. He states that "the critical distinguishing feature of a project financing is that the project is a distinct legal entity: project assets, project-related contracts, and project cash flows are segregated to a substantial degree from the sponsoring entity. The financing structure is designed to allocate financial returns and risks more efficiently than a conventional financing structure"(p. 2-3).

According to Nevitt and Fabozzi (2000), projects are rarely financed independently on their own merits without credit support from sponsors that will benefit in some way from the project. They identify a wide range of available debt and equity sources for project financing, such as:

- International agencies (The World Bank, International Finance Corporation, area development banks, etc);
- Governments;
- Commercial banks;
- Institutional lenders;
- Money market funds;
- Commercial finance companies;
- Individual investors;
- Sponsors loans and advances.

Which sources are available and most suitable varies between projects, and combination of sources is usually needed. Careful financial engineering is needed in project financing in order to allocate risks and rewards among the involved parties in a way that is mutually acceptable. Figure 3 shows the basic elements in a capital investment financed on a project basis (Finnerty, 1996, p. 3). Several different types of project financing are commonly used in the construction industry. Some of them involve public-private partnerships, while others are fully private. Finnerty (1996, p. 195) has made the following list of questions to help find the most appropriate partnership structure:

- Who will be responsible for the design and construction of the project?
- Who will provide the construction funds?
- Who will arrange the financing?
- Who will hold legal title to the project's assets and for how long?
- Who will operate the project facility, and for how long?
- Who will be responsible for each source of project revenue?

For a fully private project, the answer to all the questions is the private developer. However, some projects may have a mixture of private and public responsibilities (Finnerty, 1996).

Following is a list of some well-known project financing structures that utilize private investment to undertake public sector projects:

- BOO (build, own and operate): a private sector investor finances, builds and operates a project facility and receives title and ownership of it on an open-ended basis;
- BOT (build, operate and transfer): a project facility is built, financed and operated by a private sector entity. At the end of the concession period the facility is transferred back to the government;

- BOOT (build, own, operate and transfer):a project facility is built, financed, owned and operated by a private sector investor. At the end of the concession period the facility is transferred back to the government;
- BOOS (build, own, operate and sell): a project facility is built, financed, owned and operated by a private sector entity. At the end of the concession period the facility is transferred back to the government in a return for a residual value payment. (Buljevich and Park, 1999, p. 216)

Nevitt and Fabozzi (2000) argue that the ultimate goal in project financing is arranging a borrowing which will benefit the sponsor and at the same time not affect his credits standing or balance sheet. They state that "the key to a successful project financing is structuring the financing of a project with as little recourse as possible to the sponsor while at the same time providing sufficient credit support though guarantees or undertakings of a sponsor or third party, so that lenders will be satisfied with the credit risk" (p. 2)

Who is funding entrepreneurial start-up companies?[1]

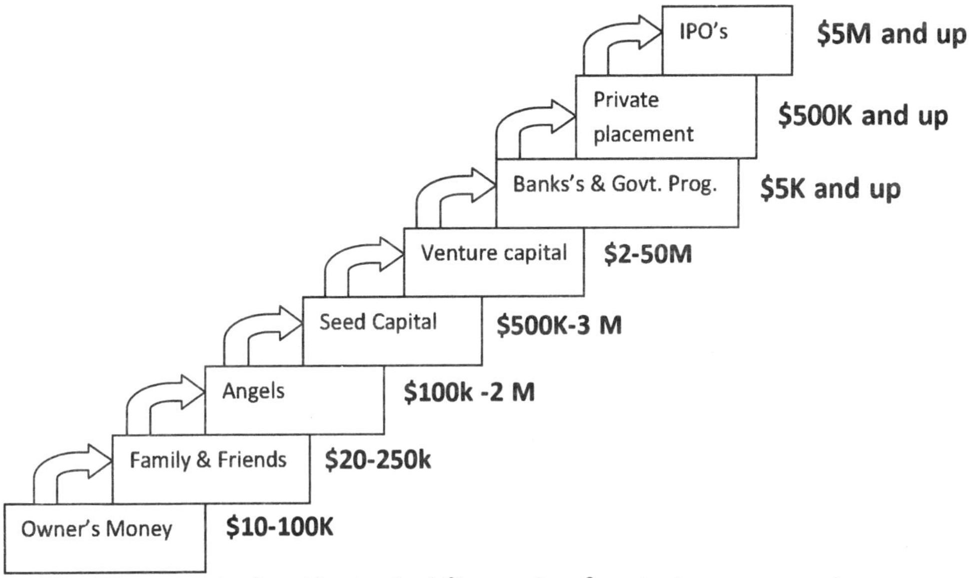

The Diagram depicts the typical finanacing for start-up companies

Fig. 17.2

17.4 SOURCES OF FINANCE

Raising finance for start-up requires careful planning. The entrepreneur needs to decide:

- How much finance is required?
- When and how long the finance is needed for?
- What security (if any) can be provided?

- Whether the entrepreneur is prepared to give up some control (ownership) of the start-up in return for investment?
- The finance needs of a start-up should take account of these key areas:
- Set-up costs (the costs that are incurred before the business starts to trade)
- Starting investment in capacity (the fixed assets that the business needs before it can begin to trade)
- Working capital (the stocks needed by the business – e.g., raw materials + allowance for amounts that will be owed by customers once sales begin)
- Growth and development (e.g., extra investment in capacity)

For the arrangement of finance various sources available to an entrepreneur i.e.:

(1) Internal Sources (raised from within organization)

(2) External sources (raised from outside)

It includes:

SOURCES OF FINANCE

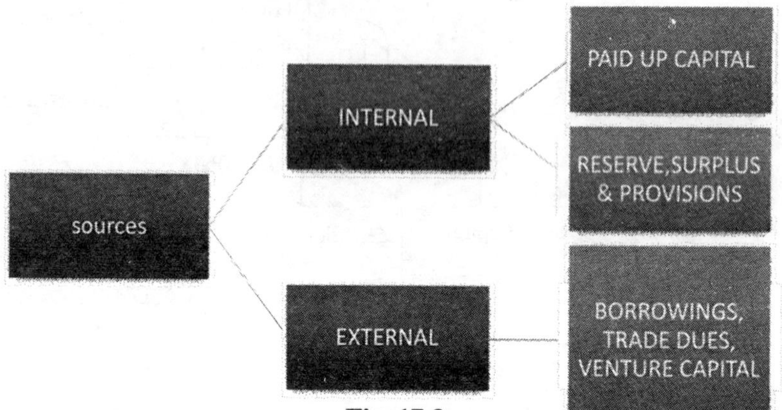

Fig. 17.3

VARIOUS SOURCES OF FINANCE (IN DETAIL)

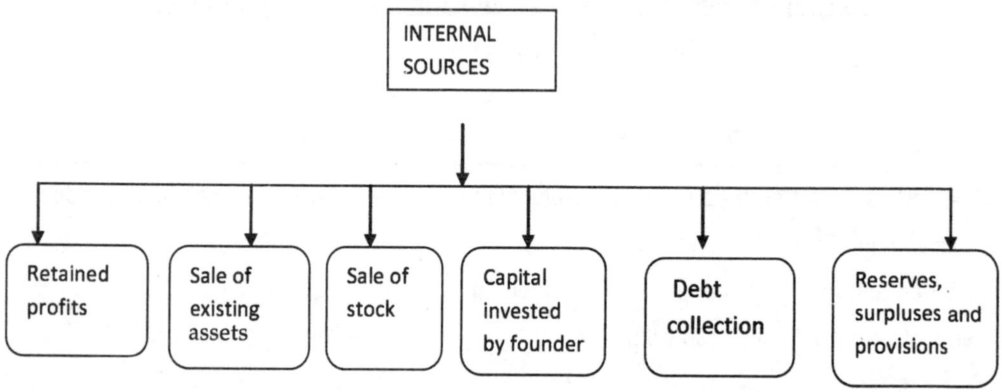

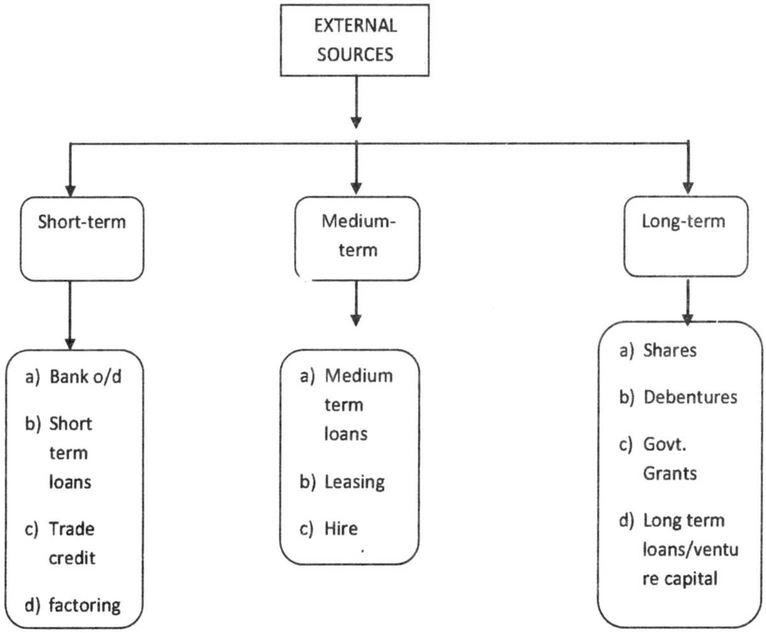

Fig. 17.4

Internal Sources :

(1) Retained profits: Businesses (especially limited companies) usually keep some part of the profit every year for future use. This is also known as **ploughed back profit**. Over a period of time it can total up to a huge amount which can be used for financing the business. This is the cash that is generated by the business when it trades profitably. For any company, the amount of earnings retained within the business has a direct impact on the amount of dividends. Profit re-invested as retained earnings is profit that could have been paid as a dividend. Characteristics of retained profits are:

(1) This source of finance is only available only for the business which has been trading for more than one year.

(2) Its made when the profits made are ploughed back into business.

(3) This is medium or long-term finance.

The major reasons for using retained earnings to finance new investments, rather than to pay higher dividends and then raise new equity for the new investments, are as follows:

(a) The management of many companies believes that retained earnings are funds which do not cost anything, although this is not true. However, it is true that the use of retained earnings as a source of funds does not lead to a payment of cash.

(b) The dividend policy of the company is in practice determined by the directors. From their standpoint, retained earnings are an attractive source of finance because investment projects can be undertaken without involving either the shareholders or any outsiders.

(c) The use of retained earnings as opposed to new shares or debentures avoids issue costs.

(d) The use of retained earnings avoids the possibility of a change in control resulting from an issue of new shares.

Advantages of retained profits

- Retained profits do not have to be repaid.
- No interest is payable if the source of finance is retained earning.

Disadvantages of retained profits

- It is not available to a new business.
- Sometimes business may not make enough profit to plough back .

(2) Sales of assets: Business might sell off old, obsolete assets which are no longer used by the business to raise additional cash for the business. This money comes in from selling off fixed assets, such as:a piece of machinery that is no longer needed. But businesses do not always have surplus fixed assets which they can sell off and there is also a limit to the number of fixed assets a firm can sell-off.

Characteristics of sale of assets

(1) This money comes in from selling off fixed assets, such as; a piece of machinery that is no longer needed

(2) Businesses do not always have surplus fixed assets which they can sell-off

(3) There is also a limit to the number of fixed assets a firm can sell-off

(4) This is a medium-term source of finance

Advantage of sale of fixed assets

It is a good way to raise finance from an asset that is no longer needed

Disadvantage of sale of assets

(1) Some businesses are unlikely to have surplus assets to sell

(2) It can be a slow method of raising finance

(3) Sale of stock: Stock means the total merchandise kept on hand by a merchant, commercial establishment, warehouse, or manufacturer. It is the total goods or raw material kept on the premises of a shop or business. The money comes in from selling off unsold stock.

Characteristics of sale of stock

- This money comes in from selling off unsold stock
- This is what happens in the January sales
- It is when the profits made are ploughed back into the business
- This is a short-term source of finance

Advantages of sale of stock

- It is quick way of raising finance.
- By selling off stock it reduces the costs associated with holding them

Disadvantages of sale of stock

- Normally business will have to take a reduced price for the stock

(4) Share capital – invested by the founder: The founding entrepreneur (/s) may decide to invest in the share capital of a company, founded for the purpose of forming the start-up. This is a common method of financing a start-up. The founder provides all the share capital of the company, retaining 100% control over the business. This is money which comes from the owner/s own savings

- It may be in the form of start-up capital - used when the business is setting up
- It may be in the form of additional capital – perhaps used for expansion
- This is a long-term source of finance

(5) Debt collection: Debt collection is the practice of obtaining payment from customers for purchases that have been made on credit. Devising and maintaining an efficient and effective system for collecting on overdue accounts should be a priority from every small business. In his book *A Practical Guide to Credit and Collections,* George O. Bancroft noted that an effective collection program "must be an integral part of the total sales process. The main objective of the collection program must be to develop customer relations and recover the company's delinquent receivables as quickly and economically as possible, while encouraging the formerly delinquent customer to patronize the company with future good business—business that is paid within the credit terms."

Characteristics of debt collection

- A debtor is someone who owes a business money
- A business can raise finance by collecting the money owed to them (debts) from their debtors
- Not all businesses have debtors, i.e., those who deal only in cash
- This is a short-term source of finance

Advantages of debt collection

- No additional cost in getting this finance, it is part of the businesses' normal operations

Disadvantages of debt collection

- There is a risk that debts owed can go bad and not be repaid

(6) Reserve, surpluses and provisions: Surplus is retained earnings accumulated from current or prior period. A surplus is used to describe many excess assets including income, profits, capital and goods. It is the amount of an asset or resource that exceeds the portion that is utilized. A surplus often occurs in a budget, when expenses are less than the income taken in, or in inventory when fewer supplies are used than were retained. There are different types of reserves used in financial accounting like capital reserves, revenue reserves, statutory reserves, realized reserves, unrealized reserves. Equity reserves are created from several possible sources: Reserves created from shareholders' contributions, the most common examples of which are:(a) *legal reserve fund* - it is required in many legislations and it must be paid as a percentage of share capital (b)*share premium* - amount paid by shareholders for shares in excess of their nominal value (c)Reserves created from profit, especially retained earnings, i.e., accumulated accounting profits, or in the case of nonprofits, operating surpluses. Reserve is the profit achieved by a company where a certain amount of it is put back into the business which can help the business in their rainy days.

External Sources

(1) Bank Overdraft: Bank overdraft is a short term finance and it is a facility given by banks to its business customers, people having current accounts. Through this facility the customers can overdraw their accounts to a greater value than the balance in the account. To overdrawn amount is agreed in advance with the bank manager. The bank assigns a limit to overdraw from the account and the business can meet its short-term liabilities by writing cheques to the extent of limit allowed. There is no need for collaterals or security. These are more flexible and the overdraft amount can be adjusted every month according to needs but Interest rates are usually variable and higher than bank loans.

(2) Trade Credit: Usually in business dealing supplier give a grace period to their customers to pay for the purchases. This can range from 1 week to 60 days depending upon the type of business and industry. By delaying the payment of bills for goods or services received, a business is, in effect, obtaining finance which can be used for more important expenditures. In this no interest has to be paid.

Characteristics of trade credit

- Trade credit is summed up by the phrase: **buy now pay later**
- Typical trade credit period is 30 days
- This is a short-term source of finance

Advantages of trade credit

- In trade credit business can sell the goods first and pay for them later.
- Trade credit is good for cash flow.
- In trade credit no interest charged if money is paid within agreed time.

Disadvantages of trade credit

- In trade credit discount given for cash payment would be lost.
- Businesses need to carefully manage their cash flow to ensure they will have money available when the debt is due to be paid.

(3) Factoring : It involves the business selling its bills receivable to a debt factoring company at a discounted price. In this way the business get access to instant cash. It is a type of financial service whereby, a firm sells or transfers title to its accounts receivable to a factoring company, which then acts as principal, not as agent. The receivables are sold without recourse, meaning that the factor cannot turn to the seller in the event accounts prove uncollectible. Factoring can be done either on a *notification basis,* where the seller's customers remit directly to the factor, or on a *non-notification basis,* where the seller handles the collections and remits to the factor.

(4) Bank loans: Banks are like the supermarket of debt financing. They provide short-, mid- or long-term financing, and they finance all asset needs, including working capital, equipment and real estate. This assumes, of course, that you can generate enough cash flow to cover the interest payments (which are tax deductible) and return the principal. Banks want assurance of repayment by requiring personal guarantees and even a secured interest (such as a mortgage) on personal assets. Unlike other financing relationships, banks offer some flexibility: You can pay-off your loan early and terminate the agreement. When a banker is asked by a business customer for a loan or overdraft facility, he will consider several factors, known commonly by the mnemonic **PARTS** i.e., **P**urpose, **A**mount, **R**epayment, **T**erm and **S**ecurity of the loan.

Characteristics of Bank Loan

(1) This is money borrowed at an agreed rate of interest over a set period of time

(2) This is a medium or long-term source of finance

Advantage of bank loan

- Set repayments are spread over a period of time which is good for budgeting

Disadvantages of bank loan

- Can be expensive due to interest payments
- Bank may require security on the loan

(5) Leasing: A lease is an agreement between two parties, the "lessor" and the "lessee". The lessor owns a capital asset, but allows the lessee to use it. The lessee makes payments under the terms of the lease to the lessor, for a specified period of time. Leasing is, therefore, a form of rental. Leased assets have usually been plant and machinery, cars and commercial vehicles, but might also be computers and office equipment. There are two basic forms of lease: "operating leases" and "finance leases". Leasing involves using an asset, but the ownership does not pass to the user. Business can lease a building or machinery and a periodic payment is made as rent, till the time the business uses the assets. The business does not need to purchase the asset.

Characteristics of Leasing

- This method allows a business to obtain assets without the need to pay a large lump sum up front
- It is arranged through a finance company
- Leasing is like renting an asset
- It involves making set repayments
- This is a medium-term source of finance

Advantages of leasing

- Businesses can have the use of up to date equipment immediately
- In leasing payments are spread over a period of time which is good for budgeting.

Disadvantages of leasing

- It can be an expensive affair.
- In leasing the asset belongs to the finance company.

(6) Hire Purchase: Hire purchase is a form of installment credit. Hire purchase is similar to leasing, with the exception that ownership of the goods passes to the hire purchase customer on payment of the final credit installment, whereas a lessee never becomes the owner of the goods. Hire purchase agreements usually involve a finance house.

(i) The supplier sells the goods to the finance house.

(ii) The supplier delivers the goods to the customer who will eventually purchase them.

(iii) The hire purchase arrangement exists between the finance house and the customer.

It involves purchasing an asset paying for it over a period of time. Usually a percentage of the price is paid as down payment and the rest is paid in installments for the period of time agreed upon. The business has to pay an interest on these installments.

(7) Issue of Share: A share is one unit into which the total share capital is divided. Share capital of the company can be explained as a fund or sum with which a company is formed to carry on the business and which is raised by the issue of shares. The amount collected by the company from the public towards its capital, collectively is known as share capital and individually is known as share. It is a permanent source of finance but only available to limited companies. Public limited companies can sell further shares up to the limit of their authorized share capital. Private limited companies can sell further shares to existing shareholders. As per the provision of section 85 of the Companies Act, 1956, the share capital of a company consists of two classes of shares, namely: Preference Shares and Equity Shares.

(8) Debentures: A **debenture** is defined as a certificate of acceptance of loans which is given under the company's stamp and carries an undertaking that the debenture holder will get a fixed return (fixed on the basis of interest rates) and the principal amount whenever the debenture matures. It is issued for a long periods of time. Debentures are generally freely transferrable by the debenture holder. Debenture holders have no voting rights and the interest given to them is a charge against profit. Debentures are a form of loan stock, legally defined as the written acknowledgement of a debt incurred by a company, normally containing provisions about the payment of interest and the eventual repayment of capital.

(9) Government Assistance: The government provides finance to companies in cash grants and other forms of direct assistance, as part of its policy of helping to develop the national economy, especially in high technology industries and in areas of high unemployment. For example, the Indigenous Business Development Corporation of Zimbabwe (IBDC) was set up by the government to assist small indigenous businesses in that country.

Characteristics of Government Assistance

- Government organisations such as Invest NI offer grants to businesses, both established and new

- Usually certain conditions apply, such as where the business has to locate.

Advantage

- Government grants don't have to be repaid back.

Disadvantages

- Certain conditions may apply for the grants, e.g., location
- Not all businesses may be eligible for a grant

(10) Venture capital : Venture capital(VC) is financial capital provided to early-stage, high-potential, high risk, growth startup companies. The venture capital fund makes money by owning equity in the companies it invests in, which usually have a novel technology or business model in high technology industries, such as biotechnology, IT, software, etc. Venture capital is attractive for new companies with limited operating history that are too small to raise capital in the public markets and have not reached the point where they are able to secure a bank loan or complete a debt offering. In exchange for the high risk that venture capitalists assume by investing in smaller and less mature companies, venture capitalists usually get significant control over company decisions, in addition to a significant portion of the company's ownership (and consequently value).

17.5 PROBLEM RELATED TO FINANCE

Finance holds the key to all business activities. It is the life–blood of any business. It also work as the guide for the regulating investment decisions and expenditures. Cash is required by a business for precautionary, speculative and transactions motives. In regard to financial characteristics, there are many differences between large and small industries in accounting practices and profitability. But all entrepreneurs face a variety of financial issues that can impact the business's profitability, and even its long-term survival. Some financial problems may be caused by factors outside of their control, like when the economy dips or a new competitor moves in next door. Other issues may be more directly related to how entrepreneurs choose to operate their business.

(1) Obtaining financing

Entrepreneurs lack their own capital and therefore heavily depend upon the institutional finance for their capital requirement. Obtaining financing for a business can be extremely difficult, especially when first starting out. Banks are reluctant to lend money to new businesses, and potential investors may steer clear of budding entrepreneurs with little or no prior business experience. A well-crafted written business plan is essential when attempting to convince lenders and investors that you know what you're doing and have thought through your idea carefully. Other possible financing sources can include loans or grants from the Small Business Administration or even borrowing from friends and family members.

(2) Problem of procuring working capital

Institutional long-term finance is given by SFC, SIDO, etc., mainly for the purpose of acquiring fixed assets. While short-term finance required for working capital are given by commercial banks .Many entrepreneurs lack knowledge about this fact. Moreover entrepreneurs finds it difficult to estimate its working capital requirement and many time they fail due to deficiency in working capital requirements. Secondly, entrepreneurs claim that their short-term requirement are not properly fulfilled by financial institutions. There remain a wide gap between the amount applied and finally sanctioned.

(3) Inappropriate financial structure

Capital structure means the permanent long-term financing of a company, including long-term debt, common stock and preferred stock, and retained earnings. It differs from financial structure, which includes short-term debt and accounts payable. Every mode of raising finance has a different cost and an optimum finance mix result in minimum cost is desirable. Rule is that the rate of profit earned, i.e., return on capital employed ratio should be higher than the cost of respective source of finance invested. Inappropriate finance mix can disturb the economic viability of the enterprise. In case of new entrepreneurs , the usual sickness is due to under-capitalisation, inappropriate finance mix and high cost of capital.

(4) Problems regarding sanctioning of loans

Normally there are lots of formalities in the sanctioning of loans by financial institutions. Financial institutions generally explore various facts like:Personal qualification, personal finance, experience, accounting policy of the firm, creditworthiness, etc. Moreover they demand security and there is always a lack of security. This problem is more acute for groups considered by lender to represent higher risk, such as 1st generation entrepreneurs, backward people and persons belonging to tiny and small sector.

17.6. MEANING OF FINANCIAL INSTITUTIONS

Financial sector plays an indispensable role in the overall development of a country. The most important constituent of this sector is the financial institutions, which act as a conduit for the transfer of resources from net savers to net borrowers, that is, from those who spend less than their earnings to those who spend more than their earnings. The financial institutions have traditionally been the major source of funds for the economy. These institutions provide a variety of financial products and services to fulfill the varied needs of the commercial sector. Besides, they provide assistance to new enterprises, small and medium firms as well as to the industries established in backward areas. Thus, they have helped in reducing regional disparities by inducing widespread industrial development.

The Government of India, in order to provide adequate supply of credit to various sectors of the economy, has evolved a well developed structure of financial institutions in the country. These financial institutions can be broadly categorised into :All India institutions and State level institutions, depending upon the geographical coverage of their operations. At the national level, they provide long and medium term loans at reasonable rates of interest. They subscribe to the debenture issues of companies, underwrite public issue of shares, guarantee loans and deferred payments, etc. Though, the State level institutions are mainly concerned with the development of medium and small-scale enterprises, but they provide the same type of financial assistance as the national level institutions.

17.7. COMMERCIAL BANKS

Commercial banks play dominant role in economic development and growth of industries ever since independence. These are the most important constituents of banking business and these banks do banking business to earn profits. Commercial banks form a significant part of the country's Financial Institution System. Commercial Banks are profit seeking institutions which accept deposits from general public and advance money to individuals like household, entrepreneurs, businessmen etc. with the prime objective of earning profit in the form of interest, commission etc. The operations of all these banks are regulated by the Reserve Bank of India, which is the central bank and supreme financial authority in India. The main source of income of a commercial bank is the difference between these two rates which they charge to borrowers and pay to depositors.

17.7.1 Classification of Commercial Banks

1. Scheduled banks: Banks which have been included in the Second Schedule of RBI Act 1934. The scheduled banks comprise scheduled commercial banks and scheduled cooperative banks. Further, the scheduled commercial banks in India are categorised into five different groups according to their ownership and/or nature of operation: (i) Nationalised Banks; (ii) State Bank of India and its associates; (iii) Regional Rural Banks (RRBs); (iv) Foreign banks; and (v) Other Indian private sector banks. Scheduled Co-operative Banks consist of Scheduled State Co-operative Banks and Scheduled Urban Co-operative Banks. They are also categorized as follows:

- o **Public Sector Banks** : are those banks in which majority of stake is held by the government. E.g. SBI, PNB, Syndicate Bank, Union Bank of India etc.
- o **Private Sector Banks** : are those banks in which majority of stake is held by private indivisuals. E.g. ICICI Bank, IDBI Bank, HDFC Bank, AXIS Bank etc.
- o **Foreign Banks** : are the banks with Head office outside the country in which they are located. E.g. Citi Bank, Standard Chartered Bank, Bank of Tokyo Ltd., etc.

At present, there are 170 scheduled commercial banks in the country, which includes 91 regional rural banks (RRBs), 19 nationalised banks, 6 banks in State Bank of India group .

2. Non-scheduled commercial banks : Banks which are not included in the Second Schedule of RBI Act 1934.

17.7.2 Financing By Commercial Banks

There are various types of credit schemes offered by commercial banks which are as under:

(a) Cash credit: It is a very popular form of advancing loan. Under this scheme bank advances loans to the customer on the basis of current assets, receivables or fixed assets hypothecated in favour of bank. Cash credit is the issuance of a short term cash loan to a business. Under this the commercial bank specify a limit called 'cash credit limit' upto which the borrower can borrow against the security. The credit is given in the form of cash. Cash credit limits are sanctioned for one year and reviewed and renewed thereafter. It is always payable on demand and the borrower has to pay interest on the amount used by him.

(b) Overdraft: Discussed above(point 8.3).It means allowing the borrower to overdraw his current account and the drawee has to pay interest on the extra amount withdrawn. This facility is available to the reliable customers only and for short period.

(c) Demand Loans: Demand loan is a loan which can be recalled on demand, i.e., this is a term loan repayable within one year in installments or lump sum. It may be clean or secured. The salient feature of demand loan is that loan amount is paid in lump sum. All the amounts credited are reduced from the amount of loan and interest is generally levied on a quarterly basis on the outstanding debit balance.

(d) Term Loan: A term loan is loan which is sanctioned for specific period and the specific period could be one year or more. These types of loans are advanced against the security. It is mostly given for financing fixed assets or working capital needs.

(e) Money at Call: It is the money lent for a very short period generally from 1-14 days. Such advances are usually made to other banks and financial institutes only. Money at call ensures liquidity.

(f) Consumer Credit: Consumer credit is granted to consumers for their consumer needs.It is a short-term loans made to enable people to purchase goods or services primarily for personal, family, or household purposes. Consumer credit transactions can be classified into several different classes: Installment credit involves credit that is repaid by the borrower in several periodic payments; loans repaid in one lump sum are classified as noninstallment credit. Installment credit has expanded in popularity, with an increasing number of consumers buying goods on credit in order to spread repayment of the purchase price and the interest owed on the principal borrowed over an extended time.

(g) Bills Purchased: Bills are written instructions of a seller of goods to the purchaser for the payment of stipulated amount at a particular date. It is approved by the buyer and if the holder of the bill requires the amount of bill before its maturity, the bills are purchased by bank from its approved customers in whose favour regular limits are sanctioned. Bills may be clean or documentary. The bank hold the documents as security against advances.

(h) Bills Discounted: Bills discounted means the discounting of bills by the banks. Bills discounted is allowed against usance bills arising out of trade transaction and maturing after a given time. Bills of exchange which are discounted by the bank are debited to the bills discounted account. The amount of the bill after deducting the commission is credited to the customer account.

17.8 TYPES AND SCHEMES OFFERED BY COMMERCIAL AND OTHER BANKS

17.8.1 State Bank of India (S.B.I)

State Bank of India (SBI) is a banking and financial services company based in India. The bank traces its origin to the first decade of the 19th century. Later on, it was merged with the Imperial Bank. In the year 1955, the Government of India nationalized the Imperial Bank along with the Reserve Bank of India. Ever since that time, the bank acquired its present name that is SBI. The

State Bank of India is India's largest commercial bank. The bank has been striving sincerely to adhere to the efforts of providing utmost customer satisfaction to the best possible extent. As of March 2012, it had assets of US$360 billion and 14,119 branches, including 173 foreign offices in 37 countries across the globe making it the largest banking and financial services company in India. In 2008, the government took over the stake held by the Reserve Bank of India. SBI has been ranked 285th in the Fortune Global 500 rankings of the world's biggest corporations for the year 2012.

SBI provides a range of banking products through its network of branches in India and overseas, including products aimed at non-resident Indians (NRIs). SBI has 14 regional hubs and 57 Zonal Offices that are located at important cities throughout the country.

Various Schemes by S.B.I

1. In 1967, the SBI launched a liberalized scheme for providing financial assistance to technically qualified or trained entrepreneurs to the extent of 100 % if necessary.
2. Under the equity fund scheme the bank may grant interest free loan for 25% of the project cost which is minimum contribution of an entrepreneur.
3. SBI has set up research and development fund of ₹ 5 crores for assisting entrepreneurial development.
4. SBI and its group offer package of financial arrangement and assistance to small scale unit in their promotional and expansion activities and act as banker to capital issue.
5. Equipment Finance Scheme offered for acquisition of machinery/equipment, both indigenous and imported. Existing units in the SSI sector with good track record and sound financial position can obtain finance through this scheme. These units should have been in operation for at least three years and have earned profits and/or declared dividend during two years proceeding to taking up the scheme. The units should not have defaulted in payment of its dues. Norms requirement of loans should not be less than ₹ 7.5 million. The limits for states of Eastern Region, North-Eastern Region, Jammu Kashmir and Himachal Pradesh shall be ₹ 5 million and Debt Equity Ratio - For projects - 2:1, for units - 1.5:1 and repayment has to made within 5 years.
6. SSI Entrepreneur Scheme of State Bank of India grants financial assistance to technically qualified, trained and experienced entrepreneurs for setting up new viable industrial projects. Loans are extended to technocrats who are unable to meet the normal margin requirements under the liberalized schemes. The borrower has to be a technically qualified person (a degree/diploma holder in engineering or technology), a craftsman with adequate experience or training or a person possessing a degree in business or industrial management, a chartered accountant or a cost accountant with relevant experience. For requirements up to ₹ 5 lakhs, no margins are involved. For needs ranging from ₹ 5 lakhs to ₹ 20 lakhs, the margin is set at 10 per cent.

17.8.2 IDBI Bank

The Industrial Development Bank of India Limited, popularly known as IDBI Bank is one of the leading public sector banks in India. Categorized as "other public sector bank" by Reserve Bank of India (RBI), IDBI Bank is also the 4th largest Indian bank. Founded in 1964 to provide credit and other facilities to its customers, IDBI Bank currently has 457 centers, 688 branches and 1020 ATMs across the nation. It is world's 10th largest development bank in terms of reach. IDBI Bank also built several institutions including the National Stock Exchange of India (NSE), the Stock Holding Corporation of India (SHCIL) and the National Securities Depository Services Ltd. (NSDL) etc. IDBI Bank was founded on July 1, 1964 under an Act of Parliament. It was established as a wholly owned subsidiary of RBI (Reserve Bank of India). The ownership was however transferred to the Government of India on February 16, 1976. It worked as the main financial institution, whose main goal was to coordinate with other institutions associated with financing, developing and promoting the industry. With the public issue of IDBI Bank released in July 1995, the share holding of the Government came down below 100%. However, the majority of the share was still owned by the government, which is currently 52.3%. IDBI Bank started offering a wide array of products and services to its customers, which covered entire range of industrial activities including services and manufacturing. Products and Services;-IDBI Bank offers a wide array of products and services to its customers. For different customer groups and needs, there are different types of products and services including Personal Banking, Corporate Banking, SME Finance and Agri Business etc.

Following products and services are offered by IDBI Bank for the corporates:

Project Finance, Infrastructure Finance, Syndication, Underwriting and Advisory Services, Carbon Credits Business, Working Capital, Cash Management Services, Trade Finance, Tax Payments, Derivatives, Technology Upgradation Fund Scheme (TUFS), Direct Discounting Bills, Rehabilitation Finance

Following SME Finance products are offered by the IDBI Bank

1. Soft loan scheme: This scheme is introduced in 1976 to provide financial assistance to productive units in selected industries, e.g.: cement, cotton, textiles, jute, sugar and certain engineering industries to modernize, replace and renovate their plant and equipment. This scheme is implemented by IDBI with financial participation of IFCI and ICICI.
2. In 1988, IDBI launched National Equity Fund Scheme (NEFS) for providing support in nature of equity to tiny and small industries engaged in manufacturing cost not exceeding ₹ 5 lakhs.
3. IDBI set up Voluntary Execution Corporation Cell (VECC) to utilize the services of experienced professionals for counseling small units for providing consultancy support in specific areas.
4. Credit Guarantee Scheme for Micro and Small Enterprises (CGMSE): Providing security for the loan availed by the micro/small enterprises units (MSEs) has been found to be a major roadblock for their inability to access banking systems. Keeping this in view, the Government of India and SIDBI had set up "Credit Guarantee Fund Trust for Micro and Small Enterprises" (CGTMSE). On the basis of the guidelines issued by CGTMSE, IDBI Bank offers collateral free loans up to ₹ 1 crore.

5. Sulabh Vyapar/ Business Solutions: Traders act as a vital link between the manufacturers of goods/commodities and the consumer. The product aims to provide hassle free finance to traders and to meet their business and financial needs at competitive interest rates. Any individual or a firm (partnership or proprietorship) engaged primarily in buying and selling mercantile goods is eligible for this mode of finance. IDBI Bank offers solutions to all the financial needs of the wholesalers/traders/retailers under the Product. Loan amount can be upto ₹ 500 lakhs on the primary security of hypothecation of stock, assets or receivables or collateral can be immovable residential or commercial property.
6. Loans to Professionals and Self-employed: All the Professionals and Self-Employed persons including:
    - Chartered Accountants, Company Secretaries, Engineers, Architects, Surveyors, Contractors, Management Consultants
    - Doctors/Medical Practitioner, Healthcare Centres
    - Packaging, Storage and Warehouse Services
    - Transport/Taxi Services, Travel and Tour Operators,Travel Agents
    - Event Management, Publicity and Media Coverage

    Fund based facilities provided to professional are:

    1. Over Draft/Cash Credit and 2. Term Loan and non-fund based : Bank Guarantee and Letter of Credit. Loan can be provided for minimum ₹ 5 lakh and maximum Rs.500 Lakh and tenor is 7 years.
7. SME Smart Line of Credit: Bank has introduced this Product where financial assistance is offered to the MSMEs by way of pre-approved composite loan. Loan amount can be maximum 500 lakhs for corporate borrowers and maximum 250 lakh for non-corporate borrowers and term loan can be for maximum 5years and for that guarantee and security has to provide to the bank.

17.8.3 SIDBI (Small Industrial Development Bank of India)

Small Industries Development Bank of India is an independent financial institution aimed to aid the growth and development of micro, small and medium-scale enterprises (MSME) in India. Set up on October 1989 through an act of parliament, it was incorporated initially as a wholly owned subsidiary of Industrial Development Bank of India.The bank commenced its operations from April 2, 1990. It is the Principal Financial Institution for the Promotion, Financing and Development of the Micro, Small and Medium Enterprise (MSME) sector and for coordination of the functions of the institutions engaged in similar activities.

Following are the financial schemes offered by SIDBI :

1. Growth Capital and Equity Assistance Scheme provides assistance in form of Mezzanine/ Convertible Instruments, Subordinated debt and Equity. It bridge the gap in means of finance for scaling up/expansion/modernization projects. It access long term structured assistance-especially for investments in intangible assets, Leverage Equity/Sub Debt Assistance from

SIDBI for raising higher debt funds. Eligibility for this scheme is an MSME as per the definition of Government of India (MSMED Act) or Units with past 3 years of profitability and 2 years of satisfactory banking credit track record (meeting internal credit rating criteria) and acceptable external rating from CRISIL, ICRA, DandB, SMERA, etc., would be desirable.

2. SIDBI Venture Capital Limited (SVCL) is a wholly owned subsidiary of SIDBI, incorporated in July 1999. It help the entrepreneur to manage his business more effectively and achieve rapid growth in internationally competitive environment SVCL use SIDBI's close functional linkages with domestic and international venture capital funds/ companies, Govt. agencies, financial institutions, commercial banks, foreign institutional investors, merchant bankers, consultancy agencies, management institutes, RandD organisations, software technology parks, etc., to provide strategic support to assisted companies of this fund.
3. SIDBI provides indirect assistance to SSIs through a large network of 913 PLIs(Primary lending Institutes), SFC's and SIDC's spread across the country .The bank provides refinance to PLIs against the term loans granted by them forsetting up of new SSI projects and for expansion, technology upgradation, etc.
4. SIDBI provides financial assistance to SSI unit under technology development and modernization fund(TDMF) scheme.
5. Direct Assistance Schemes: SIDBI directly assists SSIs under Project Finance Scheme, Equipment Finance Scheme, Marketing Scheme, Vendor Development Scheme, Infrastructural Development Scheme, ISO-9000, Technology Development and Modernisation Fund, Venture Capital Scheme, assistance for leasing to NBFCs, SFCs, SIDCs and resource support to institutions involved in the development and financing of small scale sector.
6. National Equity Fund Scheme which provides equity support to small entrepreneurs setting up projects in Tiny Sector. National Equity Fund (NEF) under Small Industries Development Bank of India (SIDBI) provides equity type assistance to SSI units, tiny units at one per cent service charges. The scope of this scheme was widened in 1995-96 to cover all areas excepting Metropolitan areas, raising the limit of loan from ₹ 1.5 lakhs to ₹ 2.5 lakhs and covering both existing as well as new units.
7. Composite Loan Scheme for equipment and/or working capital and also for worksheds to artisans, village and cottage industries in Tiny Sector.
8. Mahila Udyam Nidhi (MUN) Scheme provides equity support to women entrepreneurs for setting up projects in Tiny Sector.
9. Technology Development and Modernisation Fund: SIDBI has set up Technology Development and Modernisation Fund (TDMF) scheme for direct assistance of small sale industries to encourage existing industrial units in the sector, to modernise their production facilities and adopt improved and updated technology so as to strengthen their export capabilities. Assistance under the scheme is available for meeting the expenditure on purchase of capital equipment acquisition of technical know-how, upgradation of process technology and products with thrust on quality improvement, improvement in packaging and cost of TQM and acquisition of ISO-9000 series certification.

17.8.4 ICICI Bank (The Industrial Credit and Investment Corporation of India)

ICICI was formed in 1955 at the initiative of the World Bank, the Government of India and representatives of Indian industry. The principal objective was to create a development financial institution for providing medium-term and long-term project financing to Indian businesses. In the 1990s, ICICI transformed its business from a development financial institution offering only project finance to a diversified financial services group offering a wide variety of products and services, both directly and through a number of subsidiaries and affiliates like ICICI Bank. In 1999, ICICI become the first Indian company and the first bank or financial institution from non-Japan Asia to be listed on the NYSE. ICICI Bank is India's second-largest bank with total assets of ₹ 4,736.47 billion (US$ 93 billion) at March 31, 2012 and profit after tax ₹ 64.65 billion (US$ 1,271 million) for the year ended March 31, 2012. The Bank has a network of 2,899 branches and 10,021 ATMs in India, and has a presence in 19 countries, including India.

ICICI Bank offers a wide range of banking products and financial services to corporate and retail customers through a variety of delivery channels and through its specialised subsidiaries in the areas of investment banking, life and non-life insurance, venture capital and asset management.

Financial schemes offered by ICICI Bank:

1. Construction Equipment Loans: Bank provides loan facilities to any individual / partnership firm / company with more than two years of business experience or existing owner of construction equipment or applicants using equipment for self purpose, mine owners and contractors. It provides extended products like funding of new equipments, refinance option on existing equipment etc.
2. Assistance to projects to backward areas: ICICI has provided concessional loans and other facilities for setting up new units for the growth and development of backward areas.
3. Credit Rating Information Services of India Limited In 1987, ICICI Ltd. along with UTI set up CRISIL as India's first professional credit rating agency. CRISIL offers a comprehensive range of integrated products and service offerings which include credit ratings, capital market information, industry analysis and detailed reports.
4. Entrepreneurship Development Institute of India : Entrepreneurship Development Institute of India (EDII), an autonomous body and not-for-profit society, was set up in 1983, by the erstwhile apex financial institutions like IDBI, ICICI, IFCI and SBI with the support of the Govt. of Gujarat as a national resource organisation committed to entrepreneurship development, education, training and research.
5. MySavings Rewards;- ICICI Bank has rolled-out the programme 'MySavings Rewards' from September 1, 2012, where reward points are offered to individual domestic customers for a variety of transactions done through the savings bank account. Reward points are offered automatically to customers for activating Internet banking, shopping online/ paying utility bills with Internet banking and auto-debit from savings account towards equated monthly installments for home/ auto/ personal loan/ recurring deposit. Customers are required to maintain a monthly average balance of Rs.15,000 or more.

6. Acquisition Finance: ICICI 's acquisition financing solutions are focused on delivering innovative debt financing to companies contemplating acquisitions or mergers. The solutions are structured to leverage existing assets and those of the acquisition candidate to help finance the transaction.
7. Revolving Credit: Revolving Credit is a committed facility for a fixed tenor and is available for drawing as needed by the business. The line amount can be used, repaid and re-used within the term of the facility. Typically repaid from your business cash flow, revolving credit gives you flexibility to take advantage of business opportunities as they arise.
8. Programme for the Advancement of Commercial Technology(PACT): ICICI has set up Programme for the advancement of commercial technology(PACT) with an assistance from USAID to assist market oriented research and development activity jointly undertaken by Indian and U.S Companies.
9. Assistance under Soft Loan Scheme: ICICI operated soft loan scheme for the modernization of industrial units in cement, sugar, cotton, textile, etc., in collaboration with IFCI and IDBI. The scheme was introduced with aim to provide assistance on soft terms for modernization, replacement and renovation of plant and equipment.

17.8.5 SFC's (State Financial Corporations)

In pursuance of the SFCs Act, 1951, SFCs were set up mainly to finance small and medium-scale units. Their area of operation is generally restricted to the concerned States. The first SFC was setup in Punjab in 1953. SFCs also assist small scale units for their modernisation and technology upgradation programmes by providing soft loans, restructuring the sick small scale-units through rehabilitation schemes and through equity type assistance under SIDBI's seed capital scheme.

At present, there are 18 SFCs (including TIIC, i.e., Tamil Nadu industrial investment corp. which was set up as a company) in existence for more than 40 years and operate as Regional Development Banks. The SFCs have played an important role in the evolution and growth of small and medium scale industries in their respective states. They provide financial assistance to industrial units by way of term loans, direct subscription to equity, guarantees, etc. Over the years SFCs have expanded their activities and coverage of assistance.

One-Man Committee set up by RBI under the Chairmanship of former Secretary, SSIandARI, to look into various problems regarding credit flow to SSI sector and support appropriate measures for their redressal has given the following recommendations in its report submitted to RBI which are being processed by them:

— Restructuring of weaker SFCs by the Government.

— Funds for lending under Single Window Scheme by SFCs should be placed by SIDBI with the SFCs in adequate measures.

— Each SFC should get into an MOU with one or two Public Sector banks and participate in joint lending in which both term loan and working capital is provided jointly. For example, 80 per cent of the term loan could be given by SFC and 20 per cent by bank. In case of working capital which may be sanctioned at the same time as term loan, the proportion could be reversed, i.e., 80 per cent by bank and 20 per cent by SFC. However, the working capital account be managed and supervised by the bank through its specialised SSI branches.

— SIDBI should sign MOUs with the State Governments to provide some assistance to SFC prior to the approval of assistance packages by the Government of India/SIDBI.

— The staff of SFCs has to be adequately trained and SIDBI may be asked to make arrangements for this purpose.

Schemes by SFC's are as under:

1. **Scheme for Business Loan under Relocation:** For proposed expenditure like installation of power connection, reconditioning of existing machinery, shifting expenses, renovation of building, working capital, repayment of unsecured temporary loans taken for above purposes incurred up to one year before the date of application. Maximum Quantum of Loan (₹) is: Maximum ₹ 25.00 lakhs and Minimum ₹ 1.00 lakhs and Maximum Cost of Project : Maximum ₹ 10.00 Crore

2. **Equipment Finance Scheme:** To assist the existing SSI and service sector units for acquisition of machinery/equipment, both indigenous and imported. This would facilitate modernization / technology upgradation, expansion and diversification and quality Improvements or providing other facilities to an existing unit which is in operation for a period of at least 3 years and should have earned profits during 2 proceeding years. Maximum Quantum of Loan is: ₹ 5.00 Crore for companies and societies and ₹ 2.00 Crore for proprietorship and partnership firms.

3. **Technology Development and Modernization for SSI Units (STDM):** To encourage existing industrial units in Small Scale Sector to modernize their production facilities and adopt improved and updated technology so as to strengthen their manufacturing facilities . Maximum Quantum of Loan is Rs 80.00 Lakh

4. **Small Road Transport Operators (SRTO) Scheme:** For the purchase of new chasis including fabrication of body purchase of tool kit, stepny and insurance and registration, etc., by Small Road Transport Operators not owning more than 20 commercial vehicles including existing ones. Need based for upto 20 vehicles (incl. exiting ones). Maximum Quantum of Loan:

(i) ₹ 5.00 Crore for companies and societies

(ii) ₹ 2.00 Crore for proprietorship and partnership firms.

5. **Credit Linked Capital Subsidy Scheme:** For Technology Upgradation of the Small Scale Industries(CLCSS)

The scheme would cover the following products/Sub-sectors in the SSI: Leather and Leather products including footwear and garments,Food Processing (including ice-cream manufacturing), Information Technology (hardware), Drugs and pharmaceuticals etc. (i) Capital subsidy under the scheme shall be available only for such projects where term loans have been sanctioned on or after October 1,2000. (ii) Units upgrading with second hand machinery are not eligible. (iii) Replacement of existing equipment/ technology with the same equipment /technology will not qualify under the scheme. (iv) The beneficiary unit shall remain in commercial production for a period of at least 3 years after installation of eligible plant and machinery on which subsidy has been availed. Ceiling on loan under the scheme is raised from ₹ 40.00 lacs to ₹ 1.00 crore. The Scheme aims to facilitate technology upgradation of SSI units in the specified products/sub sectors by providing 15% capital subsidy (12% pre-revised) for induction of proven technologies approved under the scheme.

6. Mahila Udyam Nidhi Scheme (MUN): The objective of the scheme is to provide equity type of assistance to women entrepreneurs for setting up new industrial venture with the project cost upto ₹ 10 lacs in small scale sector. Terms of Assistance is Soft loan under the scheme @ 25% of the project cost subjected to the maximum of ₹ 2.5 lacs per project. The minimum promoters contribution will be 10% of the cost of project. No interest is charged on soft loan component except service charges of 5% PA. Interest on term loan is linked with refinance rate of SIDBI and repayment period is seven years (including moratorium period of three years for soft assistance and 18 months for term loan)

17.9. OTHER INSTITUTIONS

17.9.1 Venture Capital Funding

Venture capital is a new financial services and their emergence became necessary to help entrepreneurs to translate their dreams into realities. Venture capital (VC) is financial capital provided to early-stage, high-potential, high risk, growth startup companies. The venture capital fund makes money by owning equity in the companies it invests in, which usually have a novel technology or business model in high technology industries, such as biotechnology, IT, software, etc. Venture capital comprises of two words i.e."Venture" and "capital". Venture is a course of processing, the outcome of which is uncertain but to which is attended the risk or danger of "loss". "Capital" means resources to start an enterprise. To connote the risk and adventure of such fund , the generic name Venture Capital is coined. Venture capital has also been described as "unsecured risk financing" because venture capital involves investment in new or relatively untried technology, initiated by relatively new and professionally or technically qualified entrepreneurs with inadequate funds. A venture capitalist is a person that makes venture investments, and these venture capitalists are expected to bring managerial and technical expertise as well as capital to their investments. A venture capital fund refers to a pooled investment vehicle that primarily invests the financial capital of third-party investors in enterprises that are too risky for the standard capital markets or bank loans. These funds are typically managed by a venture capital firm, which often employs individuals with technology backgrounds (scientists, researchers), business training and/or deep industry experience.

17.9.1.1 Features of Venture Capital

1. High Risk: Venture capital financing is highly risky and chances of failure are high as it provides long term start-up capital to high risk-high reward ventures. Venture capital assumes four types of risks:

- Management Risk: Inability of management teams to work together.
- Market Risk: Product may fail in the market.
- Product Risk: Product may not be commercial viable
- Operation Risk: Operations may not be cost effective

2. High Tech: Venture capital investments are made in high tech areas using new technologies.

3. Equity Participation: Investments are generally made in equity and quasi equity participation through direct purchase of shares ,options , convertible debentures.

4. Participation in Management: venture capital provides value addition by managerial support, monitoring and follow up assistance .It monitors physical and financial progress as well market development initiative. They demand one seat in company's board of directors.

5. Length of investment: Venture capital help companies to grow, but they eventually seek to exit the investment in 3-7 years.

17.9.1.2 Funding

Obtaining venture capital is substantially different from raising debt or a loan from a lender. Lenders have a legal right to interest on a loan and repayment of the capital, irrespective of the success or failure of a business. Venture capital is invested in exchange for an equity stake in the business. As a shareholder, the venture capitalist's return is dependent on the growth and profitability of the business. This return is generally earned when the venture capitalist "exits" by selling its shareholdings when the business is sold to another owner. Venture capitalists typically assist at four stages in the company's development:

- Idea generation;
- Start-up;
- Ramp up; and
- Exit

Financing stages

There are typically six stages of venture round financing offered in Venture Capital, that roughly correspond to these stages of a company's development.

- Seed funding: It is the financing of the initial product development or capital provided to an entrepreneur to prove the feasibility of a project and to qualify for start up capital."
- Start-up: It is second stage . Here the business concept has been investigated and the business risk now becomes that of turning the concept into product.
- Growth (Series A round): Early sales and manufacturing funds.
- Second-Round: Working capital for early stage companies that are selling product, but not yet turning a profit.

17.9.2 Angel Capitalist

An angel investor or angel (also known as a business angel or informal investor) is an affluent individual who provides capital for a business start-up, usually in exchange for convertible debt or ownership equity. A small but increasing number of angel investors organize themselves into angel groups or angel networks to share research and pool their investment capital, as well as to provide advice to their portfolio companies. Angels typically invest their own funds, unlike venture capitalists who manage the pooled money of others in a professionally-managed fund.

An angel investor is an individual with financial resources looking to invest into an organization that personally interests him. Companies with unique business models can benefit from an angel investor, as the angel investor tends to invest into unusual business ideas but with the intention of staying with the company for the long term. It is not unusual for an angel investor to remain with a company for five years or more. Angel investors traditionally do not want to get involved in the running of your company, but they may want to have a hand in making business decisions. The term "angel" originally comes from Broadway where it was used to describe wealthy individuals who provided money for theatrical productions. Many angel investors are retired executives or business owners who have the money, knowledge, and experience to mentor new entrepreneurs so they can stay abreast of developments in a particular area of industry. An experienced angel investor can provide valuable knowledge and skills to an entrepreneur on how to run their business during its early stages of development. They may also be a good source of useful contacts, allowing the entrepreneur the opportunity to network with others in their industry

17.9.2.1 Types of Angel Capitalist

Despite this adversity, many angel investors fall into three main categories:

Core angels. These investors are individuals with extensive business experience who have operated and owned successful businesses of their own. Their vast amount of wealth was accumulated over a relatively long period of time. They are committed to their job of angel investing and continue to be involved with high risk investments despite their losses. They possess a diversified portfolio that encompasses all industries, including public and private equity and real estate. They serve as valuable mentors and advisors to their invested companies.

High-tech angels. These investors may have less experience than core angels, but invest significantly in the latest trends of modern technology. Their investments primarily depend on the value of their other high-tech holdings, which can vary considerably. Many high-tech angels enjoy the risk of their deals as well as the exhilaration of bringing a novel technology to the market place. Some may even prefer not to be actively involved in their invested companies simply because they dislike dealing with the daily challenges of operating a business.

Return on investment (ROI) angels. These investors are primarily concerned with the financial reward of high-risk investments. Their motivation behind investing is their perception of what other angels gross income may be. ROI angels tend to stay away from investing when market performance is poor and emerge once the market shows stability and improvement. They view each of their investments as another company added to their diversified portfolio and rarely become actively involved in the invested companies.

17.10. SUMMARY

Finance is the important part of every business. Finance is the lifeblood of business. It flows in mostly from scale of goods and services. It flows out for meeting various types of expenditure. For the availability of finance an entrepreneur has to depend upon various financial institutions or banks. Financial institutions provide service as intermediaries of financial markets. They are responsible for transferring funds from investors to companies in need of those funds. Financial institutions facilitate the flow of money through the economy. There are various types financial institutions like : commercial banks, development banks, venture capitalist or angel investors. These institutions provide finance according to the need and feasibility of the project.

17.11. SELF ASSESSMENT QUESTIONS

1. Discuss the role of financial institutions in the development of the entrepreneurs.
2. What are the various financial schemes of commercial banks for the enetrepreneurs?
3. Write detailed note on IDBI,ICICI and SIDBI.
4. Write a detailed note on SFC and how it helps in the development of the economy.
5. Explain the steps taken by commercial banks and development banks to improve the flow of credit to entrepreneurs.
6. What do you mean by venture capitalist and angel capitalist?

SOURCES/NOTES

1. *Source:* "Successful Angel Investing", Indiana Venture Centres
2. *The Entrepreneurial Development and Management*- Vasant Desai
3. *Entrepreneurship and Small Business*-Purnima Sehgal
4. *Management of Services–Banking and insurance*-Sukhdev Singh.